POWER, PIETY, AND PEOPLE

Power, Piety, and People

THE POLITICS OF HOLY CITIES IN THE TWENTY-FIRST CENTURY

Michael Dumper

Columbia University Press
New York

Columbia University Press
Publishers Since 1893
New York   Chichester, West Sussex
cup.columbia.edu
Copyright © 2020 Columbia University Press

Library of Congress Cataloging-in-Publication Data
Names: Dumper, Michael, author.
Title: Power, piety, and people : the politics of holy cities in the
twenty-first century / Michael Dumper.
Description: New York : Columbia University Press, [2020] | Includes bibliographical
references and index.
Identifiers: LCCN 2019053228 (print) | LCCN 2019053229 (ebook) |
ISBN 9780231184762 (cloth) | ISBN 9780231184779 (paperback) |
ISBN 9780231545662 (ebook)
Subjects: LCSH: Cities and towns—Religious aspects. | Sacred space—Political aspects. |
Municipal government—Religious aspects. | Religion and politics. | Religions—Relations. |
Social conflict—Religious aspects. | Culture conflict—Religious aspects.
Classification: LCC BL65.C57 D86 2020 (print) | LCC BL65.C57 (ebook) |
DDC 201/.5091732—dc23
LC record available at https://lccn.loc.gov/2019053228
LC ebook record available at https://lccn.loc.gov/2019053229

Cover design: Noah Arlow
Cover image: Getty Images

To Betty Pollard

Contents

Figures, Maps, and Tables

Figures

Maps

Tables

Acknowledgments

First and foremost, I thank the Leverhulme Trust. The Major Research Fellowship it awarded me has provided the most stimulating and rewarding three years of my academic career.[1] Unlike some other awards, it did not come shackled with an onerous set of reporting conditions and allowed me to immerse myself in the reading and fieldwork without distraction or interruption. It has been the highlight of my research experience, and I will always be grateful to the trust for the opportunity to open up a new direction of study. The Department of Politics at Exeter University has also been extremely supportive during this same period, releasing me from various teaching and administrative duties so that I could concentrate on the research. My thanks go to the heads of department, Andrew Massey and Robert Lamb, and to all my colleagues who covered for me while I was on leave.

Regarding my research on Cordoba, a very special thanks must go to Michele Lamprokos, who very generously shared her contacts, her profound knowledge on the Mezquita and Cordoba, and her time by reviewing my chapter on the city. I was not able to do justice to all her incisive comments and recommendations for further reading in the time available and have resolved instead to follow up this chapter with a further exploration of the feedback she gave me. Many thanks also to Lucia Solis, who acted as my research assistant and translator during my fieldwork in 2016, and to Rafael Blanco-Guzman, adjunct professor of art history at the

University of Cordoba, for his advice, comments, and willingness to discuss. In addition, I thank Irene Fernandez-Molina, my colleague at Exeter, for her introductions and for her feedback on my initial drafts. And, finally, thanks also to Ana alMuedo Castillo for her assistance in data collection on Cordoba.

Regarding Banaras, I thank Bansidhar Pradhan of Jawahlal Nehru University for his helpful advice and contacts and for recruiting two excellent postgraduate students, Riteesh Gupta and Dileep Kumar Maurya, to assist me in my fieldwork in Banaras, Sarnath, and Ayodhya (I will never forget riding pillion on their motorbikes through the traffic mayhem of these cities). Thanks also to Philippa Williams for sending me her work on the city, for sharing her contacts, and for offering advice. I extend my most grateful thanks to Rana Singh and Ashok Kumar Kaul of the Banaras Hindu University for their introductions, feedback, and stimulating observations on Banaras. Sushil Kumar and postgraduate Vivek Kumar were also most generous with their time and hospitality, and I am additionally grateful to Sushil for his assistance as translator. Similarly, I thank Sarvash Kumar, who acted as my guide and translator in Ayodhya (and also for his motorbike rides!). Linda Cooper, director of the Varanasi Welfare Foundation, was also very helpful with some essential introductions, and I am very grateful for her time and the opportunity to informally chat with her about my impressions and initial thoughts. The owner and staff of the Ganges View Hotel beside Assi Ghat were perfect hosts and very patient with my constantly changing schedule. And, finally, I thank Madhuri Desai for her advice, her comments on my chapter on Banaras, and her inspiring book *Banaras Reconstructed: Architecture and Sacred Space in a Hindu Holy City*.

Regarding my chapter on Tibet and China, I thank my colleague at Exeter Gill Juleff for her time, advice, and valuable introductions to people at various Chinese universities who were very helpful. There are also a number of people in Lhasa I would like to thank for sharing their experiences and viewpoints but will refer to them anonymously because I am not sure if a mention here would be advantageous to them. My thanks also go to Tim Niblock and Robert Barnett for commenting on the draft of my chapter on Lhasa.

Regarding my chapter on George Town, I received useful advice and introductions from my sister, Hildegard Dumper, and from Meredith Weiss, Johan Savaranamuttu, and Jomo Sundaram. Their contacts opened many doors for me, and their knowledge of the situation provided an immensely helpful starting point for my lines of inquiry. In particular, I thank Anwar Fazal, whose network of contacts in civil society, religious organizations, and the political world was invaluable. He gave generously of his time and friendship, and his "alternative tour" of George Town opened my eyes to the diversity and complexity of the communal relations in the city. Dato Ooi Kee Beng, director of the Penang Institute, was also very helpful with introductions and explanations of some of the intricacies of the historical and political situation in Penang. I am very grateful to him for his time. I thank Francis Loh for his advice, introductions, and hospitality and friendship. The opportunity to discuss politics over a plate of *kwei tiao* was one of the pleasures of my stay in the city. Similarly, I gratefully received the introductions, hospitality, and feedback to my initial ideas from Cecil Rajendra (thanks for the live music), Gareth Ismail of the Geruk Budaya bookshop, James Lockheed, Matthew Benson, and Gwynne Jenkins.

In Jerusalem, the list of people from whom I have learned about the city and who have assisted me in my various visits there over the past decades is almost too long to mention. However, I am as always very grateful to the following individuals for their willingness to update me on the situation, their advice, and their continual patience and hospitality: Amneh Badran, Ray Dolphin, Kevork Hintlian, Nazmi Ju'beh, Raja Khalidi, Menachem Klein, Awad Mansour, Rami Nasrallah, Yitzhak Reiter, Maha Samaan, Kenny Schmitt, Salim Tamari, Mandy Turner, and Ofer Zalzberg. Many thanks also to Razan Makhlouf for her photographs.

Back in the United Kingdom, I thank Abigail Grace and Rowan Dumper-Pollard for all their hard work in helping me to find secondary sources, to collect basic data for my case studies, to prepare material for my research trips, and to get the manuscript of this book in shape for submission. Their help made my life so much easier and ensured that the "business" end of this fellowship was not such a nightmare. Also, I am very grateful to Lefkos Kyriacou, the cartographer for this book. His patience, skill, and understanding were much appreciated.

I dedicate this book to Betty Pollard, my mother-in-law, whose kind and loving interest in my work I will always remember. Last but not in any way least, I thank Ann, my best friend and wife, for all her support in my work and for rallying round when I needed help. I could not have completed this book without her.

POWER, PIETY, AND PEOPLE

Introduction

Cordoba, November 22, 2015: I was not sure what to expect on this visit. My preparation had been cursory, limited to a few recent newspaper reports and readings in Arab and Spanish history from quite some time ago. The trip was just a probing visit to see if a longer one would be useful for my project. Sitting on the high-speed train from Madrid, I thought about possible signs of conflict to look out for: offensive graffiti on walls, self-censorship in official signage and information material, tension regarding dress, monitoring or surveillance based on crude demographic profiling, police patrols, and so on. Fired up as I was by two days of meetings in Madrid held under the auspices of a Spanish think-tank, perhaps I was oversensitized to the possible problems I thought I would encounter. These meetings had been devoted to the conflict in Jerusalem, specifically over the question of access to the Haram al-Sharif by Israeli Jews, which was once again spilling over into the wider Arab–Israeli conflict. The Jordanian, Israeli, and Palestinian academics and security advisers there had been discussing the Haram al-Sharif's security and trying to work out the optimum balance between respecting religious sensitivities and the logistics of containing the conflict. Daily quotas, the allocation of designated physical spaces and time slots to each side, the installation of closed-circuit TV cameras, and a heightened police and intelligence presence were options floating around my head as the train to Cordoba sped south.

In Jerusalem, the autumn of 2015 presented a period of fragile and increasingly intense stand-offs on the Haram al-Sharif enclosure. It is the site of some of the holiest shrines in Islam, the Dome of the Rock and the al-Aqsa Mosque, beneath which is also the most likely site of the great temple of the ancient Israelite King Herod. These stand-offs were between, on one hand, Palestinians and Jordanian officials who struggled to maintain control over access to the site and, on the other hand, the increasing numbers of Jewish religious radicals seeking to pray on the site. The Israeli government, through its acquiescence in the actions of these zealous outriders of the state, seemed to be on the point of finally establishing direct Israeli control over the Haram al-Sharif—a goal that had eluded it ever since the Israeli army had occupied East Jerusalem in 1967. At the same time, the recognized custodian of the shrines, King Abdullah of Jordan, identified the threat that these changes to the previously agreed arrangements posed for his kingdom and his regime. In October and November, he had made it very clear to U.S. secretary of state John Kerry that if the United States were concerned with the rise of the extremist group Islamic State (ISIS) in Syria, just across Jordan's northern border, then it was misdirecting its concerns. Unless the United States pressed Israel to hold in check its zealots entering the Haram al-Sharif, King Abdullah's kingdom would be swept away by Muslims' reaction to his perceived inactivity or powerlessness. If this were to occur, then the United States would have to deal with ISIS not only inside Jordan but also in Jerusalem.

During all this time leading up to the Madrid workshop, daily reports and videos on YouTube showed groups of Jews attempting to pray in the Haram in violation of previously agreed arrangements. They were surrounded by Israeli armed paramilitary police, who were in turn surrounded by crowds of Palestinians demonstrating their objections and fears by chanting and sometimes spitting and shoving. This was "hard-core" religious conflict being managed very poorly. In addition, it was being managed poorly under the unrelenting gaze of both social and international media, which was simultaneously fanning the anxieties of the region and the wider Muslim world. On the day of my trip to Cordoba in late November, it appeared that the prime minister of Israel, Benjamin Netanyahu, had finally blinked in this contest over control of the site. By agreeing to a series of security arrangements with Jordanian officials and Palestinian leaders, which to a large degree restored the status quo ante, he had, in effect, backed down. Yet the agreements were ad hoc, comprising personal assurances between Prime Minister Netanyahu, King Abdullah, and Secretary of State Kerry, and had not been based on any legal framework or United Nations (UN) resolutions.[1] The questions we all were asking ourselves during our meetings in Madrid were, Would the agreement hold, and had Israel let its moment to secure the holy site slip from its grasp? Furthermore, would the tensions begin to seep away, or, more likely, was this the lull before the next storm, and would the tensions reemerge more dramatically at a later date?

I gazed out the window of my train as the flat lands surrounding Madrid flashed past me. The train rounded a wide sweeping bend, and from my seat I watched the engine and the front coaches slowly climb over the mountains of the Sierra Morena before descending into the valley of the Río Guadalquivir, beside which the ancient Roman, Visigothic, and Moorish city of Cordoba stands. Further questions came to mind. Were the tensions surrounding the mosque in Cordoba anything like those I had witnessed in Jerusalem, and what could they tell us about what to do and what not to do in order to resolve the situation in Jerusalem? Happily, as I found out later that day, the tensions in the two cities were not, of course, the same— not by a long, long shot. Nevertheless, the visit was a revelation in other unexpected ways: I learned instead a great deal about the extent to which the past continues to play a role in the present, merging with current events either to stoke up tensions or to soften and dissipate them.

Despite the lack of overt conflict in and around the site, the Mezquita-Cathedral of Cordoba (also known as the Mosque-Cathedral) still blew me away for other reasons. Soon after entering the interior, I had to sit down in a quiet place along one of the darkened arcades to take in the overall impact. The eruption of the monumental, almost brutalist sixteenth-century Gothic cathedral into the center of the delicate eighth-century mosque form is astonishing. It is an assault on your visual sense. The effect is both mesmerizing and jangling. You need time to get your bearings. The composite structure, compressing a huge, high, and heavy nave and chancel inside the mosque's fragile and slender structure, is quite a miraculous feat of engineering. Putting aside the rupture to your sense of proportion, you cannot help but ponder how all that weight is spread without huge supporting buttresses or deep foundations. Aerial views of the site and views from the minaret (now a bell tower) show how the buttresses were constructed in such a way as to disguise them and minimize their impact on the more delicate mosque arcades of the interior. What struck home to me was that this apparent contradiction—between a brutal intervention and its complementariness—summed up one of the messages of the Mezquita for this book. It is both a break with the past yet also a recognition and acknowledgment of the splendor of that past. And it is a contradiction that continues to play a part in the present.

In chapter 2, I discuss the question of non-Christian access to the Mezquita in Cordoba in further detail. The controversy regarding Muslims currently wishing to pray in the building has been subsumed into a number of wider contests: between secularists and the Roman Catholic Church, between the extreme Right and the progressive Left in Spanish politics over the control over heritage sites and the narrative that accompanies them, and between the regional identities of Andalusia and the centralizing Castilian state in Madrid. But at this early stage of my research, in November 2015, I was struck by the thought of how the past in Cordoba delineated possible patterns for the present in Jerusalem. The Christian takeover of the Mezquita in the thirteenth century and the Mezquita's gradual and partial reconstruction as a cathedral can be seen as a possible trajectory of what is taking place in Jerusalem currently. In Jerusalem, you have a possible future scenario in which the Israeli government in Jerusalem gradually erodes Muslim control over the Haram al-Sharif, which leads, first, to the precedent of Jews praying there and then later to these collective prayers being accompanied by various religious paraphernalia and equipment, until, finally, a portion of the site is acquired by the Israeli state and a Jewish synagogue is built either on top of the al-Aqsa Mosque or beside it. All this is very reminiscent of what took place in 1992 in the Indian city of Ayodhya, where Hindu zealots destroyed the Babri Mosque in order to build a temple to the god Ram. Are we witnessing the start of this trajectory in Jerusalem?

At the same time, I was confronted with a parallel observation: that the present fraught situation in Jerusalem was a possible indication of the future trajectory of the controversy in Cordoba. Unless resolved, the issue of Muslims praying in the Mezquita-Cathedral threatens to escalate into something more destabilizing. If the pressure, which is at the moment contained, is not handled well, and if the numbers of Muslims wishing to pray there start to increase dramatically, then the controversy may be transformed into a more complex conflict. The controversy in Cordoba is, perhaps, only a few years away from the current situation in the Haram al-Sharif, replete with the armed guards accompanying Jewish worshippers. It is also, possibly, only a few years away from where a discussion on the monitoring of behavior, the introduction of quotas, and the allocation of designated spaces and time slots will be on the agenda of Spanish think-tank discussions concerning the future not of Jerusalem but of the Mezquita-Cathedral of Cordoba.

Why Study Cities and Religious Conflict?

This book is the product of a research project funded by the Leverhulme Trust.[2] In 2015, I received a Major Research Fellowship from the trust to carry out a comparative study of conflicts in "holy cities" and embarked upon a study of Jerusalem; Cordoba, Spain; Banaras, India; Lhasa, Tibet; and George Town, Malaysia. The purpose of the project, entitled "Power, Piety and People: The Politics of Holy Cities in the 21st Century," was to examine the relationship between the urban form and religious conflict in order to see which, if any, aspects of city life exacerbated religious tensions and transformed them into conflicts. At the same time, the project sought to identify those religious practices that also had a major influence on the development of the shape, structure, and uses of the city. The purpose was not to try and resolve the "chicken and the egg" dilemma—that is, to see which came first or which of the two was the main driver in creating conflicts. Rather, the purpose was more to identify the nature of the osmotic relationship between religion and cities and to draw out the reasons why conflicts arose in order to suggest ways in which they might be better managed or resolved.

The project is a reflection of how the study of religious conflicts in cities is emerging as a subfield in the social sciences. There are a number of reasons for this emergence. First, the rapid urbanization of the global population is a prime factor. Cities are already home to more than half the world's population, and by 2035 they are expected to absorb 95 percent of the global projected population growth.[3] At the same time, a specific urban character to violent conflict has prompted greater studies on the links between urbanization and conflict.[4] High population density, poor infrastructure, the unequal distribution of public resources, unemployment, weak governance, limited state capacity, and the absence of effective mediating institutions have combined to create conditions where violent conflict emerges as a common mode of action by competing social groups. Second, instead of modernity and technological innovation leading to the decline of religion, the twenty-first century has a seen instead a remarkable resurgence in religiosity, which necessarily has an urban dimension because it is in cities where most people now live. Currently, 84 percent of the world's population identify with a religious group: Christians constituting 33 percent, Muslims 25 percent, Hindus 15 percent, and Buddhists 7 percent. However, by 2060 the world's population is expected to increase to 9.6 billion people (a rise of 34 percent from 2015). According to the Pew Research Center, all religious groups will decline as a proportion of the global population except for Christians and Muslims, who will surpass or match the global growth rate. Indeed, due to high birth rates and a younger demographic, the increase in membership in these two religions will lead to an increase in the total number of adherents to religion in general. The growth in the number of Muslims will be twice as fast as the increase in the Christian population, so that by 2060 there will be roughly equal numbers of Muslims and Christians across the globe.[5] Thus, in this context of increased urbanization and increased religiosity, the prospect of increasing numbers of religious conflicts in cities is not really in doubt—hence the need for more studies on the reasons why and how such conflicts emerge and how they are best resolved or managed.

It is important to establish from the outset that although this project starts with the contention that all cities are arenas of contestation, only some cities exhibit specific forms of conflict arising from the salience of religious activity within them. This project focuses on the latter cities. Powerful religious hierarchies, the generation of often unregulated revenues from donations and endowments, the presence of holy sites, and the enactment of ritualistic activities in public spaces combine together to create forms of conflict that are arguably more intense and more intractable than other forms of conflicts in cities.[6] The question at the heart of the project, therefore, is: Do cities ameliorate or exacerbate religious conflicts? To answer it, we should recognize some key features of religion that bring about urban conflicts. For example, religious sites are recognized as important markers of group identities. Contestation over them, therefore, can be used to mobilize resistance and to inflame disputes. Another key feature is the way religious leaders are revered, can call upon nontangible forms of legitimacy, and are often unaccountable to state authorities. All of these qualities allow them a degree of political autonomy and, consequently, of influence that makes them significant actors when there is competition or disputes over the allocation of space and other resources inside a city. Similarly, religious communities often have revenue streams (via donations, endowments, and tithes) that offer them a degree of financial autonomy and therefore freedom from the constraints that other political parties and civil societies operate under, which, again, gives them some advantages in the arena of political contestation. Finally, religious communities are often supported by a diaspora comprising satellite communities of adherents as well as by international networks resulting from pilgrimages and outreach activities. These communities and networks together can combine to offer a degree of protection from state intervention in their activities. When we add these elements to the elements making up the urban form, we can begin to see how the evidence starts to point strongly toward an answer to the question posed earlier: Yes, cities do exacerbate religious conflicts. At the same time, as this book discovers, ethnic and religious diversity within a city does not inevitably lead to conflict.

As I explore in more detail chapter 1, cities are places where people live in large numbers, over a wide area, and in close proximity. These elements in themselves exacerbate tensions in intercommunal relations. For example, religious communities often own extensive properties in cities, so they can be segregated and form enclaves, which adds a territorial component to a conflict between religious groups. Cities that have strong religious associations are often premodern in form and layout. This usually means that access to important holy sites is often difficult, providing ample occasions for flashpoints at gateways, bottlenecks, and junctions. Another urban dimension that can exacerbate tensions is the way religious sites belonging to one community are not always located in the areas where that community resides. Over time, changes in property ownership and employment and even dispossession result in the adherents of one religion living in an enclave that is not even adjacent to their religious sites. In these circumstances, important rituals such as processions or other public demonstrations of devotion can cut across segregated residential areas or may occur at the same time as the rituals of another religion. These place and time complications can lead to disputes over precedence or other logistical inconveniences that trigger a conflict. In sum, the close proximity of large numbers of people means that incidents can very quickly be transformed from minor disputes into major confrontations. Multiethnicity and multiconfessionalism in cities can sometimes dilute tensions that build up around specific religious issues or sites, as we will see in George Town, Malaysia, but in other cities, such as Jerusalem, Banaras, and Lhasa, simple religious and ethnic binaries will exacerbate those tensions. Clearly, this interaction between the use of and control over religious sites and the ebb and flow of political power is important in understanding conflicts in cities. It lies at the heart of the discussions in this book.

Ways and Means

Before I explore these premises in more depth, I should establish what my "positionality" is, given the ethnographic material this research has encompassed. In essence, I should make explicit where am I coming from and how it affects my approach to this study. My interest in religion and its role in politics has a long genealogy. The son of an Anglican clergyman and a former Roman Catholic mother, I was born and brought up in Malaysia and Singapore. In addition to the medley of races, languages, and dress that made up parish life in Ipoh, Penang, and Singapore, there were also other colorful and dramatic influences: outside my back gate in Penang were two Buddhist monasteries, the saffron- and burgundy-robed Thai and Sri Lankan monks smiling and waving their hellos; in front of our house passed the long Hindu Deepavali and Thaipusam night processions, dramatically lit with flaming brands and with men dragging huge statues of gods and goddesses by myriad strings hooked into their bare skin; in a side street nearby, we used to watch popular Chinese opera, the *wayang*, redolent with ancient myths and legends punctuated with gongs and long high-pitched wails; Chinese New Year was a noisy school holiday engulfed by the thundering sounds of exploding red firecrackers. Our domestic and church staff were Indian and Malay Muslims, Tamil-speaking Christian and Hindu Indians, and Buddhist and Confucian Chinese. Our summer holidays were spent either trekking in the rain forests of the Malaysian interior, where we met the indigenous animistic *orang asli* in jungle clearings, or snorkeling off island reefs beside small Malay fishing villages, where the muezzin's call to prayer drew us out of the water for our supper.

Comparative religion was my daily life, and so it is unsurprising that my first degree, in the late 1970s, was in religious studies at Lancaster University in the United Kingdom under Professors Ninian Smart, John

Bowker, David Waines, and Andrew Rawlinson. Coming to grips with the ways in which the religions of the world explained the suffering of innocents and the "problem of evil" (theodicy) was a major concern of mine.[7] Later, for my PhD I switched to political science and simultaneously became immersed in the Palestinian–Israeli conflict, spending many years in humanitarian assistance and political activism. During the 1970s and 1980s, I worked with various nongovernmental organizations (NGOs) in both the ramshackle refugee camps of Gaza and the narrow alleyways of Jerusalem, and my perspectives on religious orthodoxy and personal faith underwent considerable change. I became less interested in religious teachings and practices as possible guides for my own search for answers and more in their utility as a tool for understanding the political agency of individuals and groups. In the past, I had bought into the notion of "religious language" and how, according the writings of John Hick and John Bowker, understanding of religious truths is obtained when the "penny drops" and the skeptic suddenly grasps the message behind the words. Instead, I began to see the situation in reverse and drifted closer to the skepticism of Dostoevsky's Grand Inquisitor, who maps out the gullibility of the human race in painful detail. I began to find it difficult to believe how adherents of most religions take the stories and myths of their sacred texts at such face value—to the extent that I can hardly read the Old Testament or the Ramayana now without comparing it to J. R. R. Tolkein's *Simarillion* or George Martin's *Game of Thrones*! (I exaggerate slightly, of course!)

At the same time, I fully understand how the web of socialization can be spun until one reaches a tipping point, so that belief in a particular religious system becomes the rational decision to make. If all the people around you believe that Jesus Christ rose from the dead, ascended into heaven, and is sitting at God's right hand, and if your everyday life is permeated with subtle and overt practices that affirm that belief, or if you have been raised from birth in that environment, those beliefs will quite likely make a great deal of sense to you. Religions have constructed enormously complex and sophisticated belief systems that encompass the preparation and consumption of food, attire, hygiene, personal relations, daily routines, calendars, architectural design, and social hierarchies, cumulatively providing meaning to an individual, which is a powerful driver for belief, much more so than reasoned doctrines or a colorful mythology. A belief system is not something one slots into one's mind like a DVD disc but rather is made up of hundreds of personal, cultural, and social threads that together form a powerful tapestry of one's identity and place in society. In sum, then, from background, experience, and study, I am well acquainted with most of the core beliefs that this project touches on, but, ultimately, I place myself (even now as a white, late-middle-aged, privileged professional) on the outside of all of them, looking in.

The purpose of the project is to identify, explore, and explain the religious dimension to urban conflicts. Therefore, devising a way to accurately identify cities in which such conflicts occur is important. In chapter 1, I discuss the typology of "holy cities" in more detail, so the second point I wish to explain briefly here concerns the broad steps I took to select the cities studied in this book. I started by adopting and amending the typology of "holy cities" in the Middle East suggested by Francis Peters.[8] His typology conveys the importance of both the institutional structures (religious hierarchy, property ownership) and the political economy undergirding prayer and ritual (pilgrimages, festivities, endowments) that give holy cities their distinctive character. Although useful in delineating key religious attributes and providing a starting point for analysis, the typology does not provide an explanation for *conflict* over these sites and how such conflict is played out in the urban setting. In looking for material that might offer an explanation, I also turned to the literature I encountered in an earlier project: the Conflict in Cities and the Contested State project funded by the Economic and Social Research Council, which drew attention to the interplay between the urban form and types of conflict.[9] Combining some of the findings of the Conflict in Cities project with the insights derived from Peters's approach helped me construct a more detailed framework to focus on the religious dimension of conflicts in cities. At the same time, I sought to push the explanatory aspect of the project a bit further by examining and incorporating the insights arrived at by Ron Hassner and Robert Hayden and by conflict-resolution scholars.[10] As you will read, their works highlight some of the more structural dimensions of this topic and are threaded through the following chapters.

With these approaches and insights in mind, I then identified a range of cities by the degree of their associations with religion. I go through the various steps I took to come to my selection of Jerusalem, Cordoba, Banaras, Lhasa, and George Town a little later in this introduction, but I should start with a general preliminary point regarding the possibility of selecting cities that exhibit enough characteristics of a holy city to allow comparisons to be made. My argument is based on the assumption that it is possible to identify cities with strong religious associations as a subset of cities in general. In chapter 1, I flesh out this assumption in more detail when I consider the key characteristics that suggest a city has strong religious associations: for example, holy sites, a clerical hierarchy, income derived from religious activities, and religious practices that resonate beyond the city into the hinterland and diaspora. What also needs to be established, however, is whether it is possible to consider the cities I have selected from the subset of cities with strong religious associations as having characteristics that make them sufficiently comparable to each other.

There are two ways to deal with this issue. The first is to argue that the study of a subset of cities is not an unusual exercise. A similar comparative exercise can be conducted with, say, capital cities (Washington, DC, London, Tokyo, Beijing, New Delhi) or port cities (New York, Liverpool, Hamburg, Singapore, Karachi) or frontier cities or mining cities or university cities and so on. In these comparisons, we would quickly see that it is impossible to delineate a subset of cities that are exactly "equal" or identical. There are always some similarities and some differences, often driven by geographical location. River ports, for example, are different from seaports but still generate their wealth and political influence through maritime trade and have patterns of employment and uses of public spaces and fiscal policies that are similar to those of seaports. Cities with strong religious associations are not all the same, by any means, but identifying common characteristics, as I have done and as I expand on in chapter 1, allows us to make useful comparisons. This is the reason why I look at processes and institutions that characterize a city as holy rather than embark on an impossible search for a subset of equal or identical holy cities.

Second, the social sciences have a long methodological pedigree in establishing a coherent framework for comparative study that encompasses cases that are similar and cases that are different. Derived from the philosophical writings of John Stuart Mill, this framework has evolved into what is known as the Most Similar Systems Design and the Most Different Systems Design. In essence, the former seeks to find explanatory factors for why, given similarities between cases, outcomes are sometimes different, whereas the latter provides a framework for understanding why, given important differences, outcomes can be much the same. In this way, comparative studies are not confined to the impossible task of finding identical cities to compare but can group together relevant and illustrative cases to explore some possible generalizations.

I have spent almost half of my academic career researching Jerusalem and have noted its prominence in Peters's typology, so it was the obvious place to start. Jerusalem is a city holy to the three major religions of the world—Judaism, Christianity, and Islam—and it is at the core of the protracted and at times vicious conflict between Israeli and Palestinian nationalisms. Although Jerusalem may have been an obvious candidate for inclusion in this study, I struggled with choosing others to include and on what rationale. I decided to adopt a concentric-circle framework. First, I would look at single-religion cities, such as Mecca, Rome, and Kyoto, before moving on to look at cities with more complex religious demographics, such as Lhasa and Banaras. Then I considered a couple of subcategories of cities, including borderline or "sect" cities, such as Salt Lake City (Mormonism) and the pilgrimage cities of Najaf, Qom, Bali, Lourdes, and Oberammergau. Finally, on the outer circle are cities that are not seen as "holy" but are nonetheless home to religious rivalries, such as Kaduna, Belfast, and Sarajevo. By grouping such cities inside a series of concentric circles in this way, I found it possible to create a "long list" of cities that have experienced religious conflicts and are delineated by the critical features identified by Peters and the other scholars I refer to.

The third step in the selection process was to shorten the list to a manageable five cities in order to test the hypothesis that there is a link between certain forms of urban religious activity and specific forms of urban conflict. I based the selection of the five cities on the following factors: strong religious associations (e.g., the clergy's dominant role; large endowments; proliferation of holy sites, festivities, and pilgrimages) and conflict derived from these associations (competition over ownership, over access, over use of public space for services and processions; change in use of a public space; issues of precedent; display of symbols; etc.). As I have already made clear and explore further in chapter 1, the choice of Jerusalem was incontestable. It is a city holy to three major religions and completely wrapped up in the Palestinian–Israeli conflict. Its holiest shrines are also under military occupation. The other four choices—Cordoba, Banaras, Lhasa, and George Town—need more explanation, in particular George Town because its inclusion is a juxtaposition. Cordoba, with its glorious Grand Mosque, "the ornament of the world," converted into a cathedral, offered a multilayered historical trajectory with which to explore the impact of past ruptures and transitions on the controversies of the present. It also unexpectedly introduced a feature I had not originally envisaged as being significant in the study of religious conflicts in cities: the contest between regional identities and politics and the centripetal policies of the state, which is played out in all the cities under consideration but first spotted when I examined the Cordoba case. Banaras, like Jerusalem, represents a city whose religious identity is paramount but where clashes have occurred as a result of competition over the use of holy sites and shrines. Unlike Jerusalem, parts of Banaras are not under military occupation, but inequalities of status between Muslim and Hindu residents of the city have grown and are increasingly enforced by the coercive presence of a paramilitary police force. Lhasa is like Jerusalem as well in that it is also under occupation, in its case by the People's Republic of China. Studying the Chinese government's policies there has offered a revealing comparison to the situation in Jerusalem. There are similarities in the way Tibetan political resistance to that occupation is undergirded by the dominant role of Buddhism and the Buddhist monastic hierarchy in the city and in the way that one Chinese response has been to encourage Chinese migration to Lhasa. One interesting difference, however, is that as a secular movement the Chinese Communist Party has no interest in the religious sites per se. There are no preceding Chinese shrines in Lhasa, and the Chinese state's desire to control these sites is almost entirely due to the sites' role in mobilizing political resistance to the Chinese occupation of Tibet. I chose George Town based on a consideration that emerged during the course of my research. I came to realize that although religious conflicts were the prime focus of my research, an understanding of what caused conflict and how it could be resolved would also benefit from an understanding of why conflict did *not* occur in some cities with religious associations. George Town is a city with a plethora of religious communities but apparently very little conflict, so including it in this exploration offered some useful contrasting perspectives.

Receiving the Leverhulme Trust Fellowship was like winning an academic national lottery. Generous and welcome as it was, however, the fellowship was not accompanied by huge amounts of money for research expenses. Unlike some other awards, it did not come with funds for research assistants, postdoctoral students, and so on. As a result, I had to tailor the project to a research program in which I could personally conduct all the fieldwork in five cities within a very limited budget. In essence, the fieldwork had to be more ethnographic, based on observations rather than on surveys, questionnaires, and focus groups.

For all of the cities except Jerusalem, on which I already had extensive material, I adopted a similar model for data collection. After an initial overview of the secondary literature, I undertook, as much as possible, a more in-depth survey of four areas of interest. The first area was primarily quantitative in that for each city I attempted to ascertain the key holy sites, the approximate number of clergy and other religious site employees, as well as the number of worshippers, pilgrims, and other attendees. I also sought to distinguish between major and minor holy sites. Where possible from websites and the public domain, I tried to estimate the sites' income both from internal and external sources and their contribution to the economy in the form of property development and employment. A second area concerned the functions of religious sites and practices. For example, I sought to determine the impact of major festivities and rituals through establishing their duration, the number of people attending them, the length of their stay, and their use of primary or peripheral locations. In each city, I tried to establish the role that the city or its holy sites played in prayer, liturgy, and eschatology and to identify patterns of community interaction with holy sites and other religious activity. The third area involved the data on conflict. From secondary sources and what primary literature was available, I sought to determine types of religious conflict in the cities selected. I categorized the conflicts into four main types: (1) Is the conflict over material issues—such as ownership, access, control? (2) Is the conflict over more abstract issues—such as symbolic, political, sectarian, or theological matters? (3) What are the temporal dimensions of the conflict—to what extent is it historical or contemporary? And, finally, (4) who or what are the agency and process of the conflict? For the latter, I tried to identify key actors in the conflict, delineate the types of resolution and irresolution, ascertain modes of security and policing, and determine what, if any, external intervention and monitoring have taken place. The fourth area for data collection was the urban dimension. Here I tried to assess the impact of holy sites and conflict on the city and vice versa by studying maps of religious sites and their access routes, identifying residential and other forms of ethnoreligious segregation, and locating the erection of walls, barriers, and other controlled-access points.

These four areas served as a checklist for my study of Cordoba, Banaras, Lhasa, and George Town. The next stage was to follow up with fieldwork. The fellowship budget permitted a fieldwork trip of between two to three weeks for each city. During the course of each visit, I conducted a series of observations and participant observations of the city, in particular its main holy sites and religious rituals. I also had the opportunity to meet with religious and community leaders, policy makers, planners, academics, and commentators. Collecting maps and photographs that would provide visual evidence was a supplementary part of this fieldwork.

Jerusalem is an exception in this data-collection model. In fact, I deal with Jerusalem in a completely different way from the other cities in that I use it to explore the concept of "holy cities" in general rather than as a fieldwork location to mine material for my comparative study. So chapter 1 on Jerusalem explores a range of issues, which then become the lenses through which I examine the other cities in this collection. I adopted this approach because I have already written three books as well as numerous articles, reports, commissioned studies, and encyclopedia entries on Jerusalem, so it would be difficult to avoid repeating a great deal of that material.[11] Such repetition might irritate the reader and any scholar of Jerusalem who has already read my books. At the same time, not to include Jerusalem would make no sense. It is central to my exploration of how religious conflicts can be contained or inflamed by their urban location. As a result of Jerusalem's position as a site to explore the concept of "holy cities" rather than as a fieldwork location, I have sought to combine an overview of key issues in Jerusalem regarding its historical, religious, and political developments with an exploration of how these issues in the city can set the parameters for the discussion of religious conflicts in cities more generally. For, example, since the Israeli occupation of East Jerusalem in 1967, the question of non-Muslim access to the Haram al-Sharif has become increasingly fraught. Unpacking the different stages and the different components of this pattern offers a template with which to analyze similar tensions in other cities.

Explaining Cities

Although my first degree was in religious studies, I recall dipping into Lewis Mumford's *The City in History* for one of my coursework essays.[12]

His erudition, his grasp of the long view, and his ethical slant in evaluating human achievement stayed with me. When I was preparing for this project, the first book I turned to was *The City in History*. Yet again it was rewarding with its sparkling prose, inspiring breadth of ideas, iconoclasm, and both progressive and antiauthoritarian insights. Mumford's contention that the city is "nothing less than the home of a powerful God" and that it is intrinsically religious clearly chimed with my attempts to make a link between religion and the specific kinds of conflicts it engenders in cities. "Starting as a sacred spot, to which scattered groups returned periodically for ceremonials and rituals, the ancient city was first of all a permanent meeting place."[13] For a period covering several millennia, from circa 6000 BCE to the 1960s, Mumford fleshes out in great detail how religious elites, through their fusion with the coercive power of kingship, the extraction of surpluses, and the extermination of rivals, acted as drivers in the evolution of human settlement from village to city. The European medieval city, for example, might be described "as a union of Church and community in pursuit of the Holy Life. Even when it miserably fell short of the Christian ideal, this union nevertheless had produced both institutions and buildings designed to further it."[14] Indeed, so central, in Mumford's view, is the role of religion in the development and growth of cities that I was tempted to begin this book by paraphrasing St. John's gospel (1:1): "In the beginning was the Religion and the Religion was with the City and the Religion was the City."

Although the actual shape of a city is usually determined by geographic and topographic location or in response to technological changes (such as the arrival of artillery and its transformation of walled cities) or to industrial forms of production and mass-transportation systems, Mumford identifies the three most essential functions of a city as cultural storage, dissemination and interchange, and, finally, creative innovation.[15] These functions, he argues, were performed primarily by religious institutions until they were gradually taken over by universities and more recently by multinational companies and the media. Since its publication in the 1960s, Mumford's contribution has been eclipsed in the academic literature by more contemporary studies addressing the role of cities in nationalism, the growth of capitalism, globalization, and the forensic examination of the social production of place and of group identities associated with spaces.[16] In addition, Mumford's perspective is totally ungendered: women are almost entirely absent in his consideration of history, which is surprising given the role of priestesses and the central place that the symbols of birth (renewal, continuity, hereditary) and marriage (fusion, alliance, complementarity) play in the rituals performed by the elites in early cities. Furthermore, although Mumford was prescient in foreseeing the impact of motorways on the geographical spread of habitation and revenue generation and how, as a consequence, cities would comprise a series of connected urban satellites, recent innovations have gone beyond his visionary scope. He was writing prior to the advent of the internet by several decades, and the internet has transformed the relationship among location, function, and size. One can argue that in the future the question of proximity will not play such a crucial role in city development, and, as a result, the notion of what is urban will need to be reconceptualized.

I am not an urban geographer or planner, and what I know of the academic and professional debates regarding what constitutes a city is derived from passing encounters and some reading rather than from concentrated study. I do know that it is a very large subject and that I should respectfully refrain from engaging in it. However, I cannot proceed in situating my own comparative study of religious conflicts in cities without laying out my understanding of what a city is. So much of what is written in the following chapters is based on assumptions and my own ways of seeing a city that I should make them explicit here. I am also hoping that there may also be some merit in my having a novice's perspective; however naive that perspective is, it will also be relatively free of the baggage one gets from tip-toeing around the various disciplinary agendas. In a nutshell, my view of cities is derived from a sort of *political economy of religious conflicts*. Putting aside as a given the question of size, which is a sine qua non of a city, my view is that cities are primarily spaces for human interaction that have four main characteristics: density, proximity, specialization, mobility, with competition over resources serving as the overarching dynamic. Certain combinations of these characteristics act as triggers for conflict. Let's take density and proximity first. In essence, there will be a predisposition to conflict in cities when there are too many people too close together with too few resources to survive on. In order to provide mutual security and to offer the prospect of improved conditions for, residents of cities tend to mobilize in groups along class, linguistic, sectarian, or ethnic lines or in a combination of these identities. Most cities reconcile these groups' competing interests through informal or institutionalized checks and balances, such as clientelist networks (religious leadership, corporations, unions, political parties, militia, or criminal gangs) or recognized forms of representation (councils, municipal elections, etc.).

This reconciliation leads to what I have termed an *uneasy equilibrium*, wherein resources and access to power are allocated or ceded in proportion to the influence that such groups are able to exert. I use the word *equilibrium* to convey how an approximate balance in competing social and political forces is necessary to prevent conflict from becoming so prevalent that the city fragments and breaks down as a connected urban form. Such equilibrium is "uneasy" because it is ever changing—the availability of resources or the demographic composition of the city and hence the size of the groups in competition with each other are constantly being reconfigured. For example, new population groups will emerge through migration or through natural increase, and their growth will challenge the balance of power between the city's existing constituent population groups. Governments, municipalities, and the local urban elites manage these changes through the distribution of land, housing stock, infrastructure, and other resources, which consequently becomes an arena of intense political activity. I argue that the failure to achieve equilibrium is, in fact, the norm in most cities—which is why they are the sites of so much tension and conflict. Nevertheless, governments, municipalities, and civic groups are constantly working to rectify this failure and to improve the situation to the extent that sufficient good will and cross-community partnerships are mobilized to head off the complete collapse of the city and the descent into anarchy.

Although cities in the main catch themselves or are caught by outside intervention from disintegrating, some developments do push them over the edge. Some changes—economic collapse, the introduction of new revenue-generating activities, immigration as a result of political upheaval elsewhere, natural disasters, and so on—are so great that they cannot be absorbed by the mechanisms of checks and balances usually in place. At this point, the uneasy equilibrium that somehow holds the city together starts to unravel, ultimately leading to open conflict between groups, to violence, and to the slide toward territorial fragmentation, division, or partition.[17]

As a result, the city as an integrated urban settlement is seriously impaired and so declines because the other two essential characteristics of cities—specialization and mobility—are rendered obsolete. Cities, simply due to their size, are platforms for specialization, whether in manufacturing, trade, arts, or religion: they comprise large numbers of people who can provide a sufficiently large market for niche producers in various fields. To put it simply, a village can provide for a pleasant subsistence existence, but it cannot do opera! Cities can do both. This characteristic allows for certain geographical areas or groups to specialize, which, in combination with other specializations, provide that metropolitan variety and superior quality of product one finds in cities. But for this characteristic to flourish and develop requires the additional characteristic of mobility. Unless goods, craftsmanship, artistic products, and religious sites are accessible, interact, or can be conveyed across the city and to a wider population, their value is diminished, and they do not have any greater value than what is available in a town or village. Accessibility and mobility are vital ingredients of the city in which large numbers of people live together in close proximity, and they are essential to an integrated urban form. Otherwise, the city is no longer a city but a series of smaller towns. A divided or partitioned city is in reality two or maybe more small towns. In chapter 1, I examine the subset of cities that have a fifth characteristic and are the focus of this study: cities that are holy or have strong religious associations and that generate a specific set of problems and tensions that lead to conflict.

In addition to the work by Mumford, Peters, Hayden, and Hassner, a number of publications have acted as catalysts and foils for the different avenues of thought in this project. Khaldoun Samman's pioneering book *Cities of God and Nationalism: Rome, Mecca, and Jerusalem as Contested Sacred World Cities* addresses conflicted holy cities in broad historical context. However, its main focus is not the impact of religious practice on the physical form of the cities or how the urban contributes to religious conflicts, which is the field I explore here. In contrast, *The Fundamentalist City? Religiosity and the Remaking of Urban Space*, edited by Nezar AlSayyad and Mejgan Massoumi, does give primacy to the relationship between urban form and religion in a range of cities across the world but differs from my study in that its focus is on religious fundamentalism rather than on the broader range of religious practice. The volume *Choreographies of Shared Sacred Sites: Religion, Politics, and Conflict Resolution*, edited by Elazar Barkan and Karen Barkey, has provided some of the ideas I explore further in my book but regarding a different collection of cities. Focusing on the Mediterranean region is another edited volume by Dionigi Albera and Maria Couroucli, *Sharing Sacred Spaces in the Mediterranean: Christians, Muslims, and Jews at Shrines and Sanctuaries*. This highly nuanced and empirically sound collection highlights some useful material and insights. A key work in this field is the publication edited by Glenn Bowman, *Sharing the Sacra: The Politics and Pragmatics of Intercommunal Relations Around Holy Places.* Although its main focus, like that of the previous two books, is religious sites rather than religious cities, it has a broader comparative scope, with case studies from Asia, the Middle East, and the Mediterranean. Interestingly, the latter three books are concerned, first, more with the processes of accommodating pluralism in a range of sites than with the conflict over them and, second, with the changes in religious practice that flows from this accommodation rather than with polarization and confrontation. A similar volume, *Holy Places in the Israeli–Palestinian Conflict: Confrontation and Co-existence*, edited by Marshall J. Breger, Yitzhak Reiter, and Leonard Hammer, has a number of empirically very useful chapters. Like *Sharing the Sacra*, it concentrates on holy sites but has a narrower geographical focus on sites in Palestine. I hope my book presents a broader picture and delineates more general patterns. Ron Hassner's book *War on Sacred Grounds* focuses on holy sites rather than on holy cities more generally, but it nevertheless offers ideas for policy analyses that I have found useful. Robert Hayden's notion of religious communities coexisting in a situation of "antagonistic tolerance" is also germane here. Although this notion can explain long periods of accommodation between religious groups, antagonistic tolerance is nevertheless impermanent. I have found useful Hayden's observation that as political power changes, opportunities for new relations and new precedents between religious groups unfold that can erupt into violent confrontations.[18]

Analytical Framework: Identifying Metanarratives and Other Definitions

In essence, this project is firmly empirical in orientation, and this book is a summary of my ethnographic research on the five cities. As a result, it eschews engaging with the theoretical literature on conflict studies in any depth. I have instead adopted a simple analytical framework as a key organizing structure for the study of the cities: two metanarratives and the shifting relationship between them. The first metanarrative is driven by an exclusionary vision of the city, wherein the city is part of a process termed "semitization." One of the leading social scientists on India, Ashutosh

Varshney, summarizes this vision as one where a faith has one holy book, one God, and one sacred city.[19] In this vision, the religion of the dominant political community is privileged at the expense of the other religious communities residing in the city or at the expense of other faiths that have associations with and thus some claims for recognition in the city. The most extreme manifestation of this vision is conquest, the expulsion of the other faiths, and the demolition, destruction, and desecrations of their religious sites and institutions. All historical epochs and all regions are littered with examples of such conquests: the Crusades, the Islamic conquests, the Mongol invasions, the Conquista, the Reconquista, and so on. Less-extreme versions of this metanarrative involve constraints placed on worship, construction, proselytization, and legal, cultural, or political recognition—for instance, the restrictions on Jewish worship in Jerusalem during the Ottoman period, on Christian worship during the Soviet Union era, on the practice of religion in general in China today, and on some practices of non-Muslim religions in Malaysia and many Arab states in the Middle East. I call this metanarrative the *narrative of precedence*—putting one community first and above all other communities and, where relevant, asserting the community's primacy in temporal terms: "We were here first!"

The second metanarrative I term the *narrative of transformative integration*. Although the phrase may be a bit of a mouthful, it conveys a broader, more complex meaning than the simpler phrase *narrative of integration*. By it, I mean a narrative that encourages a vision in which previous formulations or competing religious traditions are incorporated into the present so that practices and institutions of the dominant religious community are to some extent transformed by the process of incorporation. This incorporation is not necessarily a voluntary or welcome development in the eyes of those who experience it. It can be done grudgingly, reluctantly, but also realistically with a cold-eyed acceptance of the balance of power. In effect, it is on one hand a recognition that although a particular community may be dominant, it is not either so overwhelmingly dominant or sufficiently coherent or so monolithically orthodox to impose a narrative of precedence. On the other hand, it also expresses the pluralist and syncretic elements within the dominant community. This narrative is receptive to ideas and practices that emanate from the city's cosmopolitan experience and appeals to those adherents within the dominant community who are looking for inspiration for religious renewal and for supplementary forms of religious expertise.

Clearly, no city reflects one narrative or the other in its entirety, and the passage of time ensures that there is a restless rise and fall in each narrative's presence and strength. Thus, in Cordoba, the narrative of transformative integration that seeks to celebrate the city's heterodox past has been more salient at different points in its history and is currently being supplanted by a narrative of Christian precedence guided by the Roman Catholic Diocese of Cordoba. Similar changes in the salience of one narrative or another are occurring in Jerusalem and Banaras. In Jerusalem, we can see a contest between these narratives over its whole history as representatives of the three Abrahamic faiths have sought to consolidate their position in the city, largely through coercion wearing the cloak of the narrative of precedence. Since 1967, the narrative of precedence has taken modern forms in the way the Israeli government and society have sought to legitimize the exclusion of the Palestinian Arab (Muslim and Christian) minority. In Banaras, the two narratives are jockeying for dominance: the narrative of transformative integration, rooted and emanating from the local, city level, could be said to be resisting the powerful political forces of Hindu nationalism that are advancing the narrative of precedence at the state and federal level.

In addition to erecting this overarching conceptual framework to analyze and situate the data of this project, I need to unpack a number of terms. Possibly the most important question we need to hold in our minds when exploring this topic is whether the category "religious conflict" is a useful for analyzing the broad range of conflicts in holy cities. There is a strong argument that it is much too reductionist. Conflicts within cities are very rarely monocausal but almost always stem from a combination of ethnic, economic (class), and linguistic factors resulting from demographic, political, and economic change as well as from religious beliefs. To attribute a conflict to a single cause—religion—even if it is superficially and colorfully the most salient, masks other important contributing elements whose role are as important in understanding the scope, force, and causes of the conflict. In a chapter in a companion volume to this book, *Contested Holy Cities: The Urban Dimensions of Religious Conflicts*, arising out of a seminar I convened, James Anderson argues that not only are religious conflicts constituted of many causes, but they also lay dormant for long periods.[20] In the same volume, Francis Loh draws attention to the analytical discourse among South East Asian social scientists in which economic and ethnic factors are given primacy when explaining conflicts in cities. He contends that there is lack of empirical evidence for the religious dimension of intercommunal disputes and writes: "Although George Town is a multi-ethnic, multi-religious and polyglot city, it should not be presumed that diversity in and of itself results in a conflict prone society."[21] Madhuri Desai, writing about Banaras, similarly highlights how during the long periods of the (Muslim) Mughal era, state patronage of both mosque and temple construction alike was not contingent upon religious identity.[22]

We can also question whether the focus on "conflict" is misleading. Academic literature in the fields of politics, religion, and urban conflict has traditionally focused on the causes of violence.[23] As a result, insights drawn from the study of the dynamics of peaceful coexistence have been neglected. However, more recently, the notion of "everyday peace" has come to the fore and is offering a nuanced and interdisciplinary perspective on processes by which the complex personal and spatial connections among groups, institutions, and city power brokers can be understood.[24] Heterogeneous urban communities demonstrate a remarkable pattern of coexistence and intercommunal equilibrium. In fact, an insightful perspective to adopt is one in which cities are viewed as exhibiting long periods of peace or relative peace, with episodic interruptions of violence and conflict.[25]

A related issue is that of the historical context. Deterministic notions of primordial conflicts between ethnicities and sectarian groups are often skewed in their historicity and do not recognize the relativity and impermanence of conflicts. To put it more simply, a study of a contemporary religious conflict in a city will make sense only if the status quo is viewed as a snapshot and an episode between a dynamic, changing past situation and a new situation that will also change. Here, Robert Hayden's definition of "religioscapes" is useful in revealing how the evolution of a city's urban form can result in the leaving behind of religious sites and locations of religious practices from an earlier era, both geographically and resonantly. What had been a Grand Mosque in the seventeenth century may end up being a neglected shell of a building in an outer suburb as the city's administrative and political center moves across a river to the other bank.[26] One result of such changes is the phenomenon of "invented tradition," which Desai examines with regard to Banaras but is replicated in other cities that have strong religious associations. Here, new constructions of religious sites utilize previous forms and decorative architecture to convey a sense of age and to mimic a mythological past.

I also need to clarify my use of some additional terms, such as *nation*, *state*, *ethnicity,* and *community* as opposed to *group.* We should recognize the role of nation-states in exacerbating religious conflicts. The quest for the ethnic homogeneity by nationalists and racial purists is elusive, but it generates conflicts along the way. Time and again the nationalist agenda is confronted by the heterogeneity of cities, which, as I argue in more detail in chapter 1, thrive and prosper when mechanisms are found for accommodating the interests of residents from a variety of cultural and religious backgrounds. However, the role of the state as the primary actor in both the international system and the internal governance of a politically demarcated territory injects an interethnic conflict into the situation. Such interethnic conflicts can have strong religious dimensions in the competition for resources and political power that may arise between residents of a given territory. I have argued elsewhere that "cities and ethno-nationalism are an uneasy mix, particularly in capital cities. One flourishes with hybridity, the other strives for monolithic unity."[27] Anderson has made the insightful observation that in the push and pull between these two characteristics, empires are much better in managing religious diversity in cities and that it is no accident, therefore, that many of the religious conflicts in cities have taken place following the departure or eclipse of an empire.[28] In this way, the transition from the multiethnic and cosmopolitan culture of the imperial state to ethnonationalism is a major contribution to the emergence of religious conflicts in cities. We can also see how when ethnocentric ideologies such as Zionism, Ulster Loyalism, Maronite nationalism, Hindutva (Hindu nationalism), and Bumiputerism (Malay nationalism) dominate the governance of cities, counterforces are generated in the subordinate communities. The use of such ideologies in municipal governance to determine the allocation of service provision in cities can be counterproductive because such allocation leads those who are deprived of services to seek alternative sources of revenue and support, which in turn undermines the dominant group's power. As a consequence, it is possible to argue that ethnonationalism struggles to succeed in ethnically mixed cities: it has either to accommodate the minority population or forcibly to displace it. This struggle I term the "paradox of urban ethnonationalism."

I use the term *religious community* in the full knowledge that it does not sufficiently convey a number of complexities. First, as an identity marker, it is often subsumed into other identity markers, such as ethnic or linguistic community. Indeed, a religious community usually straddles several such communities. Second, the word *community* suggests a homogeneity and benign internal association that is often in fact lacking. Intracommunal conflicts are not unknown. During the Thirty Years War in Europe (1618–1648 CE), fought between adherents of Protestantism and Roman Catholicism, it would be hard to talk of a "Christian community" in any meaningful way. Referring to a "Hindu community" is particularly problematic because most adherents classified as Hindus by Western-trained scholars would not recognize much commonality with others classed in this way.[29] Referring to a demographic that espouses a particular religion as a "religious community" works best when you are discussing that demographic in relation to another demographic that espouses another religion. In this book, I use the term *religious community* extensively because the discussion is focused on religious belief and practice and their relation to cities and conflicts, but I also am cognizant of the fact that in the discussion of political and social issues, ethnicity, class, language, gender, and age are often key factors that should also be taken into account. I do not dismiss these other factors but wish to keep the focus of my study on religion.

Finally, I need to draw attention to the fact that this focus on religion as a system of belief with accompanying institutions and rituals is a Western concept that is not shared by other academic and cultural traditions. In the thought-provoking introductory essay to her book *Chinese Religiosities: Afflictions of Modernity and State Formation*, Mayfair Mei-hui Yang argues that the traditional Western academic notion of religion is both based upon its experience of Christianity and, more importantly for the purposes of this book, quite limiting.[30] She contends that the way the concept is formulated does not encompass the prevalence and full glory of local gods or of magic or superstition. These other traditions, without texts and clerical structures, are seen as marginal and confined to illiterate, rural, or low-status members of the community and thus often seen as not worthy of study or exploration. Yet, although their marginal status may be true, folkloric-type superstitions may also be adhered to by the vast majority of people within a religious community. In addition, the Western concept of religion presumes a set of institutional structures built upon a clerical–lay binary that is not replicated in some religions in the same way it is in Christianity. The concept also privileges the Protestant emphasis on private and personal intercession, or "religious interiority," and denigrates public ritualistic performance. In this sense, I can be seen as an extreme Protestant because I instinctively recoil from the showy and fussy aspects of worship that involves turning prayer wheels, wearing face markings, ostentatiously offering gifts of flowers and fruit, burning candles and incense, prostrating before or circumambulating around shrines, ringing bells and gongs, publicly flagellating oneself and piercing one's body (I recoil until, that is, my fascination with the sheer color, pageantry, and exuberance of such practices takes over). A further limitation of the Western concept of religion is that it reinforces the mind–body division that seems central to Christianity but, as Yang says, does not work so well in understanding Chinese religiosities. The limitations of the concept are also quite profound in one final way: it overlooks the different forms of modernity that have emerged throughout the world and that diverge from the Western form, and so it may result in scholars failing to recognize the reforms being undertaken in the religions being studied.[31]

The chapters here are the summary of my research and thoughts on this project. I devote each chapter to a city—Jerusalem, Cordoba, Banaras, Lhasa, George Town, in that order—and then I give a final concluding chapter with some reflections. The Jerusalem chapter is different from the other chapters because I delve into conflicts in the city to delineate some general issues, characteristics, and factors, which I then use to study the other four cities. The succeeding chapters follow roughly the same structure. First, I describe the background and context of the city before unpacking some specific conflicts to see why they have occurred and what their likely trajectory will be. Although there are clear similarities between the cities, each one is at the same time quite unique. In the final chapter, I draw together my observations and conclusions based on this research into conflict in cities with strong religious associations. Although the religiosity of a city in all its popular, bureaucratic, architectural, and ritualistic manifestations is clearly preeminent, the research also demonstrates how systems of governance play a crucial part as well. To this end, I attempt to assemble a Religious Conflict in Cities Resolution Tool Kit, which highlights the importance of the legitimacy of state institutions, a commitment to inclusivity, a respect for religious sites, a dispersed land-ownership system that discourages residential segregation, and a role for external actors. These factors are interwoven into the fabric of each city, its conflicts, and the attempts to manage those conflicts.

CHAPTER I

_____

Jerusalem

Template of a Holy City in Conflict?

L ondon, May 2, 1997: the morning after the British election that
saw the Labour Party sweep into power under Tony Blair with a
huge majority. Threading my way through the exuberant, dancing crowds between Westminster and Whitehall, I tried to focus on the
tense meetings being held in the offices of the Royal United Services Institute. I had been asked by the U.K. Foreign and Commonwealth Office to
chair a session on the future of Jerusalem at what is unofficially known as
the "London Track," a series of unofficial negotiations between Israelis and
Palestinians. The London Track was attempting to build on the break-
through in 1993 when the Oslo Accords, signed between Israel and the
Palestine Liberation Organization (PLO), took place. The Oslo Accords,
however, only laid down the framework for a transition period but did not
spell out a final agreement on many contentious issues, with the issue of
Jerusalem one of the most contentious still to be agreed upon.[1] The Palestinian team was led by the FATAH leader, Faisal Husseini, a charismatic
individual who exuded gravitas and calm.[2] The Israeli team was led by the
veteran Israeli Labour Party member Yossi Beilin, a principled operator
who was convinced that Israel had to be steered away from the populist
nationalism that was preventing the grasp of a strategic vision of its place
as a good neighbor in the Middle East. Active in his team was also the
youthful academic and peace activist Ron Pundak, one of the architects of
the secret negotiations that led to the Oslo Accords. The discussion on the

morning of May 2 did not go very well. Not only were there scratchiness and grandstanding between the two teams that had been absent from earlier meetings, but the sessions were also punctuated by shouts and victory chants from the Labour Party supporters outside as they headed down Whitehall for Downing Street and Westminster Palace. One particularly loud and prolonged roar drew all of us to the tall windows overlooking Whitehall, and we caught a glimpse of the Blairs walking into the prime minister's residence on Downing Street, waving at the crowds. Even the police were clapping!

In contrast to the celebrations outside, the mood inside the grand Royal United Services Institute rooms was increasingly somber. The particular session I was chairing did not go well either. The excitement of Oslo had faded, and the Palestinians were both confronting the cautious and legalistic pedantry of the Israeli team but also backpeddling from their own overenthusiastic embrace of a peace process that, on closer reading, did not lead to Palestinian sovereignty over East Jerusalem or to the return of significant numbers of Palestinian refugees. The Jerusalem session was turning out to be an exercise in futility. The four presentations, two from each side, were at root extrapolations from two sets of assumptions that neither side shared with the other. On the one hand, the Israelis were working on the assumption that whatever form the Palestinian presence in East Jerusalem took, Israel would remain in charge of policing and security. That was a red line for them. They were not prepared to give up security arrangements of a territory—that is, a tangible asset—in exchange for the promise of good behavior on the part of the Palestinians, particularly a territory as significant to them as East Jerusalem. The Palestinians, on the other hand, would not countenance anything much less than the status quo ante of 1967. They would consider lease-back arrangement for some of the Israeli colonies in East Jerusalem, including access to the Wailing Wall, but certainly no residual Israeli controls regarding the Muslim and Christian religious sites in the Old City. From their point of view, Israel had no right to be there, and they were not going to go down in history as the people who had surrendered control over the holy places of Islam and Christianity. I found that my work as chair of the session, to draw out the potential commonalities between the two sides, was almost fruitless. In one of the breaks between sessions, I chatted to Ron Pundak over some coffee, and he asked me what I thought was going on. I remember answering that unless Israel worked quickly and demonstrated, as the stronger party, some magnanimity over the religious sites issue, the momentum toward a peace agreement that had built up around the Oslo Accords would flounder. The Palestinian position was hardening the more detailed the discussions became. Writing as I am now, twenty years later, after many hours of such off-the-record meetings, reams of paper written and digital files made, miles of travel covered, gallons of lousy coffee consumed, the two sides are no closer to an agreement. They are possibly even farther away from one.

It is this experience of watching the possibility of peace slowly slipping through our collective fingers that in part drives this comparative project. The failure of the Oslo process has been analyzed and dissected repeatedly,[3] and it has led me to reflect personally on what lessons can be learned. As I mentioned in the introduction, the causes of religious conflicts are complex and need careful disentangling from many other factors. I hope to demonstrate this further in the following chapters as well. This chapter focuses on Jerusalem, but I want to ensure that the perspective I keep is broad and to some extent generalizable. To this end, I discuss the conflict around the religious sites of Jerusalem while I simultaneously explore and delineate the contours of the religious dimensions of urban conflicts in a wider context. This approach has the added benefit of not repeating some of the material I have already published and of allowing me to navigate around what has become a rather crowded field on the Jerusalem issue since the 2000s. In trying to encapsulate what it is about some cities with religious conflicts that is different from other cities, I draw on Jerusalem as my main case study. The first step in this exploration is to look more closely at the term *holy city*.

In Search of the Holy City

A fundamental premise of this book is that there is a subset of cities that can be designated as "holy cities" and that there are additional and possibly discrete elements that contribute to the *uneasy equilibrium* I discussed in the introduction. My argument is that such cities have particular characteristics and, as a result, engender specific kinds of conflict. Such a subset of cities, therefore, merits deeper consideration. However, there is no official "Holy Cities List." No UN body or international group of urban planners or global association of municipalities meets periodically to add to or subtract cities from an agreed register of holy cities, and no proceedings

have discussed, refined, voted on, and ratified the criteria for being designated a holy city. So how does one determine what a holy city is and what
its key characteristics are? How does one measure "holiness"? Is the mere
quantity of holy sites—such as places of worship, mausolea, shrines, tombs,
seminaries, monasteries, and convents—an adequate indication of a holy
city? Is it the number of pilgrims or citations in religious texts or the wealth
derived from religious activity or the number of persons employed by
religious administrations, among other things, or a combination of all of
these characteristics? In addition, how does one define the space or spaces
between the holy sites? Holy cities are sacred spaces whose holiness is
derived from more than the mere accumulation of sites; that is, the holiness of a city is greater than the sum of its holy parts but also includes the
use of space around those sites and the rhythms of daily life. Some holy
sites are more central to a religious faith than others are. The birthplace or
resting ground of a founder of a religion or the site of a critical event in
the formation of that religion may not lead to particularly large holy sites
or, indeed, to a plethora of them, but they nevertheless are clearly key sites
for that religion.[4] Their centrality sprinkles holy dust over believers who
live in their vicinity and on those who come to worship in them. Their
centrality to a faith is more important than perhaps the size of the site or
the number of sites in a city. Indeed, we shall see how cities encompassing
a single or dominant religion, such as Mecca, Qom, and Rome, are often
less peppered with myriad sites because the role of the dominant religion
in that city is a given, whereas a city that may be at the periphery of a religious sphere of influence or shares its spaces with a plurality of ethnicities
and religions seems to present to the world a larger number of holy sites.
The plurality engenders a greater display of territorial markings and
identity-defining symbols.[5] At root, the prospect of competition leads to
more construction. From these questions and observations, we can see
clearly that the question of what constitutes a "holy city" is complex. Nevertheless, designating a city as a holy city is very central to our understanding of the relationship between religion, conflict, and the urban form. One
can see from this how equating the number of holy sites with holiness is a
more complicated relationship than it first appears.

Second, a simple number count of holy sites in a city needs to be put in
the context of the geographic area and the demography of a city. A city
may have a large number of holy sites, but if they are spread over a wide

area, their impact on a city's urban form is likely to be less, and the possibility that conflict may be triggered over, say, disputed access and use is also dissipated. This may be particularly the case in a city where the center of the city is diffused. In the same way, a city may have a larger number of holy sites, but if the population is also very large, the sites' cumulative effect and skyline may be diluted: the per capita ratio of population to number of sites is therefore a factor. So, to some extent, the proportion of holy sites to land area or to population size can define the holiness of a city.

Third, one argument claims that the definition of holiness for a city has to take into account the proximity of major holy sites to the center of power—the royal court, the presidential palace, the seat of legislation or of the judiciary, the council chambers, or the municipality administrative center—or to the main public square. Through this proximity to the location of political decision making and the city's leadership, the religious elite not only exert influence on decision making and on the symbolic displays of the established order but also inject themselves effectively into the daily lives of the inhabitants, who look to the center for guidance and leadership.

Finally, there is also the question of who is in a position to define or designate a city as a holy city. Rather like the inscription of a site to the World Heritage List compiled by the UN Educational, Scientific, and Cultural Organization (UNESCO), labeling a city as a holy city would bring to that city international recognition, additional tourism, and the lucrative trade of additional pilgrims.[6] The incentive for acquiring that designation is considerable, and so its acquisition would be subject to manipulation and exaggeration.

These points taken together—the centrality or peripherality of the sites to the faith, the relationship between numbers of sites and geographic area or population size, the proximity of sites to political power, and the epistemological criteria for designation—demonstrate that the definition of a holy city is interdisciplinary and complex and can suck one into highly charged theoretical debates that straddle sociology, religious studies, anthropology, ethnology, political science, and the various subdisciplines of geography.

Turning to the academic community and its debates over terminology does not necessarily take us much further. One of the discoveries I made in working on this project is that, save for some recent notable exceptions, there is a clear gap in the literature on the conceptualization of the term *holy city.*[7] For example, although there is little dispute among scholars that holy cities exist as a separate category of city and have their specific dynamics and problems, there is a lack of clarity on the attributes they may have in common. Indeed, much of the theoretical debate on the nature of holy cities has focused on defining an "Islamic city" rather than a holy city in general. But even in that case, scholars have found that identifying Islamic features in the wide regions where Islam is practiced has proved to be very elusive.[8] Janet Abu-Lughod's seminal work on the subject argues that the concept of an "Islamic city" is intrinsically flawed because a "Buddhist city" or a "Christian city" is not discussed in the same terms.[9] In cities such as Banaras (Varanasi), beside the River Ganges in India, which is possibly the largest pilgrimage center in the world; Lourdes, the site of a miraculous appearance of Mary, the mother of Jesus Christ; Mecca, the birthplace of the prophet Muhammed and the site of the Kaʿaba, the holiest site in Islam; Jerusalem, a city with holy sites central to the three Abrahamic religions; and Kyoto in Japan, the location of thousands of Buddhist temples and Shinto shrines, we can see places where religion plays a dominant role in urban development. Yet is it possible to say that such a city is Christian, Islamic, Buddhist, or Hindu without acknowledging that the city's location is perhaps as significant a factor as its religiosity? Tracing the impact of religious activity on urban development and on the conflicts it might engender is in this way both fairly straightforward and quite complex. It is relatively straightforward because one can visually see the impact of religion. The location of holy sites, their size, their access routes, the construction of administrative support buildings and residences for religious personnel and pilgrims, the skyline—all cumulatively have a significant impact on the shape of the city and its urban form. It is also complex because what one sees in the cityscape is not the whole picture. Many networks and forces below the surface of our visual impressions undergird and channel the activities in holy cities and require further analysis and scrutiny.

One of the earliest explorers of the concept of holy cities as a category *sui generis* was, as I mentioned in the introduction, Francis Peters, whose quest for a typology of a holy city broke new ground in the mid-1980s. He argued that the presence of holy sites in a city leads to a number of particular characteristics: special forms of land use and property ownership, the preponderance of ritualistic activity, certain types of employment and monumental constructions that both alter the shape of the city and give it its religious character and ethos.[10] Through his comparison of Mecca and

Jerusalem, Peters was able to show how holy sites encompass much more than the footprint of the main mosque or church, including ancillary buildings for teaching, for pilgrims, for clergy, for administration, for welfare projects, and for revenue generation, including shops, hotels, warehouses, and so on. As such, large swathes of the urban property connected to a holy site, constituting what Robert Hayden was later to call the "religioscape,"[11] can be managed as quasi-monopolies connected to but at the same time slightly adjacent to the urban economy because of restrictions on their use through the form of endowments. In addition, such concentrations of religious property, usually ancient and venerated, create a distinct atmosphere and subculture. Processions, feast days, days of fasting or celebration are given an urban receptacle that not only is affected by such activities but also channels and echoes them. Clearly, the number, proximity, and interconnectedness of holy sites in a city are fundamental in defining a holy city.

To avoid many pages of discussion, evaluation, and critique of the different views regarding how to arrive at such a definition, I have resorted to a tautology. Having studied Jerusalem for more than twenty years, I am cutting this particular analytical and theoretical Gordian knot with a simple observation. I hold that I can say one thing with absolute confidence that almost everyone will agree with: *If there is such a thing as a category of holy cities, then Jerusalem is definitely one of them, and if there is such a place as a holy city, then Jerusalem is one.* Of course, I am not using the term *holy city* in a normative sense. I am not claiming that it is all peace and harmony in the city of Jerusalem. Jerusalem is an arena for an ugly nationalist conflict between Israelis and Palestinians that is appropriating the traditions, buildings, and followers of what are essentially peaceable and spiritual religions to serve political ends. But in terms of the presence of religious faiths in a city, Jerusalem is preeminent. While I was carrying out research on my previous book, it gradually dawned on me that Jerusalem is holy not just to one religion but to three. Furthermore, it is not just holy to any three religions but holy to one of the oldest religions in existence—Judaism—and holy to two of the largest religions of the world—Christianity and Islam. Not only are these three religions the main monotheistic religions of the world, but they have emerged from each other's traditions and cultures and have elements of doctrine and ritual that both overlap and are embedded in each other. In this way, layer upon layer of faith and belief has been deposited upon the city. Having lived and visited the city many times since 1977, I became so accustomed to the plurality of faiths and variety of rituals on the streets around me that for much of the time I did not recognize the utter uniqueness of this conjunction of holiness and the unlikelihood of it occurring elsewhere on the planet.[12]

So the tautology I have resorted to in drawing together a definition of a holy city is this: if Jerusalem is the Holy City per se, and if any definition that does not encompass Jerusalem is as a consequence flawed, then the characteristics that make Jerusalem holy are those that define a holy city. Jerusalem, therefore, defines the category and is also part of the category. In this way, it is possible to summarize some key characteristics of a holy city based on the case of Jerusalem. First, a holy city comprises a large number of holy sites, which may or may not be the most central sites of a faith but are nonetheless highly significant to that faith and to a high proportion of its adherents. In addition, the holy sites are located within a relatively closely defined area and are linked in function in some way. Second, a holy city supports a long-standing institutional religious hierarchy often graced by the presence of leading clerics who have considerable political influence locally, nationally, and regionally. Third, a holy city has an administrative apparatus that controls large swathes of property, offers religious, welfare, and educational services, provides the clerics and senior functionaries with an important local constituency, and undergirds a communal identity and a microeconomy. Fourth, a holy city has a semiautonomous financial base in the form of endowments, (entry) fees, and donations. This base allows the holy city to absorb external funds independent of the strength or weakness of the local economy, which in turn allows it to finance religious personnel and projects relatively free from municipal or state intervention. Finally, a holy city can point to an important network of diasporic and international contacts built up through pilgrimage and educational activities. Such contacts and interactions offer a degree of protection to the clergy and their administrations and can strengthen their immunity from state intervention. Some holy cities may not have all five features, and others may have a preponderance of one or the other. This definition or typology, however, gives us a starting point, and in the course of the book I both highlight additional features and refine the definition for both general and specific policy-orientated purposes.

At the same time, I cannot continue this discussion without recognizing that the term *holy city* is still only a partial picture of a city and hence an imperfect tool. Despite this attempt to come to a definition, it is also clear that holy cities are more than just holy cities. They are also capital cities (Rome); they are also administrative and economic centers (Istanbul); and they are also cities where their religious dynamics are subsumed within a broader touristic and heritage industry (Santiago de la Compostela, Kyoto). The search for a working definition of a holy city is rather like searching for the pot of gold at the end of a rainbow. You think you have arrived at the right place, but then you find the pot is actually somewhere else. You work away at delineating a useful definition of a holy city, but then you discover that there is always more to a city than its religious aspects, however prominent they may be. As I discussed earlier, the mobility and specializations that are intrinsic characteristics of cities work against any kind of religious exclusivity; the metropolitan nature of cities is contingent upon a complex and fluid interactivity between different revenue-generating activities and group identities. True, if the religious dimension of the city's daily life, of its urban politics, and of external actors' interest in it is either dominant or highly significant, that dimension casts other aspects of the city somewhat in the shade. Nonetheless, these aspects are still important features of a city. The subtitle of this book—*The Politics of Holy Cities in the Twenty-First Century*—is therefore misleading. A more accurate subtitle would be *Conflicts That Are Largely but Not Exclusively the Result of Religious Differences in Cities That Are Predominantly but Not Exclusively Religious in the Twenty-First Century*. That does not exactly trip off the tongue. In essence, my clarification here is that the description *holy cities* for the range of urban settlements I am examining is not exactly a misnomer; it just needs to be contextualized because the context is both a part of the city's multifacetedness and part of the conflict being studied. Thus, instead of the term *holy city*, I would really prefer to employ the phrase "a city with strong religious associations." This phrase has the advantage of avoiding the term *holy*, which has both a subjective and a normative ring to it. The phrase "strong religious associations" means that we would need to include cities such as Belfast, with its highly charged Protestant–Catholic conflict but without a particularly central position in the Christian world in terms of its place in foundational sacred texts, in pilgrimage, or in liturgy. This is a caveat we just have to live with, however. In this book, therefore, I use the term *holy cities* more in a colloquial sense and tend to use the phrase "cities with strong religious associations" when I wish to be more precise, in full knowledge of the caveat and these contexts.

Having clarified this terminology, I still need to ask why the holiness or the strength of the religious associations of a city matters in contemporary political and policy analysis. Surely the main drivers of conflict in densely populated urban settings are a blend of changing patterns of employment due to globalization, rapid urbanization, growing immigration, technological innovation, and the competition over insufficient resources. Part of the answer is that the designation of a city as "holy" or as having strong religious associations furthers our understanding of particular conflicts that may be taking place in that city. Indeed, if we drill down a little deeper to examine specific cases and religious practices, can we find specific kinds of conflicts engendered by cities designated as holy that are different from other kinds of conflicts? Cities such as Jerusalem in which there are competing religious claims over the same site provide the most salient examples of conflicts that are unique to cities with strong religious associations. Conflicts over port cities or cities adjacent to valuable mineral deposits are of a very different nature than conflicts over religious sites.

Conflicts in Holy Cities

The London Track meeting in 1997 was not my first encounter with the religious conflicts in Jerusalem. In 1991, Everett Mendelsohn and the American Academy of Arts and Sciences had invited me to contribute to a series of off-the-record discussions between Israeli and Palestinian academics on a possible agreement over the question of Jerusalem. These discussions took place just as the secret negotiations that culminated in the Oslo Accords of 1993 were also beginning, and we were confident that some of what we said was being fed into those negotiations. My participation in this series also led to my being invited to facilitate Israeli–Palestinian discussions on the future of the city at various forums. Immersed in this way in the minutiae of the topic, I often had a hard time seeing the forest for the trees. I became aware how seeking short-term political advantage over the other side often trumped the need to work toward a shared strategic goal. What became clear in the years following the Oslo Accords was that even when some formula could be invented to reconcile specific disputes, it would not hold for long because the parties were not traveling in the same direction and their hoped-for destinations were quite some distance apart. So what were the main sticking points?

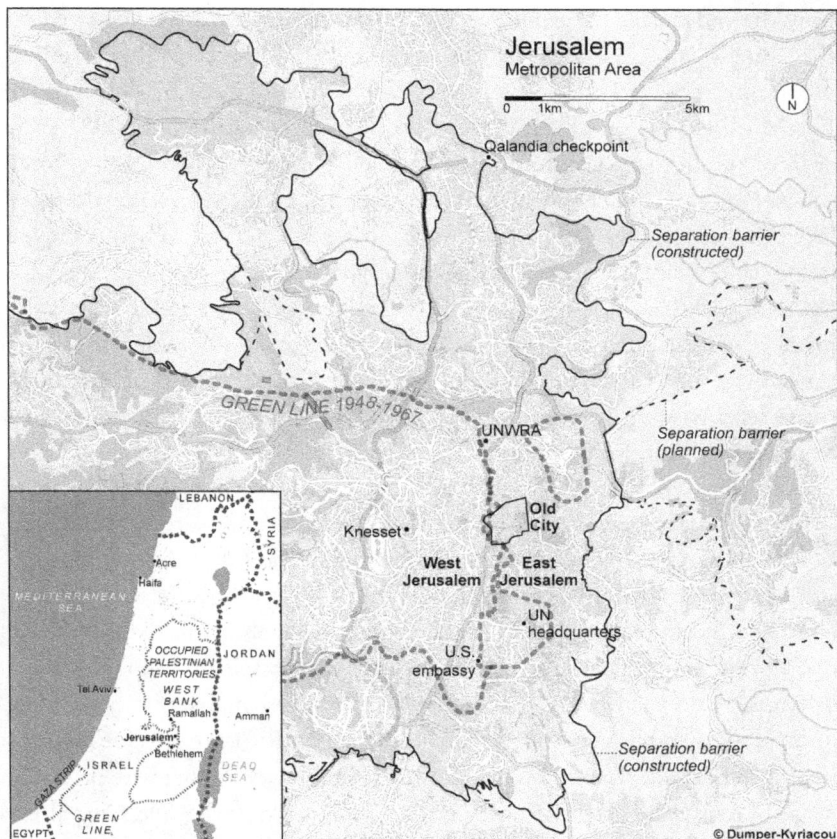

Map 1.1 Jerusalem metropolitan area. (Map by Lefkos Kyriacou and Michael Dumper)

The two main protagonists over who controls the city of Jerusalem and its holy sites are the State of Israel and the Palestinians represented by the PLO, and at its core the conflict is over which of these two ethnonational groups should have primacy in Palestine.[13] Yet we cannot get away from the fact that the city of Jerusalem, crammed full of religious sites and associated buildings, has played a key part in both framing the conflict and mobilizing its respective forces. The most important religious sites of Judaism, Christianity, and Islam are found cheek by jowl and sometimes literally on top of each other in what is a relatively small city.[14] For Judaism, the Temple Mount (Har Habayit) is the primary site and comprises the ruins of the first and second temples, with the Wailing (or Western) Wall now the only visible reminder of their destruction in 70 CE. Located on the Temple Mount is also the site of the Holy of Holies of the Israelites, where the Ark of the Covenant resided and was guarded by Levi priests. For Muslims, the exact same site is the Haram al-Sharif (Noble Sanctuary), Islam's third holiest site after Mecca and Medina. It contains the Dome of the Rock, where the prophet Muhammed is believed to have ascended briefly to heaven, and al-Aqsa Mosque, to which the first Muslims prayed before the switch to Mecca (known as *al-qibla*.) In Islam, the Wailing Wall (*ha-kotel* in Hebrew, *al-buraq* in Arabic) is also believed to be where the prophet Muhammad tethered his horse. The Golden Gate, on the northern side of the Haram, is where it is believed that Allah will sit and judge those who pass through at the End of Time. For Christianity, the Holy Sepulcher, a short walk away up the slope from these Jewish and Muslim sites in the Old City, marks the site of Golgotha, where Jesus Christ is believed to have been crucified after his celebrated punishing walk along the Via Dolorosa, which runs through most of the Old City. In addition to these primary sites, there are hundreds of related ones in the forms of churches, mosques, synagogues, prayer rooms, chapels, ritual baths (*mikva'ot* in Hebrew), monasteries, seminaries, convents, hostels for pilgrims, mausoleums, and cemeteries. One calculation in 1996 estimated that there were more than a thousand synagogues of all sizes, fifty-two mosques, sixty-five churches, and seventy-two monasteries in the city.[15] There are probably more by now. Another estimate in 2000 indicates that the Old City alone contains between 225 and 326 holy sites.[16] Given that the Old City is no larger than one kilometer square, this means that there is one holy site for every three to four square meters!

During the period of the British Mandate, these sites became intrinsically tied to each ethnonational group's sense of political, religious, and national identity and, as a consequence, have become sites of conflict. During the Jordanian annexation of the Old City (1949–1967), many traces of the Jewish presence in East Jerusalem were erased, and in 1967 Israel marked its control over the Old City by demolishing two mosques and an ancient residential area known as the Moroccan quarter in front of the Wailing Wall.[17] In the immediate aftermath of the Israeli occupation of East Jerusalem in 1967, the holy sites presented the Israeli government with a dilemma. To take over the Muslim religious sites directly would mobilize even stronger opposition by Palestinians, Jordanians, and the international community to Israel's occupation of the city, but to relinquish control over the Wailing Wall, adjacent to the Haram al-Sharif, would antagonize the state's more fervent religious supporters in Israel and abroad. Israel's initial policies were therefore double-edged. While retaining security control over the perimeter of the Haram enclosure and the rest of East Jerusalem, which marginalized the Palestinian leadership and Jordan, Israel declared that it would respect what is known as the Ottoman Status Quo of the Holy Places. To this end, non-Muslims would be forbidden to gather to pray in the Haram, and the chief Rabbinate of Israel ruled that Jewish entry to the Haram risked defiling the Jewish Holy of Holies and therefore was prohibited.[18]

In response, Palestinian leaders and Jordan set up a body known as the Higher Islamic Council and established oversight of all the Muslim endowments (*waqfs*) in the city and of the preservation of the holy sites themselves.[19] As a result, a "dual administration" emerged in the Old City and around the Haram that survived for nearly thirty years.[20] There were several serious challenges to this de facto arrangement, mostly from Israeli zealots or sympathizers but also from radical Islamic groups who saw it as Palestinian and Jordanian acquiescence to Israeli control.[21]

Ironically, what made this dual-administration model, which proved to be a working compromise between Israeli military oversight and Palestinian and Jordanian religious autonomy, untenable was ultimately the signing of the Oslo Accords. The accords transformed the PLO from primarily a military actor to primarily a political one. In addition, they led to a determination on the part of the Israeli negotiators that even if Israel were to sacrifice its settlements in the West Bank for the purposes of an agreement with the Palestinians, it would certainly not sacrifice its control over Jerusalem as well. As a result, the accords also "mainstreamed" the Israeli settler movement in Israeli political life.[22] Cooperation between settler groups operating in and around the Old City and Israeli state bodies increased to the extent that a network linking government funds, settler properties, and key state offices has transformed the settler movement from the outrider of radical Zionism to the vanguard of the Israeli establishment.[23] These groups' activities led to the crisis in November 2015 that I referred to at the beginning of the introduction.

What needs emphasizing about these post-Oslo developments is that Israeli colonization is taking place not only in the heart of the congested

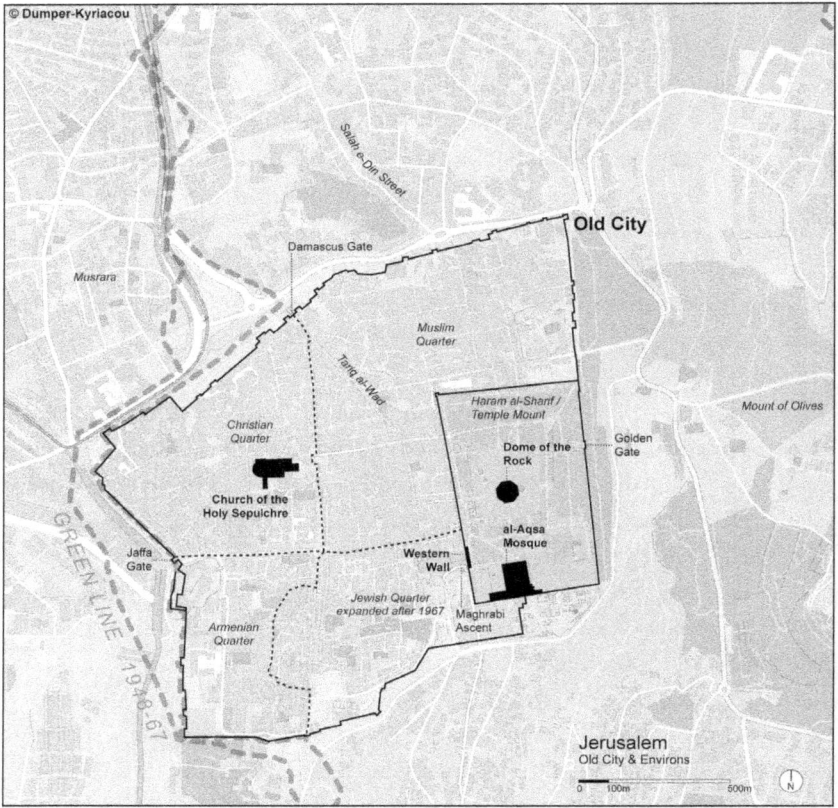

Map 1.2 Jerusalem Old City and environs. (Map by Lefkos Kyriacou and Michael Dumper)

and densely populated Old City but also, more importantly, in religiously sensitive areas close to Muslim and Christian holy sites. We should understand that the acquisition of property in these areas brings with it a panoply of security systems—Israeli armed soldiers, police outposts, Israeli private security firms, settler militia, patrols, and electronic surveillance— to protect the small Israeli groups who settle there. Palestinian residents of the city are intimidated, and their everyday life is subject to surveillance because the settlers have created a securitized culture in these sensitive areas.[24] We should also remember that these activities contribute to the consolidation of an ideological shift in Zionist political thinking. In the period following the occupation in 1967, the majority of Israeli Jews were

Figure 1.1 Dome of the Rock in the Haram al-Sharif enclosure. (Photograph by Razan Makhlouf)

content to abide by the Rabbinate of Israel's injunction not to visit or pray on the Temple Mount, but these recent developments have injected into mainstream Zionist discourse the possibility of constructing a synagogue on the Haram.[25]

Religious Conflict—the Urban Dimension

At this point, I wish to step back to explore how such religious conflicts may also be exacerbated by the fact that they are taking place in a city. I argue that cities can exacerbate religious conflicts and conflicts around holy sites for four key reasons: geography, demography, institutional transformations, and economics. At the same time, I reiterate the point I made earlier in my introduction that conflicts are highly complex and heterodox and can also flow from nonreligious dynamics in urbanism and urban development. One way of understanding the nonreligious reasons for religious conflicts is to see them as feeding into tensions that are then colored by religious symbolism and expressed as an infraction or diminishment of the concerns of that religion and its adherents. This section examines the general structural changes that take place in this process. The subsequent section examines the triggers that set off a religious conflict, which I call "flashpoints."

Geography

Changes in land use, property values, and patterns of residence due to new or depleting economic activities will affect the location of religious activities. A holy site or a ritualistic practice may find itself relocated from the center of a city to its margins or vice versa by dint of the city's changing geography, which will in turn affect its status and role in the life of the city. Conversely, a holy site may over time acquire either improved or impaired access depending on infrastructural developments elsewhere in the city and region. Better road, rail, and air links and the increased prosperity of adherents will encourage greater use of the holy site and the growth in numbers of pilgrims, tourists, and worshippers. In contrast, conflicts, wars, and changes in governance may reduce access to primary sites and lead to the use of other sites in the city or, indeed, of other cities altogether as alternative foci for worship and pilgrimage. An example of the latter phenomenon is the expansion of the site devoted to Sayyida Zaynab, the prophet's granddaughter, on the outskirts of Damascus. From a relatively small shrine in the nineteenth century, it has been transformed into a major Shi'a shrine.[26] The main reason for this expansion was the Iranian boycott of the pilgrimage to Mecca following an incident in 1989 during which more than four hundred Iranian pilgrims were killed by Saudi Arabian security services. This hiatus in Iranians visiting Mecca was lengthened by Saudi Arabia's establishment of policies to exclude and control the numbers of Iranian pilgrims entering the kingdom since that time. And so, due to the close ties between the Iranian and Syrian regimes, the Sitt Sayyida Zaynab shrine became an attractive alternative pilgrimage destination for Iranians.

In Jerusalem, the Israeli occupation in 1967 and the failure of the Oslo peace since 2000 have led to dramatic changes in land use that have affected religious practice in the city and exacerbated conflicts over religious issues. The construction of Israeli colonies on Palestinian-owned land in East Jerusalem has restricted the land available to existing Palestinian residents. A European Union report states that as a result of the Israeli government's land-acquisition policies, "around 53% of the Israeli

Figure 1.2 The "Wall" or Separation or Barrier, which divides Jerusalem from the West Bank. (Photograph by Razan Makhlouf)

defined municipal area of East Jerusalem is [*sic*] unavailable for development and 35% has been designated for settlement [colony] use."[27] This leaves less than 13 percent of land to meet Palestinians' needs, and much of this area is already densely populated and built up. Combined with a number of additional measures to reduce the Palestinian population in the city, these changes in land ownership have had two significant effects: first, they have pushed the Palestinian population both to the margins of the city and over the security border, also known as "the Wall," into the West Bank, where it is much more difficult for them to access schools, hospitals, family, and religious sites. Second, these changes have increased the housing density to a level that is physically and medically dangerous. Both of these outcomes heighten the tension in the city, so that when Israeli settlers, motivated by religious zeal to minimize the presence of Palestinians in the city, take over Palestinian properties, or when the Israeli authorities place restrictions on Palestinian males wishing to access the Haram al-Sharif to pray, the conflict is represented as a religious one and the cry "Al-Aqsa is in danger!" resonates deeply with much of the Palestinian population.

Demography

Changes in demography are often a major reason for religious conflicts in cities because, quite simply, an increase in population will inevitably lead to a larger number of worshippers, pilgrims, and visitors to a given collection of holy sites within a city. The larger numbers will take longer to "process" as civilian authorities or the military manage their attendance at rituals. Rituals will take longer; additional ones will be introduced at different times and on different days for specific demographics. In essence, the presence of people in the site, around it, and coming to it will be for a longer period of time. In addition, the increase in numbers will lead to an increase in facilities required: toilets, first-aid points, car parking, catering outlets, and water provision. There will also be more security deployed, more marshalling, more maintenance of the fabric of the sites heavily affected by wear and tear, more demand for pastoral care, and more requirement for information and interpretative literature either in the form of signage or leaflets or material on the internet. All this will warrant more administrative support staff. If the state, municipal, or religious authorities are not responsive to these changes, then tensions will arise. So without any religious reasons whatsoever, a holy site can emerge as a public-order issue by virtue of the fact that the population pool looking toward and being present at the site has increased in size.

If we focus more narrowly on how increased population numbers generally will lead to increased numbers engaged in religious rituals, we can see how the dynamics of demographic change directly lead to religious conflict. For example, rituals enacted at the site, in its vicinity, and often in relation to pilgrimage on the way to the site can also be sources of conflict. Worship at a site is both an individual and a collective activity. The act of worship creates a relationship between that person and the site. Favorite places or times are designated, memories are created, associations are made, a decision is clarified, and commitments promised. Similarly, a pilgrimage establishes the site in the pilgrim's life experience. Pilgrims have expended money and sometimes great effort; they have shared trials and tribulations; they have made friends and felt powerful emotions and possibly a spiritual fulfilment. In addition, the rituals taking place at holy sites require various religious paraphernalia and equipment, such as books, clothing, water, wine, crosses, candles, receptacles, and so on. Worshippers often like to take away mementoes, which are supplied by shopkeepers and religious retail outlets but which require space and signage and attract crowds. In sum, religious rituals mean the presence of people, and people in large numbers can both be threatening and experience a sense of threat. The behavior of rival groups can threaten the holiness of a site and lead to confrontations and violence. Worshippers, pilgrims, visitors are to religious leaders an "asset" that can be mobilized to assert a position or to resist an encroachment.

The population of Jerusalem has increased rapidly. It has tripled from 266,000 in 1967 to 883,000 in 2016.[28] Most of this increase has come from Israeli Jews being encouraged to settle in the city in order to consolidate Israel's control over it. Two important elements of this increase have an impact on our discussion. First, the Israeli Jewish population on the eastern side of the city, occupied East Jerusalem, has grown from zero in 1967 to more than 200,000 "settlers" living in in colonies or settlements strategically scattered along the hilltops and overlooking access routes into the city. In comparison, approximately 316,000 Palestinians live there. Second, for many years the Israeli authorities have sought to achieve a demographic balance of 70 percent Israeli Jewish to 30 percent Palestinian Arab, but the most recent figures show that the proportion is closer to 60:40: roughly 537,000 Israeli Jews to 336,000 Palestinian Arabs.[29] Of the Palestinian Arab population, Muslims constitute nearly 95 percent, and Christians only 5 percent. Of the total population of Jerusalem, Jews constitute 60 percent, and Muslims approximately 36 percent.[30] What this means for my purposes here is that not only are there more Israeli Jews residing in Jerusalem, but there are also more Israeli Jews residing in East Jerusalem, which is the part of the city where the most sensitive and most visited holy sites are. On top of this, the many more Palestinians living in East Jerusalem will now be encountering more Israeli Jews than ever before when engaging in religious rituals, and the increased number of Jews will be encountering an increased number of Palestinians. To add to this perfect demographic storm is the fact that in both communities we are witnessing a resurgence in religiosity, where public spaces are being increasingly utilized to demonstrate the numerical strength of each community and to assert a claim to territory. We should also note that in Jerusalem two parallel education systems reinforce separate cultures, language, religion, and history of the Israelis and Palestinians. In this context, accommodation to the other community's religious needs is seen, as Ron Hassner has elaborated, as a zero-sum game,[31] and confrontation is increasingly likely.

Institutional Transformations

Conflicts in holy cities arise from major institutional changes in and around the sites concerned. As time passes and as a site becomes a major site, a larger administrative framework is established to manage the activities of religious officials, clergy, and administrative staff. Facilities are required to house libraries, archives, and records; to hold meetings and conferences; and to service the site's employment. In our contemporary neoliberal period, during which we have witnessed a decline in the role of the state in providing safety nets and other welfare services for its citizens, a space has opened up for religious groups to take up this burden. One result has been that in holy cities the responsibilities of the clergy and other religious employees have increased. In this situation, the religious hierarchy becomes an alternative source of authority and representation. As a consequence of these developments, the number of buildings associated with a particular site or faith increases, and the site's presence in the city becomes greater and more salient. This change may affect rival or competing sects and faiths, causing friction, jealousies, disputes over precedence and access, and changes in the established arrangements for the management of rituals.

In Jerusalem, we can see how the role given to religious institution is significant. It is exacerbated in part by the lack of political representation of Palestinian Arabs in East Jerusalem. Since 2001, the PLO has not been permitted to operate in Jerusalem, and despite a peace treaty signed between Israel and Jordan in 1994, the Jordanian government has deferred formally to the Palestinian leadership. Israel has sought to encourage Palestinian residents to participate in the elections to the Israeli Jerusalem municipality, but the consensus among Palestinians has been to boycott them out of the fear that their vote will confer legitimacy upon the Israeli occupation of East Jerusalem.[32] The main consequence of these political views has been to leave the Palestinians of East Jerusalem without any formal political representation. Palestinian civil society has attempted to fill the gap, and a number of coordinating bodies have issued various statements on behalf of Palestinians residents. However, the most influential body that speaks on their behalf has been the Islamic Waqf Administration, which also acts as a custodian of the Muslim religious sites of East Jerusalem. This role has emerged more strongly since the decline of the PLO and offers Jordan, as paymaster-general of the Waqf Administration, an opportunity to recoup some of its lost influence in the city. We should remember that not all religious conflicts are interethnic or intercommunal; some are, indeed, intracommunal. In Jerusalem, the divisions between the Waqf Administration and radical Islamic groups such as HAMAS and the small jihadist group Hizb at-Tahrir are pronounced.[33] Divisions between the Greek Orthodox clergy, who tend to be Greek or Cypriot nationals, and the Palestinian Christian laity have also resulted in clashes and court cases. However, the main point is that what we see is the emergence of a powerful clerical bureaucracy that has a significant stake in the political outcomes of any agreed settlement.

The Political Economy of Holy Places

In the previous discussion, one can see how religious sites in cities become important parts of the urban economy. At a basic level, worshippers, pilgrims, and visitors require accommodation in the form of hotels, pensions, hostels, and private lodgings. They need to be supplied with food and drink via stalls, cafes, restaurants, supermarkets, and grocery shops. They often wish to replenish goods such as clothing and footwear, pharmaceuticals and toiletries. And they are a captive market for religious paraphernalia, such as rosary or prayer beads, incense, prayer rugs, icons, paintings of Christ with pulsating hearts, alarm clocks with recordings of the *azan* (the five daily Muslim calls to prayer), CDs and DVDs, olive-wood figures, candlesticks and menorah, and so on. The production and purchase of all these items inject funds into the local economy and provide employment and an income for a broad section of the population irrespective of religious faith. Many of the carnation and marigold flower sellers in Banaras are Muslim even though the flowers are used as offerings to Hindu gods. A more important level of economic input are the funds that have a direct relationship to the maintenance of holy sites, religious personnel, and the services provided by their organizations. This larger and more strategic revenue stream results in the construction of buildings and related infrastructure, the employment of personnel on a longer-term basis, and the development of programs that involve a commitment to service provision over many years. This economy flows from a more permanent presence and is often derived from funds made up of various entry fees, donations, legacies, and endowments. Control over these sources of funding and how they are disbursed can become a cause of conflict, as we will see in the dispute regarding the Mezquita-Cathedral, and, indeed, of intracommunal conflict, as we will see regarding the Thaipusam festival in George Town.

Of these funds, endowments are particularly important in the economy of holy cities and merit some further description. In addition to the blessings they bestow upon the endower, their economic and political role is threefold. First, they enhance the religious dimension of the city through the provision of places for worship, for religious propagation and training, for accommodation of pilgrims, and for the care of the poor, needy, and infirm. Second, they channel external funds into the city to support large religious buildings, institutions, or services for residents and pilgrims alike. Land and property in the city and farther afield are endowed so that the income from these assets can be used for charitable and religious purposes, in turn leading to the construction of churches, synagogues, temples, mosques, prayer rooms, public baths, schools, seminaries, hostels, and homes for orphans and the aged. Third, religious leaders often use these funds to consolidate and extend their political role in a city by investing in the construction of revenue-generating properties such as shops, hotels, and restaurants, which also support the use of the holy sites under their responsibility.

Endowments, or *waqf*s, in Palestine offer a useful example of the significant social, economic, and political role they play. It has been estimated that during the Ottoman period between 13 and 15 percent of the cultivated land of Palestine comprised Islamic endowments.[34] Between 70 and 90 percent of some towns such as Jaffa and Acre were said to be owned by *waqf*s. The political influence this gave the administrators and the wealth it gave to the beneficiaries were clearly considerable. In the latter stages of the Ottoman Empire, *waqf*s provided an independent economic base for the religious and urban elite in their resistance to the centralizing policies pursued by the authorities in Istanbul. If we turn to Jerusalem, we can see how the city was particularly "well endowed." In the period between the establishment of the British Mandate and the Jordanian annexation, 1922–1967, the role of *waqf*s in Jerusalem increased. Not only were new endowments made, but their archaic administration was reformed and made more efficient as the finances were increasingly centralized and controlled by a politico-religious elite made up of the Palestinian aristocracy. In 1967, all this was threatened by the Israeli occupation of East Jerusalem. Israeli policies introduced to acquire Palestinian land, including *waqf* land, policies to regulate the construction and use of mosques, and policies to limit the entry of Muslim worshippers to the Haram al-Sharif combined to erode the finances of the religious leaders and the institutions they ran, leading to repeated collapse in cooperation over the management of the sites and of public order on the streets of the city.

No doubt, other reasons can be offered to explain why cities exacerbate religious conflicts and conflict around holy sites, but for the purposes of this discussion these four reasons—geography, demography, institutional transformations, and economics—appear to be the most salient and relevant. In the following chapters, I cover each of these reasons in slightly different ways because each holy city has a particular context and history, and if I were to approach all of them in exactly the same way, I would fail to capture some of the emphases and nuances. Nevertheless, by examining the case of Jerusalem as a holy city per se, it is possible to identify these strong structural issues as key reasons for conflict. Before I turn to these other cities, one more step is necessary: to take these overarching reasons and unpack them a little further to see how they play out on the street. The street is the public space where conflicts swell up and are expressed, and I wish now to draw attention to triggers and catalysts of conflicts, which I refer to as "flashpoints."

Flashpoints

As I write these paragraphs, I have in front of me a photograph that I repeatedly glance at while thinking of the next sentence. The foreground depicts a Palestinian schoolgirl with a head scarf, wearing trousers and a school dress over them. She is sitting on a low wall in the Haram al-Sharif enclosure looking down at her hands, which are holding a twig or a tiny piece of paper. It is a peaceful scene. The sun is shining brightly; it is early in the morning, and she is bored and letting her heels kick gently against the wall as she waits for her friends. Several meters behind her in the middle ground there is an old olive tree growing beside a building that is part of the office selling tickets to enter the al-Aqsa Mosque. Between the olive tree and the sales window, which is not yet open, leans an Israeli policeman looking toward the photographer. He is bare-headed but has a blue flak jacket on, and there is something strapped to his back, a small machine gun or a long

Figure 1.3 Schoolgirl waits for her friends inside the Haram al-Sharif. (Photograph by Razan Makhlouf)

truncheon. To the right of the ticket office is a wide flight of steps leading up to some slender arches. Beyond them, soaring into the azure-blue sky is the golden dome of the Dome of the Rock, resting on its famous facades of blue tiles and tiny mosaics. Peeping in from the right are a few branches of a tall palm tree.

I have hundreds of photographs of Jerusalem, and this is my favorite. It tells such a complex story, full of contradictions and hidden meanings. The girl is young, living her everyday life of school and boredom; the olive tree is ancient, a symbol of peace, and stands beside an Israeli paramilitary policeman, who is ostensibly relaxing but is also alert, watching, armed. The crowds have not yet started to arrive. The spiritually uplifting beauty of the great dome overlooks the small ticket office. The office is closed and without the queues before it, as there will be later in the day, but it is waiting for the day to begin and for money to be made. The wide spaces in between are empty yet are made for the huge crowds of tourists or on Fridays for the worshippers who stand in lines across the whole of the Haram and prostrate themselves in unison. Peace, faith, and hidden conflict are all there in this picture, and conflict can be, as it has frequently been, triggered both quickly and casually. This section examines three "street-level flashpoints": that is, conflicts that are already in the making, as I discussed in the previous section, but that are triggered over time, over place, and over people. A fourth flashpoint considered here is generated by *actions* outside of the city.

Time Flashpoints

With regard to conflicts over time, we can see how in cities that are the location of several religions (i.e., are religiously pluralistic), the conjunction of different religious festivals or anniversaries of the birthday or death of a founder or other significant personages on the same day or same period can cause conflicts. As worshippers compete for priority on the streets or over access to public places where they can carry out their rituals or display their faith in front of their assembled community, an already complex web of grievances can tip over into outright conflict. This conjunction can be managed and planned through cooperation between religious leaders and the city authorities, but at the same time unforeseen events can disrupt such plans, leading to misunderstandings and heated responses. The three great Abrahamic religions have fortunately allocated different week-days as their days of prayer—Friday for Muslims, Saturdays for Jews, and Sundays for Christians—but conflicts nonetheless can occur in some circumstances when one religion's feast day falls on another religion's day of worship. One particular trigger point can be the clash of dates as some festivities are fixed by the solar calendar, whereas others are fixed by the lunar calendar. Another cause of conflict can be the conjunction of religious festivals and state-sponsored national events, such as a national day or the birth or death of a president or royal person. Such clashes can occur particularly in circumstances where the state authorities and the religious community celebrating at that time are of different religious, ethnic, or linguistic origins. Other nonreligious events can cause heightened tension if they are related to religious sites, including the visits of politicians or well-known persons to the area, which may convey recognition of one group's control over a disputed site or support for one side or the other. Finally, the acquisition of a religious property or the change of use of that property by the state or another party and the enforcement of the acquisition at a sensitive time in the religious calendar can trigger conflict if the acquisition is seen as eroding the rights of use or access by religious groups.

A good example is the management of crowds of worshippers in Jerusalem during particular festivities. During Ramadan, the Friday prayers in the Haram al-Sharif can attract up to 250,000 Muslim worshippers, who are crowded into a very small space with difficult points of entry and exit. During the Jewish High Holy Days of New Year and Tashlich, crowds of some 30,000 Jews can file through the Old City toward the Wailing Wall. Similarly, some 50,000 to 60,000 Christian worshippers will flock to the courtyard in front of the Church of the Holy Sepulcher over Easter.[35] All these festivities put enormous strains upon security and police services and require close coordination and planning with the heads of the different communities. When there is a breakdown in coordination and public trust, then incidents and confrontations occur. Because Jerusalem is one of the three holiest sites in Islam, pious acts carried out on religiously significant days are believed to be even more meritorious. One such event is Laylat al-Qadr, or the Night of Power. Laylat al-Qadr commemorates the night when the prophet Muhammad received his first revelation from Allah and thus is the foundation day of Islam. It is a night of immense religious power, and the piety of pious acts performed then is multiplied, according to Islamic scholars, by a factor of eighty-three. As Kenny Schmitt has written in his ethnographic account of the festival, "Because Jerusalem is a holy city and al-Aqsa the focal-point of its holiness, Muslims make great efforts to perform their acts of piety on the Night of Power in the sacred place."[36] On Laylat al-Qadr, many thousands of Palestinian Muslims camp out in the Haram al-Sharif enclosure in small groups, praying, reading the Qur'an, sitting in silent contemplation, being close to family members. In 2013, approximately 400,000 people filled the enclosure almost to capacity.[37] In 2015, this figure was exceeded by an additional 50,000.[38] However, in 2014, at the height of an Israeli invasion of the Gaza Strip, tensions in the city were high as Palestinians protested against the killing of more than six hundred of their compatriots in the Gaza Strip. Demonstrations took place at the large Qalandia checkpoint beside the huge wall separating East Jerusalem from the West Bank. When the Israeli authorities decided to limit access to the Haram al-Sharif only to those older than sixty, young Palestinians erupted in anger and trashed the barriers at the entrance to the Haram and set fire to a police station in the Old City.[39] Despite the protests, that year less than 15,000 people were permitted to enter the Haram for Laylat al-Qadr. Schmitt writes that on the most sacred and significant night of the year "97% of the people who would have come on previous

Figure 1.4 Israeli soldiers in soft berets, indicating a low threat level, patrol the Damascus Gate in the Old City, Jerusalem. (Photograph by Razan Makhlouf)

and subsequent years were prevented. On the night when heaven and earth intersect, Israel severed the connection."[40] Clearly, the timing of the restrictions to the Haram al-Sharif in 2014 had less to do with Laylat al-Qadr and more with the Israeli invasion of Gaza at the same time. The conflict between Israeli police and paramilitary units and Palestinians was not religious but spilled over into a religious issue as a result of an interdiction of a Muslim religious practice in the city.

Place Flashpoints

Conflicts over place—that is, over the use and access to holy sites—are also frequent. This kind of conflict is, of course, greatest when the site is contested by both parties. I use the term *contested* rather than *shared* because *shared* can imply an agreement or a degree of acceptance when a site is partitioned either spatially or temporally. In most cases, such as at al-Ibrahimi Mosque in Hebron, this is not the situation.[41] Arrangements for joint use are usually imposed by a dominant state power. Examples of such contested sites abound in the Middle East, the Balkans, northern India, and parts of West Africa. In these sites, aside from the overarching issue of ownership and control, conflicts occur at access points, with guards, marshals, or security personnel filtering and controlling both numbers and categories of people wishing to enter. When such filtering is carried out either by those who are not sanctioned by the religious custodians of the site, such as a paramilitary police force of an occupying power, or by those of a different ethnic or religious group, then the possibility of a conflict is enhanced. On top of this, the very act of filtering aggravates the congestion that is already occurring. Many holy sites are in older parts of town, with narrow streets. The slowing down of access to the site as a result of the filtering causes groups of worshippers to back up down the alleyways, thus crowding and blocking entrances and intersections, leading to jostling in the crowd and resentment by shopkeepers whose livelihood may be affected by the congestion.[42] All are fertile ground for aggravating low-level conflict. Insults are exchanged, then escalating into provocative pushing and shoving, stone throwing, and, in extremis, fights, destruction, and arson. Jerusalem's Old City is replete with such intersections, funnels, and obstacles that aggravate already existing tensions. Although Old City residents and shopkeepers in particular are generally very welcoming of tourists, I have witnessed aggressive verbal abuse and shoving directed at large coach parties of tourists who, clustering together, are unaware that they are completely blocking up the narrow thoroughfares in the Old City, which are not just there for them to stand and gawp but also routes for the transfer of merchandise as well as people.

Other possible areas for conflict are security checkpoints farther away from access points to holy sites. These checkpoints are often erected to preempt conflict at the site itself and in a space where there is room to check the eligibility of those wishing to enter the site, to do body searches, to install equipment for identity card scrutiny, to weed out of undesirables, and to house paramilitary rapid-response teams that can be deployed if a tense situation escalates. Other sources of conflict emanating from place are "transition zones." They are usually residential or retail areas straddling different religious or ethnic communities within a city and through which worshippers must pass in order to reach their holy site. Access routes become areas of contestation because their use is dominated by one religious community or another depending on the day of worship or feast day. A final typical conflict involving place concerns unresolved property disputes between religious groups. These disputes can but do not always feature the main and prominent sites but also lesser sites, such as minor entrances to contested sites, unsanctioned sales or leases of religious property to another religious group, the designation of certain places as holy by one religious group in the heart of an area dominated by another group, which as a consequence disrupts the patterns of residents' daily life.

This volatility over the use of space was vividly illustrated to me following my participation in some research conducted in 2005 by the Conflict in Cities team.[43] The team carried out a "soundscape" study of a key access route in Jerusalem for Muslims and Jews wishing to pray either at the al-Aqsa Mosque or at the Wailing Wall. We recorded sounds along the Tariq al-Wad, the street that runs through the predominantly Muslim areas of the Old City from the main entrance at Damascus Gate to the Haram al-Sharif, on both Friday, the Muslim day of prayer, and Saturday, the Jewish Sabbath. From the recordings, we were able to hear how the Palestinian Arab and Muslim character of the street changed between the two days. The sounds on Friday were composed almost entirely of Arabic conversations, Arabic market calls and sales patter, Arabic music, and sung Qur'anic prayers, interspersed with a smattering of sentences in a European language and some Hebrew being spoken into a walkie-talkie. Saturday had the same ingredients, but the proportions were different. The generalized Palestinian Arab and Muslim discourse was overlain and punctuated by much more Hebrew, Israeli songs, and smatterings of Yiddish, much more Americanized English, and much more walkie-talkie chatter by the Israeli security forces. These recordings illustrated the change of use of the streets on these two days and how the public space in that part of the city was both "jointly used" (not "shared") in temporal terms and contested overall in that when it was more jointly used, the security presence was also higher.

Another Jerusalem place flashpoint is the Maghrabi Ascent, illustrated by what has become known as the Maghrabi Ascent incident of 2007. The Maghrabi Ascent is an Ottoman ramp that leads up from the southwestern side of the Haram into the Maghrabi Gate, which is the entrance to the Haram for tourists and non-Muslims, and in 2006–2007 it began to collapse. The causes of the collapse are the subject of much dispute. Some argue that it was caused by gradual erosion and an earthquake; others are convinced that it is a direct consequence of the Israeli destruction of the Maghrabi quarter in 1967 and the building of a huge plaza in front of the Wailing Wall, which undermined the ramp's foundations. The controversy over why the ramp was collapsing and who was responsible for replacing it led to a diplomatic stand-off between Jordan and Israel and an attempt by UNESCO to intercede. Palestinians interpreted Israeli plans for the new ascent, which was much broader than the original one, as being designed to allow armored vehicles to enter the Haram to quell gatherings of Palestinian protestors. For both Jordanians and Palestinians, allowing the Israeli authorities to plan and construct a replacement ascent was also tantamount to recognizing Israeli responsibility for the Old City and thus legitimizing its occupation. Although the Israeli government clearly considered the reconstruction as an opportunity to establish a significant legal precedent and to build something more appropriate to a modern tourist economy, it also saw itself as the de facto responsible authority and therefore argued that not to take action over replacing the ramp would be seen by the international community as a dereliction of Israel's duty.[44] UNESCO, for its part, tried hard to keep the discussion restricted to technical, architectural, and engineering matters but at the same time was concerned enough about Israeli unilateral decisions to introduce a "reinforced monitoring mechanism," which was unique in its procedures, to keep a close and official eye on developments regarding the ascent.[45] The controversy fueled the bigger dispute over who controlled the Haram and the Old City. It also galvanized radical Islamic groups in Israel, who with their Israeli citizenship saw an opportunity to widen the dispute from merely a technical one to one that entailed the defense of Muslim rights in the city. More than 3,000 Israeli police and security officers were required to deal with the threat to public order this one issue caused, a force estimated to be between 100 and 150 percent larger than routine Israeli security forces.[46]

People Flashpoints

The third category of street-level flashpoints is conflicts over people. The people in these conflicts can range from merely insensitive foreign tourists to religious extremists and zealots. Their presence and behavior can provoke an angry reaction against themselves, against other members of their community, against their leadership, and against the property of the offending community. Such incidents can also lead to anger and violence against the religious leadership of the receiving community if the leadership is perceived as not sufficiently protecting the holy sites and rituals of the community. In sites where the contestation also takes on a nationalist hue, "spoilers" can be active in derailing any compromises between the various parties over access or control. There are a number of specific ways religious adherents can demonstrate their support for their holy sites and resist perceived threats that range in seriousness from the merely offensive to the seriously destabilizing. Such ways include deliberate antisocial behavior, such as immodest dress, noise, insults that can cause offense; damage to property, such as breakages, thefts, and graffiti; disruption of public order through demonstrations; the staging of prayer and chanting vigils in non-sanctioned areas; stone throwing; the planting of explosive devices; violent occupation; and hostage taking. As we shall see in subsequent chapters, all of these actions are utilized at some point or another.

In Jerusalem, it is easy to pick examples of how the behavior of individuals or groups can be provocative and trigger conflicts. On the steps of Damascus Gate, Christian pilgrims start preaching to Muslims on their way to prayer, which is perceived as offensive. Muslim youths daub swastikas on the doors of synagogues or on gravestones in the big Jewish cemetery on the slopes of the Mount of Olives, overlooking the Haram al-Sharif. But these are small-fry irritants compared to the more sustained and strategic activities of the Israeli settler movement in Jerusalem. A particularly egregious example of settler provocation eliciting a Palestinian counter-response, with the potential to destabilize the uneasy equilibrium around the Haram al-Sharif, involves the events that led up to the crisis in November 2015 that I referred to in the introduction. On July 26, 2015, an Israeli settler group working out of the Temple Institute (a settler institution devoted to efforts to rebuild the Jewish temple on the Haram al-Sharif/Temple Mount) conducted a tour of the Haram al-Sharif.[47] More than 1,200 people were on the tour, plus 40 to 50 armed Israeli police, security guards, and riot-police units.[48] The tour was ostensibly being given to commemorate Tisha B'Av and the destruction of the first and second Jewish temples, but it was also part of Israeli settlers campaign to test the limitations placed upon non-Muslims visiting and praying in the Haram al-Sharif. In the YouTube video of the tour, you can quickly see that this tour was not just for religious purposes, which in any case are proscribed by the Israeli Rabbinate. Not only was it provocative in size, but it was also accompanied by fully armed police and paramilitary units, so it appeared more like a temporary occupation. These settlers and settler supporters have broken through the taboo preventing Jews from praying in Haram and seek to do so frequently and as regularly as possible in order to establish a precedent for prayer upon which they can claim other rights, such as the construction of a temple.[49] In the video, you can see how Palestinian Muslims who had either been praying or simply enjoying the open space inside the Haram were slow in responding at first, but as they realized the extent and import of this tour, they began to congregate and to surround and harass these Jewish visitors. Hijab-clad women had walkie-talkies and were presumably summoning reinforcements. The police were fully occupied keeping Palestinians at a distance and preventing the visitors from attempting to pray. A *BBC Panorama* film on Jerusalem earlier in the week showed a similar tour being completely surrounded by *murabityyn* and *murabitaat* (male and female religious activists dedicated to preserving the Islamic character of the Haram al-Sharif), who followed the Jewish visitors en masse, harassing them by constantly yelling "Allahu Akbar" directly in their faces and spitting.[50] These *murabityyn* and *murabitaat* are aware that a violent response to the settler incursions will result in their incarceration, so they focus on studying religious scriptures in small groups scattered about the Haram and observing all the prayer times and festivals, thus ensuring there is a significant presence of Palestinian Muslims at all times on the site.[51] However, they are also on guard for the provocative entrance of any Jewish settlers or other Israeli Jews and leap to their feet to try and obstruct the Jews' progress. Their increasing numbers proved to be effective in that many of these Muslim men and women were banned from the Haram. They also succeeded in mobilizing the wider Muslim community and the religious and political leadership in both Palestine and Jordan, with the result that a crisis occurred in November 2015. Despite the Israeli government taking steps to cool the situation by reigning in the settlers and by lifting restrictions on Muslim worshippers, the situation in and around the Haram remains volatile. One gets the strong impression that the opposing groups are biding their time and strengthening their positions in preparation for the next round in the conflict.

External Flashpoints

In between these street-level flashpoints and the more structural causes of conflict discussed earlier is the international community. Interventions by the international community, at least since the end of the British Mandate, are neither a cause nor a trigger, yet they do play an important part in fanning the flames of religious conflicts in cities. Our understanding of how holy cities play a part in international conflicts is limited, and here I only wish to sketch out some possibilities to be explored in this book. Because cities are a locus for regional festivities and pilgrimages to holy sites, an international network of organizers, adherents, and other forms of transnational solidarities is created that confers significant powers upon the religious leaders and custodians of holy sites. These custodians are able, for example, to impose quotas on numbers not only to regulate excessive flows of pilgrims but also to exclude pilgrims who come from particular countries and to deny legitimacy to opposition sects. This imposition will, of course, have an impact on relations with the sending and neighboring states. For example, Sunni–Shi'a conflicts in the Middle East are frequently exacerbated as a consequence of Saudi Arabian control over the haj (pilgrimage) to Mecca. The ongoing conflict between Iran and Saudi Arabia is in part a cause and in part a consequence of Saudi Arabia's fear that a large number of Iranian pilgrims will undermine its arrangements concerning the haj and destabilize the regime. In some cases, religious conflicts in cities have led to greater involvement of the international community in the protection of religious monuments and access to them. The growing role of UNESCO in setting recognized benchmarks over acceptable activity regarding contested holy places is significant but not without its problems. Yet academic analysis of the implications of applying universal principles to confessional-based conflicts is limited.[52]

A dramatic example of how conflicts in cities with strong religious associations are both affected by and have an impact on international relations is the controversy concerning the location of the U.S. embassy to Israel. Until January 2017, along with the embassy of every other nation on the planet, the U.S. embassy was located in Tel Aviv and not in Jerusalem as a sign of the international community's refusal to accept the Israeli incorporation of East Jerusalem into Israel. In locating their embassies in Tel Aviv, states around the world were also refusing to recognize Jerusalem as the capital of the State of Israel. This is quite a remarkable fact and constitutes one of the very few total and comprehensive diplomatic boycotts of a fellow member state in the UN. Despite huge pressures from different political constituencies in the United States, despite Congress legislating to enforce relocation of the U.S. embassy to Jerusalem, and despite successive presidential candidates and elected presidents professing an intention to implement this law, the U.S. embassy remained in Tel Aviv.[53] The relocation of the U.S. embassy to Jerusalem would be hugely symbolic both to Israel and to the United States. The announcement in December 2017 that the United States would move its embassy to Jerusalem, thereby recognizing the city as the capital of Israel, broke the international consensus on the status of Jerusalem and has had deep ramifications for a negotiated agreement on Jerusalem and its holy sites. In the first place, it confirmed the bias of the U.S. position in the negotiations and removed it as a broker for any agreement between Israel and the PLO. Second, it deferred the prospect of an agreement on Jerusalem indefinitely because the U.S. recognition appeared to preempt any recognition of Palestinian counterclaims to the city. Third, it also postponed negotiations over other important issues, such as the removal of Israeli colonies in the occupied Palestinian territories, security cooperation, and Israeli recognition of the State of Palestine, because without progress on the Jerusalem issue there could be no agreement on the other issues. Nevertheless, the U.S. president seems to have calculated that the political gains he obtains from pleasing the conservative, evangelical, and pro-Israel elements of his domestic base will be greater than the political losses for the United States in the Middle East because of this decision.

At the same time, the U.S. president's announcement may also prove to be problematic for Israel. It was not clear whether moving the embassy and recognizing Jerusalem as the capital of Israel meant that the United States had ruled out a future Palestinian political role in the city. Indeed, did it mean the United States also recognized Israeli sovereignty over East Jerusalem or just West Jerusalem, and, if so, which borders in East Jerusalem— the ones established in 1967 or the security border delineated by the Wall? An analysis by the International Crisis Group unpacks this problem a little more: "Will the [U.S.] ambassador to Israel be permitted to visit East Jerusalem, including the Western Wall, in his official capacity? Will U.S. officials be permitted to meet Israelis at ministries in East Jerusalem? Will passports of U.S. citizens born in East Jerusalem say 'Israel' on them? Will settlement construction within municipal Jerusalem be treated differently?"[54] In addition, managing an ongoing conflict such as Jerusalem requires the possibility of some agreement at a future date. The removal of Jerusalem from the agenda pushes the conflict in the direction of violent action rather than negotiation. Moreover, it seriously undermines the role of the regime in Jordan, which has signed a peace treaty with Israel in which Jordan is designated a custodianship role over the Muslim and Christian holy sites of the city. In the face of mounting criticism that Jordan has either failed to protect these sites or is complicit in allowing Israel to encroach upon the sites, King Abdullah of Jordan will be under even greater pressure to demonstrate his country's support for the Palestinian position on Jerusalem and thus to strengthen the opposition to Israel. Thus, external flashpoints such as this unilateral rupture in the international consensus over the city of Jerusalem can produce unpredictable results and contribute to the fragility and volatility of an already unstable situation on the ground.

Jerusalem as a Template

The U.S. government's decision in 2017 to recognize Jerusalem as the capital of Israel in opposition to UN resolutions and international law has killed off the prospect of peace negotiations in the near future. For all the criticism directed against it, the United States has historically been a great supporter of a negotiated solution for the city, so this decision was a significant blow to that approach. Indeed, however much the United States allied itself with Israel in the negotiations with the PLO, the PLO knew that without the U.S. involvement, any agreement with Israel would not be forthcoming. By recognizing Jerusalem as Israel's capital and by moving its embassy to that city, at a stroke the United States took Jerusalem off the negotiating table and removed itself as a potential broker. Unless there is a significant shift in the balance of power in the region that can counter the relative impunity with which Israel can act both in Palestine and in the region, there is little prospect of successful peace negotiations. The Palestinians are unlikely to sign what is in effect surrender terms—not when it comes to the Muslim holy places of Jerusalem. But if we step back from the consideration of the prospects for a resolution over the holy sites in Jerusalem, we can discern a clutch of issues that are useful in examining the other cities discussed in this book: the primacy of the holy sites concerned, the role of demography, the political role of a clerical administration, issues of land and property ownership, ideology, and external intervention.

Jerusalem is unique in that it is the location of so many primary religious sites belonging to the three major monotheistic religions. Because of this unique status, employing it as a model could thus be problematic. Of the four other cities selected, only Banaras and Lhasa are comparable to Jerusalem as the location of sites central to the religious faiths involved. Nevertheless, what the case of Jerusalem does highlight is that the primacy of the sites heightens the contentiousness of any change in their status. In the introduction, I referred to how certain sites have a greater centrality to a religion than others and to the problems this centrality poses in establishing the definition of a holy city. I want to return to this notion of centrality and relate it here to the question of religious and communal identity. There may be disputes between adherents and scholars of a religion as to which sites may be more central, but the principle that some sites are more central, more important, than others is not contentious. As such, conflicts in and over primary holy sites are of a different and more profound nature than conflicts over other kinds of land and resources. The presence of these sites has resonance beyond the sphere of personal piety, and, as a consequence, a population will go to much greater lengths to protect them. Ron Hassner has pointed to these holy sites' indivisibility and "nonfungibility" as core features that make their presence in cities *politically* problematic. Unlike other territorial assets in an armed conflict, holy sites cannot be divided or partitioned without their integrity being impaired and a desecration being incurred. Neither can holy sites be exchanged for other goods or assets. Fungibility is a critical part of success in all negotiations, but with holy sites there is much less possibility for negotiations because there can be no alternative sites and no substitution for the sites. As a result of this indivisibility and this nonfungibility, disputes over holy sites in cities are usually intractable and protracted.[55] This is an important lesson to learn from the Jerusalem case.

Another major issue is surely the presence of a strong demographic binary. The ethnonational Israeli Jewish and Palestinian Arab framework within which the two main religious communities, Muslim and Jewish, are situated is paramount. Here we have a conflict where one's ethnicity, one's language, and one's religion combine to accentuate differences and to make dialogue and accommodation twice as difficult. In Belfast, at least the same language is spoken, and both sides love rugby and support the pan-Ireland rugby team. In George Town, we will see how ethnic differences are diluted by a religious diversity that straddles different groups. In contrast, in Jerusalem the divide is a defining one and undergirded by a military occupation. If we add to this divide the presence of a powerful Muslim clergy who may not be able to reverse the encroachments of the Israeli authorities but nevertheless have not been dislodged from their position, we can see how longevity, independent sources of finance, and international networks allow them to be quasi-representative of a community. This is particularly the case in Jerusalem, where political representation in East Jerusalem has been curtailed. An important buttress to this divide between the communities is also the pattern of land ownership. Despite Israel's forcible acquisition of Palestinian land and property in West Jerusalem in 1948 and in East Jerusalem in 1967, much of the land surrounding religious sites and associated with religious sites remains under the management of institutions supporting Palestinian rights in the city. This injects a territorial dimension to the conflict in that these areas, despite being constantly eroded by further Israeli acquisitions, are relatively contiguous with each other. A further issue is that of external intervention. The dispute over the future of Jerusalem is an integral part of the Arab–Israeli conflict, which has led to the passing of more UN Security Council and General Assembly resolutions on Jerusalem than on any other topic in the world. Moreover, twenty-two UN agencies with a full complement of international and local staff currently work in the city. This is emphatically not the case in the other cities studied in this book. The role of external actors in all the other cities is minimal, and what there is—for example, by Pakistan, the Arab Gulf states, and militant Islamic nonstate actors in Banaras—takes a more indirect form: the channeling of funds and the creation of local proxies. These cities do not attract the intense media and diplomatic interest that Jerusalem attracts in every violent intercommunal event.

In addition to these issues lies another one that relates to the complex nature of cities and the contradictions that are inherent when ethnonationalist ideologies determine the framework for sharing urban space and administration. In the introduction, I referred to this issue as the "paradox of urban ethnonationalism." The essential fact is that in Jerusalem since 1967 Israeli policies in East Jerusalem have been driven by an ethnonationalist political ideology—Zionism. Like in other cities that are or have been in control by groups with ethnically based ideologies, such as Ulster Loyalists in Belfast, Maronites in Beirut, Serbian nationalists in several cities in the former Yugoslavia, Han Chinese Communists in Lhasa, Hindu nationalists in many cities of northern India, Malay nationalists in Kuala Lumpur and the east coast states of the Malay Peninsula, the privileging of the dominant community leads directly to the marginalization of the subordinate community. To some extent, this takes place in all cities, but, as discussed in the introduction, most cities have processes by which the needs of the subordinate community or communities are recognized and addressed. In the case of Jerusalem, these processes are absent, and the subordinate Palestinian community is deprived of resources and the means to determine the security of its status and future due to the simple fact that it is not Israeli Jewish.

A result of this dynamic of exclusion by the dominant community is that the subordinate community will look elsewhere for representation, for funds, and for protection and will make political alliances, which can be a formidable constraint on the dominant community's attempt to control a city. Herein lies the paradox in ethnonationalist urban governance: the ideology that seeks exclusive control over a city creates the very forces that will resist it. The internationalization of the conflict that ensues is exactly what is taking place in East Jerusalem. This internationalization is exacerbated by the presence of important holy sites in the city, which serve to mobilize a wide spectrum of external players. Although the greatest ally of the Israeli state, the United States, has recognized Jerusalem as the capital of Israel, to date only Guatemala has followed suit, and not one other member of the international community has its embassy in Jerusalem. This shows the strength of the opposition to this ideologically driven attempt to incorporate East Jerusalem into Israel.

I close this chapter by simply returning the reader's attention to the analytical framework of metanarratives in my introduction as a way of understanding the religious conflicts in Jerusalem. Although in the immediate post-1967 period there were signs that a narrative of transformative integration could emerge, perhaps grudgingly, through the implementation of the "dual-administration" model I delineated, this prospect has receded completely. There were traces of this narrative being adopted in the various off-the-record Track Two discussions before and after the Oslo Accords, but these traces have disappeared in the Israeli triumphalist euphoria following the U.S. recognition of Jerusalem as Israel's capital. For now, as I write at Christmas 2018, the narrative of precedence is dominant, and it will be dominant for the foreseeable future.

CHAPTER II

The Politics of Regionalism

Cordoba's Mezquita on the Frontline

Religious conflict in Cordoba does not grab the international headlines in the media in the same way as, say, Jerusalem, Ayodhya, Najaf, and Kaguna. In the introduction, I mentioned that certain groups and constituencies wish to see the reintroduction of Muslim prayer in the Mezquita-Cathedral of Cordoba. Their view is that it is either an historical right that needs to be reaffirmed or an important symbolic act that will both reassert the city's mixed historical narrative and illustrate the beauty of religious inclusiveness in an increasingly religiously polarized world. Tensions have risen between, on the one hand, Spanish Muslim and Andalusian regionalists and, on the other, the Roman Catholic Diocese of Cordoba and the Spanish state over the question of access to and use of the Mezquita-Cathedral. Resentments, which simmer and flare up from time to time, have also been exploited by anti-Muslim and anti-immigrant political movements. I examine these issues more closely later on in this chapter. Nevertheless, in comparison to the violent conflicts around some religious sites prevailing in India, parts of West Africa, the Balkans, and the Middle East, these tensions in Cordoba are relatively minor—at this point. The inclusion of a study of Cordoba in this volume, therefore, demands some justification.

The reason for including Cordoba in this study arose during the course of my fieldwork in 2015 and 2016. As I carried out interviews and familiarized myself with the modern city and as much as possible with the historical city that lay beneath it in order to understand the context for the controversy concerning the question of Muslims' access to the Mezquita-Cathedral for prayer, I realized that I could not achieve this better understanding without a greater knowledge of the city's pre-Reconquista history. Interview after interview stressed the disagreements over the differing narratives of the site's historical past, and, as a consequence, the contemporary controversy made no sense without a better appreciation of the role that the Mezquita has played in Cordoba, in Andalusia, in the Iberian Peninsula, in the relations between Europe and North Africa, and, finally, in the Islamic world.

Yet what flowed from this research was not just a better understanding of the historical context of the Cordoba case but also an awareness that the history of Cordoba, from the late Visigothic period through to the Islamic

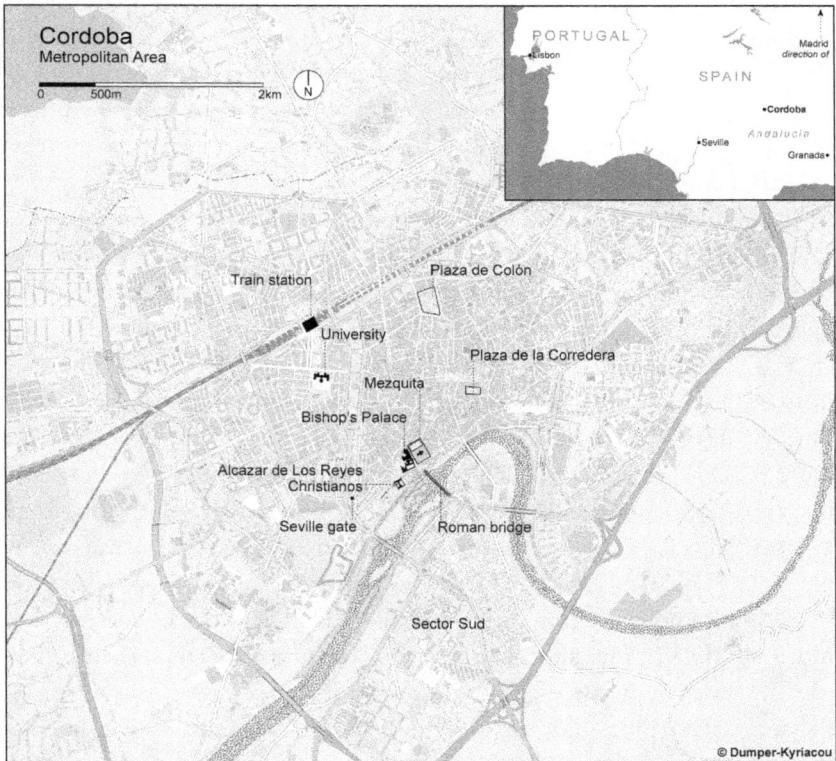

Map 2.1 Cordoba metropolitan area. (Map by Lefkos Kyriacou and Michael Dumper)

conquests and the subsequent gradual Castilian takeover of Andalusia in the thirteenth century, presented me with a rich archive of processes and dynamics associated with religious conflicts and the use of holy sites in general. Furthermore, I began to see how the case of Cordoba could be and should be mined to illustrate "la longue durée" of current controversies in other cities in order to show how they are possibly just one more stage in the ebb and flow of a tide that will continue into the future.

The current controversy over Muslim prayer in the Mezquita-Cathedral in Cordoba is in reality part of a larger range of issues, from the possible reemergence of a center–periphery tug-of-war between the capital in Madrid and Cordoba as a cultural city of some importance in the region of Andalusia to a church–secularist contestation over the ownership of national monuments and to differing visions of the role of the site in both the history and the future of the city. To what extent should Cordoba reflect a Castillian and Francoist version of history, and to what extent should the site provide a platform for an inclusive approach to religious diversity and become a symbol of reconciliation and coexistence? In the unpacking of these issues and the contextualizing of them through an understanding of the historical forces and transitions that have taken place in the southern Iberian Peninsula, more general patterns can be discerned that are relevant to the discussion in this book.

In the first place, through our understanding of Cordoban history we can see how political and military conflicts may lead to transfers of power and of ownership over religious sites from one religious community to another, but they do not necessarily take place overnight or as a dramatic rupture with the past. The transfer of ownership and control over sites may have been *preceded* by some decades, possibly centuries, of penetration by different ethnic or religious groupings and by periods of coexistence, some more peaceful than others, as a result of changing demography and shifts in the balance of power. Similarly, a transfer of control over a site may be *followed* by decades of coexistence as the new order is consolidated and people adapt to the new situation. This may particularly be the case where the site is not demolished or significantly altered. In fact, the nondestruction of important religious sites, which is possibly more prevalent than is presumed, raises many issues and interpretations relevant to religious conflicts in cities: Is it a sign of respect or a sign of weakness? Is it a demonstration of superiority and a symbol of triumphant control, or is it a constant and vivid warning? So although the focus of this book is on contemporary conflicts and controversies, the history of the Mezquita-Cathedral in Cordoba does bring to the fore both the importance of a long perspective to the discussion and a number of issues that are both historical and contemporary.

History as a Tool for Understanding the Contemporary

The cultural genealogy of Cordoba had early beginnings. A Roman colony founded in 169 CE at a crossing point over the river, Cordoba became the capital of the province of Hispania Ulterior and the birthplace of Seneca, the philosopher and the confidant of the emperor Nero, and of the poet Lucan. The archaeological evidence is not clear, but there was possibly a Roman temple close to where the Roman bridge spanned the Río Guadalquivir and over which a later Visigothic church, the Basilica of San Vicente, is said to have been built. Following the Arabo-Berber conquest of Cordoba in 711 CE, the Visigothic Christian community was permitted to remain in the city and to practice their faith. In fact, before the construction of the Mezquita (as a mosque) fifty years later, there is a tradition that the Visigothic church was partitioned between Muslims and Christians.[1] Finally, when it became clear that after many extensions there was still insufficient space to accommodate the growing Muslim population of settlers and Christian converts to Islam, known as Mozarabes, the Christian congregation was prevailed upon to sell their half of the church and were granted land for a new church outside the city walls.[2]

In 785 CE, the founder of the 'Umayyad dynasty in Andalusia, Abd ar-Rahman I, began the construction of the Mezquita, which was extended several times over the next two centuries until the final major extension in 987 CE during the reign of al-Mansur. Whether the original Visigothic basilica was incorporated into the foundations and fabric of the Mezquita is much debated because the archaeological evidence is not conclusive.[3] The Muslim tradition is not opposed to this possibility as it mirrored exactly what took place in Damascus at the start of the 'Umayyad Caliphate there and thus serves as mythological and symbolic validation of the establishment of the western 'Umayyad Caliphate based in Cordoba. However, what is not in doubt is that the end result of this extended period of construction was a building of such magnificence that it was referred to frequently as one of the Wonders of the World. The Arab historian al-Himyari, writing in the eleventh century, was not unique in his paean of praise: "In Cordoba stands the celebrated mosque, of universal renown; its vast area, its perfect design, its wealth of decoration and its solid construction make it one of the most beautiful monuments in the world. . . . This mosque does not have an equal for ornamentation, width or length among Muslims."[4] I am not an archaeologist (although I spent one summer as a teenager on a Saxon dig in County Durham, United Kingdom, and on two Roman digs in France), and I am not an architect (although in the 1980s, when acting as a consultant to a Palestinian restoration project in the Old City of Jerusalem, I worked closely with some conservation architects there), so I will not attempt to compete with others on the glorification of the Mezquita-Cathedral in this book. At the same time, it is important to give readers who have not visited Cordoba an impression of the site so that they better understand its appeal and symbolic importance.

In the introduction, I described my first impressions of sensory overload and aesthetic bewilderment when entering the Mezquita. It is difficult to imagine today how the mosque looked at the height of its glory in the tenth and eleventh centuries. Today, the interior is dark, with all four sides of the building now enclosed with walls. This alteration was introduced by the later post-Christian conquest. Previously the sides of the mosque had largely been open, creating a lighter, more delicate atmosphere. More dramatically, the central aisles of the original mosque were ripped out and now house a Gothic basilica, breaking up the integrity of the earlier site and the long vistas through the arches for which it was celebrated. Yet one is still struck by the "forest of columns," the eighteen rows of various-colored marble pillars, slender and topped by double-tiered arches of alternating voissoirs (stone stripes) of cream and terracotta red stretching out in all directions.[5] Before the Christian alterations from the thirteenth through the fifteenth centuries, there were 1,300 such pillars, and when the sides had been open, the play of light and changing strips of long shadows must have heightened the sense of never-ending vistas amid the delicate lacelike structure. The Mezquita's beauty did not stop at its light, airy, and graceful form. During the Islamic period, not only were the original twelve aisles extended three more times to an "unprecedented size," but sections and ceilings were also decorated and embellished to the very highest levels of Islamic art.[6] At its southern wall, there is a *mihrab*, or prayer room, which acts as canopy over the *qibla*, or direction of prayer, and is regarded as possibly the most beautiful of all Islamic prayer rooms.[7] Its horse-shoe arch is decorated with Byzantine mosaics and stucco work that softly gleam from all sides and from above. Nestled within the tiny mosaics are Qur'anic inscriptions made out of gold. In the vicinity are sky-lit domes and ornately carved intertwined arches, which add to the sense of palatial opulence that draws visitors and worshippers from all parts of the mosque.

It is important to recognize that this architectural splendor did not take place in a bubble of superior craftsmanship but rested upon sturdy political, economic, and military foundations. During the two centuries of 'Umayyad rule from the ninth to the eleventh centuries CE, the Mezquita and Cordoba stood at the center of the foremost political and military power in the Mediterranean and Europe, controlling all of the Iberian Peninsula south of the River Duero and the coastal area of North Africa. At one point, this power rivaled the Holy Roman Empire of Charlemagne, whose forces it pushed back as far as the Loire in France.[8] With a population of approximately 100,000 residents during the reign of the first ruler, Abd ar-Rahman I, it was the largest city in Europe.[9] In 929 CE, a caliphate was declared to supersede and eclipse that of the Abbasid Caliphate based in Baghdad at the other end of the Islamic world. Fueled by their access to Sudanese gold, the rulers of Cordoba and al-Andalus (as the Islamic region of Spain was known) were able to professionalize the army, provide effective naval defenses, consolidate trading links with the Byzantine Empire, and pour funds into embellishing monumental structures such as the Mezquita.[10] Thomas Glick refers to the "dazzling strength of the greatest power in Europe" and notes the homage and tribute rendered to al-Hakam II, who ruled al-Andalus from 961 to 976, by the rulers of Navarre, Castille, Leon, Galicia, and Barcelona.[11] The Mezquita represented and was celebrated as a fundamental shift in the Islamic community's temporal and spiritual power away from the eastern Mediterranean and Arabian Peninsula to the western Mediterranean and the Iberian Peninsula.[12]

A particularly salient symbol of 'Umayyad power in Spain was the sacking of Santiago de Compostela in 997 CE by the de facto ruler of Cordoba, al-Mansur (d. 1002). This Christian pilgrimage center was established on the mythical remains of the Apostle James, who as the brother of Christ was considered by his devotees to be of a higher rank than St. Peter. One eminent historian of Spain argues that the Cathedral of St. James aspired to rival both Rome and Jerusalem as a pilgrimage center.[13] As such, it was designed as a rival religious and ideological center to the Islam being practiced on the rest of the Iberian Peninsula and to mobilize the faithful against the strength of the ʿUmayyads and the rapid conversions that were taking place across the peninsula. Not only did al-Mansur demolish the cathedral, but he also removed the huge bells that called the faithful to prayer and transported them to Cordoba using Christian prisoners and slaves, where they were melted down and erected in the Mezquita as giant lanterns.[14] The whole exercise—the destruction of the cathedral, the towing of the bells overland through towns and villages from north to south of the Iberian land mass, the triumphant melting down, and the erection of the lanterns in the mosque—must have been both a compelling image of utter Islamic dominance and a powerful and emotive piece of propaganda designed to demoralize the remaining Christian royalty and their subjects in the northern peripheries of the Iberian Peninsula.[15]

We also need to take note of the cultural impact that the construction and extension of the Mezquita promoted and symbolized. Although the Mezquita may have constituted the largest religious building in the Islamic world and Christendom, it also supported a confident intellectual framework of inclusiveness and hybridity that acted as a conduit for the transmission of Arab and Islamic learning and as a spur for the European Renaissance. Echoing the utilization of Roman practices, Syrian styles, and Byzantine craftsmen in the actual construction of the Mezquita, Cordoba was also the home of scholars, translators, theologians, philosophers, and historians drawn not only from the Arab and Berber elite but also from the Visigothic Christian and Jewish communities and from the community of new converts to Islam.[16] They included Ibn Hazm (d. 1064), a major Muslim theologian and legal jurist; Ibn Rushd (a.k.a. Averroes, d. 1198), an influential thinker in both Muslim and European philosophy; and Moshe ben Maimon (a.k.a. Maimonides, d. 1204), a rabbi, physician, and philosopher who contributed greatly to the development of Jewish thought. This inclusivity did not mean that all was sweetness and light between the religious communities, though, and it is clear that the Arabo-Berber elite brooked little dissent to their political dominance. The frequent revolts and massacres did not cease even when conversions to Islam increased to such an extent in the tenth century that they reduced the Christian and Jewish communities into the position of minority communities with inferior rights and higher taxation.[17] Nevertheless, Cordoba became renowned for its intellectual openness and hybridity during an era of religious and political antagonisms.

In 1236, Ferdinand III of Castille (d. 1252) occupied Cordoba, ending more than 525 years of Arabo-Berber and Muslim control over the city. Although the transfer of power was effected with minimal violence, the leading Muslim notables fled the city, and the majority of Muslim residents were forcibly displaced. Some departed only to the outskirts to await better times, and they were allowed to continue to practice their religion.[18] The evidence suggests, however, that the five mosques in the city at that time were converted to churches.[19] A cross was immediately erected on the Mezquita's roof, the building underwent an elaborate purification ceremony, and within weeks it was consecrated and dedicated to the Virgin Mary. Several years later it was made into a cathedral.[20]

There are two points to note in this transfer of control over the Mezquita from one religious community to another: despite its iconic status as one of the glories of Islam and Muslim civilization, it was not destroyed and a cathedral built in its place; the alterations to the interior were for at least two centuries carried out within an architectural and artistic tradition that revealed great continuities with the earlier Muslim period. Why the Mezquita was spared the fate of many other mosques taken over by the Castillian conquerors on the Iberian Peninsula, such as the Great Mosque in Seville, is the subject of much debate and speculation. Here I look at three reasons, all of which give us some insights into the dynamics and complexities of the transfer of control over holy sites in religious conflicts.

The first and most compelling reason is political and can be drawn from the context of the period. Following a period of global Muslim expansion that reached its zenith during the reign of Abu Amir al-Mansur, the papacy and Christian rulers of Europe were gradually regrouping as Crusaders and from the twelfth century on were making inroads into Muslim-controlled territory at either end of the Mediterranean in the Levant and in al-Andalus. A symbol of their emerging power was thus required, and what could be a more effective demonstration of the rising power of Christian Castille than the acquisition and use of the greatest Muslim mosque of the period as a Christian place of worship?[21] Although there is no textual evidence to support this thesis, examples of it can be seen elsewhere in Spain, such as Valencia, where mosques were converted into churches even though there were no parishioners to populate them.[22] Indeed, as Brenda Schildgen points out, "The capture of the city of Cordoba and its wealth . . . had greater political and cultural meaning if the memory of its Islamic past was not erased because, amongst other reasons, it stood as a constant reminder of the triumph of the Christian Spanish forces over its former Arab inhabitants."[23] In this context, we should also remind ourselves that although Muslim Cordoba fell to Castillian forces in 1236 CE, it was not until 250 years later, in 1492, that the Iberian power couple, Queen Isabelle of Aragon (d. 1504) and King Ferdinand II of Castille (d. 1516) finally captured Granada, the last stronghold of the Muslim al-Andalus kingdoms. The frontier of Christendom was not so far away, and the prospect of a reversal in fortunes not so distant, either, so there may have been a certain tentativeness in the way the new rulers of Cordoba dealt with the region's greatest jewel, the Mezquita.

Another reason for sparing the Mezquita, according to historians, is the accommodation or "tolerance" shown by the monotheistic religions to each other at certain junctures in history. The coexistence that had flourished between Christians and Muslim in places such as Cordoba and no doubt the fact that many of the Muslim inhabitants of Cordoba were descended from Christian converts played a role in staying the hand of Ferdinand III and his son Alfonso X. In essence, such accommodation meant that the demonization of the Islamic prophet Muhammed that became the prevailing theme in the later Middle Ages played a secondary role in thirteenth-century Cordoba due to the fact that Muslims nevertheless worshipped the same God as Christians. The typically graphic vocabulary employed to describe the purification and consecration of the Mezquita to a Christian place of worship—"eliminata spurcicia Mahometi" (cleansing the Muslim filth)—may have been in keeping with the language of the Crusaders, but at the same time it seems not to be applied to the physical structure of the Mezquita to the extent that it would prevent it from being converted into a Christian holy site. In this way, the Mezquita site and building itself was not seen as being imbued with holiness but merely supplied the backdrop for worship. And similar to the point made in the preceding paragraph, we should recall that the Christian takeover of the Iberian Peninsula was still far from complete, and Muslim emirates continued to survive just a few tens of miles south and east of Cordoba.[24] Although relations were not good, the borders, the *banda fronteriza* or *banda morisca*, were not hermetically sealed, nor was there a state of constant warfare in the years preceding the fall of Granada. As John Edwards writes, "Recent work has suggested that the relationship between the two sides in the Reconquest was far more complex than had previously been thought."[25] In this situation, the social and economic interactions between Muslims in the unconquered parts of al-Andalus and Muslims in the conquered Cordoba hinterland were a factor to be taken into account when dealing with the iconic mosque.

A third possible reason for keeping the site rather than demolishing it lay in its potential role as a generator of lucrative revenues from pilgrims and travelers. Earlier I recounted how Muslim thinkers and writers referred to the splendor of the building and how it constituted one of the wonders of the medieval world. The beauty and hence the value of the building were not lost on the Christian leadership, either. Building something as impressive to replace it—with all its fantastic artwork and inspiring architecture—would have been an expensive and daunting task to the new Christian rulers. Due to economic and political shifts in the Mediterranean, the city no longer commanded its hitherto advantageous trading position between North Africa and the European continent, so the rulers would be killing the goose that laid the city's golden egg. There is some evidence that the Crown did not allocate much land to the Diocese of Cordoba following the conquest of Cordoba, so the diocese was relatively poor in comparison to other older, established dioceses.[26] Hence, one can persuasively conjecture that it made perfect sense to keep the site as glorious as it was and to reconfigure it in a way that would appeal to Christian sensibilities.[27] Thus, even 150 years after the takeover, a Latin scholar-monk, Jeronimo, showered almost hyperbolic praise on the Mezquita as "a temple worthy of all manner of praise, whose spectacular beauty reanimates the spirit of whoever contemplates it. It is the glory of Spain and distinctive symbol of the honour of Cordoba." Echoing the eulogies of earlier Muslim scholars, he continued: "The historians refer to the prodigious attributes of only seven buildings in the world. . . . But who will appreciate in the future these monuments as superior to others, when contemplating such a temple in our city."[28] Clearly, these arguments lost some of their force following the expulsion in 1501 of all Muslims who refused to convert to Christianity.[29] It would be interesting to discover the extent to which those who did convert were able to exert any influence on the way the Mezquita was altered and further "Christianized."

A key feature regarding the use to which the Mezquita was put following the Castillian conquest of Cordoba is the continuity in conception and style that prevailed for at least two centuries following the consecration of the alterations to the interior. Here the main point I wish to make is that the cathedral authorities continued to employ Muslim architects and designers in order to maintain the high quality of the internal additions, although the correlation between style and religion should not be taken too literally. Despite their forced expulsion in 1236, Muslims returned to the city sixty years later. It is clear from financial accounts of the period that some 2,000 Muslim artisans were being taxed. Although this number would not necessarily represent just the tip of the iceberg of the total Muslim population, it nonetheless gives an indication that many thousands of Muslims had returned. Known as *mudejar*—that is, Muslims living under Christian rule—they contributed to the upkeep and alterations of the cathedral as slaves or as artisans taxed through obligatory labor impositions or as employed craftsmen.[30] In this way, the funeral and memorial chapels along the interior walls; the chapels built for worship and the main Royal Chapel, which constituted the congregational areas close to the *mihrab*; the *mihrab* itself, which was enclosed to contain the sacraments; and the restoration of the vast ceiling of the Mezquita—all show evidence of *mudejar* craftsmanship in their fusion of Byzantine and ʿUmayyad traditions. As Heather Ecker concludes in her seminal and forensic article tracing the trajectory of these alterations and restorations, "The surviving textual evidence and, in some cases, the physical evidence make clear that prior to and following the definitive Christian conquest of Cordoba in the thirteenth century, there are few clean breaks. Muslim agency in the mosque did not cease with the conquest, and Christian agency preceded it."[31] This lack of a clean break, I argue, is a key point in assessing the likelihood of certain courses of action when examining current conflicts over holy sites in cities.

As the conquest of al-Andalus continued and Spain became increasingly centralized under the Castillian–Aragon monarchy, however, this interpenetration of Moorish and Christian culture declined, and the Christian leadership became increasingly intolerant. The stronger influence was no longer the traditions of the Iberian South and the southern Mediterranean but rather the traditions of northern Europe, with the French clericalism of Cluny Abbey becoming dominant in ecclesiastical circles and breaking the cultural links to the region and the past. The most obvious manifestation of this shift in influence was the switch from the Mozarabic liturgy to the Roman rite.[32] Nevertheless, the local residents and their notables fiercely resisted attempts to transform the Mezquita into a northern European–type Romanesque cathedral or to introduce more contemporary ecclesiastical styles.[33] It was not until the late fifteenth century that the religious authorities could propose a major architectural and structural intervention with some confidence of success. The first proposal was vetoed by Queen Isabelle, but a watered-down version retaining a Gothic nave was completed in 1496. The later Gothic cruciform design by the architect Hernán Ruiz I, inserted into the center of the Mezquita, was eventually commissioned in 1521 and finally completed and dedicated in 1607. Despite being aware of the controversy engendered by this project, the architect could not have anticipated the crushing put-down expressed by the emperor Charles V, who on inspecting the work in progress commented, "Had I known what this was, I would not have allowed it to reach the ancient part, because *you have done what could be done anywhere; and you have undone that which is unique in the world.*"[34] The contrast between the soaring new Gothic nave, bright with large windows and skylights, and the surrounding ʿUmayyad aisles and arches, their beauty and symmetry obscured by the gloom, is a marked feature of this change.

On a visit to the Mezquita in November 2015, I eavesdropped on a presentation to a touring party by an official guide, who was clearly well informed on the subject of the transformation of the mosque into a cathedral. She spoke of the conversion and alteration of the mosque as a symbol of tolerance and coexistence between Muslims and Christians. Rather than destroying the mosque, the Catholic Church made use of it. At the same time, she also pointed out that by walling in the sides and shutting the skylights, the alterations to the lighting created a very deliberate effect: the remaining "Islamic" areas are in shadow under subdued lighting, but the Gothic nave/transept is well lit and has high, clear glass windows through which sunlight pours into the chancel and choir. As a result, a simple but powerfully symbolic binary is created: dark Islamic areas and light Christian areas where worshippers walk through the dark into the light.

In retrospect, Hernán Ruiz I's design has received increasing appreciation for its clever marrying of Gothic and ʿUmayyad styles. Despite the breakup of the celebrated vistas through the colored archways, internally the fabric of the building is relatively intact. Much of the material of the demolished area was reused, and despite the fact that the Mezquita remains unquestionably a mosque in appearance, it functions also as a cathedral. There is also the argument that wherever one stands on the inflexible position taken by the Diocese of Cordoba in the current controversy, the transfer of control in 1236 and the physical alterations of 1526 could have led to a much worse result. As Michele Lamprakos argues, "It is rarely noted that Hernan Ruiz I's sensitive insertion preserved both the reading of the

Figure 2.1 View of the Mezquita-Cathedral showing the Gothic basilica extruding from the roof of the former mosque. (Photograph by Michael Dumper)

mosque and the memory of a conflict—at the very moment when the Muslim presence and cultural legacy were being erased from the peninsula."[35] Thus, the Christianization of the Mezquita can be viewed either as a glass half full or a glass half empty: one of the glories of medieval and Islamic architecture was mostly saved, but . . . it's a shame that it was not left alone. But how realistic would it be to think that the Mezquita could have been left untouched? The south of Spain had been Christianized, and it was improbable that such an iconic site would not be co-opted, if not destroyed, for the state in some way. The use of holy sites, their management, and their fate reflects the political balance of power of the times, even if there is a time lag between political changes and the changes that then take place at the sites.

Figure 2.2 Islamic doorway to the former minaret, now the clock tower of the Mezquita–Cathedral. (Photograph by Michael Dumper)

A study of the historical trajectory of the Mezquita and of Cordoba contributes to this book not only a sense of the possibility of coexistence and accommodation between religious faiths but also a realization of the dangers and opportunities of ritualistic and intellectual hybridity or syncretism. It also illustrates at least three essential points. First, a gradual transfer of power and control over holy sites in cities of religious significance can occur even when the site and the city in question have achieved preeminence and symbolic importance, as the Mezquita and Cordoba had. Centrality and salience do not necessarily herald destruction and demolition. Second, a rupture with the past is not always immediate and dramatic but sometimes incremental. These two points make a persuasive case that a useful perspective to adopt when considering current conflicts over religious sites in cities is a more longitudinal one. In essence, the conflicts we are witnessing currently in other cities with religious associations, such as Banaras, Jerusalem, and Lhasa, are part of a process that may be leading either to accommodation or to a transfer of control. Specific issues such as the installation of surveillance cameras or metal detectors, the incarceration and exile of religious leaders, the intimidation of voices calling for accommodation, all of which cause such intense public and media interest, are merely steps along the path in one direction or the other. The story of the site in question is still unfolding, and whatever resolution or arrangement emerges, that new situation will also not be set in aspic.

Third, the longitudinal study of such conflicts also reveals long-term dynamics that are often obscured by the controversy and emotions generated by specific current actions or events. For example, it is possible to interpret the increasing Christianization of the interior of the Mezquita under the current diocesan leadership and the diocese's refusal to countenance a more inclusive approach to the use of the site as the Roman Catholic Church's push back against the growing strength of the Islamic community in Spain. This would be only a partial picture, though. Not only does it ignore the lively contestation between secularists and clericalists over the role of the Catholic Church in recent Spanish history and current politics, but it also does not recognize what has been one of the most important drivers of political agency in the politics of Spain for centuries— the push and pull between the center and the periphery ever since the rise of the joint kingdoms of Castille and Aragon. The tension between the centripetalism of the regions of Spain and the centrifugalism of the state institutions in the capital, Madrid, is a dominant feature of Spanish history, economy, and politics. And the contest between Andalusia and Castille encompasses and subsumes the controversy over access to the Mezquita in Cordoba.

Whether the Roman Catholic Church can be seen as simply a powerful tool in the Castillian integralist drive is open to question. But the church's reinterpretation of the history of the region, the city of Cordoba, and the Mezquita to promote an homogeneous identity and citizenship does not necessarily reflect the experience and traditions of Andalusia. At the same time, we should not lose sight of the fact that Andalusia is also a socially conservative region in Spain, and certainly in the rural areas the Catholic Church's work is embedded in the lives of most residents. I discuss this point further when I examine the current situation in more detail. At this stage in my discussion, I want to use this point to illustrate how taking the long view throws into sharper relief trends that are not so easily discerned when one is focused on the current crisis. The power and agency of these obscured trends are not apparent when spikes of conflict occur at particular points in their history.

And it is here that the framework of metanarratives is helpful. Over the centuries, the narrative of precedence has emerged as a predominant one in Cordoba. Some skepticism may be justified regarding the view that the late-Islamic and early-Christian period was one of interfaith dialogue and coexistence. If that were the case, the narrative of transformative integration could be used to categorize that period. It is more likely, however, that this is a retrospective assessment of the historical record, a construction of a mythical Golden Age to further ethical norms in international relations.[36] At the same time, religious practices do not take place in a vacuum, and they evolve in response to social and political needs. So it is also quite likely that the syncretic elements that we see in the architecture and decorative forms in the Mezquita point to a broader mix of traditions. Therefore, although the narrative of precedence may always have been dominant and remains dominant today, the narrative of transformative integration has also been present and has appeared more salient from time to time. With these general points in mind, this chapter now turns to the current controversy in Cordoba concerning access and use of the Mezquita.

Background to the Current Controversy

Before zooming in on the present day, we need to capture some of the main developments in the early–modern period that affected the Mezquita. It is quite astonishing to find that the current controversy is part of a long-running debate that reflects both local and national moods and perspectives. However, by the mid–seventeenth century it would have been clear that with the expulsion of the Moriscos, the descendants of Muslims, at the beginning of the century, which was echoed by the dedication of the new altar in the transept, the Christianization of the Mezquita was complete. The installation of elaborate baroque choir stalls and the whitewashing of the red and white arches were hardly a necessary confirmation of this last phase.[37] However, by the nineteenth century the pendulum began to swing back again with a revival of *mudejar*-style architecture in Spain.[38] In Cordoba, there was a renewed interest in and appreciation of the Islamic fabric of the building: the whitewash was removed, and the *mihrab* was revealed in all its glory. Even more significant was the restoration work carried out on the external facades, in particular the eastern portals with their elaborate Moorish designs and Arabic inscriptions, which reconfirmed the site's non-Christian origins.

Prior to the Spanish Civil War (1936–1939), Spain's regional identities came to the fore once again, and Lamprakos writes of how some Republicans wanted to turn the Mezquita into a museum, whereas others argued that Muslims should be allowed to pray in the building again. One radical proposal taken up by the Franco regime, despite its strident defense of the conservative religious establishment, was that the transept should be removed entirely and the demolished Islamic parts be reconstructed. That this was not the wild-eyed dream of some prototype Usama bin Laden but a serious proposal supported by significant professional backing can be seen in the way it was submitted to the International Commission on Monuments and Sites in 1973.[39] We should recall that after the Second World War, Spain was internationally isolated, not being admitted to the UN until the 1950s, and it sought to exploit its Muslim heritage in order to obtain Arab backing for its policies in Africa and the Mediterranean. The proposal to remove the transept was formally debated at the International Commission on Monuments and Sites Conference in 1973, held in the Mezquita as the prelude to inscribing the site onto the UNESCO World

Heritage List. Although the site was inscribed onto the list in 1984, it was decided that the transept and other Christian introductions should remain as they were because they demonstrated the values of religious and cultural coexistence. This decision was seen as a defeat for Franco's policy of establishing closer links with the Arab and Islamic world, but it also signaled the beginnings of a renewed "Christianization" of the Mezquita in the face of growing opposition to the influence of the clergy in Spanish society. And it heralded the reemergence of the post-Franco autonomy movements of Spain's regions.

Governance

Thus, the current controversy, as we can see, is not new. However, the context and the factors that give it more dynamism and salience have changed once again, and at this point in the chapter we should take stock of some of the major developments that frame discussion of the controversy, including issues of governance, demographic change, the economy, and the role of religious communities in modern Cordoba. Regarding governance, one should note that Spain, although not fully federal, has many features of a highly devolved state, with many powers exercised by regional governments, more accurately known as the "autonomous communities" (*comunidades autónomas*).[40] Cordoba is located in the Autonomous Community of Andalusia, whose capital is Seville, and Cordoba, although socially conservative. has traditionally opposed the centralizing policies of the national state. In the twenty years following Franco's death in 1974, Cordoba was the only city in post-Franco democratic Spain to elect Communist mayors; one such mayor, Julio Anguita, whose tenure lasted from 1979 to 1986, also later became the leader of the Spanish Communist Party at a national level.[41]

Another notable feature of Cordoba is its "strong participatory tradition," which has clearly affected the debate over the role of the Mezquita.[42] A key illustration of this tradition is the introduction by the Municipal Council of Cordoba (Ayuntamiento de Córdoba) in 2001 of a consultative process known as *participatory budgeting* in which residents could decide how to allocate part of the municipal budget to address local needs. Nevertheless, the domination of the Andalusian government by the Socialist Party since the transition from the Franco era led to entrenched bureaucratic fiefdoms and corruption. In 2014, according to a report in the British newspaper *The Guardian*, the Spanish Socialist Workers Party was accused of misusing public money for artificial redundancy payments to so-called employees of companies close to the party, totaling some hundreds of millions of euros. The regional government, which the party controls, is also under investigation for the misuse of 17 million euros in European grants designated to help unemployed people retrain.[43] So on one hand you have a tradition of an anticentralizing and active civil society, but on the other hand you have disaffection with the established channels of political agency. The emergence of La Platforma de la Mezquita-Catedral de Córdoba (Platform for the Mezquita-Cathedral of Cordoba) is clearly an attempt to find alternative ways to influence the political actors involved in the current controversy.

The Role of Demography

The second major factor contributing to the controversy over access to the Mezquita is the demographics of Cordoba and of Spain more widely. During the Franco era, Spain suffered from population losses due to emigration, but since the transition to democracy in 1975 and particularly since Spain's entry into the European Economic Community (the precursor to the European Union) in 1986, there have been shifts in migratory patterns. As the country liberalized and synchronized its norms with the rest of western Europe, it became both more accessible and more desirable to Europeans as a place for vacation, retirement, and business. In addition, between 1986 and 1999 it experienced significant emigration from North Africa, followed in the 2000s by an increase in migration from Latin America. This latter wave was actively encouraged due to the similarities in language, culture, and religion. As a result of these successive waves, the population of Spain grew exponentially, with a migration of 279,000 in 1990 rising to 5.7 million in 2010. Because of the financial crisis of 2008, however, many of those migrants have returned home (and many young Spanish people have since emigrated in search of work), so today the population is estimated to have decreased to 46.5 million.[44] There have also been many changes to the demography of both the province and city of Cordoba in the past forty years. During the twentieth century, although the city saw a strong growth in population—increasing from 56,000 in 1900 to 232,000 in 1970—the population of the province as a whole fell, corresponding with the general trend of rural emigration in Spain.[45] In 2011, the census recorded a city population of 328,326, and more recent estimates from 2016 suggest a decline to 326,606.[46]

The Economy

Many of the geographic advantages that made Cordoba an economic powerhouse in the Middle Ages have disappeared. The river that runs through the city can take only small boats, so that the location of the city astride a key river crossing and the trade routes between Europe and North Africa no longer applies. Its intellectual and cultural eminence has been eclipsed by Madrid and Barcelona, and Seville is the seat of regional government. As a result, Cordoba is not in a strong place economically, and recent unemployment rates have touched 39 percent—more than one in three employable residents do not have a job.[47] Although this rate is higher than the national average, Cordoba's current economic woes are very much in line with changes to the Spanish economy and labor market nationally.

Clearly, in a country where tourism is a key industry, Cordoba—with the Mezquita-Cathedral, the Alcazar de los Reyes, the Roman bridge, the winding streets and garden patios of the Old City and the Judería (Jewish Quarter), the grand expanse of the Plaza de la Corredera, and the imposing Puerta de Almodóvar—retains its status as a major draw for external revenues. The inscription of not only the Mezquita but also of the southwest quadrant of the historic city onto the UNESCO World Heritage List provided a significant boost to the city's international appeal from the mid-1980s on. In addition, there is a city-wide effort to exploit the "Cordoba Paradigm" of interfaith coexistence in the economic sphere. For example, there are reports that business, municipal, and community leaders in Cordoba are working in concert to position the city as a major destination for Muslim tourism and that city officials are working in partnership with the Junta Islámica of Cordoba as well as with other Spanish Muslim organizations to create a halal "cluster" in Cordoba.[48] This development would host up to 1,300 businesses devoted to halal food and service, creating a new industry in the region.[49]

Thus, in Cordoba we can see how there is a heady and possibly dangerous mix of rural in-migration with all the attendant challenges of deracination and changing social mores, high youth unemployment, and a discredited political class. Combined, these features provide a potentially toxic cocktail for radicalization, whether it be left-wing extremism, ultra-conservative nationalism, or militant fundamentalism. Certainly, in cities where there is great religious and ethnic diversity, language and religious differences become both a cause and a result of conflict. Sarajevo, Belfast, Jerusalem, and, increasingly so, Brussels are good examples. With this in mind, I turn to the last key factor we need to look at in understanding the current controversy in Cordoba—the religious composition of the city—but first let's take a quick look at the national picture.

Demography of Religion and the State's Relations with Religious Communities

Spanish law prohibits the collection of census data based on religious belief, so in order to obtain a snapshot of the religious breakdown of the population scholars rely on reports and the statistics collated by NGOs and think tanks. One such source is a survey conducted in 2015 by the Centre for Sociological Investigation, which found that 72.9 percent of people on average in Spain identify as Catholics—nearly three-quarters of the population. Nevertheless, significantly, this figure is a drop of nearly 10 percent from the proportion given in a similar survey carried out in 2005, 79.3 percent. An additional nuance to the more recent survey is that nearly 50 percent of those identifying as Catholics said they did not attend mass or collective worship in any form. This seems to indicate that although Roman Catholicism remains the largest nominal religion, a large number of Spaniards, presumably younger Catholics, have rejected or have largely ignored the church's teachings and religious practices.[50] A similar survey in 2015 for all the autonomous regions of Spain found that in Andalusia 78.8 percent of the population identified as Catholic, which is higher than the national average at that time.[51]

According to figures for 2005, there were 400,000 evangelical Christians and other Protestants, one million Muslims, 50,000 Jews, and 9,000 Buddhists in Spain.[52] In 2015, these figures rose to 1.4 million evangelical Christians and other Protestants, 2 million Muslims, 45,000 Jews, and 80,000 Buddhists, with Andalusia being one of the regions containing the most non-Christians (the others being Catalonia, Madrid, and the exclaves of Ceuta and Melilla).[53] Many Muslims are immigrants from Morocco, who make up the largest immigrant population in Spain.[54]

In order to understand the full meaning of these bald statistics, we also need to understand the profound change that has occurred in Spain since the end of the Franco era in 1975. During his tenure, the Roman Catholic Church hierarchy closely allied itself to the regime. Thus, an essential part of the transition to democracy has been the loosening of church–state relations and an attempt to extricate the church from both the formal state structures and the daily lives of its citizens.[55] However, despite adopting a new constitution in 1978 that proscribed the status of a state religion, the Roman Catholic Church continued and continues to this day to enjoy preferential treatment from the state in many ways.[56] The clearest example of this treatment is how the Spanish taxation system provides taxpayers with the option of hypothecating 0.7 percent of their income tax to the Roman Catholic Church or to NGOs, but significantly not to other religious groups.[57] This percentage was based on estimates of how much the church would need if the state subsidies that had been allocated before 1978 were continued. The irony—or, indeed, the scandal—is that the government has agreed to continue to cover any shortfall so that, irrespective of the hypothecation, those residents of Spain who are not Roman Catholics— that is, Protestants, Jews, Muslims, and others—continue to subsidize the Roman Catholic Church. One key battlefield in the war over the church's influence in the Spanish state—education—left the church constrained but still powerful, with "one child in every seven" going to a school owned by a religious order or association.[58] More importantly, the Roman Catholic Church has retained oversight of all religious education in public schools as well.

Certainly, during the governments of the conservative Popular Party, which had many Franco sympathizers in key positions, relations with the Roman Catholic Church were very good. For instance, the government supported the church's attempts to register ownership over important monuments and large quantities of properties. This support led to protests nationally and fueled the controversy in Cordoba. For example, a law in force since the Franco era allowed the church to register itself as owner of goods and properties that were without title but where the church could justify its presence and ownership. The exceptions to these provisions were places of worship. In 1998, this exception was revoked by the government of Popular Party prime minister José María Aznar, and since then the church has registered its ownership of more than 4,500 properties and places of worship, causing a vociferous reaction from secularists, socialists, and followers of non–Roman Catholic faiths.[59] This controversy as it pertains to Cordoba is explored in greater detail in a later section.

The Muslim Community in Cordoba

According to the Association of Muslims in Cordoba, the Muslim population of Cordoba is approximately 3,500. They are largely of Moroccan extraction, whether first, second, or third generation, and the majority are

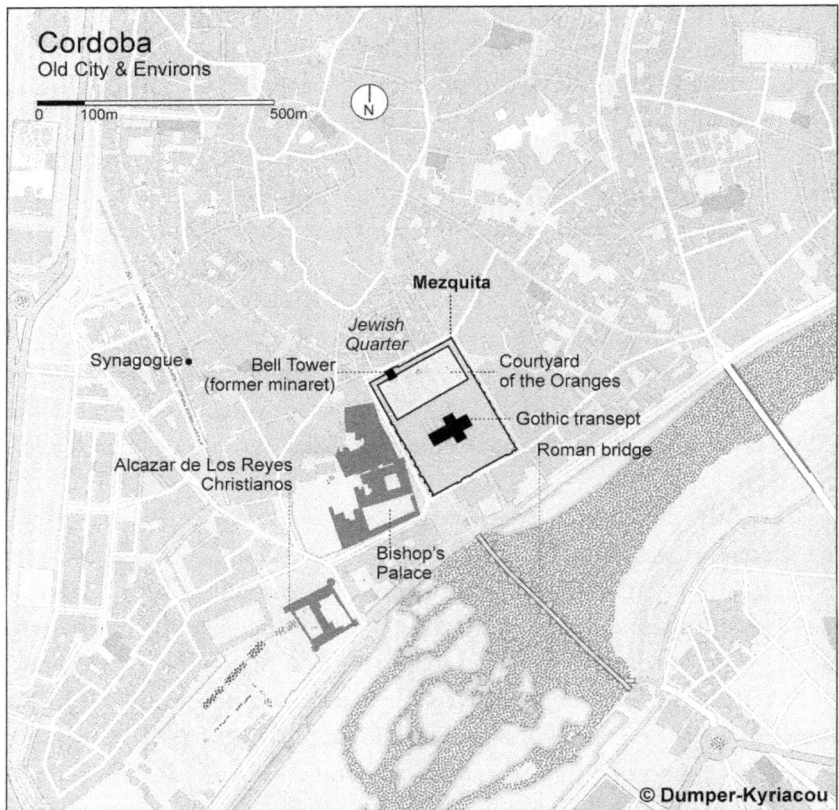

Map 2.2 Cordoba Old City and environs. (Map by Lefkos Kyriacou and Michael Dumper)

younger than fifteen. The greater part consists of small businessmen or workers in the informal sector, such as having stalls at the local bric-a-brac or flea markets, while a proportion work as laborers in agriculture. Very few are wealthy, and the community tends to be concentrated in the poorer area of the city, Sector Sud, south of the Guadalquivir River, where the rents are lower (see map 2.1). There the association has established a small mosque in one of the rooms in a former unemployment office. The main mosque, however, is located in the Plaza de Colón to the north of the Old City and was built by General Franco for his Moroccan troops. After the civil war, it was closed and abandoned but was reopened in 1986. The association, comprising about 150 people, was set up in 1991 to meet the needs of the Muslim community in Cordoba. As well as maintaining the very small mosque, the association pays for a Moroccan imam, holds Arabic classes for children (for a nominal payment), and liaises with the Cordoba municipality. Currently, the two most pressing issues facing the Cordoban Muslim community, in the association's view, are the need for a dedicated Muslim area in a cemetery and a plot of land or public space for a larger mosque and meeting place.[60]

There is little radicalization among the Muslim youth of Cordoba.[61] This is partly because the community is smaller and relatively well integrated into the political, social, and economic life of the city, and individuals are well known to each other, Nevertheless, as a consequence of the bombings in Madrid in March 2004, surveillance of the community does take place, and community leaders are invited for interviews with the Ministry of Interior from time to time. There is growing skepticism among Cordoban Muslims regarding the government's antiradicalization program, which many Muslims claim does not take into account that Muslims are also victims of terrorism. Islamophobia in Spain has reportedly increased by 500 percent, most of which is directed against women in traditional Islamic dress but also against men sporting long beards. In Cordoba, it is difficult to identify whether abuse is Islamophobia or more generally anti-immigrant. There is a view that since March 2004 the Spanish government is being much more interventionist in the field of education and mosque management, particularly since the growth of the Muslim population in Spain is through the conversion of the indigenous Spanish population and not just through immigration of Muslims. Generally, however, relations between community leaders and local politicians have been good, fluctuating according to their political orientation. For example, when the United Left was in power in Cordoba, the relations between the Association of

Muslims in Cordoba and both the city and regional government bodies, the Municipal Council of Cordoba and the Junta de Andalusía, tended to be cooperative. But with the right-wing Popular Party in government, this has not been the case in either forum.

The Mezquita Controversy Today

This, then, is the overall context in which the controversy over Muslim prayers in the Mezquita is occurring. A small local minority community with a low demographic, economic, and political profile is nevertheless swept up in the wider national concerns regarding economic decline, immigration, the role of the Catholic Church in a modern Spain, and the relations between the center and the regions. It is also caught in the slip-stream of broader international issues regarding the West's cultural and political relations with the Middle East and the South and the rise of terrorism as a military tool for both state and nonstate actors.

The Mezquita dispute does not fall easily on either side of the Christian–Muslim divide.[62] It is quite common for Cordoban Roman Catholics to say, "I am going to the mosque (Mezquita) to pray" or "My daughter got married in the mosque (Mezquita)" without any sense of irony or incongruity. The debate is more nuanced and relates as much, if not even more, to the tensions between Spain's political center and its regions, between Castillian centrifugalism and Andalusian centripetalism. And it is in this area that the debate over public ownership and the extent to which the Catholic Church is entitled to own the site and to the revenues it generates resonates more widely and is of greater political significance. Shared worship would be a nice symbol for some, but public ownership and management are an issue that exercises many more in Cordoba and Spain. That revenues from tourists visiting the site go into the church's coffers when the Mezquita has received considerable funding for its restoration and upkeep from national, regional, local, and international agencies is regarded as a flagrant exploitation of a local resource that is not benefitting the residents of Cordoba.

In this way, pinpointing the exact year in which the controversy blew up is very difficult because many developments both internationally and nationally fed into the events that constitute the controversy. And, indeed, the issue of Muslim prayer becomes eclipsed in the wider contestation over narratives, legal ownership, and the status of religion in the state. I take each of these issues in turn to show how when we examine the context of shared prayer, there is a widening circle of concentric rings that have less and less to do with Muslim prayer. Nevertheless, the issue concerning Muslim prayer in the Mezquita is one that, if poorly managed, threatens to trigger religious tensions and racial conflict and to inflame the passions generated by these other issues.

In 2003, the controversy reemerged as a result of the forcible eviction of a group of Muslim women from the Mezquita when they attempted to pray. The women were participants in the conference "Women and Islam" organized by Junta Islámica. Part of the program was a visit to the Mezquita, where the women were apparently so moved by the experience that at one point they automatically began praying and were subsequently thrown out.[63] To the Junta Islámica, this ejection was a deliberately aggressive symbolic response to the growing debate in Cordoba and Spain about how Spain in general and Cordoba in particular offer a bridge between the cultures of Europe and the Middle East. The sentiments of inclusivity had seemed to flow seamlessly from the inscription of the Mezquita to the UNESCO World Heritage List, which emphasized the Islamic history of the site, and in the application by city authorities for Cordoba to be the European Capital of Culture in 1992 and 2000.[64] However, departing from this overall trend, the Roman Catholic Diocese seemed to be setting out a new set of exclusivist protocols in an emphatic way and ignoring precedents where prayer by Muslims had previously taken place and been permitted by the diocese. In 1931, for example, the Muslim poet, thinker, and reformist Muhammed Iqbal was permitted to pray in front of the *mihrab* and wrote a poem as a memorial to that honor.[65] In 1974, President Saddam Hussein of Iraq is reported to have also prayed in front of the *mihrab*, and it is believed that many senior politicians and diplomats, including President Muammar Gaddhafi of Libya, have prayed in private visits.[66] The director of the Junta Islámica, Mansur Escudero, tried to open up a dialogue with the church, suggesting that the Mezquita become a center for ecumenical dialogue.[67]

The diocese rejected these overtures, with the then bishop of Cordoba, Juan José Asenjo, stating that "it would not contribute to the peaceful coexistence of different creeds. . . . [T]he shared use of temples and places of worship would not help to create this dialogue, and would only generate confusion among the faithful and give rise to religious indifference."[68]

Escudero also wrote to the pope and during the next few years prayed outside the Mezquita in protest to the diocese's response, an act that attracted a great deal of media attention to the affair.[69]

The debate over access had wider reverberations and threatened to bring in external actors. In 2007, secretary-general of the League of Arab States Amr Moussa pitched in and added the weight of the league behind calls for a Friday afternoon Muslim prayer service to be allowed in the Mezquita. In the same year, the World Islamic Peoples Leadership organized a conference in Cordoba, which called on the Spanish government to grant citizenship to the descendants of the Moriscos and Jews who were expelled from Spain in the fifteenth and sixteenth centuries.[70]

The controversy took another turn in 2010 when a group from the Association of Young Austrian Muslims had a confrontation with staff from a private security firm who accused them of attempting to pray in front of the *mihrab*.[71] Reports suggest that after the security staff asked them to desist, some members of the group refused and continued to pray. The clash became violent, and the security guards called the police. The security guards accused the young Muslims of consciously planning to conduct Muslim worship and coordinating a human barrier to be able to do it. On their part, the Austrians argued that they were not aware that Muslim prayer was forbidden and insisted that they did not physically attack the security guards. A Spanish court later absolved the eight Austrians who had been charged with confronting the security guards on the grounds that the security guards presented contradictory testimonies.[72] The situation threatened to escalate, with a number of other protests against the diocese's position.[73] As of 2017, there had been no incidents of similar proportions, but visits by Muslims to the Mezquita have in many instances been very fraught. Cathedral wardens and private security guards so closely monitor the behavior of tourists with "Middle Eastern appearance" that these tourists have felt harassed and unwelcome.

My own visits to the Mezquita in November 2015 and 2016 confirm that the controversy over shared worship has led to the presence of a large number of wardens and security staff. Excluding those at the door and at the ticket offices, I counted at least fifteen on one visit and sixteen on another. All of them male, they were dressed fairly uniformly in dark-blue blazers but not uniforms, although photographs of uniformed security personnel are extant.[74] At the close of visiting hours, their firm and respectful channeling of visitors toward the door was a polished operation. I did not witness any overt "profiling" of visitors who wore traditional Muslim attire or were of "Middle Eastern appearance," but certainly a subtle and covert monitoring did take place, with security staff hovering at a distance in a coordinated way when Muslim visitors stood for a long time or gathered in the vicinity of the *mihrab*.

One small incident that I did witness had little to do with attempted Muslim worship but instead took place during a mass I attended in November 2016. It revealed the efficiency and slight paranoia of the monitoring operation. Although the Mezquita was closed for the Sunday morning mass, there was no problem entering. I just followed other members of the congregation walking through the Patio de los Naranjos, and when challenged at the door, I just said, "Mass," and my companion and I were let through without much ado. The congregation was mostly Spanish with, it transpired, attendance from many local parishes in the region. There were some tourists, of whom a high proportion seemed to be East Asian. Many male wardens stood at the periphery of the transept, helping with chairs but also constantly observing the congregation. Photography during the service was forbidden. The service was led by the dean and was largely traditional in form and, as one would expect, male dominated. At the same time, there was a noticeable amount of lay participation in the readings and the prayers, and the choir was mixed male and female and also lay. After the service, the senior clergy stood at the front on the chancel steps to allow parishioner groups to stand beside them holding signs with the names of local villages and towns written on them to have their photographs taken. I had the strong impression that this service was designed to extend links to the rural hinterland and had the effect of a small pilgrimage.

The incident I refer to involved an East Asian–looking tourist. Going up to receive the wafer bread with other communicants, the tourist did not swallow the bread but held it in his hands. On returning to his seat, he drew attention to himself by appearing to giggle. Immediately two or three of the wardens approached him and quite assertively gesticulated that he should eat the wafer, which he rather shamefacedly did, while the wardens stood around him to make sure he did. The scene was quite jarring and dramatic. It was not clear what the problem was, and, having a church background myself, I do not ever recall the nonconsumption of a wafer being an issue. My supposition is that it may be a new phenomenon resulting from social media: a photograph of the wafer could be posted on Facebook, or the wafer itself could be sold on sites such as eBay, which may offend some Catholics. However, in terms of the control of behavior and the monitoring taking place in the Mezquita, what was quite remarkable were the close observation of each individual and the speed with which the wardens took action. The incident demonstrated both effective team work and significant degree of surveillance taking place, even during a relatively "closed" period for the Mezquita, such as Sunday morning Mass..

The issue of denying Muslims access to the Mezquita or shared worship is part of the diocese's more generalized reaffirmation of the Christian nature of the building—a second re-Christianization. The most of obvious aspect of this trend is what the tourist-management trade calls "interpretation" of the Mezquita, which emphasizes its Christian history through signage, websites on the internet (with maps, links, and contacts), information leaflets, and audio recordings. I do not have space here to examine each one and so illustrate the issue with just two: the amendments to the official Mezquita website and the revisions made to the official information leaflet for tourists. The official name of the Mezquita has been "Mosque-Cathedral," and the original UNESCO inscription even designates it as the "Great Mosque of Cordoba." Before November 2014, all official tourist material used either one or the other designation, but then the Diocese of Cordoba changed the Mezquita's official website address to www.catedraldecordoba.es, and Google Maps was somehow persuaded to follow suit, thus erasing the name "Mezquita" and the word *mosque* from any searches. The indignation this change provoked was widespread and immediate. Within three days, an online initiative on the activist website Change.org collected 55,000 signatures. By November 25, Google beat a retreat, and the original search name was restored.[75] The website name, however, remained the same for some time after and was not changed back to the original until 2016.

Public pressure took longer to produce a similar result over the publication of leaflets by the diocese and distributed to tourist visitors to the site. I visited the site in 2015 and again in 2016, picking up the official leaflet on each visit, and could see how it had changed in an almost unrecognizable way from one visit to the next. Sometime in the mid-1990s the name "Mosque" was removed, leaving the official name of the site as "Cathedral of Cordoba."[76] The leaflet I picked up in 2015, *The Cathedral of Cordoba: A Live Witness to Our History*, opened with the following: "The Mother Church of the Diocese: The Cathedral Chapter welcomes you to

Cordoba's Holy Cathedral Church. The entire grounds of this outstanding building that you are going to visit was consecrated as the mother church of the Diocese in the year 1236." It continued with a potted history in which the site's Islamic features were downplayed, while the Visigothic past and the later Christian additions after 1236 were brought to the fore: "It is an historical fact that the San Vicente Basilica was destroyed during the Islamic period in order to build the subsequent Mosque. Originally it was the city's main church . . . [and] continued to be remembered and worshipped by the Christians, centuries after its disappearance."[77] In contrast, for the leaflet in 2016 the title had reverted to *Monumental Site: The Mosque-Cathedral of Cordoba* (in place of *The Cathedral of Cordoba*). This leaflet stated, "The Mosque-Cathedral of Cordoba is one of the most exceptional monuments in the world, a testimony to the ancient alliance of art and faith. Its Islamic architecture, with Hellenistic, Roman and Byzantine touches, comes together with Christian architecture to create one of the most beautiful examples of its kind."[78] These denials of the Islamic past and the focus on the Christian heritage had outraged local residents and many others in the public sphere in Spain. In 2013, they triggered the formation of the citizen activist group La Platforma de la Mezquita-Catedral, which comprised a coalition of grassroots community leaders, politicians, intellectuals, and former high-ranking public officials. Their mobilization of public opinion in Cordoba and farther afield succeeded in making the issue a central feature of the municipal elections on May 24, 2015. Four former mayors of Cordoba organized a public debate on the status of the Mezquita.[79] The grassroots initiative received the support of thousands of intellectuals, politicians, writers, and high-ranking public officials.[80] Four hundred thousand signatures were collected.[81] On March 29, 2016, following lobbying and pressure from the minister of culture of the regional government of Andalusia (the Junta de Andalusía) and former mayor of Cordoba, Rosa Aguilar, the diocese finally announced that it would restore the name "Mosque-Cathedral of Cordoba" to its official documents, sites, and leaflets.

The second issue where the question of Muslim access to the Mezquita and shared worship are entangled with broader conflicts is that of property ownership by the Roman Catholic Church. It will come as a surprise to many that in modern Spain the church did not have title to most of the properties it was using and managing. This is largely a consequence of the close political ties that historically the church had with the state, and so the issue did not arise. In the post-Franco period of the transition to democracy, these close ties, as we have seen, were loosened, particularly during periods of Socialist Party rule, when a more secularist agenda was pushed by some party factions. In an earlier section, I referred to how in 1998 the government of José María Aznar, leader of the right-wing Popular Party, which is close to the church's senior hierarchy, modified the law to allow the church to formalize its use of places of worship. The Mortgage Act, which had been in force since Franco, had allowed the church to register under its name any assets that were untitled if the church could justify its presence and use. The exception was places of worship, and it was this exception that was revoked by an amendment to the act in 1998. Since then, there has been a flurry of registration of the title of properties by the Roman Catholic Church, including the Diocese of Cordoba. The exact number has not been publicly disclosed because the amendment does not oblige the church to do so, but it has been estimated at more than 4,500 places of worship.[82]

In 2005, the Diocese of Cordoba registered, for thirty euros (no less!), 22,000 square meters of the Mezquita as its own property.[83] What was quite shocking to the residents of Cordoba is the surreptitious, underhand way in which the registration was put into effect. It was not until 2009, four years later, that this lack of transparency and the absence of open discussion were revealed: a resident, smelling a rat because of the church's attitude to the controversy over the changing of the name of the Mezquita and the rewriting of the tourist leaflets, examined the public registry and discovered that the registration and transfer of title to the diocese had taken place. The public outcry both in Cordoba and throughout the nation, where similar registrations were also taking place, obliged the government to repeal the amendment in 2014.[84] However, the repeal was equally damaging to those who sought public ownership of such properties. First, it was not retroactive, so properties registered in the church's name could not be de-registered, and, second, the repeal took place before a ruling could be passed as to whether it had been constitutional in the first place. Therefore, challenges to completed registration of property under the title of the church on the grounds that the amendment was unconstitutional are no longer possible. The end result of the repeal is that it is now more difficult to reverse any registration than if the repeal had not been passed in the first place.[85]

Part of the anger directed against the Diocese of Cordoba concerns the revenues that accrue to it following the registration of the Mezquita in its name. In essence, the registration is seen as a disguised raid on the public coffers—bearing in mind, its opponents say, that the Mezquita is the most important site in Cordoba and that without it Cordoba would have no tourist industry. "It is," a leading opponent of the registration has said, "like the Eiffel Tower to Paris or the Sistine Chapel to Rome." La Platforma estimates that the Diocese of Cordoba receives from ticket sales alone between 12 and 13 million euros (approximately U.S.$13.3–$14.4 million) every year.[86] This is a conservative estimate because it does not take into account the evening Son et Lumiere shows (at a cost of 50 euros per person) and another 50,000 euros per year from visits to the Bell Tower (at a cost of 2 euros per visit). On top of these figures are also the revenues obtained from visits by VIPs and senior executives of multinationals, who pay corporate rates for a private guided tour when the Mezquita is closed to the public. None of these charges are declared as income because they are accepted as donations (the entry tickets clearly state "donation") and, as a consequence, are not taxed. In addition, the ticket offices do not accept credit cards or electronic transfers, and all payments are made in cash, rendering it difficult to trace as income. I did not witness this, but apparently after dark, bags of cash are carried surreptitiously from the ticket offices in the Patio de los Naranjos across the street to the Bishop's Palace, to the west of the Mezquita, to be counted and made secure.

The slightly farcical nature of this operation and the embarrassment it causes the diocese, not to say the chance of theft along the way, are among the main incentives behind the proposal by the diocese in 2016 to relocate the ticket offices to the Bishop's Palace. This move will oblige all tourists to visit the Bishop's Palace to buy their entry tickets and to pass through a room showing, it is believed, videos of the history of the Mezquita from the perspective of the Roman Catholic Church. This change will, La Platforma argues, continue to reinforce the Christian historical narrative of the site, and it is feared that the video, like the revised leaflet, will not present the full story, which should include the proper consideration of the site's role during the Islamic period. The diocese's proposal also includes a gift shop and a café, which some residents see as a means for the church to exploit its monopoly over the site to the detriment of the local shopkeepers and the public investment. Furthermore, the "Bishop's House" as a location for the ticket office will reinforce the impression of the clerical and nonpublic nature of the site's administration.

This issue has provided avenues for political cooperation between secularists opposed to the Catholic Church's domination in the political, social, and cultural life of modern Spain and those seeking to maintain a strong Andalusian identity in the face of the centralizing forces of the center, perceived to be dominated by the Castillian elite.[87] Particularly irksome to these two groups and to politicians across many stripes in Andalusia is the extent to which the registration of the Mezquita as a diocese property ignores the public subsidy for the upkeep and preservation of the Mezquita over many decades. This subsidy has taken the form of not only direct subventions for repairs, restoration, and general maintenance but also support for applications to various international and intergovernmental bodies.[88] For example, applications for inscription to the UNESCO World Heritage List—which leveraged funding and expert advice for restoration works from different sources, including the European Capital of Culture, and entailed considerable public expense, personnel investment, reorganization of administrative systems, interagency coordination, as well as ongoing commitments to adhere to benchmarks and to carry out monitoring and evaluation—were assumed to be for the benefit of the public purse but ultimately has solely benefitted the diocese treasury.[89]

The political ramifications of this controversy in all its dimensions—access for non-Christian prayer, contesting narratives, transfer of ownership, secularism, and regionalism—have been heightened by its conflation with immigration, the growth in the Muslim population, and the rise of Islamic terrorism in the contemporary period in Spain. As I wrote the first draft of this chapter in August 2017—in the immediate aftermath of the Barcelona attacks, in which a member of a Islamic terrorist cell ran down pedestrians along the popular thoroughfare Las Ramblas—the role of Muslims in Spain was once again thrown into sharp relief. The issue of Muslim access to the Mezquita for prayer becomes highly symbolic, and it may only be a question of time before the far-right political party Vox updates its "incendiary" YouTube video from 2015 portraying a future Muslim takeover not only of the Mezquita but also of Cordoba.

The Diocese of Cordoba has not played an uplifting role in this maelstrom of myths, symbols, fears, and prejudices. As we shall see in the next chapter on Banaras, some of the religious leaders of that holy city adopted a different course of action. In 2006, when Muslim militants carried out an attack on a Hindu temple, prominent leaders of both the Muslim community and the Hindu sect whose temple had been attacked came together to issue joint statements condemning such atrocities and participated in each other's prayers and devotions. Their joining had a spell-binding effect upon a nervous population and marginalized the extremists and militants on both sides. In contrast, the Diocese of Cordoba has made no attempt to reach out to the Muslim community in Cordoba. One wonders if in the case of the Mezquita the diocese is missing a golden opportunity to take the initiative in positioning itself as the responsible guardian not only of the site but also of mature relations between different ethnic and religious groups.

During my visits in 2015 and 2016, I was unsuccessful in obtaining interviews that would have given me a better understanding of the diocese's position. However, as a son of an Anglican bishop, I am familiar with some of the concerns that ecclesiastical authorities have regarding the use and management of religious property—the topic was the staple diet of breakfast-table discussions at home—and with the imperviousness to criticism that senior clergy often have in the face of what they see as volatile populism and opportunistic politicians.

In this context, I recall a private conversation in 1993 with one of the most senior clergymen in the Greek Orthodox Patriarchate of Jerusalem. It took place in a shady hotel garden during a break in a conference in Rabat, Morocco on the topic of Jerusalem. He was responding to my presentation of research on property sales by the patriarchate to Israeli government bodies in Jerusalem. As we walked up and down the pathways, cloistered by flowering trees and large shrubs, he suddenly stopped, turned to me, and looked directly into my eyes. What I failed to understand, he said, is that the actions taken by the patriarchate should be seen in the light of thousands of years of history. In order to survive in Jerusalem over this long period and, more importantly, into the future, it was necessary to be careful of how closely the patriarchate allied itself with ephemeral popular movements such as Palestinian nationalism and Zionism. Maintaining good relations with the ruling authorities down the ages was an essential ingredient in shoring up the patriarchate's preeminent position in Jerusalem. Selling property at key junctures, he implied, was a judicious use of the patriarchate's assets in its determination to survive the maelstrom of competing nationalisms that characterize the Middle East region.

This ultralong historical view has both a theological and an institutional basis and is, I would argue, an important lens through which to analyze the Diocese of Cordoba's position regarding the Mezquita. Setting a precedent of allowing Muslims' to pray in the Mezquita or even of conducting some shared prayers in the Mezquita would lead to unintended consequences that might diminish the role of the Catholic Church and the diocese in the city and in Andalusia.[90] To introduce change is a heavy responsibility, and the direction modern Spain is traveling, with its secular trends, changing demography, and external and internal threats, means that a cautious and careful approach that stresses continuity is required. Monopolizing the access and management of one of the most important cultural and religious shrines in southern Spain, if not the whole of Europe, would place the Roman Catholic Diocese of Cordoba and the Christian community in a sound cultural and financial position for decades to come. Who can blame the diocese for seizing this opportunity?

Nevertheless, one can see how the diocese could be misreading the range of options available to religious people in addressing the tensions between faith and secularism and between national and regional values. The diocese appears to be narrowly focused on consolidating its position culturally and financially and to be out of step with some of the key milestones in the history of Cordoba. Emphasizing the establishment of a separate Christian identity and narrative in the Mezquita seems to be, in the light of the more fundamental environmental and nihilistic threats facing modern society in general, a Huntingdonian and retrogressive approach, part of a tired, worn-out, and unimaginative worldview. It may serve specific internal ecclesiastical purposes and short-term populist trends, but it lacks a universal vision and a sense of greatness.

Using the mixed architectural heritage, rich history, and religious traditions of the Mezquita and Cordoba, the diocese could offer an inclusive and embracing view of Christianity as a great facilitator of pathways to God. Yes, it may have to surrender some control—inclusiveness is inherently democratic and a little messy—but it could establish itself as a beacon of interfaith understanding, coexistence, and dialogue in the city without compromising its essential Christian message. In place of the tribal and grasping approach it seems to be currently taking in the controversy over access and ownership, this inclusive approach would be a much greater contribution to Cordoba's past, present, and future and one that many Christians would be proud to be associated with.

Cordoba's Mezquita: Past, Present, and Future

My overall impression is that the issue of shared access to prayer and worship, although highly charged, is ultimately a minority interest among the residents of Cordoba. It certainly is not emanating from the Cordoban Muslim community, which, as we have seen, is small and more concerned with improving their standard of living and the facilities available to them. This chapter has shown how the controversy is subsumed by a cultural and political debate and contest over rival interpretations of the historical narrative of the city and hence of its current identity as a cultural beacon not only for Andalusia but also for Spain. The debate centers on the extent to which the city's Islamic past should be recognized and celebrated or minimized and made secondary to the dominant Christianized culture of Spain. By examining the controversy over Muslim access to the Mezquita in this broader context, we can see how cooperation and accommodation can still both enrich and consolidate the Mezquita's contribution to Cordoba and to the vexed state of sectarian relations in Spain. The late Mansur Escudero, a former secretary-general of the Islamic Commission of Spain and resident of Cordoba, has always maintained that the request to share prayers or to have access for Muslims to pray in the Mezquita was not an attempt to muscle in on the diocese's control of the site but more a response to the diocese's exclusivist view and Christianized narrative of the site and city. "We are not trying to take the Mezquita away from anyone," Escudero is reported to have said, "just open it up."[91] Following his death, the Junta Islámica in Cordoba, of which Escudero was also director, has retracted its demands, and a consensus has emerged in the Muslim community of Cordoba to let rest the issue of Muslim prayer and shared space for worship.[92]

Nevertheless, if this dimension of the controversy has lost some of its inflammatory potential, the question of control over the Mezquita is not being dropped by those opposed to the diocese's actions. La Platforma is continuing to mobilize civil society in favor of some form of public oversight of the Mezquita. Commissioning reports by experts, it is fleshing out proposals based on the "Alhambra model," which outlines a shared-management structure comprising the three main actors involved: the central government, which would have responsibility for funding; the regional government, which would have oversight of restoration and maintenance; and the diocese, which would have use of the building for church activities. It is unlikely that the diocese will cede any title or responsibility in this way, however, and the ball is very much in the hands of the regional government as to whether it wishes to expend political capital in pressuring the diocese on this issue. It remains to be seen whether the Barcelona attack by a Muslim immigrant from Morocco in August 2017 will once again lead to the conflation of terrorism, Islam, and immigration in the politics of Spain and thus permit the Diocese of Cordoba to position itself as the defender of Christian and Spanish values, using the Mezquita as an iconic symbol to promote its views. It also remains to be seen if the recent revival in 2019 of the Socialist Party of Spain and its return to government will constrain the activities of the Roman Catholic Diocese of Cordoba.

The Mezquita case suggests that the drivers for a change in its status are relatively weak. In the absence of any major demographic challenge to the Christian majority in the city, and in the absence of geostrategic considerations such as those espoused by General Franco in his search for Arab and Islamic support to break out of Spain's isolation, pressure for change will come mostly from supporters of Andalusian regional identity. In addition, the Roman Catholic Church remains a dominant force in the region and city, with no strong countervailing religious organization to keep it in check. To some extent, the Socialist Party could offer that opposition to the church's ideological hegemony, but there is little evidence that it will risk its political control over the main governing institutions in the region to do so. The management of the Mezquita site by the church may be contested, but the legal and political framework within which it operates and that affirms its continuing hold is, although under dispute, not contested in the same way as Israel's legitimacy in East Jerusalem is contested. In this sense, the Mezquita controversy can be said to be contained. The narrative of precedence is unlikely to be significantly challenged. However, what is interesting and relevant to this study is how the history of the site continues to throw long silhouettes down the ages to the present day. The Roman Catholic Church's position may be overwhelmingly the dominant one, but it still needs to be asserted, the church still has to maneuver to strengthen its position, and it still feels on the defensive. The controversy over the access, use, and management of the Mezquita is clearly longstanding and unresolved. The passions and political forces it engenders have risen and fallen and will continue to rise and fall in decades to come. It also sends an ambiguous message to those who study and attempt to resolve the conflicts over holy sites in Jerusalem: there may be worse to come. But at the same time there may also be a swing in the pendulum away from confrontation to accommodation. In the next chapter, we turn to Banaras, where a similar kind of site, the Gyan Vapi Mosque, is believed by Hindus to be built over the ruins and with the spolia of a Hindu temple, the Vishveshwur Temple, in a city that also once had a glorious Islamic past. Here we will see how contained and dormant passions can be roused by changing political, social, and religious factors to create a volatile and unstable new situation.

CHAPTER III

Hindu–Muslim Rivalries in Banaras

History and Myth as the Present

The Hindu festival of Holi, known as the "Festival of Colors," celebrates the coming of spring with great exuberance and humor. Indians of all castes and creeds join in the carnival-like atmosphere, which includes the throwing of colored dyes and powder over fellow revelers. In March 2006, however, one week before the festival was to commence in Banaras (also known as Varanasi), the festival ended in tragedy. The courtyard of the Sangkat Mochan Temple, dedicated to the Hindu deity Hanuman the Monkey God, was brimming with devotees preparing for the evening prayers. The courtyard was particularly crowded with wedding parties gathering under the shady trees and covered walkways because spring is also a popular time for marriages to take place. But disguised among the wedding gifts was a shiny new pressure cooker crammed with explosives, which when detonated ripped through the crowd, killing twenty-one worshippers and wounding scores of others. Among the dead was a bridegroom. Later, television footage of the temple showed abandoned shoes scattered in pools of blood and chunks of flesh spattered on walls and pillars. Crowds screamed and shouted in fear, anger, and grief, and newspaper reports wrote of a stampede of thousands narrowly being averted. Bicycle rickshaws, *tuk-tuk*s, and volunteers threaded their way through the throng carrying the dead and wounded to the nearest hospital. Fifteen minutes later, two more blasts rocked the Varanasi Cantonment Railway Station, leaving a foot-deep crater and shattering nearby windows.

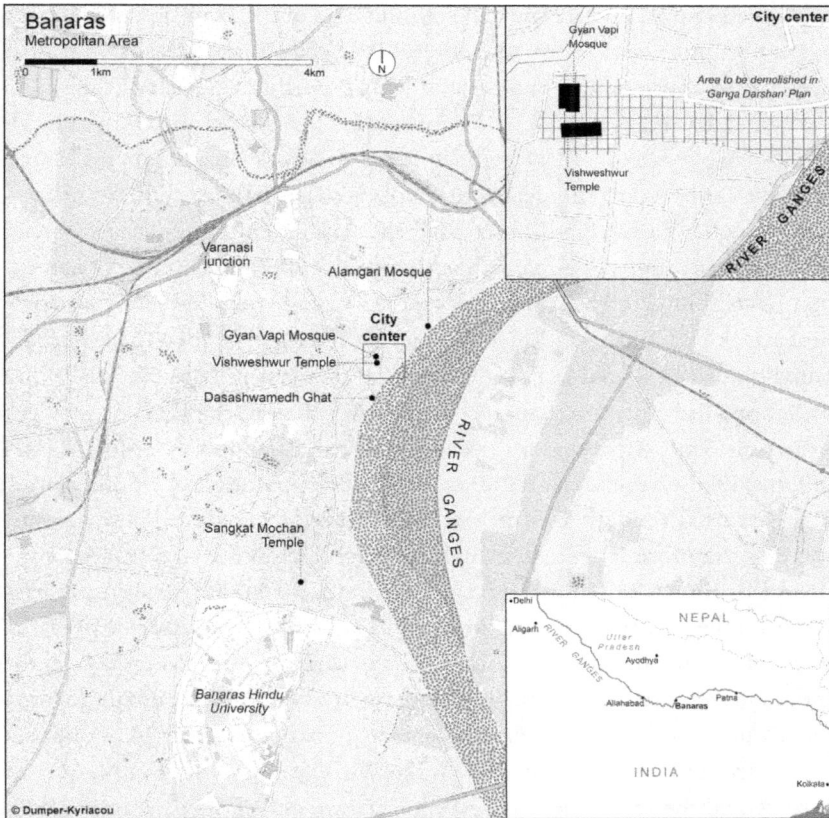

Map 3.1 Banaras city center and insert showing Gyan Vapi Mosque and Vishweshwur Temple. (Map by Lefkos Kyriacou and Michael Dumper)

One bomb had been placed beside an inquiry kiosk, and the other on a crowded platform where an express train for Delhi was about to depart, leading to seven more fatalities and many more wounded.[1] Four more unexploded bombs were also found close to a popular site for ritual bathing along the shores of the River Ganges, which flows nearby. A curfew was imposed across the city.

It is not clear exactly when the atrocity began to be attributed to Muslim terrorists, but it is quite likely that it was fairly soon after the shock receded. Although no formal claim was made by any group, that conclusion was nevertheless an understandable one for the traumatized crowds to draw.[2] Tensions between Hindus and Muslims, long a feature of Indian local and national politics since the closing days of the British Raj, had once again been growing. Since 2001, there had been a series attacks on Indian national institutions and civilians by Muslim militants, such as the group known as Lashkar-e-Taiba, and supported, it is alleged, by the Pakistani intelligence services.[3] In December 2001, an attack on Parliament House in New Delhi led to the deaths of 6 police officers and a civilian; in September 2002, Lashkar-e-Taiba raided the Akshardam Temple in the state of Gujarat, killing 33 people and wounding 70; the next August, twin car bombs attributed to Lashkar-e-Taiba killed 52 and wounded 150. The deadliest attack by Lashkar-e-Taiba came in October 2005, when three coordinated bombs exploded in two markets and on a bus in New Delhi, killing 63 and wounding more than 200.[4] A few days before the Banaras incident in March 2006, there was a violent conflict in Lucknow, the state capital of Uttar Pradesh, between Hindus and Muslims as a result of Muslims' protests against President George W. Bush's visit to India.[5] These are just some of the more salient events taking place within the overarching context of Pakistan–Indian maneuverings over long-standing grievances arising from the partition of India, in particular the disputed province of Kashmir, where jihadi teachings, recruitment drives, and atrocities against Indian targets are some of the tools utilized to weaken the Indian government's position.[6] There is also the wider global context of Islamophobia arising from the al-Qaeda attacks on the World Trade Center in New York in 2001 and the sectarian polarization leaching out of the various conflicts in the Middle East—Palestine, Iraq, Libya, and so on.

The result of these developments was an atmosphere of mistrust that Hindu nationalist leaders could easily whip up against the Muslim community in India. In Banaras following the explosions in 2006, the leader of the right-wing Hindu group Bajrang Dal, Vinay Katiyar, attempted to rouse his supporters by organizing a sit-in demonstration inside the Sangkat Mochan Temple courtyard, replete with the blowing of conch shells and cries of "Jai Shri Ram" (Hail, Lord Rama), while L. K. Advani, the leader of the main Hindu nationalist party in the state parliament, the Bharatiya Janata Party (BJP), sought to organize a procession from the temple through the city.[7] But in contrast to the riots that took place in 1992 in the aftermath of the destruction of the Babri Masjid (Mosque) in Ayodhya by Hindu nationalists, which I examine more closely in a later section, key religious leaders in Banaras worked hard to diffuse sectarian tensions and prevent revenge attacks. The chief priest of the Sangkat Mochan Temple,

Mahant Veer Bhadra Mishra, sought to calm the situation by ensuring that the evening prayers, *aarti*, were carried out as normal within a few hours of the atrocity, and in his media appearances he stressed the importance of not blaming the Muslim community of Banaras.[8] He discouraged politicians from exploiting the incident and fanning the flames of sectarianism.[9] Foremost among his endeavors to restore calm was a meeting with a delegation of Muslim leaders led by the mufti of Banaras, Maulana Abdul Batin Nomani, a well-respected cleric who had previously established a personal rapport with the *mahant*. Publicly receiving a gift of holy water from the Ganges from the hands of the *mahant*, the mufti spoke of the shared heritage and economic bonds that bound the Hindu and Muslim communities of Banaras together. In a visually dramatic gesture that reverberated throughout India, young Muslim women, in head scarves and Islamic dress, gave a recital of the Hanuman Chalisa—a hymn to the temple's deity—to demonstrate their commitment to communal harmony.[10]

If the perpetrators of the Sangkat Mochan Temple and Varanasi Cantonment Station bombings intended to deepen the sectarian divisions in the city, they seemed to have failed. The following year, in 2007, a Hindu religious procession was jointly led by the *mahant* and the mufti, and a nationally renowned Muslim woman activist, Noor Fatima, was a guest of honor at the ceremony. Although it would be going much too far to say that sectarian grievances have been resolved and the Hindutva (Hindu-ness) nationalists' aspirations neutralized, displays of intercommunal solidarity in the streets of Banaras have become more commonplace. A Christian-run center for interfaith dialogue, Maitri Bhavan, or Friendship House, hosted a series of meetings and collective prayers with members of different faiths to convey the message of religious harmony and peace.[11] The Sangkat Mochan Temple now holds an annual music festival at which musicians from a range of religious traditions perform, including famous artists from Pakistan.[12] As such, the Banaras example offers an important insight into how religious conflicts are managed in cities where different religions and religious communities live cheek by jowl and are going through both local and national transformations.

The main exploration of this book has been the degree to which the two metanarratives, the narrative of precedence and the narrative of transformative integration, are in competition or in equilibrium in the cities under examination. In Cordoba, we found that the contemporary debate was concerned with how the narrative of transformative integration was being supplanted by the narrative of precedence, exemplified by the Roman Catholic Diocese's initiatives, which were aided and abetted when the central government in Madrid applied the brakes on the devolution of power to the Spanish regions. Similarly, since the Israeli occupation in 1967, we see how in Jerusalem a narrative of transformative integration has been totally eclipsed by the narrative of precedence, although it briefly flickered to life again during the period immediately following the Oslo Accords in 1993.

Banaras offers us a useful addition to this way of viewing changes and conflict in a city and the role played by its religious sites. We can see how the narrative of precedence, pursued by the supporters of Hindutva and Hindu nationalism, has since independence in 1948 increasingly come to the fore, particularly since the demolition in 1992 of the Babri Masjid in Ayodhya. As a result, the push to emphasize the association of Kashi/Varanasi/Banaras with Hinduism and a Hindu identity has led to the marginalization of historic Muslim associations in the city and to neglect the contribution made by the Mughals and other Islamic dynasties to the development of the city. Nevertheless, the narrative of transformative integration retains much resonance at the city level. The culture of communal interdependence conveyed by the description of Banaras as a city of *tana bana*, "warp and weft," is based on the textile and weaving industries in Banaras as joint intercommunal enterprises.[13] It places the Muslim community at the heart of the city's economic prosperity and commercial reputation and in this way fuels much of the dynamism that resists the total eclipse of this integration narrative. Similarly, the public discourse concerning coexistence, using terms such as *bhai-bhai* (Urdu) or *bhaiachara* (Hindi), meaning "Hindu–Muslim brotherhood," and "Ganga Jamuni *tahzeb/sanskriti*," which expresses the shared North Indian culture of the Ganges plain, undergirded much of the response to the incident in 2006.[14] In Banaras, then, we can see how national-level political debates over the preeminence of Hinduism and its status as a signifier of Indian identity are strongly countered by the local celebration of heterodoxy and inclusiveness. The relative positions of the two narratives have continued to change to this day, receiving both setbacks and assistance from many different political, demographic, international, and social factors that this chapter attempts to unpack.

The focus of religious tension in Banaras is around what is popularly called the "Golden Temple": the Vishweshwur Temple.[15] The current edifice, built in the late eighteenth century, was located as close as possible to what was thought to be the site of the original Hindu temple, which had been demolished in 1669 by the Mughal emperor Aurangzeb.[16] In its place, he built the Gyan Vapi Mosque, which remains open today, which is controlled by a Muslim board and to which Hindus have limited access and a proscribed involvement in the maintenance works carried out. We should recall that Banaras—or Kashi, City of Light, its Hindu name—is one of the most sacred cities in Hinduism. It is, among its many other important roles in Hindu mythology, the home of Shiva, one of the greatest of the gods in the Hindu pantheon, and his consort, Parvati; the location of Shiva's *jyortilinga*—the emblem of sheer light; and the site where if a devotee of Shiva were to die, he or she would be freed from the never-ending cycle of reincarnation—that is, he or she will attain *moksha*, or liberation. Its centrality to Hinduism is akin to Jerusalem's centrality to Judaism and Christianity, Mecca's to Islam, and Rome's to Roman Catholicism.[17] Banaras does not, however, have the same resonance and centrality to Islam as a world religion as it does to Hinduism, although, as I describe, the imprint of its Islamic past is deep.

Due to the long and checkered history of northern India, with political power alternating between Buddhist, Muslim, and Hindu rulers, we have a situation in Banaras where at the epicenter of Hinduism there lies a mosque on the very site of what is believed to be the most famous linga (a phallic stone column representing Shiva) of all. To most Hindus, the demolition of the original temple housing the linga and its replacement with a mosque are a tragedy to be regretted and mourned. To contemporary Hindu nationalists, they are a desecration and an outrage that must be reversed. For centuries after the construction of the Gyan Vapi Mosque, the power of Islamic state authorities and subsequently the British colonial administration prevented any such reversions, and Hindus made do with a number of replacement sites close by. The important role that Indian Muslims played in the economic life of the city also tempered the wilder extremes of Hindu nationalists in the city. However, since independence and particularly since the rise of Hindutva parties in state and national legislatures and their success in the demolition of the Babri Masjid in 1992, the Gyan Vapi Mosque is now in the nationalists' crosshairs—its time possibly numbered and contingent upon the balance of demographic trends and political forces in the city, in the region, and across India.

As a result, entrance to the mosque is highly restricted: along the narrow streets that ring the mosque and adjacent temple are a series of police checkpoints, backed up by paramilitary Rapid Action Force (RAF) units. The mosque is surrounded by barbed wire, and a tall watchtower rises above the hodgepodge of roofs, small courtyards, and alleyways in the vicinity. Nevertheless, the current situation is extremely fluid. While Hindu nationalists consolidate their power in state-level institutions and circle round Muslim sites said to be built upon Hindu temple ruins, the dispersal of Islamic State forces in the Middle East into South Asia as a result of the collapse of the Raqqa-based Islamic Caliphate in 2017 may yet provide a dangerous foil to the growing power of Hindu nationalists in the city.[18] The prospect of another Islamic militant reaction manifesting itself in an atrocity similar to the bombings in Banaras in 2006 cannot be discounted.

It is in this context of swirling national and religious ideologies and political forces that the study of Banaras becomes so important. At the same time, my focus is this chapter is twofold: it seeks to identify some of the key developments and sites concerning religious tensions in the city and examines whether a grasp of these tensions in Banaras and their political and social context can add to my understanding of some of the more general dynamics of conflicts in other religious cities, such as Cordoba and Jerusalem. In approaching this topic, I ask whether there are sufficient similarities to make a comparison worthwhile. But, perhaps more importantly, I also ask if the differences bring to the fore hitherto overlooked factors that need to be taken into account when examining religious conflicts in cities. Furthermore, the so far relatively successful attempts to neutralize the impact of militant and radical attempts to promote the narrative of precedence in the city prompt the following questions: Is there a possible "Banaras model" for managing and resolving religious conflicts in urban settings, and, if so, how transferable to other locations is it?

This chapter is divided into six sections. The first describes the city's context and examines the factors that could lead to religious conflict and violence as a result of its location in the national political discourse. The second section explores the role of the Muslim community, which is increasingly beleaguered in the face of institutionalized Hindu nationalism. The third returns to the broader context by deconstructing some of the drivers of community and sectarian tensions in the city through an examination of the issues of governance: the role of the state on the federal, state, and municipal levels, the role of the economy, and the extent to which these factors play a part in the managing of religious conflicts in Banaras. The fourth section discusses the city's strong religiosity due to its preeminent role in Hindu mythology and pilgrimage rituals and, furthermore, what impact this role has on the appeals made by political ideologies and parties. To demonstrate the tensions that exist regarding the Vishweshwur Temple's history of past demolition and reconstruction and its location abutting an historic mosque, the chapter examines the temple's history and current role as a key Hindu site in the city. In this section, I also examine the impact of the demolition of the Babri Masjid in Ayodhya and its impact on Muslim–Hindu relations in Banaras. The fifth section focuses on the tensions arising from the campaign to rebuild a temple to Shiva on the site of the Gyan Vapi Mosque and considers ways in which these developments may precipitate further conflicts. A concluding section draws together the chapter's themes and attempts to relate them to this study's overall focus.

The Potential for Conflict in the City

Despite the efforts made by the *mahant* of the Sangkat Mochan Temple and the mufti of Banaras in 2006, the potential for conflict in Banaras remained. Indeed, in December 2010 another extremist Muslim group known as Indian Mujahideen detonated a bomb among a crowd of worshippers and bathers on the steps of the Shitala Ghat, close to the access route to the Vishweshwur Temple.[19] Yet again Muslim–Hindu tensions were inflamed, and Hindu nationalists felt that their denunciations of Islam as an alien presence in India were vindicated. However, not all religious conflict in Banaras is sectarian; intra-Hindu disputes as well as disputes between religious groups and the state authorities are also known to take place. In October 2015, for example, a curfew was imposed in the central districts of Banaras after a *yatra*, or religious procession, descended into chaos and a melee. Following some stone throwing and the setting of motorbikes and police vehicles on fire, local police units assisted by the elite paramilitary RAF carried out a series of baton charges to disperse the crowds.[20] This confrontation between a fundamentalist Hindu sect and the police arose as a result of a state policy to reduce the high levels of pollution in the River Ganges by banning the common and deeply felt ceremonial immersion of idols of Hindu deities, which are unfortunately decorated with highly toxic paints.[21]

As these examples show, the potential for violence over religious disputes is significant and arises from several factors, both internal and external to the city. Later sections of this chapter focus on the internal factors, and in this section I establish the overall context and focus on the primary arena of religious conflict—that is, the arena of Hindu–Muslim relations. For reasons of space and to avoid repeating what is already well covered in the academic literature, I do not enter into the history of these relations in any great depth but summarize the main points before highlighting some specific issues that underlie current developments in the city.

Muslim–Hindu tensions in India originate from the period of Islamic conquest of parts of the Indian subcontinent in the twelfth century CE. During the sixteenth and seventeenth centuries, Turkic-Persian rule reached its apogee during an Islamic golden age under the Mughal rulers in northern India, with the glorious Taj Mahal as the iconic manifestation of that dynasty's religion, culture, and artistic achievement. The gradual British takeover of India from the eighteenth century to the mid–twentieth century introduced a lasting conflictual dynamic that has not yet been resolved. On the one hand, British colonization may have acted as a catalyst toward a nonsectarian Indian nationalism incorporating the major Hindu–Muslim religious divide, but, on the other hand, it also resulted in more self-conscious separate Muslim and Hindu political identities, identities that the British authorities encouraged to fragment the political opposition to their presence.[22] By the turn of the twentieth century and on the eve of the departure of the British Raj in 1947, political action among Indians was highly sectarian, characterized by a Hindu-dominated Indian National Congress and a Muslim All-India Muslim League as the key actors.

The collapse of a shared nonsectarian vision for the state that was to follow decolonization and independence led to the partition of the subcontinent into two countries: India and a geographically split Pakistan based on parts of the Punjab in the West and parts of Bengal in the East. Pakistan was declared the first modern Islamic state, and some 10 million people moved in two disastrous and bloody directions from India to Pakistan and vice versa. India was established as a secular but multicultural country under the aegis of the Congress Party, but with a sizeable Muslim minority remaining. In fact, only a small proportion of Indian Muslims availed themselves of the opportunity to live in Pakistan. However, despite the fact that more Muslims remained in India than settled in Pakistan, and despite the fact that they make up by far the largest religious minority community in India, since independence they have experienced considerable discrimination and violence.[23]

A comparison among the censi of 1991, 2001, and 2011 reveals an overall slowdown in the population growth rate of both Hindus and Muslims, but the Hindu growth rate slowed less sharply than the Muslim rate, although the Muslim growth rate is still overall higher.

The minority position of Muslims in India has been made even more marginal by the relatively untrammeled growth of Hindu nationalism and its more extreme elements. Hindutva, or the promotion of a Hindu-centric concept of Indian citizenship and identity, may have started as an attempt to create political unity among Hindus, but its success was contingent on creating an idealized ethnically homogenized community that excluded sectarian differences. For Hindu nationalists, if Hindus cannot be accorded legal primacy in the new state, then at the very least they should be given social and cultural primacy.[24] As a result, Muslims in India, who are highly heterodox theologically, linguistically, socially, and economically, have been "Othered"—reconstructed as a monolithic political threat and designated as an obstacle to national unity.[25] Such reductionism has elided the divisions within Islam, which has strands of Sunni personal law, numerous Shi'a sects, Sufi orders, and other perceived heretical offshoots, such as the prosperous Ahmadiyya sect. Ashutosh Varshney, one of the foremost analysts of sectarian conflicts in India, lays out the overgeneralization very clearly: "By often flattening all Muslims into an anti-Indian mold, the Hindu nationalists embitter even Muslims who are syncretistic in their religiosity and culture, as well as those for whom Islam is a faith, a way to

TABLE 3.1

Population of India by Religion (Hindu and Muslim) by Percentage, 1991–2011

Religion	1991	2001	2011
Hindu	82.0	80.5	79.8
Muslim	12.1	13.4	14.2

Sources: Census of India 1991, cited in Ashutosh Varshney, *Ethnic Conflict and Civic Life: Hindus and Muslims in India* (New Haven, CN: Yale University Press, 2002), 56; Government of India, Office of the Registrar General and Census Commissioner, "Census Data 2001," 2001, http://www.censusindia.gov.in/2011-common/census_data_2001.html; Government of India, "Religion Census 2011," 2011, https://www.census2011.co.in/religion.php.

sustain troubled private lives, but not a political ideology, and who have remarkable pride in India."[26] Although Islam as a religion, with its powerful emphasis on the uniqueness and unity of a single deity, Allah, may be highly resistant to theological syncretism, Islamic social practices in India have been open to many influences, not least the Hindu caste system, but also music, art, poetry, and various celebrations, such as popular festivals. Thus, with Hindutva, one could argue that an inclusive Indian culture encompassing different social and religious legacies has been sacrificed upon the altar of militant Hindu nationalism.

The capture of local, state, and federal institutions by Hindu political parties and movements since the mid-1990s flowed from the extensive mobilization of pro-Hindu sentiments in increasing dramatic and unchecked ways. Large-scale demonstrations and religious processions centered on themes derived from Hindu mythology, the takeover and demolition of mosques, the intimidation and finally displacement of Muslim residents from districts and urban quarters became a fact of political life in India. From the mid-1980s, increasing acts of violence and rioting, particularly in northern India, the location of the majority of the Muslim population, took place.[27] A crescendo of triumphant Hindutva occurred on the occasion of the forcible destruction of the Babri Masjid in Ayodhya in 1992, which was followed by riots in in Mumbai in 1993 and the widespread destruction and displacement in Gujarat in 2002, which resulted in the eviction of more than 100,000 people from their homes and the injury of more than 1,000 Muslims.[28]

The Muslim Community in Banaras

How does this tension between the Hindu and Muslim Indians in the national sphere affect Banaras? We should recall here the observation made in the introduction that the lens of confessionalism, or the focus on religious identities, can accentuate perceptions of a religious divide. Tensions between different religious, linguistic, and ethnic groups in cities are often derived from class (or, in the case of India, caste) identities and economic conditions. I examine this issue in the third section. In this section, though, in order to understand some of the religious dynamics played out in the city, we need to gain some understanding of the city's demographic makeup. The most recent census for Banaras district, which also includes the city of

Banaras, was carried out in 2011. By looking at trends between the 2011 census and the previous one in 2001, and by combining the data from the 2011 census with the data given in several other sources and reports, we can begin to gain an insight into the region's and city's demographic profile.

In 2011, the total number of people residing in the district of Banaras was 3,676,841.[29] The majority of them live in nearly 1,300 villages in the district's rural parts. Meanwhile, the city of Banaras had a population of 1,198,491.[30] This concentration of just less than half of the population into the city indicates a high density, which in 2011 was 2,399 people per square kilometer for the whole district of Banaras compared to the national average of 382 people per square kilometer.[31] When these population statistics are broken down by religion, the figures broadly mirror national trends. As seen in table 3.2, Hinduism is the predominant religion in the district, with 84.5 percent of the population being Hindu, in comparison to the Uttar Pradesh average of 79.7 percent and the India national average of 79.8 percent. The second-largest religious group is the Muslims, amounting to 14.8 percent in the Banaras district, as opposed to 19.2 percent in Uttar Pradesh and 14.2 percent in the nation as a whole.

Table 3.3 provides a detailed breakdown of the city's religious profile. It reveals that the city, as opposed to the district, is, according to the 2011 census, basically a two-to-one split between Hindus and Muslims, with Hindus making up just a little more than 70 percent of the population and Muslims a little less than 30 percent. Banaras thus bucks the national and state average quite significantly. Whereas Muslims compose roughly one-sixth of the population of India and one-fifth of the population of Uttar Pradesh, in Banaras they compose almost one-third of the population.[32]

TABLE 3.2

Population (Hindu and Muslim) by Percentage for Banaras District, Uttar Pradesh, and India, 2011

Religion	Banaras District	Uttar Pradesh	India
Hindu	84.5	79.7	79.8
Muslim	14.8	19.2	14.2

Sources: Government of India, "Religion Census 2011," 2011, https://www.census2011.co.in/religion.php. See also Government of Uttar Pradesh, *Human Development Report* (Lucknow: Government of Uttar Pradesh, 2007), http://hdr.undp.org/sites/default/files/india_uttar_pradesh_2007.pdf.

TABLE 3.3

Population of Banaras City by Religion, 2011

Description	Total Population	Percentage
Hindu	840,280	70.11
Muslim	345,461	28.82
Christian	4,034	0.34
Not Stated	3,995	0.33
Sikh	2,610	0.22
Jain	1,417	0.12
Buddhist	461	0.04
Other	233	0.02

Source: Government of India, "Varanasi (Varanasi) District: Census 2011 Data," Census 2011, https://www.census2011.co.in/census/district/568-varanasi.html. A proposal submitted to UNESCO for the inclusion of Banaras on the World Heritage List gives, also citing the 2011 census, the figure of 35.7 percent for the proportion of the population who are Muslims. The proposal is undated, and this figure may be the result of an extrapolation from the growth rates at the time of submission. See Rana P. B. Singh, "Proposing Varanasi as a Heritage City for Inclusion in the UNESCO World Heritage List," n.d., draft approved by Manoj Kumar, divisional commissioner, Society of Heritage Planning and Environmental Health and Vrinda Dar-Kautilya Society, Varanasi, copy in author's files.

This dominance of the two main religious communities is highlighted in the 2011 census by the fact that the members of all the other religious groups combined—Christians, Jains, Sikhs, Buddhists, and others—do not add up to more than 1 percent of Banaras's population.[33] A high proportion of the in-migration to the city is by elderly Hindus and Hindu widows who seek to pass their final days in the holy city, believing in this way that they will escape the never-ending cycle of reincarnation. At the same time, part of the growth is due to in-migration from the rural hinterland of Banaras, especially from Bihar and West Bengal, which can be attributed in part to the availability of good schools and the opportunities for higher education in Banaras.

Some historians have traced the emergence of a Muslim community in Banaras to the eleventh century following the Islamic conquests of northern India by the Afghani-Turkish tribes under Mahmud al-Ghaznawi in 1021 CE.[34] However, it was not until the establishment of the Mughal Empire and the conquest of Banaras under Akbar between 1574 and 1576 that material traces of Islamic presence in the city can be definitively identified. As Madhuri Desai has observed in her authoritative and forensic examination of the archaeological and architectural evidence of the earliest buildings in Banaras, "Mughal intervention established the city's forms, spaces and land use patterns."[35] In fact, there is little evidence of construction prior to Akbar's conquest, and whether this lack of evidence indicates the absence of any monumental and lasting structures prior to this point or the wholesale demolition of earlier structures at this point, including a temple housing the Shiva linga, is the focus of much polemic debate and controversy, which I explore further in the next section. What is certain is that it was during this period through to the mid–seventeenth century that Mughal rule dominated. One notable feature of the Mughals' rule was the co-optation of many of the Hindu elite into their system of government and dominant social mores, leading to a degree of syncretism that, one can speculate, laid the foundations of the *bhai-bhai* and *bhaiachara* practices and discourse mentioned earlier. During the reign of Emperor Aurangzeb (1658–1707), a more orthodox Islam prevailed, but it was short-lived as the Mughal Empire gradually disintegrated. By the time the British East India Company took over Banaras in 1781 under Warren Hastings, the city had become a much sought-after prize by competing Hindu, Shi'a, and Mughal princes and sultans.

Governance

Banaras is not only a site of spiritual and religious significance but also a key seat of political power and influence in the country. It falls under the governance of the state of Uttar Pradesh. A state governor is elected every five years who acts as the constitutional head and is responsible for appointing a chief minister and some members of the upper house, the Vidhan Parishad—a council of 100 ministers who have the power to legislate. The lower house, the Vidhan Sabha, has a total of 404 members and acts as a legislative assembly. The seats are contested by four main parties, two of which are "caste-based" regional parties and two are national parties—the right-wing BJP and the center-left Samajwadi (Socialist) Party (a coalition comprising the Congress Party as its largest member).[36] Uttar Pradesh is important nationally because it sends the largest number of representatives to the federal Parliament, and therefore its elections to both state and federal parliaments are contested vigorously. During federal and state elections, Banaras is often the location for rallies and speeches from all candidates. The Congress Party singles out Uttar Pradesh as having the "distinction of providing many illustrious and top grade leaders to the Indian National Congress" and uses the region as a base for its Youth Congress.[37] The website of the current prime minister of India, Narendra Modi (leader of the BJP), proclaims that because Banaras is the only place in India where the River Ganges turns direction to flow north, "the start of the biggest change will also happen from Varanasi. The country is moving towards GOOD GOVERNANCE and this message initiated from the Varanasi will light a NEW HOPE in the entire country."[38] Varshney observes that electoral politics in India give Muslims disproportionate voting power. In 10 percent of constituencies, they constitute 50 percent of the electorate, and because minorities tend to vote en bloc, Muslims thus wield greater influence than their actual numbers seem to indicate on the electoral roll.[39] In this way, the Muslim electoral districts in Banaras are much sought-after prizes by the different political parties. In this context, however, it is also worth noting Philippa Williams's findings that Hindus and Muslims in Banaras share very similar concerns regarding scarce resources, the poor delivery of services, and the bias in favor of the well-to-do that is so prevalent in Indian politics.[40] One result of these shared concerns is the Ansaris' (Muslim weavers') "self-provisioning." Since 1970s, in one neighborhood alone, Madanpura, three private hospitals have been established and funded by Ansari businesspeople weavers.[41] Such self-provisioning is the Muslim community's response to the failure of the state at both federal and state levels to deliver adequate services and to protect the Muslim community's interests.

The Economy

The largest economic sectors in Banaras are manufacturing and commerce, which in 2006 employed approximately 40 percent and 26 percent of the workforce, respectively. A further 19 percent of those are in "other services.[42] The city's religious significance also provides the opportunity for a substantial tourism industry. More than 3 million domestic and 200,000 foreign tourists visit annually, with the peak season being between October and March. As a result, many thousands are employed as tour guides or tour operators, hotel or hostel owners, catering and hospitality workers, and bus, taxi, or rickshaw drivers. It is estimated that about 12,000 beds are available to tourists—of which about one-half are in inexpensive budget hotels and one-third are in *dharmashalas* (Hindu religious guesthouses). In addition, the city is home to the largest residential university in Asia, Banaras Hindu University. Not only has it attracted a sizeable student population, but it is also a large employer of academics, administrators, and grounds staff (its 1,300 acres are described as having "extensive greenery, a temple, an airstrip and buildings, which are an architectural delight"[43]). Finally, Banaras has a reputation for fostering employment based around classical arts, cultural history, and humanities in keeping with its aspiration to be inscribed on UNESCO's World Heritage Site list.

Among these features, the silk trade of Banaras requires further discussion. By the seventeenth century, the Muslim community had settled in sufficient numbers and adapted to urban life. Accompanying the conquerors were skilled Muslim weavers from West Asia, who also settled in Banaras and introduced the *kinkhaab*, the weaving of brocades with intricate designs in gold and silver thread, which became the hallmark of Banaras. Later the fusion of Hindu and Muslim designs in silk made the city weavers' products exceptional and unique, and Banaras became a famous center for handlooms making silk saris.[44] The weaving industry became the city's economic hub, and it still constitutes its main employment. Rana Singh estimates that in 2013 there were about 50,600 looms in the city, employing approximately 60,000 weavers directly.[45] Taken as a whole, the silk-sari industry employs approximately 500,000 people in various trades, such as dyeing, sari polishing, and trading. Given that the total population of Banaras is approximately 1.2 million, this means that nearly 50 percent of the population is engaged in the sari industry in some way.[46] The manufacturing of saris is confined largely to certain Muslim-majority neighborhoods, notably Saraiya on the outskirts of the city, Alaipura in the northern part, Madanpura just south of the Chowk, the main bazaar area in the center, and Lallapura to the south. Whereas the weavers are in the main Muslims, the suppliers of raw material and traders are traditionally Hindu, with the result that most trading transactions take place in and around the tiny shops of central Chowk, which is a Hindu area.[47] As described in the next section, it is erroneously assumed that current Muslims in Banaras are descendants of the Mughals, when in reality they are most probably low-caste Hindus who converted to Islam to escape their confining caste status.[48]

The first two decades of the twenty-first century have been a period of decline in the sari industry, a result due to globalization, cheaper products being produced by China, the appearance of fakes of the traditional bro-cade on the market, and changing consumer fashions and tastes.[49] This decline has affected the fortunes of the Muslim community and contrib-uted to periods of heightened intercommunal tension.[50] Nevertheless, the industry's resilience can be seen in its extensive commercial networks across the state, across India, and sometimes all the way to the Middle East, North America, and Europe.[51] Because of the industry's critical importance not only to the Muslim community in Banaras but also to the Hindu traders and suppliers—a key political constituency for the ruling BJP—and to the city's broader prosperity, some economic support has also been forthcom-ing from the Indian government.[52]

As a result of all of these factors, an economic interdependence between the two communities constitutes the backbone of the Baranasi shared iden-tity. Although in recent years the division between weavers on the one side and the suppliers and traders on the other is being eroded by online marketing and the emergence of a small group of Muslim master weavers as wholesale traders and entrepreneurs, the two main communities' eco-nomic interdependence still remains largely intact. One important conse-quence of this interdependence, which I expand on in the following sec-tions, is that on both sides of the sectarian divide there is little appetite for supporting polarizing political activities that would damage this trading relationship..

Muslim weavers are popularly referred to as "Ansaris" and in Banaras are predominantly Sunni and belong to the *barelwi* (40 percent) and Deo-bandi (35 percent) sects. The former sect is seen as more moderate and Sufi inspired, whereas the latter is more influenced by puritanical Wahhabism. Shi'as constitute a minority of Muslims in Banaras, although Shi'a festivi-ties have become part of the calendar of Muslim celebrations. A small group of Sunnis, formerly Deobandis who converted in the 1930s and 1950s, belong to the Ahl-i-hadith sect, which is even more closely aligned with Wahhabism.[53] This drift to Salafism has been given additional momentum in the past few decades as a result of Saudi Arabian and other Arab Gulf state funding, specifically targeting Sufism and its offshoots for its openness to syncretism and thus for what is perceived as its compromises regarding the core tenets of early Islam.[54] Cumulatively, the result of these develop-ments is that to Hindus living in adjacent quarters, some Muslim quarters give the impression of an exclusive and forbidding Islamic conservatism. In addition, Ansaris, as the dominant component of the Muslim community in Banaras, are recognized as a significant political force. I explore this dominance in greater depth in a later section but suffice it to say here that in the eyes of the Banaras police force, which is predominantly Hindu, Banaras Ansaris are historically an unruly threat to the establishment and difficult to police.[55] Williams recounts how during the course of her fieldwork between 2006 and 2008 her Muslim interviewees ironically referred to their neighborhood as "mini-Pakistan."[56]

Although the Ansari community may be the largest of the Muslim communities in Banaras, it is also important to recognize the pervasiveness of the Indian caste system and its penetration into the Muslim community as well, which has led to the fragmentation of the Muslim community. The lack of homogeneity also plays out in the political sphere: higher-caste Muslims who due to their wealth, connections, and education seek to play a leadership role have repeatedly been marginalized by the political activism of the lower castes, in particular the occupational castes, which have closer kinship ties and clearer politicoeconomic goals.[57]

Mitigating the Communal Divisions

This element of sectarian geographical divide and residential segregation aside, scholars of Banaras have in the main noted the dynamics that mitigate separation and contribute instead to the sense of a joint Baranasi shared culture. These dynamics include the lack of Muslim homogeneity, as seen in the community's internal makeup, the economic ties between Muslims and Hindus, and other links with the Hindu community through the practice of Islam and associated festivities and rituals. Rana Singh has carried out a useful survey of the key Muslim sites in Banaras, enumerating and classifying them and then examining the rituals surrounding five sites that illustrate a range of intercommunal exchanges. The survey, carried out in 2000 and 2009, establishes that out of nearly 1,400 Muslim sites, 415 are mosques, 299 are tombs of martyrs (mazars), and 197 are imamchauks, which are ceremonial buildings that house religious images (tazia) and that play a central part in processions.[58] The number of mosques in Banaras is almost certainly much greater in 2018 than in 2009. As indicated in the 2011 census, not only has there been an increase in the Muslim population since 2009, but the flow of funds from the Middle East, the Arab Gulf states in particular, for the construction of mosques has been a noteworthy phenomenon.[59]

Singh divides the list of 415 mosques into two groups: 15 "historical" mosques and the rest.[60] Among these 15 sites is the famous Gyan Vapi Mosque, believed to be built on the site of the first Vishweshwur Temple to Shiva. There are also the Alamgari Mosque, whose minarets tower over the bend in the River Ganges, adorning many an orientalist painting of Banaras, and whose foundations are said to be those of a Hindu temple, and, finally, the mosque of Sultan Raziyyat adjacent to the Adi-Vishweshwur Temple, which has been posited as an alternative location for the original Vishweshwur Temple.[61] For the purposes of this book, a more useful division would be a list of those mosques that are in active use and within a predominantly Muslim neighborhood and another list, à la Hayden, of those mosques that were built in previously significant parts of the city but are now marooned as a result of demographic changes. From my own brief observation, many of the historical mosques are, indeed, marooned, located strategically in the center of the city close to where both wealth and power historically lay but now, because of Banaras's expansion during the twentieth century, no longer serving a vibrant community. They appear not to be fully functioning as centers of life for the quarter with an active congregation but are more historical monuments than places of worship. The Alamgari Mosque is certainly of this sort. A visit on a Friday in May 2017 revealed a very small collection of worshippers at the midday prayers but at the same time a fairly convivial mix of Hindu residents taking the opportunity to stretch their legs and meet in the open space of the courtyard with its fountains and views.[62] Another more useful list for this discussion would be of those mosques that Hindu nationalists have slated for demolition because they are believed to be located on the site of a previous temple.

Singh's case studies of the rituals associated with five Muslim shrines are of great interest. These shrines are devoted to saints, healers, and Sufis dating back to the eleventh century and have continued to provide a platform for celebration and the public displays of faith to this day. Each shrine has a *mela* (fair) dedicated to it that comprises a variety of rituals but mainly a circumambulatory procession carrying effigies of key figures; dramatic reenactments; offerings of holy water, flowers, and sweets to the tombs and effigies; collective public prayer; as well as singing and sometimes ecstatic dancing. Indeed, all the pageantry, color, and variety of Indian cultural life are incorporated in these Muslim *mela* (so you can understand why, in the face of such blatant syncretism, Salafi purists are outraged!). What is significant, a factor not confined by any means to Banaras but a common phenomenon across India, is that the festivities attract not only Muslim residents of the adjacent quarters and farther afield but also many Hindus in the city, who revere the healing and holiness of these celebrated persons.[63]

In addition to the religious aspect of the rituals associated with a shrine, a commercial aspect that consolidates the Hindu–Muslim intercommunal relationship in Banaras should also be noted. In designated open areas and sometimes along roadsides during the period of the shrines' festivities, scores of stalls sell foodstuffs, drinks, and other items. Singh has compiled indicative lists of the numbers of stalls selling *pakora*, *sharbat*, *kulfi*, ice cream, biscuits, *nan-khatai*, *sewada*, tea, fruits, betel leaf, flowers, toys, and other items for offerings.[64] Of particular interest here is that although the number of Hindu proprietors fell between 1989 and 2009, when Singh conducted his survey, they still accounted for roughly one-third of the shops overall. One can imagine how any objections Hindu residents may have to the noise, congestion, and general upheaval created by these Muslim festivities are in part mitigated by the economic opportunities they open up. A popular, well-attended Muslim festival will bring additional wealth into the access routes going through Hindu areas. And this semitransactional relationship is reciprocated: most of the flower and religious paraphernalia vendors outside Hindu temples either are Muslim or obtain their supplies from Muslim market gardeners.

The contribution and participation of many different groups in the annual cycle of rituals and festivities is replicated in Banaras in many other instances, in particular the big festivals celebrating the Shi'a Muslim holy month Muharram and the fabulously large, long, and multiple-sited Hindu Ramlila, or reenactment of the life of Rama. Although there is some evidence that Muslims' participation in the Ramlila festivals has declined as a result of Hindu nationalists' representation of the drama as an articulation of Hindu supremacy and precedence, the pull of the festival remains strong across all sects and communities.

This complexity in the social and cultural practices of the Muslim community life in Banaras indicates the absence of simple binaries so beloved of ethnonationalists and religious fundamentalists. Immigration to Banaras for religious and economic reasons over the centuries has led to a marked heterodoxy of the city in general. As in other large urban settlements, in Banaras such patterns simultaneously provide a potential trigger for intercommunal confrontation and, due to the sheer variety of backgrounds of the communities, lead to a dilution of the potentially polarizing communal solidarities. Williams records that there is a Hindu disdain for Islamic culture, but this disdain is at the same time mixed with support for good Hindu–Muslim relations as cause for maintaining peace in the city. "Inter-religious harmony," or "Ganga Jamuni *tahzeb/sanskriti*," may be the discourse of the elite, but it also percolates down to the street level. The popularity of the poetry and music by Muslim artists Bismillah Khan and Nazir Baranasi attests to this process.[65] Other examples include how the *mahant* of the Sangkat Mochan Temple and the mufti of Banaras were asked to broker peace between Muslims and Hindus in the dispute over the installation of a Shiva linga in a temple next to a mosque in the Hartirath neighborhood.[66]

One can argue that as important as it is that the Muslim community is criss-crossed with internal cleavages, the almost identical heterodoxy of the dominant Hindu community is perhaps more important in terms of the city's political dynamics. Hinduism is both very accommodating and very diverse; it has scores of sects, castes, and philosophical schools, and its believers speak a range of languages and come from a wide geographical area. Banaras is a magnet for all kinds of Hindus and "Hinduisms." There is no monolithic Hindu community. There is not, therefore, an overwhelmingly strong sense of a Hindu "Us" opposed to a Muslim "Them." The binaries and polarization you find in Jerusalem are not expressed in Banaras. This means collective and concerted action on a communal basis is less easy to engineer, which reduces the number of levers available to politicians to promote activities that may polarize the city. Nevertheless, despite the presence of such heterodoxies, the potential for conflict fueled by religious antagonisms still remains and, given the particular set of political constellations being formed, is likely to grow.

Banaras as a Hindu City

A first-time visitor to Banaras experiences an overwhelming impression of Hindu religiosity and spirituality in the city's daily life. From my own experience, I think spirituality is embedded in Banaras to a much greater extent than in any other holy city I have visited, including Jerusalem. This impression stems not just from the 3,000 (and counting) temples and shrines on every street, every corner, every courtyard, every hallway and interior, shrouded in incense smoke and garlanded with flowers, but also from the crowds of pilgrims and devotees striding determinedly to the bathing *ghats* that line the west bank of the River Ganges, the joy of the bathers both young and old, the daily *aarti* and *puja* rituals of worship beside the river, accompanied by songs and slow stylized dances, with flames from censors swirling around.[67] It stems from the constant referencing to events and relationships in the lives of gods, goddesses, demons, and saints in daily and casual conversations, so much so that one almost turns around to see if these figures are indeed as present in the room as one's interlocutor seems to believe. Staying any length of time in Banaras is like experiencing two parallel worlds—a material, Newtonian world to which one is accustomed and a spiritual world that overlays it like a translucent sheet decorated with the pantheon and dramas of Hinduism. With this image, one can see how daily life is given a resonance and meaning that goes beyond what is immediately before one's eyes. As a Banaras novice, I took an early-morning boat trip—as one does—along the Ganges waterfront to watch all the *puja* ceremonies, to wave to the bathers, and to observe the rays of the rising sun lighting up the huge steps of the *ghats*, their palaces and temples behind them. It was, as the myths and guidebooks said, quite a "timeless" sight, and I could not help experiencing a great sense of how religion was bringing people together in the simple act of a cleansing ritual: a pleasing mixture of cosmic drama and banal quotidian human task.[68]

For Hindus, Banaras is Kashi, the City of Light, and stands at the center of the earth, the place of creation, yet it is also a *tirtha*—a crossing point between this world and what is referred to in the Vedic scriptures as the "far shore" of the Brahman, the Reality that is the source of all being.[69] As the geographers Wilbert Gesler and Margaret Pierce put it, "Everything that is powerful and auspicious is present in Varanasi as a microcosm of the universe."[70] The medieval Hindu collections of myth, legend, and ritual known as the puranas state that the city is where Shiva, one of the three main deities in Hinduism, and his wife, Parvati, chose to make their home after many years of living in the Himalayas, and so it holds a unique and prime position in Hindu beliefs.[71] According to the highly respected Sanskrit scholar and Banaras expert Diana Eck, a popular saying in Banaras is, "Kashi ke kankar Shiva Shankar haim—The very stones of Kashi are Shiva!"[72] It is also the site where the Ganges—regarded also as a goddess and the Mother of Life, having fallen from heaven to earth—turns from its eastward flow and curves north for several kilometers before turning east again. In this movement, a wonderful bend that catches the morning light of sunrise is created. This bend is taken as a sign of both the blessed nature of the city and a symbolic movement from death to rebirth and so is considered a site where a ritualized bathing will cleanse one of sins and disease.[73]

As a result of this conjunction of critical components of Hinduism, Banaras has become one of the most important pilgrimage centers in Hinduism. Indeed, the Vedic scriptures and puranas have also determined that by dying in Banaras, beside the Mother Ganges and close to the home of Shiva, one can be released from the constant cycle of reincarnation and achieve *moksha*, liberation from death and rebirth, and be reunited with the Brahman, regarded as the source of all being. Death in Banaras is a kind of eschatological fast-tracking that is not replicated in any other Indian city. Banaras is therefore not only a magnet to ordinary Hindu pilgrims from all over India but also the destination of many elderly devotees who seek to end their twilight years, happy in the prospect that this will be their last death, that there will be no reincarnation if they die in Banaras. In a religious cosmology that measures time in eons, this is a major attraction. The puranas also describe Kashi as "the Forest of Bliss," a forest paradise full of Shiva lingas as well as flowers, groves, streams, pools of clear fresh water, birdsong, and the tinkling of the ankle bracelets of "lovely women": "In its blessed groves even animals who are natural enemies dwell in peace with one another. The mouse nibbles the ears of the cat, the cat sleeps peacefully in the tail feathers of the peacock, the crane leaves the fish alone, the hawk pays no attention to the quail, and the jackal befriends the antelope."[74] Having experienced the Forest of Bliss, the gods themselves became dissatisfied with heaven! Over time, therefore, Banaras, the puranas tell us, became the sylvan setting for temples and ashrams, where teachers of yoga, ascetics, and hermits found beautiful places among the shady trees and bushes where they could practice their disciplines. Little remains of this forest in the modern bustling and congested city, but eighteenth-century sketches of the riverbank do in fact show that the broad sweep of the bluffs overlooking the Ganges were crowned with trees. Similarly, maps from the early twentieth century reveal that large areas in the southern part of the city consisted of gardens and fields. Even in the urban center, locals, according to Eck, refer to the Chaukhamba and Thatheri Bazaar as the "Ban Kati" or "Cut-Down Forest" quarter.[75] Evidence of a more verdant past can be seen in the numerous pools, or *kund*s, scattered prolifically across the city. Most are now empty and rubbish strewn and have been transformed by clay and or stone and concrete walls so that they more resemble large tanks and cisterns, but in the past they were reputed to be places of tranquility and beauty. Furthermore, before the construction of the huge *ghat*s lining its banks, the Ganges used to flood, replenishing these pools and even linking them up so that parts of the city became an island. The times of such floods are regarded as particularly auspicious.[76]

Banaras also represents in Hindu mythology the microcosm of India as a subcontinent. The seven holy cities of India have representative temples and shrines in Banaras. Ayodhya, the capital of Lord Ram, for example, is revered at a former pool known as the Rama Kund, which has a small temple, the Rameshvaram Temple, beside it (according to Eck, this pool is "more attractive to water buffaloes than to bathers"[77]). Similarly, Banaras contains what the scriptures call the four abodes of the gods, specific shrines that enhance the city's status even further. It is also the site of what are known as the twelve lingas of light, representing the twelve places in India where the divine broke through to the earth in a blinding shaft of light. So for the pilgrim as well as for the resident, everywhere they turn in Banaras there is a connection to a story or a belief on quite a cosmic scale.

Over time, therefore, a series of pilgrimage routes around the city evolved, irregular concentric circles that demarcate the city's sacred zones. The longest, the *panchakroshi yatra*, takes five days to complete, comprises visits and offerings to important shrines and temples on the way,[78] and concludes with ritual bathing at the Manikarnika Ghat and worship at the Vishweshwur Temple. In completing this pilgrimage, the pilgrim is "liberated even while living" and "gets the merit of going round all the Tirtha Kshetras [main pilgrimages] on earth."[79] The shortest pilgrimage route takes a little more than an hour and is a circumambulation of the Vishweshwur Temple. It is carried out by every Hindu pilgrim who comes to Banaras. One can only speculate on the congestion that this causes. Take the medieval area of a city in Britain—say, the Shambles quarter in York, close to York Minster. Halve the width of the narrow streets there, and then imagine the thousands of tourists who would be reduced to a shuffle as they make their way to the minster. On a normal day, the alleyways around the Vishweshwur Temple are like this—*all the time.*

Banaras's preeminence in Hinduism injects a form of religious chauvinism into the arena of contestation between the Hindu and Muslim communities. As the paramount holy city of Hindus, particularly of the Shaivite tendency (devotees of the Shiva tradition), the Muslim presence and contribution necessarily have to be eclipsed or diminished. This attitude feeds into and fuels the narrative of precedence that pervades so much Hindu argument over the future of the holy sites in the city. Yet the Banaras of mythology and faith sits uneasily with the archaeological and architectural evidence. Mark Twain's description, "Benares is older than history, older than tradition, older even than legend, and looks twice as old as all of them put together," is almost complete nonsense.[80] As Desai demonstrates in her close reading of the architectural provenance of the oldest buildings in Banaras, very little construction preceded the building spree during the Mughal period.[81] All those orientalist descriptions and paintings of the bathing *ghats* that are intended to evoke the city's timelessness lack historical foundation. The Hindu rituals associated with the Ganges and the city of Shiva are indubitably premodern and pre-Islamic, but the edifices that are imputed to them do not exist and may not ever have existed.[82] This is not to say that there was not an ancient Hindu city on the same site prior to the one built by the Mughal Empire. There clearly was an urban settlement of sorts, even if it was purely in the service of the pilgrimages that prospered in the pre-Islamic period. But the monumental vestiges are absent, and even the age of the foundations of the Gyan Vapi Mosque, attributed to a pre-Islamic Hindu temple, is open to debate. The irony of this situation is that the ancient character of the city is nonetheless affirmed in a different way—the discovery in 1794 of the Buddhist religious complex at Sarnath, just north of Banaras, indicates a continuity of settlement in the area that has still not been explored sufficiently by archaeological excavations. Thus, in addition to the cosmopolitanism inherent in any large city, Banaras's antiquity also makes it more likely that other religious and cultural influences have at some stage been present there and formed its development. In this way, the narrative of transformative integration is also given salience and stands in opposition to the other narratives.

The Vishweshwur Temple

The absence of pre-Mughal structures is laid at the feet of Islamic conquerors. In the popular Hindu imagination and in the writings of Hindu militants and some scholars, the Mughals zealously destroyed important symbols of Hinduism. Even if the evidence for the perceived wholesale and systematic destruction of Hindu religious sites is sparse, the notion that it indeed took place is embedded in popular culture and quickly surfaces in any discussion over the origins of religious sites in Banaras. But, again, as Desai emphasizes, the historical record is more complicated than that. Even the rebuilding of the Vishweshwur Temple can be attributed to the Mughals, whose role as patrons of temple (as opposed to solely mosque) construction is well attested. Noting the close affinity between the Hindu pilgrimage rituals and the circumambulation ritual of the Ka'aba in Mecca, the Mughals were attracted to these types of religious display. As Desai concludes,

> The shifting sites of temples and mosques in Banaras have usually been explained through simplistic narratives of Islamic invasions that resulted in inflexible animosities between Hindus and Muslims in the city and indeed in the entire subcontinent. . . . This is largely a history of adaptation and transformation, accompanied by a few memorable instances of the actual destruction and desecration of religious sites, particularly temples.[83]

The main point to grasp is that Muslim/Mughal control over Banaras in the seventeenth century did not lead to the exclusion of Hindus from the city or from positions of economic, religious, and political influence. Cooperation, co-optation, and varying degrees of sponsorship were reflected in the continuance of the court–temple relationships that had prevailed in pre-Islamic periods.

These subtleties and dynamics can be seen quite clearly when one focuses on the main Hindu holy site in the city—the Vishweshwur Temple. As is the case for many ancient holy sites, the origins of the temple are disputed and contingent upon which sources scholars base their discussion. Three small hills in Banaras (so small, in fact, that unless you are cycling or walking, you are unlikely to notice them) cause the Ganges to bend once again from its new north direction toward the east. Traditionally, the larger middle hill is where Shiva made his home and where the oldest linga in Banaras was to be found.[84] Smiting the ground with his powerful trident, he dug a hole for the first waters of creation to emerge, waters said to be so pure they were a liquid form of enlightening wisdom and were used to cool the burning power of the linga. Pilgrims today still bring waters that have been blessed and pour them over the linga. Even Diana Eck, who argues that the textual sources are clear that the original temple housed the preeminent Shiva linga in the city, acknowledges that the Shiva linga

Figure 3.1 View of northern Banaras and the Ganges River from the roof of Alamgari Mosque, with mosque courtyard in the foreground. (Photograph by Michael Dumper)

usurped the previous lingas celebrated in the ancient puranas and thus was not always so preeminent.[85] What is clear is that an important Shaivite temple did exist in Banaras for more than a thousand years, but the exact location of the original site is not known. Determining this site is made more complicated by not only the destruction of temples in Banaras during this long period but also by the reconstruction of this key temple on different sites and the incorporation of possible alternative lingas into it, so that the nomenclature of these temples has become confusing.

There is also no doubt that Muslim dynasties demolished the original temple or temples, but whether the destruction was as extensive and as repeated as some scholars claim is not clear. Desai claims that there are no textual accounts of the destruction before the seventeenth century, although both Singh and Eck refer to demolitions in the twelfth century, citing those, for example, that preceded the construction of a mosque known as "Razia's Mosque," built, it is thought, by a sultana in the early thirteenth century. The construction of mosques close to or on top of Hindu sites has been, in some scholarly circles, interpreted as a Mughal strategy to preempt the

Figure 3.2 View looking south from the roof of the Alamgari Mosque toward the Vish-weshwur Temple and showing the *ghat*s that line the River Ganges. (Photograph by Michael Dumper)

reconstruction of a demolished temple. The evidence is clear that this is exactly what the Mughal emperor Aurangzeb (1618–1807) intended. Renaming Banaras "Muhammadbad" in 1669, he also set about replacing the Vishweshwur Temple with a mosque, which incorporated not only the temple's foundation plinth but also its southern wall. Nevertheless, if Aurangzeb's intention was to establish the dominance of Islam in the city, he manifestly failed. More than that, as Desai observes, such is the power of myth and popular memory that he may have unwittingly reinforced the preeminent status of the Vishweshwur Temple: "In a contradictory turn of events, and far from overturning religious sentiments and identities, the sheer act of dismantling may have transmuted Vishweshwur into the undisputed centre and fulcrum of the city's ritual landscape. . . . As a consequence, the Shaiva vision for the city became its dominant identity."[86] As in the cases of Solomon's and Herod's temples in Jerusalem, removing a temple does not suddenly void its role. Despite the loss of the Vishweshwur Temple edifice, the myriad rituals of devotion and the economic activities associated with them carried on. The site continued to figure significantly in the pilgrim circumambulations, and Hindu devotees continued to visit and make offerings to the plinth and the remaining wall. Brahmins reestablished themselves in the precinct just in front of the mosque, where Shiva's well was located, and carried out their ritual duties. More and more property in the vicinity was gradually purchased from Muslim landowners.[87]

As Mughal power receded, the Hindu religious leadership and aristocracy grasped the opportunity for reconstruction. The current Vishweshwur Temple was built around 1781 by Ahilyabai Holkar (1725–1795). She was the daughter of a Maratha chief who, as a symbolic response to the Mughal rulers' religious injustices, had originally intended to destroy the mosque and rebuild the temple on the exact same site but demurred as a result of political pressures. Ahilyabai chose a site just south and adjacent to the Gyan Vapi Mosque. Interestingly, there is evidence that for a time the new Vishweshwur Temple was in competition with the Gyan Vapi precinct, where the Brahminical ritual activity was still honoring the old destroyed temple, which, despite its simply being just a courtyard, had the priceless prize of the Shiva's well, into which a quick-witted Brahmin is said to have thrown the original linga when Auranzeb came to destroy the old temple.[88] Eventually there was convergence, and the pilgrimage routes and rituals were reconfigured accordingly. By the time of the British period,

Ahilyabai's Vishweshwur Temple was the principle destination for pilgrimage in Banaras.[89]

Eck writes how the temple, despite its fame, "has none of the magnificence, architectural splendour, or antiquity of India's great classical temples in Orissa or South India."[90] I concur. It is actually a quite small, poorly maintained, and, for a nonbeliever, rather underwhelming holy site to visit. Setting aside the rather tortuous queues for security clearances and what Eck would call my "Protestant sensibilities" about the noise, bustle, and jostling of crowds, the litter of discarded flowers, used sweet wrappers, and plastic water containers in a place where silent reverence and cleanliness would be, for me, a more familiar response, the aesthetics are still disappointing. Photographs and designs of the structure showing its ornate spires and central domes suggest a building of some style, but there is nowhere in the small interior courtyard to appreciate these elements. Crammed between narrow alleyways, overshadowed by the domes and spires of the Gyan Vapi Mosque, hemmed in by the quarter's poor, crowded, and run-down tenements, the Vishweshwur offers no vistas, no long pools or splashing fountains—just a rather tightly proportioned tiled courtyard with small, open-sided rooms housing a succession of effigies of deities and lingas. The Golden Temple of Amritsar or the Taj Mahal it certainly ain't.

But to the devoted Hindu these considerations are immaterial because the power of the site lies not in its architectural beauty but in its centrality in Hinduism, a significance that is made demonstratively visible by the hundreds and thousands of worshippers who line up there in all weathers at all times of the year to make their offerings. Ninety-five percent of the temple's income comes from donations (with the remaining 5 percent coming from interest on bank deposits).[91] The temple is open from 2.30 a.m. to 11.30 p.m. daily, and all through the day crowds from all parts of India throng the narrow streets leading up to its two entrances.

In terms of temple administration, it should be recalled that Hinduism is a complex and multifaceted amalgam of many traditions that do not cohere into one organization at a senior management level. Unlike the Roman Catholic Church, it is not hierarchically structured. Although a priestly caste, the Brahmins, forms a religious elite, Hinduism comprises many disparate and unconnected schools and traditions. In addition, many ancient and large temples are wealthy and powerful and assert a degree of autonomy that national, state, and municipal authorities are reluctant to challenge. With independence, most large Hindu temples came under the control of the government authorities through a board of trustees. The board usually includes respected Sanskrit scholars, some hereditary officials, and priests known as *karsevak*s, but the state government also ensures that many of the trustees are ex officio members of various state departments.[92] Since 1983, the Vishweshwur Temple has been administered by a board of trustees set up by the state government of Uttar Pradesh.[93] More than half of the trustees are ex officio members of the Uttar Pradesh Departments of Cultural Affairs, Finance, Social Welfare, and so on as well as senior legal and police officers. The Executive Committee is chaired by the Banaras division police commissioner! It is hard to imagine a closer relation to state authorities than this and suggests a need to keep a firm control over the activities in the temple to ensure that the priests and other employees adhere to government and state policies regarding the use of access routes and relations with the temple's Muslim neighbor, the Gyan Vapi Mosque. Given that the Vishweshwur Temple is the center of the belief that by living and dying in the city one achieves salvation (*moksha*) from the cycle of reincarnation, there are political implications over and above the activities of the Hindutva movement. Such a belief offers an egalitarian and overwhelmingly precious reward to its believers that cannot be matched by any political ideology or movement. The promise of better sanitation, education, health, and housing, for example, pales into insignificance in the face of the belief that, after uncountable previous incarnations, one is living one's final life in Kashi/Banaras and will at last be reunited with the source of all being—the Brahman. In this sense, the Hindu priests hold all the trump cards in mobilizing people and creating solidarities. The material rewards dangled by the politicians cannot match those offered by the gods and their avatars.

Religious Tensions in Banaras

Religious tensions in Banaras have both a long genealogy and a national political context. And it needs to be emphasized that religion can often be an excuse and a mask for other areas of contestations, including new immigration as well as economic and class differences. In this context, one's faith is a badge or moniker of and not necessarily a cause for tensions. At the same time, religion provides a useful tool for mobilizing communities who feel under threat and are experiencing damaging change to both their position in society and their access to their share of limited economic or state resources. There are numerous examples of this nexus between sectarian mobilization and other issues driving change. In the 1920s and 1930s, an economic downturn in the weaving industry in Banaras occurred at the same time as the rise of the militant Hindutva movement. One particularly contentious plank of the Hindutva platform advocated *shuddhi*, the conversion of Muslims to Hinduism. As a result, Ansaris in Banaras began to mobilize along sectarian lines and formed the core of a new movement among Muslims in northern India, *tanzeem*, meaning quite simply "organization." In the early 1930s, some 25,000 to 30,000 people attended public meetings and rallies held by the prominent *tanzeem* leader Baba Khalil Das.[94] *Tanzeem* volunteers were increasingly seen sporting green badges, Turkish caps, and red flags with white crescent moons—all popular Islamic monikers—and forming *akhara*s (martial groups), which staged drills and parades with weapons. A kind of mobilizing "arms race" was triggered as, in response, Hindu activists formed counterdemonstrations. As Nandini Gooptu observes, "Animosities and tensions in urban neighbourhoods increased and took the form of defence of space and territory through neighbourhood patrols and vigilante organisations. This created a relentless cycle and an escalating spiral of mutual competition and hostility among local Hindu and Muslim religious organisations."[95] As a result, in 1931 riots between the two communities in Banaras broke out. The Ansari community was blamed for provoking the violence, and the police clamped down severely upon activists in Muslim quarters in Banaras. Nevertheless, despite such incidents and compared to other cities in Uttar Pradesh, such as Aligarh, Allahabad, and Ayodhya, Banaras since independence has experienced relatively few incidents of Hindu–Muslim violence.[96] Indeed, in his forensic study of the causes of ethnic violence in India, Varshney has compiled a list of "riot-prone cities"; Banaras comes in at lowly twenty out of twenty-eight cities.[97] Similarly, Paul Brass's survey also concludes that very few fatalities have taken place in Banaras.[98] Indeed, there are no recorded incidents of Muslim–Hindu violence in Banaras between independence and 1966, and there were only twelve recorded incidents between 1966 and 1991.[99]

In 1977 and 1979, violent sectarian conflict did occur in Banaras as a result of processions celebrating Durga Puja through a conservative Muslim area, Madanpura.[100] Similarly, a procession in honor of the goddess Kali in 1991 led to riots after an altercation between Kali devotees and Muslim bystanders.[101] In these incidents, however, we also see how what can be framed as a sectarian conflict also had overtones of regional tensions. Both processions were organized by members of relatively newly arrived immigrants from West Bengal determined to assert their status in the city against the established Banarsi community, who, in both cases, were also Muslims and thus a relatively "soft" target. Since the Ayodhya-triggered riots of 1991 and 1992, there have been no large-scale incidents of violence in Banaras. We should also note that the bombing incident in the city in 2006 also included an attack on the main railway station, which resulted in some Muslim fatalities as well. As Williams notes, such indiscrimination by the Muslim militants provided the opportunity for religious and most civic leaders to foster the impression that the Banaras Muslim community should not be blamed for the work of "outsiders."[102]

The Precedent of Ayodhya

However, the demolition of the Babri Masjid in Ayodhya, only five hours drive away, still casts a dark shadow over the city of Banaras and the relations between Hindus and Muslims there. Anxiety over a possible similar outbreak of Hindu nationalist violence against Muslim holy sites in the city, in particular the Gyan Vapi and Alamgari Mosques, results in a sense of fear and gloom among Banarsi Muslims whenever new developments in the Babri Masjid controversy unfold. To counter such tendencies, some religious and civil leaders have sought to be proactive. In 1993, for example, the Hindu business community was able to head off the growing triumphalism of the Vishna Hindu Parishad (VHP), which announced that following Babri Masjid it was aiming to "recover" the Gyan Vapi, by threatening to withdraw its political support for Hindutva parties.[103] Similarly, in September 2010 a "peace march" was held in Banaras ahead of the Allahabad High Court judgment on whether the demolition of the Babri Masjid should stand, in order to quell such fears and demonstrate intercommunal solidarity.[104]

The destruction of the Babri Masjid in Ayodhya in December 1992 is a defining moment in Hindu–Muslim relations in India. Not only was the mosque demolished by extremist Hindus, but it was also demolished with impunity, the government standing by without lifting a finger to prevent its destruction. Its destruction shattered relations between the two communities in the city and other parts of India and discredited both Muslim leaders and Congress Party leaders who were in government but were completely passive in the face of such militant activity. It sent shock waves through Banaras because the arguments put forward for the narrative of Hindu precedence in Ayodhya are identical to those put forward for Banaras and the preeminent role of Hinduism in the city. Understanding the issues that surrounded this controversy help us see the broader picture regarding the relations between the Hindu and Muslim communities in Banaras and the role that the two main religious sites of each community play, the Vishweshwur Temple and the Gyan Vapi Mosque.

The Ayodhya controversy originated in 1528 when the Mughal conqueror Babur (1483–1530 CE) constructed a mosque in the city. In doing so, he reputedly destroyed a Hindu temple to the Lord Ram, an avatar of one of the greatest gods in the Hindu pantheon, Vishnu. The archaeological evidence for such a temple is very thin, and even that slim evidence is disputed. It is an historical fact that Ayodhya's previous name was "Saketa," but it was renamed in the fifth century CE by a king of the Gupta dynasty who wished to associate himself with the mythical birthplace of Lord Ram.[105] Over time, the symbolic name became the real name, and the mythical birthplace of Lord Ram has become, in the eyes of many Hindus, the real birthplace now. We need here to remind ourselves that, as we have seen in the Ramlila festival in Banaras, the Ramayana is an immensely popular epic, especially in northern India, and appeals to a wide spectrum of classes, castes, and faiths.[106] The epic's popularity adds significantly to the popular appeal of the Hindu claim in face of the historical facts.

One is reminded of the disputes concerning the location of Solomon's temple in Jerusalem. Here, too, the archaeological evidence exists but is similarly thin. Yet the discourse among the Israeli public and more broadly the Jewish community is such that the evidence is sufficient for the claims to be regarded as conclusive. In a detailed study on the Jewish temple in Jerusalem, John Lundquist argues that "the single most important fact regarding the Temple of Solomon is that there are no physical remains of the structure. There is not a single object or artefact that can be indubitably connected with the Temple of Solomon."[107] However, as he goes on to make clear, this statement is controversial and provocative mainly in a political sense and should be seen in that context. Analysis of other evidence, mostly textual and archaeological, Lundquist concludes, suggests that the claim that there was a temple on this site is not so much certain as believable. As any archaeologist will attest, 100 percent indubitable evidence is a rare occurrence. Most claims rest upon a balance of probabilities.

The implication one draws from Lundquist's research on Solomon's temple and discussion of the evidence is that for any other site such a body of evidence would probably be sufficient to become the scholarly consensus, but because of the political sensitivity of this particular site, a higher burden of proof is expected. The same could be said of the Ayodhya controversy, although the archaeological evidence appears to be much, much thinner. Nevertheless, by focusing on evidence, the Muslim camp apparently missed and continue to miss the point that what actually happened or what actually took place or what the facts are not what ultimately counts in this kind of contestation. Instead, what is "believed in" motivates and engenders the passion around such holy sites. Indeed, this denial of the other side's religious and historical narrative for the site is a cause for the chasm between the two positions and the bleak prospects for a possible negotiated solution. As Varshney points out about Ayodhya, "Muslim leaders kept harping on the religious meaning of Ayodhya, refusing to encounter the nationalistic meaning. Worse, the various mosque action committees (and the secular historians) initially argued that Rama was a mythological figure, for there was no historical proof for Rama's existence or his birthplace. This was a gratuitous argument. . . . Religious belief does not depend upon rational evidence."[108] At the same time, up to the 1980s there was little tension over the site, particularly because the Muslim community was increasingly centered in Faizabad and the Babri Masjid itself was little used. In addition, a number of other places in Ayodhya were also believed to be the birthplace of Rama.[109] Given the lucrative revenues associated with Rama pilgrimages, this is not surprising, but it had the effect of dissipating the focus of activists.

In the mid-1980s, however, two significant events took place. The first was the Shah Bano affair, in which the Supreme Court ruled that India's secular laws took precedence over Muslim personal law and the Islamic courts. However, the government of the day, under Rajiv Gandhi, equivocated and tried to reverse the ruling through Parliament. There was a Hindu backlash, and in an attempt to allay Hindu anger the Babri Masjid was ordered to be opened for Hindu worship, which in turn caused a Muslim outcry.[110] The second event was closely related. The VHP, a militant Hindu nationalist organization, launched a campaign to "liberate" Hindu temples from Muslim control. A very successful mass program of dedicating bricks for the reconstruction of the new temple in Ayodhya drew in masses of ordinary Hindus and culminated in an equally successful and visually dramatic *yatra* incorporating a vehicle dressed up as Rama's chariot that slowly made its way through cities and towns of northern India to Ayodhya.[111]

In December 1992, thousands of Hindus converged on Ayodhya, completely overran the Babri Mosque, and demolished it. Despite the fact that the Hindu militant groups' leaders had agreed to stand by the court's decision and had declared that only a religious ceremony would be held to symbolize the laying of the first bricks of the proposed temple, a crowd more than 200,000 strong broke through police cordons. Wielding hammers, they scaled the roofs of the mosque, knocked down its three domes, and then prized away the bricks with their bare hands until the building was totally destroyed. Eyewitnesses reported that the hundreds of police drafted to control the crowd stood by and allowed the destruction to take place. Encouraged by such passivity, breakaway groups turned on Indian and foreign journalists recording the scene and then rampaged through the city center, targeting Muslim houses and property. Residents recall being terrified as mobs of triumphant and hysterical young men, *sadhus* (ascetic holy men), and *karsevaks* ran through the streets looking for Muslims to attack. Fifteen Muslim residents were beaten to death. Paramilitary reinforcements were eventually sent to the area to quell the unrest.[112] Nevertheless, more than 2,000 people were killed in riots across India, and damage to commercial and private property costing over 3 billion rupees was caused.[113] Ten years later there were still tensions. In February 2002, the VHP mobilized hundreds of *karsevaks* to the mosque site to begin construction of the temple, and a train carrying Gujarati activists was attacked by Muslim militants seeking revenge, resulting in the death of at least 58 people. This, in turn, led to another wave of rioting throughout India, particularly in the state of Gujarat, where up to 2,000 people, mainly Muslims, died.

Despite this violence and despite the constant pressure from Hindu nationalists, the issue remains unresolved and is being contested in both the Supreme Court of India and its lower courts. In 2010, the Allahabad High Court, after many years of deliberation by various commissions, ruled that the site should be divided into three parts and allocated to the Sunni Wakf Board, a Hindu political party, and a Vaishnavite *akhara*, but the

Indian Supreme Court subsequently overruled this decision. It is possible to see, however, that, in contrast to the status of the mosque in 1850, significant changes have taken place and that a Hindu takeover and construction of a temple are ever closer. The appointment of a militant BJP Hindu, Yogi Adityanath, as chief minister of Uttar Pradesh has reinvigorated the political push for the construction of the Hindu temple. Although he has acted cautiously in terms of challenging the various legal rulings that are delaying the commencement of the construction, he is also arranging the political pieces so that action can take place swiftly and is consolidating the popular Hindu discourse concerning its construction.[114]

Ayodhya is still recovering from the violence of 1992 and fears the threat of either more violence or actions of impunity. The Muslim community in Ayodhya still feels very vulnerable. Out of a total population of approximately 45,000, there are little more than 5,000 Muslims living in Ayodhya and Faizabad. There are four madrasas and ten mosques.[115] Most Muslims are employed as tailors, shoemakers, carpenters, and food retailers. Some also work in trades that supply the pilgrims who come to Ayodhya and in the manufacturing of religious artifacts and souvenirs. The Muslim community has one representative on the Ayodhya Municipal Council, a member of the Peace Party, which is a local list. All the other councilors are members of the BJP. The views of the Muslim community in Ayodhya concerning the future of the Babri Masjid are conveyed to the Babri Masjid Action Committee, which is based in the state capital, Lucknow. The local Muslim consensus, I am told, is that some compromise and concessions can and should be offered to the Hindu community. Because the actual site of Lord Ram's birthplace is believed to be approximately one hundred meters away from the mosque itself, these Muslims feel it should be possible to come to some agreement on the shared use or access to the site. As one local Muslim leader expressed it, Babri Masjid is simply a mosque, but because of the activities of the Rashtriya Swayamsevak Sangh (RSS, National Volunteer Organization), a right-wing, Hindu nationalist, paramilitary organization, it has become more important as a symbol of the nature of Muslim–Hindu relations in India and also of the role, if any, of the government in protecting the rights of Muslims. The broader issue now appears to be that of preventing the establishment of a precedent that has been achieved by force. Because the RSS has a target list of more than three hundred mosques that it claims are on the sites of Hindu temples and that it intends to demolish, the concern among Muslims, secularists,

Figure 3.3 Decorated stones prepared and waiting for the building of the Ram Temple (Ram Janmabhumi) in Ayodhya to commence. (Photograph by Michael Dumper)

and moderate Hindus is that if Muslim leaders agree to Babri Masjid remaining demolished without any reparation or a return to the status quo ante, this acquiescence will open the doors for the RSS to start attacking the other mosques. Hence, the shadow that Ayodhya casts over the Gyan Vapi Mosque in Banaras. As I finish writing this book, the Muslim community was terrified yet again by a rally of more than 50,000 Hindu nationalists in Ayodhya, demonstrating to put pressure on the Indian and Uttar Pradesh governments to implement plans for the construction of the 221-meter statue of Ram in the city, making it one of the tallest statues in the world.[116]

A new Supreme Court judgment in November 2019 allocated the demolished structure and some surrounding land to a Hindu trust for the purposes of building a Hindu temple dedicated to Lord Ram. The Muslim community will be allocated land in an alternative "suitable" location for the erection of a mosque.

Temple and Mosque in Banaras

The events of Ayodhya have had their impact on Banaras. The Gyan Vapi Mosque has been the target of the VHP, which has threatened to demolish the mosque in the same way the Babri Masjid in Ayodhya was.[117] Like the Babri Masjid in Ayodhya, the Gyan Vapi Mosque in Banaras may be underused and a vestige of a past when Muslims in the city were the ruling elite. Unlike in Ayodhya, however, in Banaras the Muslim community is a significant presence. As noted in a previous section, it constitutes one-third of the population and provides the workforce behind the most important industry in the city. The Samajwadi Party, which represents low-caste "untouchables" and Muslims, plays a significant role in the city's politics, having secured a majority in the state legislature in recent times.[118] Its vote is sought after by both local and national parties. In addition, as we have seen, the Ansaris have a track record of defending their interests, and any attack on the Gyan Vapi Mosque would be seen as a threat to their position in the city's power structures. It is unlikely that they would take it lying down. In this context, we can return to the bombing incident of 2006 and ask, What if Vishweshwur Temple had been the target of the attacks by Muslim militants in 2006 and not the Sangkat Mochan Temple? What would have been the outcome of such an attack?

As we saw, the Sangkat Mochan Temple is a popular Banaras temple. It carries out not only religious ceremonies but also a wide range of social and charitable works inspired by the poetry of Tulsi Das, renowned for his inclusivity and liberal views. Williams highlights its unique role in Banaras in this way:

> This temple is open to people of all castes, classes, religions and nationalities, and its community extends beyond immediate devotees to the sweet-makers, milkmen, chai wallahs (tea vendors) and flowersellers who work in and around the temple. . . . The temple has subsequently earned a citywide reputation as an inclusive space. This perception shaped the psychological impact of the terrorist attack on the temple; it was not just regarded as an attack on Hindus, but also the wider community of Varanasi.[119]

But the Sangkat Mochan Temple is not the main temple in the city and not the temple to Shiva, the greatest god in the Hindu pantheon, and thus, it could be argued, not the raison d'être for the city of Banaras. The Vishweshwur Temple has a pan-Indian position that the Sangkat Mochan Temple does not have. It is also a government-supervised temple whose administration is enshrined in national legislation. An attack on this site would have been an attack upon a state institution and would have broader and deeper political implications than an attack on the Sangkat Mochan Temple. In this context, one can understand the sensitivities around security of the Vishweshwur Temple/Gyan Vapi Mosque complex. Williams records that over the past twenty-five years the Banaras city administration has deployed security around the Vishweshwur Temple and Gyan Vapi Mosque at an annual cost estimated in 2009 to be 10 million rupees.[120]

During my visit to the Vishweshwur Temple in May 2017, it was clear that security was tight, although not as thorough and extensive as in Ayodhya. Non-Muslims are not permitted into the Gyan Vapi Mosque, so I was not able to enter there. Entry to the temple was via a narrow and congested alleyway leading off from the road to Dasashwamedh Ghat, one of the most popular *ghats* along the Ganges. At the entrance to the alley, there was a light police checkpoint, but only in the sense that there was no boom preventing access, no scanner, and no frisking. Instead there were approximately eight policemen observing the movement of people through a rough metal archway with the words "Kashi Vishvanath Temple" written on it. The police wore soft hats, not helmets, and were armed with long sticks, known as *lathi*s, although some vintage-looking rifles were leaning against a wall behind their chairs and gear. From the alleyway, there are three entrances to the temple, two of which are for visitors. I encountered pairs of policemen in the alleyway at different points, some armed with what seemed to my untutored eye to be more old rifles, but certainly not automatic weapons. Continuing down the alleyway, I came to the first entrance, which is not for foreign tourists. Here there was a metal-detecting scanner, and people were frisked and searched, with separate routes for male and female visitors. No bags were allowed. As I was passing, a unit of the RAF in camouflage uniforms (but not helmeted) exited through this entrance, carrying automatic weapons, and as I made to grab my camera to take a picture, I was quickly informed by nearby policemen that no photographs were permitted. Looking up, I caught sight of other RAF personnel on the roofs of inner buildings, and there was also a thirty-meter watchtower immediately beside and overlooking the alleyway. Barbed wire covered the tops of adjacent walls and shop roofs. Making my way farther along the alley, around the back of Gyan Vapi Mosque, I arrived at the entry for "foreigners." Here a guard recorded my passport details, and I was asked to deposit my bags with a nearby shopkeeper for safekeeping and to place my mobile phone in a locker. As a foreigner, I was permitted to skip the long queue of pilgrims holding up garlands of flowers, sweetmeats, containers of milk with brightly colored petals on top, leaves, and other offerings and, following a quick frisk, to enter the temple. Inside the temple, there was no security or surveillance equipment in the courtyard area that I could see, although I noticed RAF personnel patrolling adjacent roofs, and I could see the watchtowers I had noticed earlier from the alleyway.

After Ayodhya, this level of security around this key religious site in Banaras has become the "new normal," and clearly the status of both the temple and the mosque make them a lightning rod for both city-wide intercommunal relations and national issues concerning the role of the Muslim minority in a BJP-dominated government. In 2018, the situation appeared relatively evenly balanced. On the one hand, the two main communities are sufficiently fragmented to reduce the possibility that a concerted Hindu takeover of the Gyan Vapi Mosque can be effected. There are too many cross-cutting alliances and cleavages for that to take place without either a major provocation or a dramatic change in the city's demographic, economic, and political balance of power. At present, the Muslim community in Banaras has sufficient access to levers of power and capacity to mobilize itself that the political capital required to alter that status seems to present too high a price for the Hindutva sympathizers in power to pay, for the time being at least. Feeding into this dynamic is the narrative of transformative integration and inclusivity prevailing in Banaras. Although integration and inclusivity may be primarily an elite -level preoccupation and discourse, the alternative narrative of precedence is not sufficiently supported by the wider Hindu population.

Figure 3.4 Rapid Action Force watchtower beside the Gyan Vapi Mosque. (Photograph by Michael Dumper)

On the other hand, these factors in favor of the status quo around the Gyan Vapi Mosque do not rest on a solid foundation. In the first place, by all accounts the mosque is not well used, and although it may serve the immediate neighborhood, it lacks the stature, profile, and outreach activities of a city-wide institution, which would offer it a greater degree of protection. Nor is it embedded in the life of the city in the same way as the temple. Civic functions incorporating activity in the mosque are rare. In addition, Hindutva support in the national, state, and municipal governments is strong. Therefore, although a direct takeover of the mosque may be deferred for the time being, a financial and administrative framework in which the temple is given preeminence and Hindu preferences are prioritized over Muslim ones is gradually being introduced. In addition, popular Hindu opinion and discourse regarding the narrative of precedence may not yet have peaked. As recent events suggest, the destruction of the Babri Masjid in Ayodhya in 1992 is not necessarily the high-water mark of Hindutva, and although there may be some disarray and disagreement among Hindu activists, the tide has not receded and may yet rise again.

To some extent, these trends—Banaras inclusivity and increasing Hindutva sentiment—are cancelling each other out, and what we may be witnessing in the controversy concerning the future of the Gyan Vapi Mosque is an interesting reversal of the role of religious conflicts in political life. Rather than political conflicts being given a religious mantle to wear in order to assist in the mobilization of a range of ethnic, class, and regional groups, what we can see in Banaras is how religious sites have become symbolic of a quest to define a national identity. The way such religious conflict is managed will answer the question "What kind of India are we?" Will it be an inclusive or majoritarian democracy? In this context, we can see how specific events in the city may tip the balance in favor of one set of factors over the other. There are a number of challenges, some of which are specific to Banaras and some of which are also fairly typical of cities with complex religious and ethnonationalist identities. Two challenges face the prevailing uneasy equilibrium in Banaras: first, the celebration of religious festivities in the city and how important it is that they are managed with care and sensitivity and, second, the implementation of proposals for better access to the temple.

One of the main causes of conflict in cities with religiously mixed and heterogeneous populations are festivities and public displays of religious faith, such as processions. As noted in the discussion of time flashpoints in chapter 1, processions or parades in particular have the potential to trigger a reaction by nonparticipants and bystanders who do not belong to the group conducting the procession. The reason for this is that processions have other functions that belie the ostensible demonstration of faith. It is often overlooked that they have positive functions, such as the recognition of the legitimacy of those in authority or acknowledgment of a relationship and historic ties with institutions of other denominations or the expression of gratitude to neighboring quarters.[121] However, they also have other functions: they act as a show of strength and wealth, serve to mobilize the faithful, encourage the recruitment of waverers, and provide an opportunity for training in organizational and leadership skills. In cities, they have an important function in demarcating territory or, indeed, the expansion of that territory through incremental advances in either the direction or the length of the procession route. In this way, processions reflect social and demographic changes and, more importantly, the relative power and status of different communities in the city. In Banaras, there are many historical precedents for such conflicts.[122] Williams's ethnographic study analyzes a number of more contemporary occasions when Hindu and Muslim religious festivities clashed in Banaras, such as in 1982 and 2006, when Bengali Puja processions coincided with the Muslim celebrations of Muharram and Eid al-Fitr.[123]

Another challenge to the uneasy equilibrium in Banaras is the management of the huge numbers of tourists and pilgrims who wish to visit the temple and to a lesser extent the mosque. As described earlier, access to the Vishweshwur Temple and the Gyan Vapi Mosque is via narrow alleyways and even narrower entrances. For much of the day, the alleyway is clogged with slow-moving queues, and the facilities for visitors are very poor. Not only do these negative physical factors mar the pilgrims' spiritual experience, but they also affect the tourist potential of the site and its proximity to the main bathing *ghat*s on the Ganges. The area is also suffering from poor infrastructure and poor services. In addition, the houses in the vicinity are badly maintained due to both chaotic legal title and depopulation as people seek better services in neighborhoods away from the old city. As a result, the Varanasi Development Authority has been drawing up various plans that would make access more convenient and more pleasant and with a greater capacity to process more pilgrims and visitors. Recent iterations of this plan, known as the Ganga Darshan (Offering to Ganges) Plan, involve the demolition of more than 150 residences to create a four-hundred-meter corridor connecting the Vishweshwur Temple with the Ganges and its *ghats*. Although previous political parties considered the plan, the appointment of the BJP activist Yogi Adityanath as chief minister of the Uttar Pradesh government has given it renewed impetus. Many who reside in the area object to the plan and will see their neighborhood change irrevocably, and others argue that it will destroy the specific heritage of the city, which comprises the houses, alleys, and courtyards that cluster round the backs of the *ghats* and give this sweep of the Ganges its distinctive visual character and atmosphere.[124]

But there is also a more disturbing political aspect to this plan, and it is not clear to what extent this aspect is an accurate reflection of policy or a side effect that is being construed to have sinister overtones: the impact that the plan has on the Gyan Vapi Mosque. The plan involves the demolition of several houses and *haveli* (large private mansions that over time may have been extensively subdivided to create a mini-neighborhood) around the mosque and a compound around the temple.[125] As one journalist recently wrote, "The real intentions behind the rejuvenated 'Ganga Darshan' project are now out in the open and people are afraid of a repeat of what happened in Ayodhya on December 6, 1992. . . . The mosque has been on the radar of the Hindu right wing ever since Independence."[126] A number of houses have already been knocked down, reducing the number of people in the neighborhood who would make the mosque a viable and vibrant religious institution. Suspicions that this is only the first step in a program designed to take over the mosque are merely heightened when it is clear that both the Indian prime minister and the Uttar Pradesh chief minister strongly support the plan.[127]

Banaras: An "Uneasy Equilibrium" at Tipping Point

I selected Banaras for this project so that I could obtain a much better understanding of some of the dynamics that lie behind conflicts in cities with a strong religious association. What could a grasp of the main issues in Banaras add to my understanding of such conflicts derived from my previous research work in Cordoba and Jerusalem? Are there sufficient similarities to make a comparison worthwhile, but also do the differences point to an alternative approach to understanding these dynamics? Indeed, is there a possible "Banaras model" for managing and resolving religious conflicts in urban settings, and, if so, how transferable would it be to other locations? As this chapter has outlined, the potential for religious conflict in Banaras is quite high, arising from several factors. These factors include the aftermath of the Ayodhya/Babri Masjid riots in 1992 and uncertainty over the future of the site stemming from the long and convoluted Supreme Court judgment process; the elections of an explicitly pro-Hindutva state government in Uttar Pradesh in 2014; the impact of funding from the Arab Gulf states and the fallout from the dispersal of Islamic State forces in the Middle East into South Asia; and an increased religiosity in society in general, compounded by the Indian political class's adoption of a neoliberal model of the small state that contracts out its functions to the private sector.

Nevertheless, it is important to be clear that, unlike Jerusalem and Lhasa, Banaras is not a contested city. There are clearly intercommunal tensions between the dominant Hindu community and the smaller Muslim one, but the city is not occupied, like East Jerusalem or Lhasa: the place of Banaras in the Indian state is not in question. The rule of law under the Indian Supreme Court, even if differentially and erratically applied, is accepted by all sides as the framework for dispute resolution, and the Constitution offers a degree of protection for religious freedoms and minority rights. Similarly, although the different religious communities may emphasize and celebrate different aspects and periods of the city's history, they do not hold competing narratives concerning the role of Banaras as a supremely holy city in the long span of Indian history. The genealogy and founding myths may be derived mostly from Hindu mythology, but the narratives emanating from the Buddhist, Jain, and Muslim communities are seen to be supplementary, if not complementary, to the Hindu myths and certainly not negating them.

In attempting to perceive the relative strengths of the components in this Banaras dynamic, we can see how the narrative of precedence has gradually emerged as the dominant narrative. As would be expected given the role of Hindu myths in the construction of a Banaras identity, religiosity and spirituality are embedded in the daily life of the city to a much greater extent than in any other city I have seen. The prospect of salvation (*moksha*) from the cycle of reincarnation by living and dying in the city offers an egalitarian and overwhelmingly precious reward that cannot be matched by any political ideology or movement. As I observed earlier in this chapter, the promise of better sanitation, education, health, and housing, for example, pales in significance to the belief that, after uncountable previous incarnations, one is living one's final life in Banaras. In this sense, the Hindu priests hold most of the trump cards in mobilizing people and creating solidarities. We should be careful not to overstate this simplistic opposition, though. The religiosity of the city has, on one hand, the effect of weakening the opportunities for Hindu nationalists to push the agenda of their narrative of precedence in the political sphere, but, on the other hand, the heterogeneity of Hinduism provides ample scope for nationalist politicians to find a reservoir of potential supporters. For example, a closer study of the demographic foundations of the various Hindu belief systems in Banaras would highlight the non-Brahminical beliefs held by the lower-caste Dalit community, who are less in thrall to the priests and more responsive to the promises of politicians.

The city's heterodoxy is exacerbated by significant immigration. Such immigration simultaneously provides a potential trigger for confrontation between different communities and a dilution of potentially polarizing communal solidarities due to the sheer variety of the immigrants' backgrounds. As important as this variety of immigrants is, more important, in terms of city's political dynamics, is the heterodoxy of the dominant Hindu community. Hinduism is both very accommodating and very diverse; it has scores of sects, castes, and philosophical schools, and its believers speak a range of languages and come from a wide geographical area. Banaras is a magnet for all kinds of Hindus and "Hinduisms." Its Hindu population is not a monolithic community. To a lesser extent, something similar applies to the Muslim community, which is going through processes of transition, renewal, and consolidation. There is not, therefore, an overwhelmingly strong sense of a Hindu "Us" to oppose the Muslim "Them." The binaries and polarization you find in Jerusalem are not expressed in Banaras. This means collective and concerted action on a communal basis is less easy to engineer, which, again, reduces the number of levers available to politicians to promote activities that may polarize the city. In this context, two further elements are clearly relevant. As we saw, the economic interdependence between the Muslim community weavers and the Hindu community entrepreneurs constitutes the backbone of a Banaras shared identity. Although this division in economic roles is currently being eroded, it still remains a strong feature of the city. One important consequence of it is that the appetite for supporting political activities that will damage this trading relationship is not great. To be sure, grievances have led to violent confrontations between the two communities, but these confrontations have lacked central direction and have been sporadic and unplanned. Again, channeling community grievances regarding the economic situation into a program of political action is not an option easily available to political leaders.

Another key feature underlying the potential for religious conflict in Banaras is the predominance of private-property ownership. In Jerusalem, much of the city's land is owned by religious foundations and trusts of the three faiths. A significant proportion has also been acquired by the Israeli state, which by its own statutes can only lease the land it owns to Israeli Jews. In East Jerusalem, some Palestinian aristocratic families also own large tracts of land, but the Israeli state has also confiscated Palestinians' land for colonial construction. This form of state and ethnically based landownership provides a platform for consolidating a territorial presence of one community at the exclusion of the other community. In Banaras, the dispersed, fragmented, and multiple agencies involved in property ownership reduce the possibility of ownership being directed toward political ends. In addition, the prevalence of squatting, forcible acquisitions, and wildcat occupations of derelict, rundown, and neglected properties, particularly in the Old City of Banaras—all without the prospect of legal intervention due to the time lag in Indian courts—suggests an unplanned and opportunistic character to the dispersal of the population. An important consequence of this characteristic of property ownership in Banaras is the lack of rigidly demarcated residential areas. Clearly, there are predominantly Muslim and Hindu neighborhoods, but, unlike in Jerusalem, such ethnic neighborhoods appear to be permeable, the borders between them blurred. They are certainly very different from the semifortified hilltop Israeli settlements or the segregation caused by the "Green Line" of 1949 that divides Israeli West Jerusalem and Palestinian East Jerusalem. In Banaras, the daily interactions between Hindus and Muslims while they are shopping, going to school, entering hospitals, witnessing festivals and other rituals, and so on are clearly much greater.

An additional feature of the situation in Banaras is the lack of capacity of government institutions at both the federal and the state level to deliver resources to the population. In order to mobilize its citizens, a state needs to be seen to deliver decent housing, minimal sanitation, good roads, electricity, a credible education system, and accessible health care. Unable to provide these things, it will have limited credibility and tools at its disposal to demand adherence to a political program. Government discrimination in the allocation of resources to the Hindu community clearly is an issue across India, including Banaras, but what is of greater significance is the general paucity of resources altogether. This lack of state capacity is experienced by all residents and unites Hindus and Muslims in their struggle against poverty and their search for alternative sources of economic support. This inability to intervene is mirrored in a final feature to be noted: the lack of international intervention in Banaras's affairs, which is in stark contrast to the dispute over the future of Jerusalem. As we saw in chapter 1, the conflict in and over Jerusalem is an integral part of the Arab–Israeli conflict. More UN Security Council and General Assembly resolutions have been passed on it than on any other issue in the world. Moreover, twenty-two UN agencies with a complement of international and local staff currently work in the city. This is emphatically not the case in Banaras. The role of external actors is in fact quite minimal, and what there is—for example, by Pakistan, by the Arab Gulf states, and by militant Islamic non-state actors—takes a more indirect form: the channeling of funds and the creation of local proxies. You certainly do not have in Banaras the intense media and diplomatic interest in every violent intercommunal event that you have in Jerusalem. Although this absence of interest means that discriminatory actions can go unchallenged and unscrutinized and therefore allows for incremental changes that erode the rights and religious practices of subordinate communities, it also allows for local agency to exercise restraint without passions being excited by external actors' concerns and interventions. It is here that we can see how Banaras's demographic and religious heterodoxy, its economic interdependence, and the permeability of its residential areas all combine to provide a platform for a Banaras-wide identity within which religious elites can engage in dialogue and negotiation.

CHAPTER IV

A Very Secular Occupation

Buddhist Lhasa and Communism

S ix hundred miles east of Lhasa lies the small rugged Tibetan town of Machu. It serves as a market center for nomads whose yak herds graze along the edge of the vast Tibetan mountain plateau. One spring morning in March 2012, a young nomad woman, Tsering Kyi, emerged from the public toilets wrapped in blankets that were tied around her with wire. The blankets were soaked in petrol, and as she approached the vegetable market, she set them alight and was promptly engulfed in flames. Reports do not specify how long it took for her to die but refer to her "charred remains," which suggests that the petrol blankets were effective and that she died in situ and not later from her burns in a hospital.[1] As shocking as the manner of her painful death is the fact that she was not alone in taking such drastic action but part of a pattern that was spreading across areas where large numbers of Tibetans live. A promising twenty-year-old student, Tsering Kyi was one of 95 Tibetans who by December 2012 had set fire to themselves, or "self-immolated," in protest against the Chinese government's policies toward Tibetans.[2] By the middle of 2017, the U.S. Congressional Commission on China reported that 144 Tibetans living in the western provinces of China and in the area known as the Tibetan Autonomous Region (TAR) had self-immolated.[3]

Although the Chinese government labeled these Tibetans as either unstable individuals or terrorists or delinquents lacking in self-control or being manipulated by the Tibetan government in exile, particularly by the spiritual and political leader of Tibetans, the Dalai Lama, it was unable to disguise the fact that such actions were a damaging critique of its policies in the extensive regions inhabited by Tibetans. This series of actions reverberated around the world and as such was a serious setback for the Communist Party of China and the Chinese state.[4] Not only were the majority of the self-immolators Tibetan Buddhist nuns and monks who had been the target of intensive Communist Party reeducation campaigns stretching over several decades, but the majority were also younger than thirty—that is, the very generation who should have been exhibiting signs of severing their links to the religious and cultural life of "Old Tibet" and embracing the secularism and materialism of modern China and its "socialism guided by scientific principles." Furthermore, the vast majority of self-immolators were Tibetans who were not living either in Lhasa or in the TAR, but adjacent to the TAR in provinces in China: Sichuan, Gansu, and Qinghai.[5] And in virtually every case, those who took their lives in this way made it clear that they supported the exiled Dalai Lama and were protesting a particular egregious form of Chinese persecution and control. Finally, this wave of self-immolation, as well as being extremely damaging to China's projection of its economic and soft power, also pointed to the failure of its twin-track strategy of containing Tibetan dissent: policies of economic development and material prosperity on the one hand and hardline coercive repression on the other. Coming hard on the heels of protests and riots in Lhasa and other Tibetan cities and towns in 2008, and after many years of Chinese government investment in agriculture, infrastructure, education, and institution building, the continued Tibetan resistance to Chinese rule and presence began to suggest that the government would soon run out of options and that there were not many tools left in its tool kit.

The emergence of this radical form of protest in the Tibetan areas of western China calls into question the focus on Lhasa in this chapter. What does it mean that only 3 of the 144 self-immolators came from Lhasa—the capital of the ancient kingdom of Tibet, the administrative center under Chinese rule since 1950, and, until the later wave of self-immolations in 2012 on, the center of Tibetan Buddhist resistance to Chinese secularizing policies? Did this shift in the location of resistance mean that the Chinese government has been successful in breaking the power and influence of the large and ancient Tibetan Buddhist monasteries of Sera, Drepung, and Ganden in Lhasa, which have until recently led the resistance to the

Chinese government takeover of Tibet? And does it mean that the Chinese policies of economic development, the migration of large numbers of ethnic Han Chinese into the city, and the co-optation of much of the Tibetan middle class have succeeded in turning Tibetans away from their religious culture and separatist aspirations? If this is the case, then the Chinese authorities must still be both perplexed and dismayed at the resurgence of Tibetan nationalism in areas outside the TAR because the resurgence conveys a sense that trying to contain political resistance in one geographical area merely serves to push it into the open in other areas. The recent introduction (in 2018) of new regulations severely restricting the activities of Tibetans to organize any form of mutual assistance and welfare smacks of a desperation and a degree of micromanagement that is possibly unsustainable but that the Chinese government clearly sees as a prerequisite for achieving its ambitions both to integrate its national minorities into the state and to project Chinese soft power and economic power to its neighbors.[6] In this changing context, what role does the city of Lhasa play in the conflict between Tibetans and the Chinese government? Does its urban form exacerbate or ameliorate the range of tensions and disputes that arise? Do the conflicts over the control of religious sites act as a microcosm of the wider conflict between Tibetans and Chinese? Are the conflicts in the city more intense as a result of the presence of these sites, and do they lead to deeper and wider repercussions?

Having never visited China, Tibet, or Lhasa prior to this research project commencing in 2015, I am a novice on the area. In addition, I speak neither Tibetan nor Mandarin. Nevertheless, having studied several other cities with religious sites at the heart of their conflict, I was equipped with a set of analytical tools and was able to use the opportunity to watch and observe and to listen and learn. Basically, despite being a novice, I felt that my previous research experience allowed me to hit the ground running. So, despite what amounted to a very introductory glimpse of the city's complexities, I was able to glean much information that was useful and to add greatly to my understanding of both the role of the city in contemporary Sino-Tibetan politics and, more generally, the role of religious sites and institutions in the generation and management of urban conflict.

After two and half days of train travel from Chengdu northward to Xining and then southwest across Tibet's high plateau, I arrived at Lhasa's large new railway station. Peering through the bright early-morning sunlight, I could immediately see that contemporary Lhasa was not in any way the Shangri La of yore and myth. Despite extensive preparatory reading, including books by Robert Barnett, Emily Yeh, and John Powers,[7] I still had not anticipated the miles of skyscraper apartments, the wide tree-lined boulevards, the pristine parks and tightly regulated road junctions, the swirling ring roads, the deep and long but also fast road tunnels, and the delicately spun bridges over the River Kyichu. Instead of a city on the "roof of the world," steeped in magic, mist, and folklore, I found a city pulsating with new construction, new suburbs, and new satellite towns on its eastern and western approaches. The former Tibetan city is now confined to a central "Old City" quarter, which you could easily miss during a quick drive around the "new city," and even there much of the eighteenth- and nineteenth-century housing, with its characteristic stone walls tapering upward from a wide base on the ground floor, has been demolished and replaced by modern, straight-up vertical lookalikes.[8] If you were to be parachuted down into the city without knowledge of its past, you would be struck quite forcibly with how modern, how extensive, how Chinese, and how dynamic it is. Apart from the shuffling streams of bonneted and be-robed

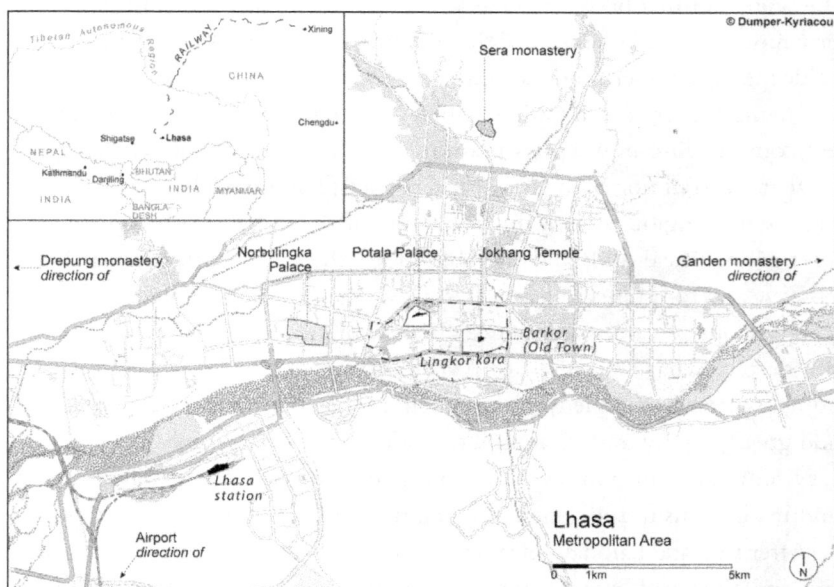

Map 4.1 Lhasa metropolitan area, with inset of the region. (Map by Lefkos Kyriacou and Michael Dumper)

Tibetan pilgrims along certain roads, you would hardly be aware of its Tibetan past. Yes, you still have the wonderfully nearby snow-capped mountains encircling the city and the spectacular Potala Palace sitting like a queen on her throne at the city's center, but, despite Lhasa's remote and distant location, its urban structure is decisively modern and Chinese. My romantic and orientalist preconceptions took a severe battering within an hour of my arrival.

The current eclipse of Lhasa by other Tibetan areas in the resistance to Chinese rule and the dominance of Han migrants over Tibetan residents in the agricultural, commercial, and political life of the city do not mean, however, that Lhasa no longer plays a key role in the unfolding drama of Sino-Tibetan relations. Its unquestionable place in Tibetan history and Tibetan Buddhism ensures that it will continue to do so. Indeed, it is the very fluctuation of its centrality that gives scope for a useful analysis of the various events and policies and will help shed light in the identification of specific kinds of conflicts that relate to religious sites and practices in cities and how conflicts regarding them can be managed or resolved. In comparing the situation in Lhasa to the situation in Jerusalem, Banaras, Cordoba, and George Town, we can see how Lhasa has both strong similarities and significant differences. For example, it would be possible to argue that similarities between Lhasa and East Jerusalem are the greatest of all. Lhasa has been occupied (or liberated), just as East Jerusalem has been occupied (or reunited, depending on one's political perspective), and the role of religious sites as symbols of national identity as well as the equally important role of the clergy who run these sites have been central in mobilizing resistance in both cases.

Yet there is a major difference between the two: the Chinese government and the Chinese community in Lhasa do not claim prior possession or ownership of the major religious sites in Lhasa—namely, the Potala Palace and the Jokhang Temple. Although the Chinese narrative is that Tibet is indeed part of China and Tibetan Buddhism is an offshoot of Chinese Buddhism, the sites themselves are not contested in the same way as the Haram al-Sharif in Jerusalem or the Mezquita in Cordoba or the Gyan Vapi Mosque in Banaras is. The conflict between the Chinese government and the Tibet government in exile over the control of these sites is not because they are *shared* religious sites but because they are symbols of Tibetan independence. Furthermore, in Lhasa there is a slightly different dynamic at work. In situations of shared and conflicted religious sites, the state can act and is expected to act as arbiter between two or more nonstate actors or religious groups. In Jerusalem and Banaras, the position of the state in this dynamic has been strongly influenced by strident religious nationalism and, as we have seen, possibly even been "captured" by religious nationalist political parties in recent years, but it has not always been that way. The successes of the settler movement in Israeli politics and the Hindutva movement in Indian politics, where this capture has taken place, are relatively recent phenomena. In Lhasa, the Chinese state has always been, from the inception of its takeover in 1950, the main opponent of any substantive Tibetan autonomy and independent political control over these sites, and, as a consequence, the interface between the state and the devotees of Tibetan Buddhism and their leadership is totally unmediated. What is even more subtly expressed in the Lhasa case and needs careful exploration is the role of ethnonationalism in the colonizing process. Has the Chinese Communist Party ideology of economic development and ethnic integration masked a privileging of Chinese interests in Lhasa in the same way Zionism as the explicit ideology of the dominant Israeli power has privileged Jewishness and Jewish interests in Jerusalem or as the Malaysian Constitution has promoted Malay Muslim interests in George Town or as the Bharatiya Janata Party and its Hindu nationalist agenda have performed a similar function in Banaras?

In addition, such policies based on a Chinese and Han ethnonationalism often play out in terms of residential segregation: certain areas, as we have seen, become monocultural and exclusive. Here there is one very obvious contrast between Lhasa and Jerusalem: the absence in Lhasa of walls and fences separating the Han Chinese and local Tibetan communities. Lhasa is not divided in this simplistic way. This absence of walls is a reflection of the complete military dominance of the Chinese state over Tibet and the city, although at certain given points during the riots in 2008 some streets in the Barkor or old parts of the city were temporarily rendered no-go areas.[9] Nevertheless, despite the absence of such "hard" borders in the city, it is easy for a longtime resident to discern ethnic divisions crisscrossing the city in the gated communities differentiated by poor-quality housing and service provision and not least in the profusion of colored Tibetan prayer flags flapping in the wind over some rooftops but not others.

Furthermore, the emergence of an ethnonationalist strand in the imposition of political control by the Chinese state and the dominant Han community over the subordinate Tibetan community reveals a pattern similar to that which has occurred in Jerusalem and other divided cities, such as Belfast and Beirut—a phenomenon I referred to in the introduction as the "paradox of ethnonationalist urban governance." As I discussed in chapter 1, ethnocentric ideologies such as Zionism, Ulster Loyalism, and Maronite or Hindu nationalism that drive the allocation of service provision in cities can be counterproductive in similar ways. As a dominant community seeks to establish control over minority and subordinate communities in a city by means of exclusionary and discriminatory policies, those who are deprived of services are driven to seek alternative sources of funds and means of representation and will make external political alliances that can be a formidable constraint on the dominant community's attempt to control the city. Herein lies an important contradiction in the politics of urban ethnocracy: the ideology that seeks exclusive control creates the very forces that will resist it. What can ensue is the internationalization of a city's conflict, and this is exactly what is taking place in East Jerusalem, an internationalization that is furthermore exacerbated by the presence of important holy sites in the city, which serve to mobilize a wide spectrum of external players.[10] However, in the case of Lhasa, what is striking is the *absence* of external intervention in the form of international NGOs, foreign consulates, media, educational and cultural exchanges, and so on that cumulatively are in a position to constrain the exercise of Chinese control in the city. The inscription of the key religious sites, the Potala and Norbulingka Palaces and the Jokhang Temple, on the UNESCO World Heritage List notwithstanding, the international community's leverage on the situation in Lhasa appears to be minimal.

The four sections in this chapter cover the main issues raised so far. The first offers some background on the city, providing readers with a sense of its geography, history, and role in the politics of the region. As well as providing an overview of Tibet's long history, it focuses on the periods immediately prior to the Chinese occupation in 1950 and the period between that occupation and the riots in Lhasa in 2008. The second section examines the impact of Chinese developmental policies on the city's growth and how the city's physical, demographic, and economic profile has completely changed over the past seven decades since 1950. The third section explores the ways in which the Chinese state has addressed the powerful role of religion in Tibet and has attempted to curtail the monastic leadership's influence over the resistance to Chinese rule. It looks at both physical measures taken to erode the centrality of Tibetan Buddhism in the city and ideological and legal approaches used to challenge its moral authority. The final section examines current trends and events not only highlighted by the wave of self-immolations mentioned earlier but also encompassing the Chinese state's apparently unstoppable ability to impose its policies on the Tibetans in Lhasa and discusses whether this ability will lead to different forms of resistance or a resigned accommodation to a Chinese fait accompli. A uniquely interesting but vitally important aspect of this peering into the future concerns the various options open to both the Chinese government and the Dalai Lama in making arrangements for his reincarnated successor!

A note on terminology. As in the Arab–Israeli conflict, in the Sino-Tibetan conflict the use of certain terms in Tibetan studies can be controversial in that they can convey the political legitimization of an act that is against international law. For example, Chinese scholars and official Chinese government and Communist Party documents refer to the Chinese takeover of Tibet and Lhasa in 1950 as a "peaceful liberation," whereas many Tibetans and their supporters refer to it as an invasion, conquest, or occupation. Robert Barnett's approach is to adopt the Tibetan terminology because "those events are and were perceived in that way by many people in Tibet" and not because he seeks "to antagonise the Chinese government."[11] An additional guide is to adopt terms used in international legal documentation, as in reports by UN agencies, although UN terminology regarding the situation in Tibet is, compared to the terminology it uses for the Arab–Israeli conflict, somewhat lacking in clarity and has also changed over the decades since 1950. By extension, it is also important to note that the Chinese government's designation of parts of the Tibetan Plateau as the Tibetan Autonomous Region is also contentious. The TAR does not encompass all the areas in which Tibetans live but can give the impression that it does. The TAR is roughly congruent to the area that was under the control of the thirteenth and fourteenth Dalai Lamas prior to the Chinese invasion in 1950, but previous rulers in Tibetan history have held sway over larger areas to the north, south, east, and west, implanting Tibetan culture and language and Tibetan Buddhism in those regions. In fact, to this day more Tibetans live outside of the TAR than in it. More than half live in several western provinces of China, in particular Qinghai and Sichuan. Approximately 20 percent of the population of Qinghai is Tibetan (mostly nomads), and Qinghai encompasses most of the former Tibetan region of Amdo, which is administered currently through subdistricts of the

Qinghai province known as "Tibetan autonomous prefectures." Similarly, Sichuan comprises the Tibetan autonomous prefectures of Kardze and Ngaba. Kardze was formerly the eastern area of Tibet known as Kham, and Ngaba was part of the southern Tibetan area of Amdo.[12] In fact, the wider Tibetan region constitutes almost one-quarter of the land area of the People's Republic of China, which accounts for the Chinese government's resistance to any idea of cultural autonomy.[13] In this chapter, I attempt to be consistent in referring to Tibet as the "wider Tibetan region," which includes the TAR and the prefectures of Qinghai and Sichuan, and in using the abbreviation TAR to refer explicitly to the smaller truncated areas created in the 1950s. In this chapter, I also refer to the dominant ethnic group in China, the Han, as "Chinese" because referring to them as "Han Chinese" can give weight to the Communist Party argument that all the minority ethnic groups— Uighur, Mongol, Tibetan—in China are essentially Chinese and thus that the Hans are simply the largest and most dominant group. I also use the names "China," the "People's Republic of China," and "Chinese government" interchangeably.

Prelude to Transformation

The most striking aspect of Lhasa is its location. The steep-sided valley in which the city is built is 3,000 meters above sea level, and the snow-clad peaks that surround it reach to higher than 5,000 meters. Visitors usually take at least three days to acclimatize to the high altitude, as I found out to my dismay. No matter how fit you think you are, climbing a short flight of steps on your first day in Lhasa can bring on nausea and headaches. As a result of its altitude, Lhasa experiences long hours of bright sunlight and very low night-time temperatures. In addition, both low rainfall and a dry climate often result in both frost and drought.[14] The winters from mid-November through to mid-February are bitterly cold, and the city almost shuts down as a tourist destination; construction work and agriculture are suspended, while many Chinese residents return to their homes in the Chinese interior. Lacking in both the traditional important mineral resources such as iron ore and coal and a fertile agricultural hinterland, largely bypassed by the ancient Silk Road trading routes running thousands of miles to its north, cut off from India to the south by the highest mountain ranges in the world, the relatively inaccessible, Lhasa has never been a large or cosmopolitan city—that is, until the past few decades. Nevertheless, despite its diminutive size for most of its existence, Lhasa was the preeminent city of Tibet for much of its history, given Tibet's small population and the culture of nomadism that prevailed across the whole of the Tibetan Plateau.[15]

Lhasa emerged as a significant political and religious center in the seventh century when from 629 to 649 CE its king, Songsten Gampo, ruled an empire that stretched across the whole of the Tibetan Plateau and into northern India. He and his successors established a formidable dynasty that lasted for two hundred years and was regarded as a regional power by its neighbors. Songsten Gampo was not just a military ruler. He encouraged the absorption of both Chinese and Indian cultural influences, which over time transformed the rough-and-ready, subsistence-based culture of Tibet into one with its own distinctive script, renowned centers of learning, and its own version of Buddhism. Symbolic of this transformation was the marriage of Songsten Gampo to Nepalese and Chinese princesses. Each bride brought with her a statue of especially venerated Buddhas, which were housed in the Jokhang Temple, built for this purpose.[16] The Jokhang Temple became the most important religious site in Tibet and the main center for pilgrimage in Tibetan Buddhism; it also, as a consequence, has been the focus of much contention since 1950.[17] Songsten Gampo also built his palace on the small hill overlooking the Jokhang Temple, which later became the site of the Potala Palace. Following the decline of the Gampo dynasty in the twelfth century, Lhasa was eclipsed by the power of kings based in the rival city of Shigatse but reemerged as the capital of Tibet when these kings were defeated by the Mongol-assisted army of the fifth Dalai Lama in 1640–1642. It was during his period of office that the fifth Dalai Lama, as the head of the ascendant Gelugpa monastic order, was able to combine the roles of spiritual leader and temporal leader of Tibet and to unite and extend the territory under Tibetan control. Commensurate with establishing this enhanced role, he set about building the Potala Palace on a scale much grander than its previous form under Songsten Gampo. Regarded as one of the architectural wonders of the world, it has been the seat of government and the winter home of the Dalai Lamas down through successive centuries until the exile of the current Dalai Lama, the fourteenth, in 1959. The palace comprises more than 1,000 rooms and has schools, chapels, jails, and tombs for all the Dalai Lamas. A small village to

Figure 4.1 Monks' Assembly Hall in the Potala Palace, Lhasa. (Photograph by Michael Dumper)

house all the servants and retainers nestles at the bottom of the small hill on which the palace is built.[18]

The death of the fifth Dalai Lama in 1642 was followed by a series of Mongol and Chinese interventions in Tibet as they wrestled with the political vacuum caused by power-hungry regents and successive Dalai Lamas who were either too young or too weak to establish their authority. From the seventh Dalai Lama (d. 1757) on, Chinese influence under the Qing (sometimes referred to as the Manchu) dynasty (1644–1911) in Tibet grew, which set the precedent for later Chinese interference in Tibetan politics and for the invasion in 1950. It was during the Qing period that Tibet began to acquire its mythological status as a forgotten, cut-off kingdom ruled by holy men and child kings. But as the Qing Empire weakened during the nineteenth century, both Russia and Great Britain began to explore opportunities for extending their own influence in Tibet. Intending to preempt a possible Russian invasion, a British force took over Lhasa in 1903 and imposed a treaty upon the thirteenth Dalai Lama's regent. This treaty, in turn, prompted a fresh Qing invasion in 1910. However, the Chinese return to Lhasa failed to establish their dominance in Lhasa or Tibet because the Qing emperor in China was soon ousted in a nationalist revolution in 1911.

By 1920, taking advantage of the turmoil in China and the preoccupation of the nationalist government with internal affairs, Great Britain was back on the scene, and a mission took up residence in Lhasa. Headed by Sir Charles Bell, who had become a close friend of the thirteenth Dalai Lama during a period of his exile in India, the mission took on the role of facilitating the modernization program adopted by the Dalai Lama. The program included training Tibetan military officers, furnishing the army with modern weaponry, building a hydroelectric plant to supply power to Lhasa, and setting up a small English school. Nevertheless, despite the fact that the thirteenth Dalai Lama was the head of the dominant Buddhist monastic order, his reforms alienated the conservative religious hierarchy. Opposition to the Dalai Lama formed and crystallized around the figure of the Panchen Lama, who is historically regarded as second to the Dalai Lama in spiritual authority in Tibetan Buddhism. When the Panchen Lama failed to obtain British support, he fled to China, but the opposition remained strong, and following the death of the thirteenth Dalai Lama in 1933, the country was riven with factional strife. These conflicts provided a timely opportunity for the new Communist government in China to intervene, and in 1950 it invaded Tibet to reestablish order and its influence over Tibetan politics.

China's Takeover of Tibet

The next section looks in more detail at the impact of the Chinese takeover of Tibet on the city of Lhasa itself and on its role as the religious and political center of Tibet. In this and the next subsection, however, I cover two contextual areas: first, I provide an overview of the imposition of Chinese policies in Tibet to show the context of specific actions in Lhasa; second, I give an overview of Chinese policies regarding its minority groups in general so that we can understand better the reasons for and background of its policies toward Lhasa and Tibet. The general view is that in 1950 the resistance by the Tibetan army and the Tibetan people to the Communist takeover was badly organized, and the army was defeated. The Tibetan military were outgunned, outnumbered by a factor of ten, outmaneuvered by the generals of the battle-hardened People's Liberation Army (PLA), and suffered very badly from a poor and fragmented leadership.[19]

As an act of defiance, the Tibetan government enthroned the fifteen-year-old Dalai Lama, two years earlier than a reincarnated Dalai Lama is normally enthroned. Despite this provocative act by the Tibetan leaders, one of the Dalai Lama's first significant acts was to reluctantly agree to a document drawn up by the Chinese government in 1951. Without an army and without the hoped for support from the United States, the United Kingdom, India, and the UN, he signed the Seventeen-Point Agreement on Measures for the Peaceful Liberation of Tibet, which recognized a degree of autonomy for Tibet within the People's Republic of China.[20] Several articles in the agreement revealed a tightening of the Chinese grip over the administration of the plateau through the introduction of oversight committees and were thus distinctly unpalatable to the Tibetan leadership. However, other articles were more accommodating. Article 4, for example, stated that "the central authorities will not alter the existing political system in Tibet. The central authorities also will not alter the established status, functions, and powers of the Dalai Lama," and Article 7 declared that "the religious beliefs, customs, and habits of the Tibetan people shall be respected, and lama monasteries [sic] shall be protected." Interestingly, it also stipulated that "the central authorities will not affect a change in the income of the monasteries."[21]

This view of a general Tibetan military capitulation and Chinese relative moderation is widely challenged. What appeared to be a compromise between the Tibetan goal of independence and the Chinese Communist Party plans for the incorporation of Tibet into the Chinese state was in fact Mao Zedong's playing of a long game. Mao recognized that in 1950 the Tibetan army was sufficiently strong to counter the PLA. In addition, he saw that the PLA would also be confronted by the significant logistical obstacles in conquering Tibet: the roads were not good enough to transport the large numbers of PLA troops that would be required to subdue the plateau or to supply them with food and equipment in the event of a long campaign; the terrain to be occupied was vast and exceedingly difficult to traverse, and the climate and altitude would adversely affect the army's operational effectiveness. As a result, Mao bade his time while major roads were being built and the PLA troops acclimatized to the altitude. He was also able to court the Dalai Lama with his friendship and adherence to the Seventeen-Point Agreement.[22]

Which perspective is the more accurate does not alter the fact that following the PLA's entry into Tibet and Lhasa, there was a period of coexistence between the government of the Dalai Lama and the Chinese authorities, and only minor reforms were introduced. It proved to be a lull before the storm. As China consolidated its position, as the city's population doubled through the stationing of 8,000 PLA troops there, as food was increasingly requisitioned to feed them, as isolated monasteries were sacked, and as a large part of the eastern Tibetan province of Kham was annexed to the Chinese province of Sichuan, stirrings of revolt by the Tibetans grew more and more pronounced. By 1956, guerrilla resistance threatened to erode Chinese control in Kham, and armed revolt broke out in other areas in central Tibet and in Lhasa. The famous Lithang monastery in Kham was besieged by the PLA for sixty-seven days and finally bombed into submission.[23] Tibetan anxiety and resistance were fueled by fears that the harsh measures introduced by the policies known as the Great Leap Forward, such as collectivization of farms, and imposed upon the Han Chinese population and in other areas of China would also be introduced in Tibet.[24] Despite many attempts at dialogue and negotiation, trust between the Tibetan and Chinese governments broke down, and by 1959 Lhasa was in ferment. During the New Year celebrations in February that year, rumors circulated that the Dalai Lama would be arrested while attending a ceremony at a Chinese military base outside the city. This rumor prompted up to 30,000 Tibetans (several thousand more than the entire population of Lhasa at that time) to surround the Dalai Lama's summer residence, the Norbulingka Palace, to prevent his abduction. As a result, violence broke out, and the PLA shelled the palace. In order to prevent further bloodshed, on March 17 the Dalai Lama fled to southern Tibet and then on to India.[25] During the fighting in Lhasa, many hundreds of Tibetans died, and key sites such as the Potala Palace, the Norbulingka Palace, and the highly politicized Sera monastery were bombed. The Jokhang Temple was also shelled, and it was estimated that hundreds of Tibetans sheltering inside died.[26]

Following the flight of the Dalai Lama, the Chinese government sealed the borders with India; dissolved the government of Tibet; launched an all-out assault on the guerrillas; introduced a program of sequestration of property, reeducation, and work camps for the nobility and monastic orders; and established controls over the income that monasteries and nunneries could receive. From the perspective of the Chinese Communist Party, not only was the old Tibetan order a challenge to the party's political and military hegemony, but it was also an appalling example of the worst kind of feudal oppression, characterized by mass servitude and grotesque inequalities and legitimized by an irrational and superstitious thought system. Yet despite the possibility of liberation from what the Communist Party characterized as their mental and physical bondage,[27] thousands of monks and nuns voted with their feet and made their way to India. For his part, the Dalai Lama did not relinquish plans either to return to Tibet or to create a Tibetan state, albeit perhaps with some associational arrangements with China. He continued to reject the Seventeen-Point Agreement and campaigned for independence well into the mid-1970s. In 1989, he proposed associative arrangements with China and later, in 1992, diluted these arrangements further by showing a willingness to discuss Tibetan autonomy within the Chinese state, provided it had substance and was not a cosmetic arrangement. To these ends, he established a government in exile, the Central Tibetan Administration, based in Dharamsala in northern India and staffed by exiled monks and former administrators in the Tibetan government.

China and Its Minorities, Including Tibetans

Why has the People's Republic of China been so adamant that Tibet remain part of its polity, and why has it expended huge amounts of bullion and political capital in consolidating its control over Tibet? In the literature covering events in Tibet, there is a risk that focusing on the mistakes and the excesses of the Chinese Communist Party policies, from which many minority groups and even the Han Chinese have suffered, obscures the strategic and bigger picture. As we shall see, Chinese financial and political investment in Tibet has been huge and therefore possibly irreversible. I argue that unless we appreciate the reasons why there has been this degree of commitment (and risk), we may not understand what is driving the Chinese state's development and integration juggernaut in Lhasa, which has been so unrelenting that the term *cultural genocide* is often applied to it.[28]

The first thing to recognize is the complex challenge that the presence of minorities in China poses to the Communist government. Modern China is a state based firmly on a socialist ideology that considers ethnicity both an obstacle to the advancement of proletarian unity and a category set of relationships and networks used by reactionaries to maintain their power and privileges over less-advantaged community members.[29] This ideology is maintained despite the fact that minority groups in China constitute a very small portion of the huge total population of China. Apart from the Han Chinese, there are fifty-five recognized minority groups in China, and in 1949 the percentage of minorities (i.e., non-Han Chinese) in the newly created republic was a mere 6 percent. In 2010, it was approximately 8.3 percent.[30] Of this small percentage, Tibetans make up an even smaller number. In 2010, they constituted only 0.47 percent of the total population of China! They are not even the largest minority group, coming in at eighth in 2000 and ninth in 2010, just ahead of the Mongol minority.[31] Indeed, there are three times as many Zhuangs and twice as many Manchus as there are Tibetans. In 1990, according to official government sources, in all areas of China, including the TAR, there were 4.6 million Tibetans; in 2000, there were 5.5 million; and in 2010 there were approximately 6.2 million.[32] Yet the role of the minority groups in China remains an issue of great strategic and political concern for the government, and at different junctures in post-1950 Chinese history priority has been accorded to their political, social, and economic development. Identifying explanations for this concern is an important part of trying to understand Chinese policies toward Tibet, Tibetans, and Lhasa.

One of the key explanations is that even though the numbers of China's minorities may be a small percentage of the total population, that 8.3 percent still amounts to almost 107 million people, exceeding the population of most countries of the world, including France, Germany, and the United Kingdom. Thus, the absolute numbers are significant and constitute a policy challenge of the first order. Second, the geographic location of most of the minority groups is critical for the Chinese government. Han Chinese are situated largely on the coastal areas and the interior, but China's minorities are frequently found close to or straddle China's borders with other countries. The Kazakhs in the far west, for example, live on both sides of the China–Kazakhstan border. The same applies to the Mongols on the China–Mongolia border and to the Miao (sometimes referred to as the Meo or Hmong) along the southern Chinese border with Myanmar, Thailand, Laos, and Vietnam.[33]

The fear in Beijing is that unless such minorities are closely integrated with the economic and administrative structures of mainland China, their ethnic links and kinship ties across these borders may pull them away from

China, or, even worse, their grievances may be exploited by neighboring states either to destabilize China or to promote irredentist aspirations. These fears were heightened following the dissolution of the Soviet Union, which resulted in the opening of some Central Asia countries bordering China to Islam and to the support of Muslim community activities. Similarly, in 1990, the Mongolian People's Republic was transformed into a non-Communist regime, which led to a revival of Tibetan Buddhism, an increase in students learning Tibetan, and a state visit by the Dalai Lama despite strong Chinese objections. In this context, the Chinese government is very sensitive to any concrete Indian support for the émigré Tibetans along the India–China border, which, we should recall, is more than 4,000 miles long.[34] These border areas provide a base for ideological and material support for Tibetan separatism. Thus, the presence of minority groups close to the borders of China and just over them intrinsically has the capacity to internationalize what the Chinese government and the Communist Party see as an internal domestic issue. China's creation of the Shanghai Cooperation Organization in 1996 was an attempt to elicit the cooperation of its neighbors in combatting possible separatist activities emanating from those bordering countries.[35]

A third explanation for the seriousness with which the Chinese government regards its minority groups is that the areas where most of the minority groups live are rich in natural resources, such as fossil fuels and minerals, and, more important in more recent times—given the overcrowding of the coastal areas—rich in space.[36] Eighty percent of China's meat, milk, and wool-supplying animals are found in these areas. China's rapid urban expansion and huge infrastructure projects have led to a huge demand for concrete, which has been supplied in part by open-cast mining all over Tibet. In these latter respects, Tibet is a precious and huge slice of real estate that is increasingly vital for the Chinese economy.[37] Minerals aside, Tibet's natural resources alone are of great political significance. The Tibetan Plateau, for example, contains more than 46,000 glaciers, constituting the largest river run-off from any single location in the world. It has been estimated that approximately 1.3 billion people living in more than 5.6 million square kilometers of drainage basin are dependent on the major rivers that originate in Tibet, including populations in India, Bangladesh, Thailand, Vietnam, and mainland China. Think of the influence that Turkey has over Iraq by virtue of its control of the headwaters of the Tigris and Euphrates Rivers or, similarly, that Sudan has over Egypt and the political implications of this geographical advantage. As a strategic asset, Tibet is therefore an immensely valuable prize for China.

A fourth reason why minority areas are so important to China is ideological. If the Chinese model of communism is to be attractive to other societies in different parts of the world, the successful integration of its minorities into the communist system is important. By demonstrating how different ethnic groups can prosper under its tutelage, China strengthens its case in the clash of ideas and values on the world scene. At the same time, the opposite would be damaging. As June Dreyer argues, "Having discontented and rebellious ethnic populations would be, and continues to be, an embarrassment for the [People's Republic of China]. Ethnically based discontent could also compound China's strategic problems, in that dissident minorities would be more receptive to subversive influences from foreign powers."[38] The prospect of having hostile émigré communities on its borders, which is what occurred in both Tibet and Xinjiang in 1959, is a challenge to be taken seriously. Creating conditions where photographs can be taken of happy, smiling, folklorically dressed workers and peasants has been an essential tool in this propaganda effort.

Closely connected to this ideological reason is the final reason: the huge revenues derived from tourism. China's cultural riches and colorful heritage are a lucrative resource that is only beginning to be exploited. In the same way, its landscapes are only recently beginning to be recognized as among the wonders of the world, and most of these natural wonders are located in the remoter regions, away from the cities and the Han Chinese–dominated areas. Ensuring that these areas are well connected with good facilities and a welcoming population is thus an important policy priority. At the same time, the increase in traffic of tourists and commercial people has caused frequent anxiety among Chinese local party officials, who have not mastered whatever minority-group language is relevant and are as a consequence sometimes bypassed in any transactions. In addition, the liberalization of the economy and travel has led exactly to that greater degree of contact between minority groups on both sides of the border and to their mutual expressions of dissatisfaction regarding their situation in China when they see and experience the greater prosperity and opportunities available to their distant relatives outside China.[39]

The Chinese Communist Party's policies toward minority groups have undergone a number of changes since 1949. Depending on the nature of the regime in Beijing, at times policies were more coercive and sought to assimilate minorities into the dominant culture and at other times were more accommodating and operated under a framework of pluralism. Dreyer argues that during Mao's ascendancy there was greater stress on assimilation, but in the immediate aftermath of the Cultural Revolution and with the advent of Deng Xiaoping a more pragmatic approach was adopted.[40] In the light of China's current drive for greater influence in world affairs, the approach favored by the current regime of Xi Jinping could be characterized as a mixture of both—a hardline emphasis on closer integration but also recognition of the value of co-optation and devolved decision making. Minorities were thus occasionally exempted from laws and regulations applied to the majority Chinese. For example, in some areas traditional village elders were co-opted into the top-down party system of management, or minority groups were exempted from the one-child-only policy of population control and allowed to continue to practice polygamy or, in the case of some Tibetans, polyandry.[41] One indicator of these shifts in policy was the support or lack of support for minority-language instruction: since 1949, the Chinese state has switched repeatedly back and forth between policies that have either suppressed or subsidized minority-language instruction. A constant element in the central government's policies, however, has been the investment in economic development and infrastructure, but unfortunately for the government this investment has not always had the impact the government sought. In many instances, the Chinese migrants to the minority areas have been the ones to benefit from it. In addition, the alleviation of poverty and support for educational advancement have resulted in a growth rather than a decline in dissident activity.[42]

One result of these pendulum swings between a pluralist approach and coercive assimilation has been the creation of a series of administrative structures with different degrees of devolved local decision-making powers. Ben Hillman argues that by examining the expenditure of the different levels of government, we can say that China is "one of the most decentralised countries in the world—more decentralised, even, than many federal states such as Germany, Australia, and the United States. The decisions made by local party and government leaders have a greater impact on Chinese society and economy than at any time since the founding of the People's Republic."[43] Although on paper government and administration in China is divided into provinces, within which there are prefectures, counties, and townships, the actual implementation of policies is filtered through a bewildering array of other national, regional, and local bureaucracies.[44]

Not only is there a parallel and more powerful decision-making structure in the form of Communist Party oversight, but there are also discrete regional administrations accountable directly to central state bodies. Thus, for example, Inner Mongolia is administered by the Inner Mongolia Autonomous Region, Xinjiang by the Xinjiang Uygur Autonomous Region. As we have seen, part of historic Tibet is administered by the Tibetan Autonomous Region, but there are also Tibetan autonomous prefectures within the Chinese provinces surrounding the TAR.[45] In these administrative districts, there is a mixture of, on the one hand, greater control and surveillance and direct financial accountability to state-level institutions and, on the other hand, a degree of special exemptions from laws applied to the rest of Han-dominated China.[46] This level of control has led to the argument that the terms *autonomous* and *devolved power* are not appropriately applied to these autonomous prefectures, although there are consistent attempts to ensure that ethnically Tibetan officials are given senior posts.

In discussions concerning the future of Sino-Tibetan relations, the granting of greater autonomy to either the TAR or the autonomous prefectures is not under serious consideration by the Chinese authorities. Tibetan exiles and some senior Tibetan officials in the Chinese Communist Party cite the Hong Kong example of "one state two systems" as a possible model to be emulated, but the view from Beijing is that applying this framework to Tibet would open a Pandora's box of demands from other minority groups across China.[47] Indeed, states Dreyer, "there has been no indication that the central government is willing to accede to these demands, and it is not difficult to understand why. . . . What appear to be reasonable calls for a devolution of decision making may prove to be the slippery slope toward gradual erosion of all government control and de facto independence. The risks of liberalisation would seem to be greater than the risks of continued repression."[48] In addition, similar to the situation of second- and third-generation Israeli settlers in the occupied Palestinian territories (the West Bank and East Jerusalem), Chinese government policies of the past twenty years have created a new status quo of Chinese settlement in the TAR and Tibetan autonomous prefectures. The settlers' accommodation into a new political structure or their evacuation poses a serious challenge to any change regarding Tibetan autonomy. It is in this context of both ongoing Tibetan separatism and Chinese government rejection that we should turn to the role played by the government's development policies in Lhasa.

Lhasa and the Development Juggernaut

In the next section, I examine the key role played by Tibetan Buddhism in the conflict between Tibetans and the Chinese authorities in Lhasa. Yet if the main focus of this chapter were to be solely upon lay and clerical religious practices, religious ideas and beliefs, and monastic structures, it would obscure the direct interplay between the social, economic, and political context in Lhasa and the role of religion in the conflict. It would divide into segments what is a highly complementary and symbiotic bundle of related factors. Although the idiom and channels for expressing dissent, protest, and rebellion in Tibet seem primarily formulated in religious terms, it is clear that the triggers and tipping points for this expression are varied. Therefore, to illustrate this interplay more clearly, this section examines three main features of the situation. First, the urban landscape of Lhasa has changed so rapidly and so greatly that a returning exile from the revolt of 1959 would not recognize her city, and the changes have been disorientating, alienating, and disempowering for long-term residents as well. The second feature—demography—is closely linked to the first, and I unpack some of the data behind what is accepted as immense growth in the total population of the city and the implications of this growth for the political and religious dynamics between Tibetans and the Chinese authorities. The final feature is the "museumification" of Tibetan cultural and religious life. Iconic sites such as the Potala Palace, the Jokhang Temple, and the Norbulingka Summer Palace as well as popular religious rituals such as the *kora*, once at the heart of government and religious life in Lhasa, are rapidly being repackaged as lifeless heritage sites on tourist itineraries, emptying out their role in the governance of Tibet and the city and detaching them from the life of ordinary Tibetan residents and visiting pilgrims.

Changes in the Urban Landscape of Lhasa

In examining the urban landscape of Lhasa, we should not forget that it was the preeminent city of Tibet throughout Tibetan history. In her study of Chinese development policies in the city, Emily Yeh observes that Lhasa's "importance lies in its privileged position in the imagined geography of the Tibetan nation and its place as a powerful symbol of Tibetan cultural identity." And, very relevant to our discussion, she goes on to add: "Recognition of these symbolic valences has also made Lhasa the site of the most intense application of state policies at enforcing 'harmony' and quelling dissent."[49] The radical changes effected by the Chinese government's development and surveillance policies since 1959 have had an impact not only on the city's spatial organization and visual aesthetic but also, perhaps more significantly, on its Tibetan identity and its sense of belonging and community. If the city is no longer culturally "Tibetan," but merely a satellite or replica of, say, Cheng Du, then what is its purpose anymore in contemporary Tibetan politics, religion, and society? Are the transformations so great that they account for the drift in the center of gravity of Tibetan revolt away from Lhasa to the eastern Tibetan areas in Chinese provinces, as exemplified by the self-immolations?

On the eve of the Chinese takeover in 1959, a Tibetan Buddhist pilgrim standing on the small hill known as the Chakpori, which is slightly to the southwest of the Potala Palace, would have seen all of the ancient city of Lhasa at her feet. Stretching eastward, a dense clump of houses and alleyways would be the Barkor neighborhood, the muddled collection of traditional courtyards and markets enfolding the Jokhang Temple, whose golden roofs would be flashing in the bright noon sun. The observant pilgrim would have also been able to pick out the two main *kora*s that defined the city in different ways.[50] The Barkor *kora*, along a street lined with houses, shops, and market stalls, was approximately one kilometer long and encircled the kernel of the city, including the Jokhang Temple. The Lingkor *kora* was the outer ritual circumambulation of about eight kilometers that swung round the eastern edge of the Barkor neighborhood, followed a tract of the River Kyichu to the south, and wandered along the western edges of the Chakpori before running around the lake and gardens at the foot of the Potala Palace to the north. Until the late 1980s, the expansion of the city was primarily within this outer *kora* route.[51]

Much of the expansion of the city began in earnest in the late 1990s as economic reforms opened up the possibilities for private enterprise. Chinese migrants flowed into the city, encouraged by subsidies for land conversion and housing to set up market gardens and to assist in the development of tourism. But it has been mainly from the late 2000s that Lhasa has expanded at such a ferocious rate. From 1990 to 2008, it expanded from half a square kilometer per year to nearly one and a half square kilometers per year. From 2008 to 2014, this growth rose exponentially to more than

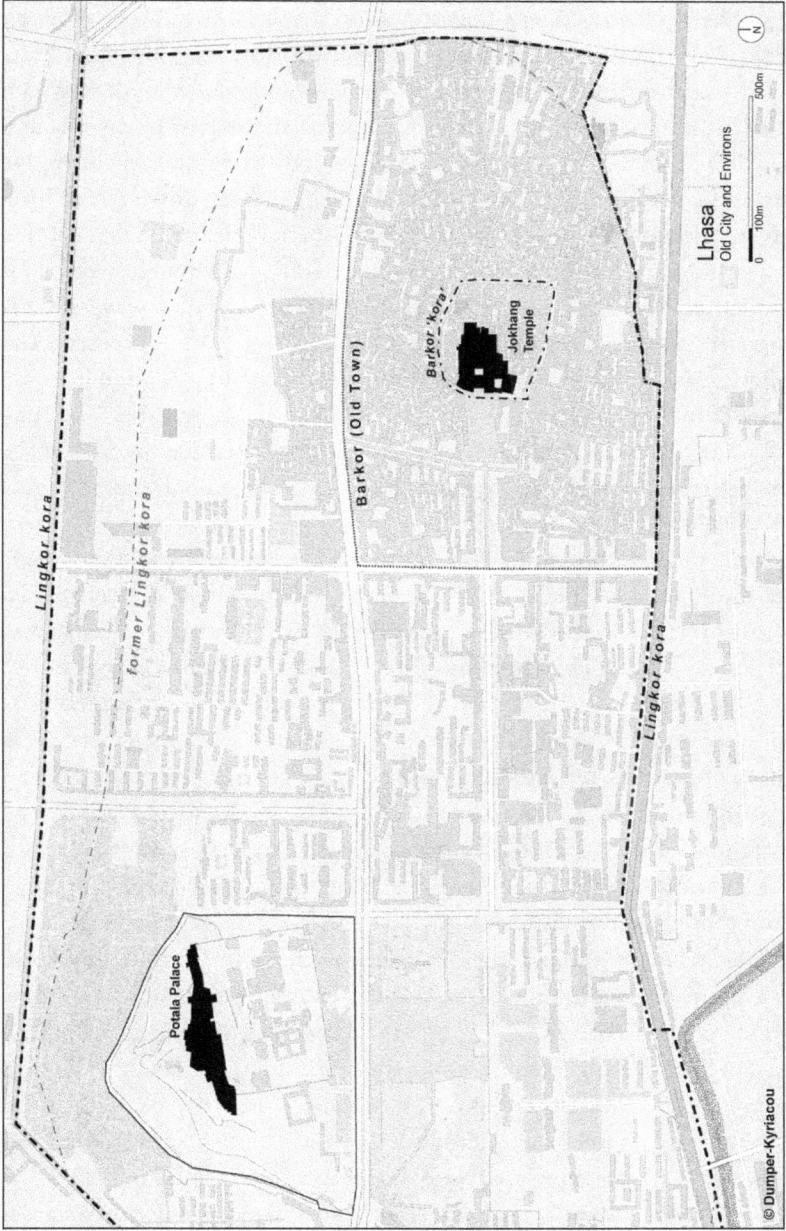

Map 4.2 Lhasa Old City and environs. (Map by Lefkos Kyriacou and Michael Dumper)

Lhasa
Old City and Environs

0   100m   500m

Lingkor kora

former Lingkor kora

Lingkor kora

Barkor (Old Town)

Barkor kora

Jokhang Temple

Potala Palace

© Dumper-Kyriacou

five and a half kilometers per year, with the result that the city has burst out of its traditional location clustered around the base of the Potala Palace and gobbled up land between the mountains north and south and all along the river.[52] Lhasa is now made up of four main districts—a central business district, encompassing the traditional Barkor neighborhood, in which most of the religious and heritage sites are located; districts to the east and west, where most of the new housing, light industry, and administrative construction are located; and, finally, a smaller southern district straddling the river. Prior to these developments, Lhasa's spatial orientation was defined by the circumambulation routes that connected the different key religious sites together. These routes were generally circular. The new wave of Chinese government construction pushed these patterns of movement and connection aside and introduced a gridlike rectilinearity defined by wide thoroughfares that cut through the medieval circular clustering. The rupture with the Tibetan past was further exacerbated by the renaming of the old roads—for instance, the Tibetan "Happy East Road" became the Beijing "East Road."[53]

Significant government investment in roads and housing and the opening of the Qinghai–Tibet Railway in 2006 (a prodigious engineering feat that cost more than all Chinese government expenditure on health and education in Tibet for the previous fifty years) has increased prosperity to an unprecedented height. A tripling of public-sector salaries and the provision of comprehensive health care and adequate schooling where there had been little before seem to have resulted in the co-optation of the Tibetan middle and professional classes into the Chinese development plans for the city and for Tibet in general.[54] During my visit to Lhasa in May 2018, one sight I had not expected to see was the number of shiny new SUVs clogging up the roads at rush hour!

Similar to many other Chinese cities that have undergone rapid and state-assisted development, one of the key characteristics of Lhasa's new urban form has been created through the allocation of housing according to certain criteria. The residency registration system (*hu kou*) in China is too complex to be discussed here; it has undergone many changes and is subject to many regional variations, which would be too confusing for our purposes.[55] In Lhasa, there are two basic categories of household. The first is the "individual urban household," found mostly in the older urban areas and consisting mostly of homes in the vernacular architecture and layout.

Figure 4.2 View northward from the Potala Palace, showing the new suburbs of Lhasa. (Photograph by Michael Dumper)

Most households in this category, possibly up to 95 percent, are Tibetan households and are registered under district offices and residential committees supervised by public-security stations. The second category is the "unit household" and comprises employees of government institutions delivering services such as health and education or employees of large commercial government enterprises. These units have their own shops, restaurants, dining halls, transport, and kindergartens; larger units have also built their own primary and secondary schools and often buy consumer goods and foodstuffs in bulk. As such, they are "more or less self-supporting communities."[56] On a walk around the more modern areas of Lhasa, it is quite easy to pick out what appears to be gated communities, with walls and fences separating them from other gated communities and with security checkpoints at the entrances. These unit households are roughly half Chinese immigrants and half Lhasa or TAR Tibetans in government service, but these two communities live in different gated communities, with the result that they rarely intersect.

Demography

No one can be blind to the huge demographic transformation that has taken place in Lhasa over the past seventy years. From a city of less than 30,000 in 1950, it became a city of approximately 220,000 residents according to the 2000 census. Yet there are several problems with these figures. The first figure is based on estimates by travelers, and it is not clear if the monastic population is included in them or not.[57] The second figure and other later figures supplied by the Chinese authorities are in the form of censuses or annual surveys or extrapolations from studies, making them difficult to compare on several accounts. For instance, some of the figures refer to the administrative area of Lhasa, which is much larger than the built-up urban area in that it includes rural land and many villages. Some population figures include those who are registered to live in Lhasa but not those who reside there illegally. Furthermore, some figures include Chinese migrants who either reside in the city only during the course of a work contract, which may be for only a few years, or are seasonal workers who return annually to their towns of origin in China. Some figures include military personnel; others do not. Some figures are collected in November, when many of the Chinese temporary residents are absent and others who are connected to the tourist trade and transport industry have returned to their towns and villages in China. And, finally, some figures are collected in the summer, when the city is full not only of temporary migrants but also of mostly Chinese tourists.[58]

In this muddle of figures, it is quite easy for pro-Chinese government supporters and Tibetan separatists alike to claim support for their claims from the population statistics. On the one hand, the Chinese government has used its figures to demonstrate how Tibet has benefitted from Chinese migration in terms of a range of development indicators. On the other hand, many Tibetan leaders in exile can point to the disappearance of a Tibetan majority in Lhasa to bolster their accusations of "cultural genocide."[59] In a measured and astute article, " 'Population Transfer' Versus Urban Exclusion in the Tibetan Areas of Western China," Andrew Fischer makes two important observations that shed a useful light on how best to interpret these figures. First, Tibetans have lagged behind the Chinese and other Asian groups in what in development studies is termed "the demographic transition." This is the common pattern in the socioeconomic development of countries undergoing urbanization and industrialization. In this pattern, a rise in key development indicators—health, education, and economic prosperity—is accompanied by fertility rates that fall below replacement levels. In essence, more people are dying than are being born. The decline in Tibetan fertility and thus in Tibetan population growth has coincided with exactly the period when Chinese migration into Tibet has increased, vividly encapsulated by the opening of the Qinghai–Tibet Railway in 2006. The impression that Tibetan residents of Lhasa may have of being swamped by new Chinese migrants, therefore, is reinforced at the same time by the exponential increase in domestic Chinese tourism. The second observation is that Chinese migration into the TAR is almost entirely an urban phenomenon. Fischer writes: "In the TAR, the contrast between the rurality of Tibetans and the urbanity of the Han and Hui is extreme. Therefore, the key issue is not the overall size of the population balance between Tibetans and outsiders, but the fact that outsiders have dominated urbanisation."[60] Although he goes on to observe that the Tibetan exile view of a population invasion of the TAR is valid, it is only partially so in that it applies only to towns and cities, while in the rural areas there is still Tibetan dominance—97.6 percent of the TAR is Tibetan, according to the 2000 census.

Nevertheless, in Lhasa itself the change has been swift and dramatic, to the extent that Lhasa is jokingly referred to as "Little Sichuan."[61] The 2000 census indicates that the Chinese population of Lhasa falls short of a majority and comes to just a little more than 34 percent, but it is acknowledged that these figures, collected in November, do not include the migrant population who left the city before then to avoid the long cold winter or the residents of some of the gated communities on the urban periphery.[62] Other figures derived from Lhasa Public Security Bureau (i.e., Chinese government) sources suggest that the number of temporary migrants not covered in the 2000 census ranges from an astonishing 100,000 to an even more astonishing 200,000![63] Aggregating these figures and updating them, therefore, can convey a very different picture of Chinese dominance in Lhasa from the one given in the 2000 census. It is a picture that seems to bear out the concerns expressed by Tibetans, who increasingly feel marginalized in their capital. Certainly, I recall a conversation in May 2018 with a Tibetan acquaintance and resident of Lhasa. While I was politely drinking my yak butter tea in a Lhasa café courtyard, we were chatting about the ways in which the city was very different during the winter than in the sunny summer months, and my interlocutor concluded with a telling phrase: "At the end of the tourist season, many of the Chinese leave, and we feel as if we get our city back."[64] However, even if we should treat all these figures with the utmost caution and go along with the notion that Chinese dominance in Lhasa is perhaps overstated, it is difficult to disagree with Andrew Fischer's further point that because urban areas represent the centers of economic and political power in China, "the real issue is economic and political dominance rather than population dominance."[65] The value of this argument is borne out when we look at the interlinked patterns of employment and education in Lhasa and their impact on the levers of power and influence in the city.

The Chinese government's system of guaranteeing employment in the public sector, known as *fenpei*, was of great benefit for non-Han minorities in China, such as the Tibetans. The Tibetans were educated mostly in Tibetan-medium schools, so their Chinese-language skills were generally inferior to that of Chinese, making the Tibetans less attractive to private employers in Lhasa, who in any case tended to be Chinese. Guaranteeing employment, particularly to Tibetan university graduates, was a direct form of positive discrimination. However, one result was a rapid increase in urban incomes, exceeding in some cases those in other parts of China, and this included the pay packets of middle-class Tibetans, who were able to spend their newfound wealth on consumer goods, probably explaining all the SUVs I saw choking up the roads during my visit in 2018. As Emily Yeh writes,

> The raising of administrative wages for cadres, which happened again after the completion of the Qinghai–Tibet Railway, was explicitly designed as a means of securing loyalty and political stability after the protests of 1987–89. Disproportionately high urban salaries have given rise to a small but highly visible class of wealthy Tibetans and

considerable conspicuous consumption of largely imported goods. Lhasa's per capita car ownership is almost equal to Beijing's.[66]

However, in the late 1990s the *fenpei* guaranteed-employment system was gradually phased out across China and in Tibetan areas, including Lhasa. In what appears, in hindsight, to be a monumental miscalculation by the Chinese authorities, the termination of the system occurred roughly at the same time as the new schools and universities, which had been established in the 1980s, began to churn out Tibetan graduates. So not only were there larger numbers of Tibetan graduates than in previous years, but also the levels of educational attainment and expectations of employment had risen, and there were no public-sector jobs for them. Demand had increased at exactly the time that supply had been deliberately reduced. Further exacerbating this policy miscalculation at the same time were the drastic reforms of the monastic system that began to take effect. I cover these reforms in more detail in the next section, but relevant to the discussion at this point are the numerical caps on the size of monasteries and nunneries, the expulsions of monks and nuns from the monasteries, the banning of recruitment of novices younger than eighteen, and so on, so that many of the monks, nuns, and novices were thrown onto the streets or into the arms of their already struggling families.

We should recall here the decision made by the U.S. government after its invasion of Iraq in 2003, which has now been accepted as a strategic blunder: the banning of the Baath Party and the demobilizing of the Iraqi armed forces. This action left thousands of educated Iraqis, both young and mature, unemployed and with nothing to do, with no stake in the political system, and with no hope of a future. But, crucially, they had been trained to shoot! The net result was an uprising of the Iraqi Sunni tribes against the U.S. Army and interim administration, culminating in the rise of the Islamic State. Though not quite on the same scale as in Iraq, in Lhasa by the mid-2000s it was becoming clear that a similar blunder was taking place. The hosting of the Olympic Games in Beijing in 2008 and the accompanying arrival of the foreign media provided the match to light the tinder that had been inadvertently prepared. The abolition of the *fenpei* system in the TAR took place in 2007, and it has been estimated that as a result job allocations dropped from about 6,000 per annum in previous years to a low of approximately 2,300 in 2007. Many thousands of educated young Tibetans were left unemployed and were easily convinced to blame the Chinese Communist Party.[67] The abolition of the system may not have caused the riots in 2008, but it clearly provided much of the fuel for them.

Andrew Fischer and Adrian Zenz have discerned since the riots of 2008 an almost complete reversal of the abolition of the *fenpei* system, albeit within a changing political and economic context, which they have termed a "neo-*fenpei*" system.[68] In 2011, coinciding with the wave of self-immolations taking place across Tibetan regions, the Communist Party announced the aim of providing full employment for Tibetan graduates of the TAR. To some extent, this goal was achieved, with more than 61,000 graduates being offered employment between 2011 and 2016.[69] However, as significant as the timing of the reintroduction of the *fenpei* system are two other aspects of this new policy: first, many of the posts available are security related—that is, young Tibetan graduates are being channeled into positions in which they can be both closely scrutinized by their Chinese superiors and used to police their own compatriots; second, local residential requirements are used to discourage non-TAR Tibetan graduates from applying for jobs in Lhasa and thereby keeping in check the opportunities for wider pan-Tibetan networking.

Overall, this policy has had a number of other impacts. First, it has emphasized the importance of a university education as a vehicle of entry to state employment. Given the poor quality of rural schools in Tibet, it therefore has served to increase the rural–urban divide in Tibetan society. Second, although the reincarnation of the *fenpei* system was very similar to the old one, nevertheless public-sector employment as a proportion of total employment in the TAR has been much reduced in the post-2008 period. Thus, most university-educated Chinese are recruited for better-paid jobs in the private sector, which in turn accentuates the linguistic and ethnic divide in Lhasa by adding income disparities between the Han and local Tibetans. Finally, Fischer and Zenz point out that the policy itself may have run out of steam. The jobs available under this scheme have dropped by half since 2016, and in 2017 there were seven times the number of applicants than jobs available.[70] Whether this incapacity or unwillingness by the Chinese to absorb the growing number of Tibetan graduates presages the kinds of political turmoil Lhasa has seen in the past, it is too early to determine.[71] But, whatever the reason, we can be pretty sure that it will fuel the grievances that the educated and more articulate Tibetans feel toward Chinese policies in the city.

The "Museumification" of Tibetan Governance
Structures and Culture

The "museumification" of Tibetan governance and culture in Lhasa is part and parcel of the Chinese government's development juggernaut. By examining it, we can see how those policies affect not only the use of space in Lhasa and the rapid change in demography but also its decision making, its culture, and its society. Such an examination is also an opportunity to draw attention to the role of external actors. I noted earlier in this chapter that one of the striking characteristics about Tibet, in common with many Chinese cities of the interior, is the absence of visible signs of external and foreign intervention. Although foreign retail outlets operating under Chinese license and franchises are not rare, there is very little NGO, media, diplomatic, or UN presence in Lhasa. This is in marked contrast to Jerusalem, where there are literally hundreds of NGOs, scores of consulates, multiple media bureaus, and more than twenty UN agencies with offices and personnel, their white vehicles with blue UN signs painted on them scurrying around the city at all times.[72] As in many highly centralized and autocratic states, foreign intervention and even foreign presence are highly controlled in China and even more so in the areas where national minorities live. The periodic imposition of martial law since 1959, which also has included the expulsion of the media and all foreigners, has interrupted any pattern of external intervention. Of course, the glaring exception to this policy of excluding foreigners has been driven by economic policies, which are designed to encourage tourism. Tourism is clearly a welcome source of income for Lhasa. Not only do tourists bring in external revenue, but the need to provide hotels and restaurants, to improve transportation links, and to provide the upkeep of monuments and sites leverages additional Chinese government investment and employment. Nevertheless, of interest to this discussion is the impact tourism has on both the city and the religious conflicts that emanate from the presentation and transformation of religious sites.

The growth of tourism in Lhasa has been spectacular. Between 1995 and 2000, the TAR received 2 million visitors, the vast majority of whom were Chinese, and virtually all of whom probably visited Lhasa because of the key historic sites there.[73] It has been estimated that in 2007 there were more than 4 million visitors to the TAR.[74] In 2014, Lhasa received more than 9 million tourists and is projected to cater to more than 20 million by

2030!⁷⁵ Between 1990 and 2014, the proportion of Lhasa gross domestic product derived from tourism rose from 0.65 percent to more than 32 percent.[76] The impact on the urban landscape and the fabric of those parts of the city that are of great historical interest is therefore immense. Access roads are widened; historic pilgrimage routes such as the Lingkor *kora* are altered to fit into the modern grid system; renovations are carried out quickly and superficially without authentic materials; and the provision of catering outlets, hygiene and medical facilities, security, and parking have transformed the city from a small and rather mysterious place into a large pleasure resort. Widespread prostitution and the proliferation of high-end casinos and bars are new additions to Lhasa and spin-offs from the migrant-led development policies of the Chinese government.

Obviously, as we have seen elsewhere, these challenges precipitated by migration and modern tourism are not unique to Lhasa. Much of my research in Jerusalem's Old City in the early 1980s took place amid piles of rubble, excavations, the intrusion of heavy machinery, incessant drilling and hammering, and the rumbling of concrete mixers. It was a difficult challenge to distinguish the improvements being carried out on the infrastructure of the Old City by the Israeli authorities from their deliberate harassment and displacement of Palestinian residents. Certainly, when "improvement" was accompanied by property confiscations and evictions, as in the Jewish Quarter, it was easier to see.[77] And as is the case for the Palestinian residents in Jerusalem, Lhasan Tibetans have no ownership over deciding how to manage and channel Lhasa's cultural assets or over the revenues that those assets generate, which must add to their sense of disenfranchisement and disempowerment.[78]

Two aspects of this phenomenon illustrate the impact of these policies. The rapid expansion of Lhasa was accompanied by the widespread destruction of its older neighborhoods and replacement with modern look-alikes. According to a Norwegian survey produced in *The Lhasa Atlas*, the adoption of the Chinese government's Lhasa Development Plan, 1980–2000, and its sister plan the Barkor Conservation Plan, 1992, was a turning point in the city's history. One of the authors of the atlas concluded that between 1995 and 2005 "most of Old Lhasa's historical-traditional buildings were demolished and 'reconstructed' as larger monotonous housing developments in a 'Neo-Tibetan' style."[79] Of the nearly seven hundred historic buildings that existed before 1950, only fifty have survived, and most of them are connected to monasteries or nunneries in some way. One of the most egregious examples is the complete destruction of the iconic village of Shol at the foot of the Potala Palace and its replacement by simulacra of traditional Tibetan buildings to house administrative, security personnel, and a rather clumsy museum focusing on the injustices of the old Tibetan aristocracy.[80] Part of the village is now an enormous plaza similar to Tiananmen Square in Beijing and Wenceslas Square in Bucharest and serves much the same function as a site for officially approved celebrations. Redolent of the plaza constructed in front of the Wailing Wall in the Old City of Jerusalem on the site of the old Moroccan quarter and the plans linking up the Vishweshwur Temple in Banaras to the River Ganges, "Potala Square" has become the most popular site in Tibet for selfies and group photographs, thus reducing the Potala Palace to ethnic Disney World backdrop.[81]

Those sites that have been spared destruction have nevertheless undergone a transformation of their role. The buildings may have been preserved, but the radical change in their function is gradually emptying them of meaning. For example, the Potala Palace, which was simultaneously a temple, a monastery, a residence for the Dalai Lama, a fortress, and an administrative center, has been hollowed out and presented to the world as exotic but at the same time backward and irrelevant. It is no longer the heart of Tibetan society and politics, with instruments for devotional rituals and tools for government and administration, but instead a unique museum full of cultural relics. The message is clear that the site belongs to the past, which will never return, and that the future lies elsewhere.[82] In 1961, the Potala Palace was placed under the protection of the Chinese state and in this way spared the looting, the damage, and the demolition that other Tibetan religious sites suffered during the Cultural Revolution from 1965 on.

Although this action may have preserved some of the most important treasures in Tibetan culture and Buddhist religion, at the same time two other less-benign things happened. First, the palace and its contents were made the property of the Chinese state, which underlined the imposition of the new political Communist Party order and its refusal to brook any partnership with the Tibetan leadership on the exercise of power in Tibet. In addition, this state acquisition deprived Tibetans of a say in how the site or its contents were to be used. The renovation work undertaken prior to 1994 is thought to have been extremely poor, leaving some of the oldest chapels, such as the Avalokiteshvara Chapel, in ruins.[83] Second, the site and its contents were re-presented to Tibetans and to the millions of

Chinese and foreign tourists who traipsed through its halls and corridors and viewed the displays in the Tibet Museum as relics of a bygone era and a backward past that was depraved and debauched and only improved upon by the Han elder brother's intervention. In this way, many items were wrongly classified and inaccurately portrayed as symbols of oppression and luxury in order to consolidate the impression that Tibetans had been freed from serfdom and a medieval tyranny.[84] As Clare Harris writes,

> By 1999 the world's first Tibet Museum opened in Lhasa, where some of the most significant items from the Potala were prominently displayed. The purpose of the move was clear: it would define the accoutrements of power associated with the dalai lamas as defunct and position the period of Tibet's theocratic government firmly in the past. It would reclassify Tibetan objects according to Chinese categories as "Cultural Relics" to be viewed in glass cases, and redesignate the buildings they derived from as heritage sites to be photographed by tourists.[85]

UNESCO received a great deal of criticism for its apparent complicity in this transformation. Tibetans had high hopes that UNESCO, as one of the few international organizations that are allowed to work in China and the TAR, would temper the Chinese authorities' determination to appropriate such symbols of Tibetan culture history and society. As the Chinese authorities began to understand the value of Lhasa as a major tourist site, they welcomed the visits of officials and technical advisers from UNESCO's World Heritage Center. By obtaining World Heritage List status for the Potala Palace, the Jokhang Temple, and the Norbulingka Palace, not only would the Chinese receive valuable expert input and funds for renovation and preservation, but they would also receive international legitimacy for their actions in Lhasa to date.[86] As the application for World Heritage List status went through the various stages and UNESCO committees, some resistance could be discerned in the public debates and private discussions, but the formal procedures merely noted technical shortcomings and the need to consider possible reappraisal of the overall plans for the historic fabric of Lhasa.[87] Potala Palace, Jokhang Temple, and Norbulingka Palace were awarded UNESCO World Heritage List status in 1994, 2000, and 2001, respectively, and another ninety-three buildings were listed as protected. As Robert Shepherd concludes in his examination of the politics of cultural heritage in Tibet: "UNESCO marks sites as worthy of protection because of their cultural value, and Chinese authorities comply by transforming these sites into the elements in the state narrative of Chinese culture and civilization."[88] The development juggernaut in Lhasa has continued apace, and the impact of the Chinese urban policies has prompted international experts to press UNESCO to take a stronger stand against what is increasingly being regarded as a machine out of control.[89]

Taken altogether, these transformations of Lhasa from a city at the center of the Tibetan Buddhist world to one that is hard to distinguish from a city in the Chinese interior and that lacks the cultural markers that would offer a connection to the meanings of its recent history have led to a degree of cultural dislocation not uncommon when indigenous peoples have been robbed of their patrimony. Among the manifestations of anomie have been the breakdown of family ties and the reputed prevalence of alcoholism in contemporary Tibetan society.[90] The transformations are also perceived as a Chinese colonialism masquerading as a Communist-inspired egalitarian development that marginalizes and derides Tibetan culture and Tibetan systems of governance. The official characterization of the Han as the "elder brother" of non-Han siblings, such as Tibetans, in the Chinese family is a patronizing formulation of an unequal subservient relationship with racist undertones.[91]

Tibetan Buddhism in Lhasa: An Enduring and Future Legacy

Clearly visible from the Jokhang Temple in Lhasa, the most revered holy site in Tibetan Buddhism, is a plain but domineering thirteen-story building overlooking the serried rows of prostrating pilgrims and the temple's golden curved roofs. This building houses the Chinese government's Public Security Bureau. It has become an equally significant landmark in a city that has been transformed from a backwater to a focus of global attention. The juxtaposition of these two buildings symbolizes the tension in Lhasa between a heightened religiosity with nationalist overtones and a controlling secular authority with settler-colonialist undertones. This section delineates the main phases and features of this fractious and destabilizing relationship. It begins with an overview of the Chinese government's policies toward religion and the struggle to shoe-horn Tibetan Buddhism into them. It also tries to convey the central role that Tibetan Buddhism plays in Tibetan society and how, despite its superficial eclipse in Lhasa by rapid urban development and the Chinese state's secularizing policies, it continues to affect the city's dynamics. The section then examines Chinese policies and Tibetan resistance in two main phases: the period of radical reforms leading up to the riots in 2008 and the period after 2008 until the present day. It concludes with an examination of a number of themes that encapsulate the relationship between the city, its politics, and its religion.

Government and Religion in China

Prior to the Cultural Revolution, the Chinese Communist Party superficially adhered to the Constitution of 1954, which guaranteed the "freedom of religion." The Religious Affairs Bureau (RAB) was established, and a number of umbrella religious organizations were created to oversee relations between the recognized religious communities of China on the one hand and the Communist Party and Chinese state institutions on the other.[92] These umbrella organizations included the Buddhist Association of China, the National Taoist Association, the Protestant "Three-Self Patriotic" Movement, the Chinese Catholic Patriotic Movement, and the China Islamic Association.[93] One of the key tasks of these state-sponsored organizations was to ensure that the legitimacy of their religions was derived from the Communist Party and not from external sources, such as the World Council of Churches or the Vatican. However, much of this initial edifice was sidestepped by the Smash the Four Olds campaign, unleashed against religious groups by the Red Guards during the Cultural Revolution.[94] The American Chinese scholar of contemporary Chinese religiosity Mayfair Yang refers to the Cultural Revolution as "the most severe religious decimation and persecution in the twentieth century." Indeed, she elucidates how this campaign was in fact part of a three-decade period of "anti-religious terror" starting in 1949: "Monks, nuns, ritual specialists, shamans, and devout lay practitioners in all the different religious traditions were harassed and terrorized, made to undergo 'thought reform,' imprisonment, sent to labour camps, forced to marry against their will, and even tortured and executed by overzealous local cadres or ordinary thugs who took matters into their own hands."[95] The Red Guards ransacked temples, mosques, and churches across the whole of China, sparing neither priceless religious artifacts nor ancient books, paintings, or other valuable antiquities.

Since the 1980s, there has been a gradual relaxation of these coercive policies stemming from a series of initiatives derived from a text issued by the Communist Party known as "Document 19." Although the general oversight by the state religious organizations remained, Document 19 allowed the revival of religious practices and a restitution of places of worship to their congregations. In 2004, the State Council issued the revised Regulations in Religious Affairs, which restored many of the rights that religious communities had exercised previously but which still ensured a high degree of state intervention. Parallel with the drive toward a "socialist market economy" following the fall of Mao Zedong, the revival of religious life has been remarkable in China.[96] Temples, monasteries, and nunneries have been allowed to open their doors, and thousands of worshippers, pilgrims, and tourists have flooded in, generating revenue streams that have raised their profile and their role in Chinese life and society. Fenggang Yang writes: "Economic development remains the central task of CCP [Chinese Communist Party] top leadership. Many local governments have used this to justify the pragmatic and tolerant approach to various religions . . . [and] government agencies have tried to put religion to use for economic development, such as building temples for tourism or allowing more churches in order to attract overseas investments."[97] New religious academies and centers of learning and training have opened, and recruitment has flourished. In fact, in order to counter the influence of the unrecognized Falun Gong cult and the growth of Christianity in China, government agencies have more recently adopted a more instrumental approach and promoted the more endogenous and Sinified religions of Buddhism and Taoism through a number of international conferences.[98] On a visit to Cheng Du, the capital of Sichuan province, in May 2018, I was quite struck by the numbers of people visiting the Buddhist Wenshu Temple. The grounds and gardens were well maintained; the extensive buildings, including offices and dormitories, were clean and newly painted; and the numbers of young monks carrying out duties and assembling for communal prayer were quite striking. Also revealing were the lay devotees circulating in the courtyards and joining in the prayers: the greater number of them were young people and young families—that is, the very demographic one would expect to have been thoroughly secularized by the decades of a Communist Party–inspired education system. Some of these young people and families were clearly on holiday and were probably curious tourists, but, judging from their familiar interactions with the monks, a great proportion of them seemed to be locals and regulars.

Despite this religious revival, which has accelerated in twenty-first century, the Chinese state authorities continue to monitor religious practices closely.[99] All religious groups must register and submit to the authority of one of the umbrella associations mentioned earlier. Unregistered religious associations are persecuted, and places of worship can be seized and destroyed. Even apparently benign interventions show the strong hand of the state's controlling instincts. In order to redress the decline in "quality" of the senior clergy of the five recognized religious communities, a training program has been established at the People's University in Beijing. Here the intention is not only to improve managerial skills but also to improve the clergy's understanding of their own religious history, doctrines, rituals, and theologies![100] The subtext of these endeavors is clearly that the practice of these religions must be closely aligned to the principles of the Chinese Communist Party.

Governing Religion in Tibet and Lhasa

The situation in Lhasa and in Tibetan areas in general and the policies toward Tibetan Buddhism have both conformed to these trends and sharply diverged from them. Before examining the situation in more detail, we should take a brief look at the extent to which Tibetan Buddhism is central to the lives of Tibetan residents of Lhasa and elsewhere. Such an examination necessarily focuses on the role of the monastic life. As Jose Cabezon has summarized, "Religion is at the very heart of Tibetan ethnic identity, and monastic institutions are one of the hallmarks of Tibetan religion."[101] Before the Chinese occupation, monasteries and nunneries were sites of devotional practices, collective celebrations of annual events, regional or district festivals, and pilgrimage. They were also important employers of labor and consumers of local products. Loseling College, for example, part of the major Drepung monastery in Lhasa, managed more than 180 estates and employed 20,000 people, who worked the land but also paid taxes to the monastery.[102] It has been estimated that prior to 1959 between 10 and 12 percent of Tibetan males became monks, and a lower proportion of Tibetan females became nuns.[103] As a result, all Tibetans had a relative, often more than one relative, who was at some stage of initiation or membership in a monastery or nunnery. The monasteries were not only sites for pilgrimages but also places for family visits and reunions, which doubled up as both meretricious actions as well as family holidays.[104]

In obtaining a picture of the role of Tibetan Buddhism in Lhasa, we should focus not only on the great holy sites and temples but also on its role in affirming a Tibetan identity. The Tibetan Buddhist practice of circumambulation, or *kora*, of such sites is shared by all ages and draws together Tibetans from across the Tibetan region. *Kora*s have a religious role in that they take place around and inside holy sites, but they are also social and nationalist in the way they promote a Tibetan community cohesiveness and solidarity.[105]

*Kora*s are accompanied by many other distinctive Tibetan Buddhist practices. A circumambulation may be punctuated with prostrations or even completed entirely in a prostrated posture in order to obtain additional merit. Many *kora*s are lined with prayer wheels, which passing pilgrims conscientiously turn, and with stalls selling yak butter, which is later deposited into the various lit receptacles in front of statues and icons. Prayer flags, normally in red, blue, saffron, white, and green, are seen on mountaintops, high passes, and bridges, and in Lhasa they also adorn roofs and entrance ways. The presence of Tibetan Buddhism is thus constantly being reaffirmed by practice and in spectacle. Ignoring this presence has political risks. In his book on Tibetan guerrilla resistance following the flight of the Dalai Lama in 1959, Mikel Dunham observes how the Chinese misjudged the importance of the Great Prayer Festival, or Monlam, which is celebrated after the Tibetan New Year and draws large crowds. In the lead-up to the disturbances in 1959, anti-Chinese feelings were running high, and the festival provided a forum for their expression, catching the Chinese military commanders off guard.[106] Similarly, the *kora* in Lhasa has become the prime platform for protest against Chinese policies since the formal takeover of Lhasa in 1959.

The whole of the Tibetan region is peppered with monasteries and nunneries, but three of the most important ones are located in and around Lhasa: Sera, Drepung, and, a little farther outside the city, Ganden. Known collectively as the *densa chenmo sum*, "seats of learning," these three are, according to Cabezon, the "elite monasteries of the Geluk school that before

1959 were the largest monasteries in the world."[107] Prior to 1950, they together comprised approximately 17,000 monks, constituted more than half the population of Lhasa, and exerted considerable influence on the government of Tibet, so much so that it was commonly perceived that they were indeed part of the government. *Densa* abbots were appointed by the Dalai Lama; specific aspects of their finances were regulated by the government; promotions of monks to certain ranks, such as lamas, required government approval; disputes were adjudicated by government officials, who were also empowered to issue permits for a range of minor activities. At the same time, the *densa* monasteries wielded a significant degree of internal autonomy and self-governance and dealt with minor crimes through their own disciplinary procedures. The monasteries were known to appoint large and muscular monks as a private police force. Known as *dob-dobs*, these monks were feared for their punishments but also respected for the vehemence with which they defended the premises against hostile opponents, hence the remarkable militancy of some of the monasteries. The Lhasa *densa*s were organized around a college system, and within them monks were allocated residences associated with certain regions. Colleges also specialized in intellectual disciplines such as rhetoric, logic, law, and philosophy and had their own eminent scholars, libraries, and classrooms. Competition between colleges, which was often colored by regional identities, produced gifted debaters and scholars and was responsible for the reputation that Tibetan Buddhism and the monasteries of Lhasa in particular held in the wider Buddhist world.[108] All these activities and institutions were supported by large estates and income derived from produce, land taxes, large donations, and offerings both in kind and in cash (entry fees).

Despite this dynamic balance between self-governance and state regulation, after 1950 the Chinese authorities in Tibet began a long campaign of attrition in which they sought to erode the independence of the monasteries. In turn, this meant that the monasteries' capacity to question the authority of the Communist Party and the legitimacy of the Chinese takeover of Tibet was undermined. To Mao Zedong, monks and nuns were unproductive parasites. In 1959, just after the flight of the Dalai Lama from Lhasa, Mao declaimed, "There are 80,000 lamas in a population of 1,200,000 and these 80,000 lamas do not produce matter nor [*sic*] produce people. . . . Lama[s] must engage in production, farming or industry."[109] On the surface, the Chinese state's policies in Tibet were little different from those in

Han areas of mainland China and possibly no worse than those carried out against the Muslim Uighurs in Xinjiang.[110] Where they departed from those applied in the Han areas is the way in which the loosening of restrictions over worship that took place after the Cultural Revolution across China was not applied to Tibet. Tibetan Buddhists instead found themselves more tightly controlled and regulated in all Tibetan areas, but particularly in Lhasa. Tibetan resistance to these Communist Party controls was too closely associated with separatism and the rejection of the incorporation of Tibet into the Chinese state for Tibet to be included in the general relaxation of state control over religion. As Ninian Smart observes in his magnum opus *The Religious Experience of Mankind*, the Achilles heel of Buddhism as a political force has been its reliance on the monastic system. The Mughal conquerors of northern India learned in the sixteenth century that if they removed the monasteries, they opened the way for their dominance of the people.[111] The Chinese authorities seem to have taken a leaf out of the Mughal book.

Chinese state controls on Tibetan Buddhism have taken two main forms. The first is an overall framework in which institutions and their leadership are allowed to operate. Senior clergy, temple administrators, and monastic orders are made accountable to national advisory bodies such as the Buddhist Association of China, which in turn is accountable to the RAB and the United Front Work Department, which is a Communist Party body responsible for relationships with nonparty organizations. Each of these bodies also has regional-level supervisory responsibilities. In the TAR, however, it appears that the Buddhist Association of China has only limited functions. Monasteries, for example, are directly regulated by the municipal or county arm of the RAB. In fact, the three Lhasa *densas*, which are regarded as a potentially destabilizing force, are supervised by a mosaic of bodies, such as the regional RAB, the regional Commission on Nationality Affairs, the Lhasa Municipality, and the Lhasa and TAR Public Security Bureau.[112] This complex and overlapping system of governance and management ensure that the great monasteries of Lhasa have retained no autonomy whatsoever in their decision making.

The second form of Chinese state control is direct intervention in the way the monasteries and nunneries are run. This intervention encompasses not only their management but also, quite unbelievably, the content of what monks are taught, which is confined to only "normal religious activities."[113]

The key tool of supervision is the Democratic Management Committee in each monastery or nunnery, which comprises a chair who is the local senior Communist Party official, a deputy who is the monastery's or nunnery's abbot or abbess, several party-approved monks, and possibly a representative of the police or the Public Security Bureau. Among the committee's duties is the collection of information on all nuns and monks: their family background, their home village or town, who they associate with, and their education attainments. The committee also issues certificates with photographs, without which no nun or monk is allowed to continue to reside in a nunnery or monastery. In some large monasteries, there are variations. In Sera monastery, for example, the committee has fourteen members, eleven monks and three nonmonastic Tibetan officials. It functions as two units: a directorate with five members (four monks and one local party official) and a council with eight members (one police representative, one RAB official, and six monks). There are no elections, and when vacancies in the committee occur, the directorate's nominee is vetted for approval by the RAB.[114] The abbot of Sera monastery is nominated by the Democratic Management Committee and is approved by the RAB. As Cabezon writes, "In short, the government has veto power over any monk who occupie[s] any kind of administrative position within the monastery. The abbotship is today largely ceremonial and has no real power."[115] Alongside these restrictions, a "Patriotic Education" program was introduced, whereby teams of specially trained Communist Party officials are stationed in monasteries and nunneries and compel their members to attend intensive classes.[116] Monks and nuns of all ages and seniority receive lectures on Marxism, the policies of the Chinese Communist Party, patriotism, and interpretations of Buddhist theology that conform to the Chinese government's notions of the Communist Party as the sole legitimizer of beliefs. In many instances, the so-called Buddhist beliefs in these lectures are barely recognizable to the students.[117]

The net result of these two facets of control has been the overall decimation of the monastic population and the transformation of its central role in the culture and identity of Tibetan society to one of mere guardian of touristic sites and the relics of a marginalized tradition. One cannot help thinking of the Native Americans on reservations in the United States, who before the Wounded Knee incident in 1973 were expected to dress up in Hollywood-type "Red Indian" costume and to sing and dance for tourists.

It is not quite as bad as that in Tibet, but that seems to be the direction it is heading. In 2018, I visited the Sera monastery during one of its renowned debating sessions for novice monks. Along with scores of tourists with their expensive, ostentatious cameras and smartphones at the ready, I was directed to a courtyard garden. Inside were more than one hundred burgundy-robed monks with their shaven heads, assembled in small groups of five or six. After all the tourists positioned themselves round the outside of the courtyard, sitting on a paved path or among the shrubbery, a bell rang out like a starter gun, and immediately in each of the small groups of novices one of them began declaiming an argument loudly, almost shouting. The din rose and fell as arguments were laid out with one hand raised high, then cut through the air to land in a sharp smack on the other hand to emphasize a point. Feet were stamped, and shouts of triumph or derision would ring across the courtyard if the groups failed to provide a counterargument. It was a dramatic, colorful spectacle full of noise and the long burgundy robes in constant swirling movement. Yet I was left feeling very uncomfortable. On the one hand, it was a fascinating demonstration of how debating skills are taught and fostered, an archaic pedagogy that has some lessons to teach the modern world. On the other hand, the American "Redskin" analogy was also very present in my mind. This performance was staged for the tourists, for the revenues they brought, and was clearly impinging on the authenticity of the exercise. Some novices seemed to resent our presence, turning their backs to the gawping crowds, while others played to the gallery with a smile or a smirk. I felt complicit in the debasement of an important educational ritual.

Enrollments into monasteries and nunneries have been capped, age limits for entry set, cooperation and exchange between institutions constrained by restrictions on mobility, approval of rituals and the display of images or symbols required, the content of religious instruction and the conferment of qualifications monitored, the annual religious calendar altered, repair works focused on exploiting tourism, and revenues in general monitored.[118] Of the 2,500 monasteries in existence in 1959, only 70 remained in 1962.[119] If these figures are correct, that is an astonishing rate of closure over a mere three years. Some scholars have estimated that by the mid-1990s more than 11,000 monks and nuns had been expelled from the monasteries, mostly for refusing to denounce the Dalai Lama. In the Lhasa *densas*, approximately 20 percent of the monastic population were expelled.[120]

Response and Resistance

Such dramatic interventions into the monastic system have not occurred without side effects. The "blowback" has been persistent and at times deeply challenging to the Chinese presence in the TAR and Lhasa. It can be divided into two types: ideological resistance and active resistance. First, there has been a significant fall in the quality of monks and nuns. The sharp reduction in the numbers of monks and nuns through capping and expulsions led to a collapse of the college system, which had served to refine and sharpen the monks' and nuns' intellectual skills. It also led to the decrease in the pool of members from which senior monks and nuns can be selected. This decrease has been exacerbated by a "brain drain" of bright and able monks and nuns fleeing to India, where they can continue their studies and spiritual development unfettered. Concern over the poor quality of senior clergy was one factor that led the Chinese authorities to introduce the remedial step of additional training in specially designed courses in Beijing. On top of this, the reeducation campaigns have been largely ineffective in challenging the tenets of Buddhism.[121] The poor-caliber Communist Party tutors display a profound ignorance of Tibetan Buddhism, often conflating it with other strands of Buddhism and folk religion. Ultimately, these efforts are thought to have been counterproductive in terms of influencing the beliefs of the monks and nuns they sought to convince.[122]

The second form of blowback is active resistance, mostly nonviolent but sometimes quite violent and bloody. Although some of this resistance has been provoked by a range of nonreligious factors, such as dispossession of property and the loss of traditional employment, and thus has involved ordinary lay Tibetans, the presence of monks and nuns and the use of religious rituals and symbolism have been striking features of the resistance to Chinese interventions.[123] Lhasa has been at the forefront of this resistance. For example, in 1987 a group of thirty monks from the Sera monastery used the *kora* of the Jokhang Temple to stage a demonstration of loyalty to the Dalai Lama, chanting "Long live His Holiness, the Dalai Lama" and "Independence for Tibet." Despite arrests being made, the demonstration snowballed when passers-by joined in large numbers. A few days later a similar demonstration took place, with Tibetan flags being flourished, and it attracted between 3,000 and 4,000 Tibetans, who overturned police cars before being broken up by police shooting into the crowd.[124] Martial law was declared, but the disturbances carried on into the following year. In 1989, another large demonstration, possibly the largest since the Chinese takeover in 1959, took place in Lhasa, which triggered the further imposition of martial law. Despite Chinese efforts to integrate Tibet into China, it paradoxically was becoming increasingly a unique region with a special security status and, as a consequence, less accessible to Chinese and foreign visitors.

Although the Chinese security clampdown and suppression of political activity (known as the Strike Hard Campaign) led to a period of relative calm, dissent continued in coded ways: celebrations of the Dalai Lama's birthday, the wearing of Tibetan dress, increased participation in religious festivities, the throwing of *tsampa* (barley flour associated with religious festivals) in the air to mark the awarding of the Nobel Peace Prize to the Dalai Lama, and other activities.[125] Yet even these coded expressions of dissent provoked a strong Chinese response. For example, in 2005, following the arrests of the abbot of Drepung monastery and other senior monks who refused to denounce the Dalai Lama, four hundred monks staged a silent protest in the main assembly hall "in what was probably the largest act of resistance the monastery had seen to that date."[126] A military occupation of the monastery, arrests, and expulsions followed, leading to a further standoff between the monks and the Chinese authorities. Cabezon suggests that these actions in Drepung were a key factor leading to the riots that took place in 2008.[127] As noted earlier, taken together with the termination of the *fenpei* system, they were quite likely to have been the tipping point for the later riots.

The staging of the Olympic Games in Beijing in 2008 was a kind of "coming out" party for the Chinese Communist Party, an opportunity to showcase the enormous and impressive strides the country had taken in economic development, the completion of infrastructure projects, and the distribution of prosperity. It also provided an opportunity for Tibetan separatism activists to spoil the party. By taking advantage of the access to Tibetan areas granted to the international media, they were able to draw attention to the situation. The initial event that triggered the later riots was a small protest similar to that which took place in 1987. Fifteen monks from the Sera monastery circumambulated the Jokhang Temple and began to hand out leaflets denouncing the Patriotic Education program and shouting pro-independence slogans. Although all of the demonstrating monks were arrested, the Chinese authorities and police also revealed an unexpected degree of hesitation and restraint because of the unusual political conditions brought about by the impending Olympic Games. In addition, a significant difference from the demonstrations in 1987 was the presence of online social media, which relayed the events and the uncertain official response instantaneously. These factors, it has been suggested, emboldened other Tibetans to join in public shows of dissent.[128]

The arrival of paramilitary forces; the searches of homes, monasteries, and nunneries; the closure of downtown businesses; and the arrests of monks marching from Drepung monastery combined to inflame the situation. Further demonstrations by hundreds of monks took place in Sera and Ganden monasteries until finally, on March 14, monks marching in central Lhasa were confronted by paramilitary police, who then came under attack by Tibetan supporters of the monks. Paving slabs were ripped up from the ground and hurled at the police lines. Chinese and Hui migrants were also attacked, and businesses and shops torched, leading to the imposition of a curfew and the expulsion of all foreign media.[129] Protests spread across Tibetan areas; Chinese soldiers fired upon demonstrators, killing dozens; and the Sera monastery was occupied by 2,000 troops.[130] Between March and July 2008, approximately 30,000 demonstrators participated in more than two hundred public events. Although the demonstrations were instigated primarily by monks and nuns, over the course of the disturbances the demographic changed to include university students, school children, and laborers. More than one hundred people were killed, and in Lhasa alone more than five hundred people were arrested.[131] All foreigners were expelled, and Lhasa was under a comprehensive military lockdown, with many Chinese returning to their homes in China either to avoid the violence or because businesses were shut and tourists unable to enter Lhasa.[132] The Chinese Olympic parade had been well and truly rained upon.

It is in response to these events in 1987 and 2008 that Chinese policies in the TAR and Tibetan areas diverged significantly from those in predominantly Chinese areas. Whereas a relaxation of controls over religious activity corresponding with the opening up of the economy took place in mainland China, the fear of separatism being mobilized as part of religious revival made such relaxation too great a risk to take in Tibet. Lhasa and other Tibetan areas instead saw an intensification of regulation and state control. During the course of 2008, Chinese authorities stepped up their public-relations campaign to reassure their citizens that the situation was contained and that the malcontents were few in number and misled by the traitorous Tibetan leadership in exile. At the same time, curfews were enforced; schools, monasteries, nunneries were closed; and trials resulting in confessions were publicly broadcast. When martial law was lifted and the tensions in Lhasa eased, instead of a reflective assessment of what lessons could be learned, there was a ratcheting up of the internal controls on monastic institutions and of the Patriotic Education program. In a report in the *Tibet Daily*, the head of the Communist Party Publicity Department in Tibet declared: "We must clean out the monasteries and strengthen the administrative committees. After that we will absolutely control them."[133] This focus on monasteries and nunneries was supplemented by the targeting of an increasing number of hermits, who by virtue of their solitary and remote existence were evading party control.

The crackdown on Lhasa has also had an unintended consequence. The majority of the protests took place in the city, but it became clear that many of the Tibetan areas inside China proper were also affected. Despite the Chinese government's attempts to fragment the Tibetan areas, its coercive policies have in fact helped to generate a growing communal solidarity and ethnic identity.[134] Monasteries in Sichuan, Gansu, and Qinghai provinces have seen numerous acts of protest in response to the physical occupation of and increased state control over the Lhasa *densa*s. This response can be seen particularly in the dissent that has appeared since 2008. In addition to the self-immolations described at the beginning of this chapter, there have also been more coded acts of resistance, in which one emphasizes one's Tibetan identity by speaking only Tibetan, removing Mandarin neologisms from Tibetan dictionaries, wearing Tibet attire, consuming Tibetan products and cuisine, visiting temples, carrying out *kora*, and maintaining the yak-butter lamps in shrines—all of which reaffirm a Tibetan national identity. However, these actions have been given extra meaning by being exercised particularly on what has become known as "White Wednesdays"—regarded as the Dalai Lama's "life-force day."[135] Tibetan restaurants have refused to serve customers who on Wednesdays order food in Chinese, and Chinese businesses are boycotted. The effectiveness of these steps can be seen, perhaps, in the new proclamations by the Chinese authorities banning the wearing of Tibetan attire on Wednesdays![136]

At the same time, despite these widespread and inclusive acts of cultural resistance and despite the wave of self-immolations, the Chinese authorities have continued to pursue the control of Tibetan Buddhism. The paramilitary forces dispatched to Lhasa and the TAR during the demonstrations in 2008 are now a permanent presence, and the city has been divided into neighborhood grids that are monitored for any suspicious activities among the residents.[137] Paramilitary patrols along key streets in Lhasa remain a regular feature of city life. In addition, Tibetans from outside the TAR are not allowed to enter it, and other restrictions on festivals and telecommunications have been introduced to curtail opportunities for Tibetans to communicate or to meet in public. Police checkpoints at county and region borders are now a common sight. The most recent annual report of the U.S. Congressional-Executive Commission on China supplies details of demolitions and expulsions taking place in

Figure 4.3 Chinese paramilitary police patrol the *kora* around the Jokhang Temple, Lhasa. (Photograph by Michael Dumper)

two monasteries in Ganzi Tibetan Autonomous Prefecture, Sichuan province: the Larung Gar Buddhist Institute and the Yachen Gar.[138] Larung Gar is one of the world's largest Buddhist institutes and has had its numbers reduced from 10,000 to just a little more than 5,000. Similarly, Yachen Gar, comprising mostly nuns, has had its numbers reduced from 10,000 to 9,000. Most of those expelled are reported to have come from the Tibetan Autonomous Region.

The pressure on the Communist Party cadres is also immense. Hillman analyzes the ways in which the Chinese and Tibetan Communist Party officials are haunted by the prospect of blame or career stagnation and even punitive sanctions if any disturbances occur under their watch, to the extent that they consequently exceed the instructions for monitoring and controlling Tibetans.[139] In this context, it is significant that a fire in the Jokhang Temple in 2018 resulting in the serious damage of one of the most revered statues in Tibetan Buddhism, the Jowo, was not extinguished more quickly. Given the presence of an ever-greater number of fire extinguishers and Chinese official fire wardens stationed in and around Tibetan holy sites to prevent self-immolations, this delay reveals perhaps a close adherence to instructions to concentrate on self-immolations at the expense of any other event.[140]

Religion and Ethnicity in Lhasa

On my last morning in Lhasa, I carried out a final *kora* around the Potala Palace, known as the Tsekor *kora*. The air was fresh and cool, and despite its being only around 7:30 in the morning, the sun was high and bright—remember, Lhasa is on Beijing time, even though it is several thousand miles to the west.[141] There were already queues at all the security gates in front of the Potala, but I was struck by how many of those lining up to have their bags searched were Tibetans. Obviously, the Chinese and other foreign tourists were still having breakfast while the local Tibetan residents were squeezing in a *kora* before they set off to work or to school. The cross-section of people was quite astonishing. There were admittedly a large number of elderly ladies slowly walking along the inner curve, spinning the hundreds of golden prayer wheels that lined the northern edge of the Potala Palace. As in most other religious sites, this demographic was to be expected. However, I did not anticipate the large numbers of teenagers and twenty-something-year-olds who were walking together in groups that continually merged and broke up, taking photographs, skipping along, stopping to text on their smartphones, sharing snacks, laughing, and chatting all the time. Strolling along in the sunshine, watching the crowds, seeking out glimpses of the palace high above, I must have caught the attention of one such group just ahead of me. They slowed their pace, and a couple of young women peeled off and tried to engage me in conversation in broken English. Where was I from, did I like Lhasa, did I have a family, what were my children doing, why was my wife not with me, did I like Beyoncé, Ronaldo, who did I prefer—Prince William or Prince Harry? Soon their companions joined in, and I finished the rest of the *kora* as part of a small crowd of friendly, curious, and confident young people. Apart from feeding off the buzz of energy that groups of young people sometimes have, I finished the *kora* somewhat elated. I could not help thinking that these youngsters were not browbeaten, broken Tibetans. Some were students, and some were working in the tourist trade. They must have been younger than ten when the last major uprising in Lhasa took place in 2008, so their overwhelming teenage experience of Lhasa was as a Chinese-occupied and a Chinese-controlled city. But they were unashamedly Tibetan, chatting in Tibetan to each other, and although they were not in traditional costume, there was something in their attire that was different from the few Chinese also doing the *kora* and something in the ease with which they occupied the space around them. Despite the armed police and CCTV cameras, this was their space, this was their custom. In 1981, I lived for several months in a Palestinian village in northern Israel and met scores of Palestinians who live in Israel and have Israeli citizenship. They often will speak to you first in Hebrew, rather than Arabic, and they are sometimes cautious about revealing their Palestinian heritage. Their reasons for these choices can be complex and are usually understandable, but they are also quite telling. In contrast, nothing in this bubbly crowd of young Tibetans conveyed fear, shame, pragmatism, evasion, or guile.

This is a snapshot, an anecdote, and I am not an experienced enough Lhasa hand to be able to say whether it encapsulates the zeitgeist of the emerging generation or presages a direction of travel for the future. Nevertheless, it provides a counterpoint to the sense of overwhelming Chinese dominance in Lhasa and Tibet. The latter sense is buttressed by an awareness of both the sheer size of the country of China, the numbers of people involved, the surveillance resources the government has available, the capacity for effective and transformative economic development, and the strength of the state's institutions. Whatever its financial problems and mounting debts, China is not a country that will fall apart or withdraw from any part of the wider Tibetan region. However badly it is playing its cards by crudely asserting a Han ethnic dominance, a withdrawal from Tibet is not part of the game. Tibetan separatism and independence will need to be a very long game—one played over several generations—and any gains will be minor, cosmetic, and incremental. Only an economic collapse in China will result in Lhasa reverting back to a Tibetan city, with Chinese immigrants leaving and the huge government investments and subsidies drying up.

In fact, *reverting* is not the right word. Too much has changed, and even if there is a return to Tibetan demographic dominance, the city's now modern gridlike features will take many decades to soften and be reindigenized. Even if there is a loosening of controls over Tibetan Buddhism, it is also hard to see the monastic system's dominance returning in its old form. The landownership system that provided the income for the great monasteries has been comprehensively dismantled, and the likelihood that Tibetans will opt to restore such a feudal system is zero. In addition, in a globalized world the opportunities for other forms of livelihood are much greater, so the number of young people entering monasteries and convents is also unlikely to reach the levels that existed in Tibet prior to 1959.

A critical moment for Sino-Tibetan relations in the future will be the death of the currently exiled and ageing fourteenth Dalai Lama. At eighty-four years old, the Dalai Lama still serves as a unifying force in Tibetan politics and society even though he has stepped aside from active politics by arranging for the election of a prime minister (Kalon Tripa) for the Tibetan government in exile.[142] The replacement of the Dalai Lama as the head of Tibetan Buddhism with someone more pliable is therefore an important goal of the Chinese government.[143] The system of identifying the reincarnated Dalai Lama has become a matter of intense scrutiny. I would speculate that the Chinese government is busy ensuring that whatever Regency Council is established after the Dalai Lama's death, it will be stuffed with supporters of the Communist regime. The government will ensure that when the Regency Council discovers and nominates a baby as the reincarnated Dalai Lama, that baby, as he reaches maturity, will be more compliant. However, this avenue is strewn with complications for the Chinese government. Its previous poor track record of attempting to ensure more compliant senior figures in the Tibetan Buddhist hierarchy, as in the Panchen Lama and the Karmapa successions, does not augur well for it.[144]

The case of Lhasa offers a great deal to this research on identifying specific kinds of conflicts that relate to religious sites and practices in cities and how they can be managed or resolved. It raises a number of revealing similarities and contrasts to the situations in Jerusalem, Banaras, Cordoba, and George Town. Similarities between Lhasa and East Jerusalem are the most salient: Lhasa has been either liberated or occupied, like East Jerusalem has been either occupied or united, depending on your political position. The role of religious sites and of the clergy in mobilizing resistance to this watershed change has been central in both cases. Indeed, in the absence of strong political institutions and movements, the religious leadership of Tibetans has been much more prominent and active in decision making and in implementing resistance activities than, say, the Muslim religious elite in East Jerusalem have been. Another similarity is the role of ethnonationalism in the colonizing process in Lhasa. The ideology of the Chinese Communist Party and its policies of development and integration clearly mask a privileging of Chinese interests in Lhasa in much the same way Zionism as the explicit ideology of a colonizing Israeli government privileges Israeli Jewish interests in Jerusalem. Similar privileging of the Hindu community is also attempted in Banaras and by the Malay Muslim community in George Town.

Lhasa differs from Jerusalem in three key areas. The first is the striking absence of external intervention in the form of international NGOs, foreign consulates, media, educational and cultural exchanges, and so on. The leverage that the international community exerts over the situation in Lhasa is therefore minimal. Despite the inscription of some key religious sites on the UNESCO World Heritage List, this mechanism has apparently had little impact on the implementation of the Chinese government's centralizing policies. In contrast, we can see how external intervention has provided the subordinate Palestinian Muslim community in East Jerusalem with considerable assistance in resisting Israeli attempts to encroach upon Muslim religious sites and practices in East Jerusalem.

A second area of difference is housing. The absence of a highly homogenized and segregated housing provision is a surprising facet of Lhasa's urban profile. It mitigates, to some extent, the impact of the development policies that favor migrants at the expense of Tibetan residents. Although there is evidence of distinct Tibetan residential areas, it is not as much as one would expect given the incentives afforded to Chinese migrants. The Old City in Barkor aside, the ghettoes that one might have anticipated in these circumstances do not exist. It is here that the purported Communist ideology of egalitarianism in housing provision in Lhasa can be contrasted with the state-sponsored Zionist ideology of Israel, which has led to Jewish-only colonies in East Jerusalem. Again, in East Jerusalem the role played by religious institutions in preserving extensive property holdings (land endowments such as the *waqf*) has also led to a high degree of residential segregation. The irony of the Lhasa case is that the total control over land ownership by the Chinese Communist Party has prevented the same kind of urban ghettoes and fragmentation experienced in East Jerusalem.

The final area of difference between Lhasa and Jerusalem is the nature of the conflict over religious sites. In situations of shared religious sites or sites that are revered by more than one religion, the state can act and is expected to act as arbiter between two or more nonstate actors. This arbitration has taken place, however imperfectly, in Banaras and Cordoba. One can also argue that immediately after the 1967 War the Israeli state played a similar role in restraining the zeal of Jewish militants seeking to take over the Haram al-Sharif or Temple Mount. It was not until the capture of state institutions by Israeli settler groups and the ideological hegemony of the Israeli militant nationalists that the Israeli state ceded this arbiter role. In Lhasa, however, the conflict over its religious sites is strikingly different: there is a direct interface between the state and the devotees of Tibetan Buddhism and their leadership. The Chinese government and the Chinese Communist Party are not in conflict with Tibetans and Tibetan Buddhism over Lhasa's holy sites because of a prior claim on the sites. In a narrow sense, the conflict is not a religious one. Rather, it is an ideological conflict over which principles should frame the ordering of society and the relations between the various centers of power in the areas under Chinese rule. The religious sites in question symbolize and encapsulate in a powerful way an opposing view to the Chinese government and therefore, according to the government, must be contained and transformed. At this point, we can return to the question posed at the beginning of the chapter regarding the continuing centrality of Lhasa as the location of Tibetan resistance to Chinese rule. Is Lhasa still relevant in the resistance? The answer is clearly yes. No other major population center in the wider Tibetan region rivals Lhasa's paramount role in Tibetan history, politics, and religious life, and as such it still remains the pivotal point of contact with the Chinese state. It is still the front line. But two other major factors point to its continuing paramount role. It has unrivaled symbolism as the seat of religious power in Tibetan society, and although acts of resistance may be taking place in other parts of Tibet and the world, the point of reference still remains the Potala Palace, the Jokhang Temple, the Norbulingka Palace, other key sites in the city, the monasteries, and the *koras* associated with them—all in Lhasa. Finally, as we have seen in Jerusalem, Cordoba, and Banaras, these sites and their symbolism have long, dynamic, and continually unfolding histories in Lhasa. The past is not a passive ruin but a kind of spirit running through the present, and although the religious role of Lhasa is much diminished and constrained and the people subjugated, the current situation is unlikely to be the end of the story.

CHAPTER V

Branding Religious Coexistence

Malaysia's George Town as a Model City of Harmony?

T
he city of George Town in Penang, Malaysia, has a special resonance for me in this study. I was born in Ipoh, just a ferry hop
and two-hour bus journey away, but I spent my early childhood
in Penang. Between 1956 and 1963, my father was the vicar of the main
Anglican church in the city, and my mother was very active in community affairs, running a choir, a charitable secondhand clothing shop from
the ground floor of the vicarage, youth clubs, summer camps, and a mem-
orable badminton club that met twice weekly in our spacious garden. As a
child, I was given astonishing freedom to wander the streets, markets,
beaches, and hills of the island with my Malay, Indian, and Chinese companions, speaking to each other in an ever-changing street patois that my
parents could hardly make sense of. All around us were dramatic manifestations of religious practice, with frequent noisy and colorful processions,
gongs, bells, pounding drums, thunderclap bangs of firecrackers, tuneful
prayers, flagellation and self-mortification, garlands of flowers, and exotic
fruits. As an introduction to religious diversity, these early experiences were
ingrained into my memory.

Fast-forward fifty years, and I find myself doing this research into religious conflicts in cities. In attempting to identify case studies that would
provide material for analysis and reflection, I constantly had a sense I was
overlooking an important element. Something was missing. Studying the
various cities that could have been included in this study, I had trouble

identifying what the missing element was. At that point in my research, I also started reading the literature on "everyday peace" in much greater depth, and I began to see more clearly how scholars of conflict studies have a tendency to end up focusing so much on conflict that they can lose track of a wider perspective. This wider perspective suggests that harmonious coexistence between religious groups is also an important and sometimes a more prevailing phenomenon.[1] As already noted, Robert Hayden has been assiduous in showing how despite many instances of violent and protracted intercommunal conflict in cities, there are also decades of grudging accommodation and "antagonistic tolerance." So in progressing further into this subdiscipline, I began to find that images of the religious diversity that characterized the George Town of my younger days gradually began to seep back into my memory, and I decided to take a closer look at it as an adult and as a scholar. I argued to myself that given my early experiences I would have a sort of "inside track" into the city and the pitfalls that its residents were navigating. In addition, I felt it was important to examine in this study at least one city where the dominant discourse, both official and unofficial, is that of accommodation and coexistence. The contrast with Banaras, Lhasa, and Jerusalem would be, I believe, revealing. Furthermore, through the city of George Town it would also be possible to examine whether there are policies, institutions, and processes that indicate better ways of reconciling differences over religious beliefs, over religious practices, and over holy sites in cities.

One of the main thoroughfares of George Town, Pitt Street, is replete with almost a score of different religious sites—St. George's Church, the Kuan Yin (or Goddess of Mercy) Buddhist temple, the Kapitan Keling and Acheen Street Mosques, the Khoo Kongsi (Clan) and Yap Kongsi Centers, and the Sri Maha Mariammam Temple. As a result, in the promotional literature about the city, Pitt Street has been renamed the "Street of Harmony."[2] Similarly, George Town received international recognition in 2008 for its successful management of its cultural diversity by being inscribed onto the UNESCO World Heritage Site list. As I write this chapter, I have in front of me half-a-dozen maps and brochures with various titles such as *Journey of Harmony: A Self Discovery Walking Tour* and the *World Religious Walk: Penang*, produced by the Penang Global Ethic Project and by George Town World Heritage Inc., identifying key religious sites to visit along the so-called Street of Harmony. The branding of the city as a model of interreligious harmony is explicit, confident, and celebratory and consequently demands further interrogation.

This chapter, therefore, seeks to probe deeper into the apparent success of George Town as a multiethnic city and its presentation to the world as a site of harmonious interactions between different religious communities. If the key actors, such as the Penang state administration, the George Town Municipal Council, civil society, and community leaders, have successfully found a formula or a model by which religiously and ethnically diverse urban communities can manage and resolve their differences—thus avoiding the kind of carnage we have seen in other similarly diverse cities such as Beirut, Sarajevo, Jerusalem, and Ayodhya—then academics and policy makers should start a serious and important discussion of the extent to which some policies and features in George Town can be replicated. For researchers who, like myself, have been engaged in the study of the Arab–Israeli conflict and its cruel impact on the city of Jerusalem, the failure of the Middle East peace process has led to a search for alternative approaches. This redirected focus toward understanding the causes of peace in order to understand the dynamics of religious conflicts in occupied or divided cities may prove to be useful. The overarching questions I intend to try and answer, then, are: What can the "culture of accommodation" (a phrase beloved of scholars of Malaysia) that appears to prevail in George Town tell us about managing religious diversity more generally? Are the institutions and processes concerned with dispute resolution in the city robust and embedded, or are they contingent upon the existing political architecture or upon local agency and the charisma of individual religious leaders? In essence, does the rhetoric indicated by the name "Street of Harmony" match the reality?

Before I embark upon an examination of George Town, I want to take stock of some of the main observations and arguments of this book thus far. The main focus has been to identify key constitutive elements in conflicts that are generated by the associations a city has with religious beliefs and practices. I can pinpoint five main elements. First, the most obvious and perhaps most powerful element and trigger of a conflict in a city due to its religious associations has been the close proximity of important religious sites to each other. Even more complex and intractable than that are holy sites that are shared or claimed by different religious groups. The conflict between Palestinians and Israelis over the Haram al-Sharif/Temple

Mount in Jerusalem is the foremost example of this element. The second important element is the ownership of land and property by religious communities. Landownership patterns in the form of religious endowments or other forms of institutional religious ownership can give a spatial and territorial foundation to social and economic activities of particular religious communities and can lead to varying degrees of residential, educational, employment, and political segregation. As I discussed in the introduction, when there is a breakdown in the processes that tie the various communities of a city together, not only can these geographical areas become enclaves and markers of community identity, but religious practices and rituals, such as processions and public worship, that include crossing from one area into another or intruding into an area are also frequently seen as transgressions that need to be resisted. The Roman Catholic and Protestant communities' parades and marches in Northern Ireland are regarded as egregious examples, but as we saw in the chapter on Banaras, such transgressions also take place on a regular basis in many other cities. In Lhasa, Buddhist ceremonies and festivals in public spaces are closely regulated by the Chinese Communist Party and have even been banned due to their symbolism as demonstrations of the strength of the Tibetan community in Lhasa.

Closely connected to the element of land ownership is the third element: how competition between different communities over access to land, revenue streams, and other resources is exacerbated by the density of a city. A change in resource allocations tends to be a zero-sum game that can disadvantage one community as opposed to another. Because of a city's density and the close proximity of large numbers of residents, the affected community can be quickly and easily mobilized in response to this disadvantage. As seen in the discussion of flashpoints in chapter 1 and in the cities already examined, this is especially the case if that change is seen as a threat to a religious site or a religious ritual. This nexus between change and the potential to mobilize resistance is a marked feature of urban as opposed to rural politics. The fourth key element is also closely connected. In cities where the institutions of the state are weak and ineffective or where political resistance has been decapitated, religious leaderships and senior clerical figures are often thrust into the role of key political actors. As we have seen in Cordoba and Banaras, some religious leaders are committed to dialogue and coexistence and work across the religious divide, whereas others have used religious differences to advance more sectarian interests.

Finally, as the fifth key element, external interventions on religious grounds can also play an important part in triggering conflicts. Cities that have important religious sites and are centers of religious learning or pilgrimage generate attention among devotees and the wider public beyond the immediate confines of the state in which they are located or even of their own religious community. Events in the city that have an impact on those sites and rituals resonate far and wide. In some instances, such external connections can protect those sites from the depredations of an opposing religious community or state. Jerusalem, again, is a good example of how the power of the Israeli state and its religious nationalist supporters is constrained by external intervention, whether in the form of UN resolutions or of financial and political support from other Islamic states to Palestinian religious institutions. Lhasa, in stark contrast to Jerusalem, has minimal external intervention. Nevertheless, the international role of the Dalai Lama and the energy and tenacity of Tibetans in exile have played a significant constraining role. By publicizing widely the Chinese authorities' policies that are deliberately eroding the position of Tibetan Buddhism, they have succeeded in tempering some of the Chinese state's more coercive acts. At the same time, the importance of sites can also draw in unwelcome political interference that can exacerbate the tensions that have arisen. A minor infringement or dispute that might have been resolved locally can reverberate globally, which may inflame the situation.

The dynamic between these elements needs explaining. In previous chapters, I explored religious conflicts in cities also on the more abstract level of metanarratives. I posited that it was possible to view the religious conflicts arising from the competition between the narrative of precedence and the narrative of transformative integration. In Jerusalem, we saw how a very qualified narrative of transformative integration has been eclipsed by the narrative of precedence since the collapse of the Oslo peace process. In Cordoba, I observed that the controversy over the use of the Mezquita was a reflection of how the emerging narrative of transformative integration was being resisted by the Roman Catholic authorities espousing a narrative of precedence. I also argued that this resistance should also be viewed in the political context of a centralizing Spanish state restraining the centrifugal tendencies of the regions. A similar and potentially more destabilizing contest over metanarratives has been taking place in Banaras, with the Hindutva movement challenging the heterodoxy and relative inclusiveness that has prevailed hitherto in that city. In George Town, I argue that we find a variant of the Banaras metanarrative competition. Here the uneasy equilibrium between the main ethnic and religious communities has prevailed—just. The narrative of Malay Muslim precedence has been given increasing force by the Malaysian Constitution and the capture of the federal government institutions by a Malay Muslim political party, but in George Town itself, as in Banaras, there has been a powerful pushback by the narrative of transformative integration. Unpacking the ingredients of this pushback is part of this chapter's task.

Contemporary George Town is certainly not the utopian idyll of my childhood memories. It has expanded fourfold in size, doubled in population, become exceedingly congested, and, despite its bleached and palm-fringed beaches, become disturbingly polluted. Nevertheless, given the city's complex and continuing religious diversity, the absence of both persistent and pervasive violent conflict in the city is remarkable. The absence of the coercive apparatus of the federal Malaysian government on the city streets is also quite striking. In contrast to, say, in Jerusalem, Banaras, and Lhasa, in George Town there are no checkpoints on the streets leading up to its holy places or heavily armed paramilitary snipers on the roofs overlooking them or an atmosphere of brooding surveillance. At the same time, however, before we can authoritatively suggest that the city has something to tell us about managing religious diversity in urban settings more generally, this phenomenon needs testing, probing, and accounting for.

During a visit in June 2017, I systematically visited the various religious sites on the island. Many of them were almost unchanged from my childhood memories, but many were also very different: they were larger, wealthier, less peripheral and more part of the urban sprawl, and more integrated into the global economy of tourism, endowments, welfare provision, and public relations. A good example of these changes is the Buddhist Kek Lok Si Temple on the outskirts of the city.[3] Formerly a relatively quiet temple with a monastery built upon the side of one of the small hills of the island's interior, the site is now a bustling tourist honey pot with rows of souvenir stalls lining the steps, ramps, terraces, and corridors that channel you up through gardens, meditation rooms, chapels, and ultimately up to the largest pagoda in Malaysia.[4] From its pinnacle, you can see all of George Town spreading out from its farthest point at the seashore and covering the expanse of the low-lying land in between, right up to the foot of Penang Hill. This vantage point I am sure is significant.

Figure 5.1 The Ten Thousand Buddhas Pagoda at the Kek Lok Si Temple, George Town. (Photograph by Michael Dumper)

Indeed, from the pagoda, almost half the island is visible, and when the sun sets, you can catch the twinkling lights of Butterworth on the Malaysian mainland across the sea. But surely as important as what the pagoda's gaze falls upon is the fact that the temple itself can also be seen from half the island. Like a soaring minaret or a high church spire, it has become a point of reference and orientation in people's daily lives in the city. Indeed, at Chinese New Year, the temple guardians put on a spectacle lasting for thirty days that is famous for its thousands of lanterns and light shows. Such is the prominence of the temple, these lights can be seen from the city center as well as from many parts of the island to the south.[5] Absorbing these impressions, you begin to realize that there is something slightly sensitive about this visual "outreach," particularly when you also learn that the Malaysian government limited the height of the huge one-hundred-foot statue of Kuan Yin, the Goddess of Mercy, erected behind the pagoda. This restriction was not established for safety purposes. It was to prevent the statue's shadow falling on the Penang State Mosque some three kilometers away.[6] Add to this the fact that donations for the Kuan Yin statue were collected not only from wealthy Malaysian Chinese businesspeople but also from devotees in Taiwan, Hong Kong, and mainland China, and you can begin to see the temple as a formidable expression of a resurgent Chinese Buddhism in Malaysia.[7] So I began to ask myself: Is there more to these changes in the religious sites of George Town than initially meets the eye? In the context of the Chinese government's huge regional investment program in Southeast Asia, known as the Belt and Road Initiative, does the increasing salience of Chinese religiosity suggest a subtle change in the balance of power between Malays and Chinese, the two main ethnic communities on the island? And is this change taking place when the radicalization of Muslim Malay groups has also led to an erosion of the culture of accommodation that has been the dominant discourse on the island?

Thus, in delving below the surface of the branding of George Town as a city of harmonious interactions between different communities, we can significantly add to the analysis in this book. Having mapped out in previous chapters how frictions generated by some religious practices can coalesce and evolve into more serious and violent conflicts between religious communities or between residents and the state, I can now examine religious diversity in George Town and its political context to figure out how conflict has hitherto been avoided there. It will be an informative exercise in understanding the relationship between urban demographic heterogeneity and state power. To this end, the chapter is divided into five sections. The first sets out some of the historical background and overview of the city's religious and ethnic composition. It also unpacks some of the demographic trends and classifications used to describe the city's population and analyzes the economic and political structures that provide the framework for civic and political agency. The second section discusses the culture of accommodation that prevails despite the privileging of the Malay Muslim community in the Malaysian Constitution and the government administration. The third section explores the culture of accommodation in more detail and describes some of the conflicts over religion that have taken place. It uses as case studies the Kampong Rawa Temple-Mosque Incident of 1998 and the contemporary dispute regarding the organization of the annual Hindu Thaipusam festival. The fourth section examines the mechanisms and processes that attempt to consolidate the "culture of accommodation" in Malaysia and assesses their prevalence in efforts at dialogue and coexistence. The fifth and final section delineates the main reasons why religious diversity has not led to conflict in George Town and assesses the extent to which some aspects of this coexistence can be utilized elsewhere.

Historical Background and Overview of George Town

The Emergence of a Unique City Status

The urban morphology of George Town is a direct result of its rather contradictory location. Sitting on the entranceway to the Straits of Malacca, it lies on several important trade routes, but it also has a peripheral status for being on the edge of successive empires in the region. The eclectic architecture of its important buildings and the evolution of its urban design provide accurate visual snapshots of its geography and its historical trajectory.[8] We should also remember that in relation to some of the other great cities of the world, George Town is a very young and a very small city. Its rapid expansion to the second-largest conurbation in Malaysia didn't occur until after the 1970s. The orthodox historical narrative is that in 1786 George Town emerged as a trading city as a result of its role as an outpost of the East India Company. It was during this year that Sir Francis Light leased the island from the sultan of the Malay state of Kedah on the Malay Peninsula. What this narrative overlooks, however, is, first, the centuries of Penang's maritime interactions with what pan-Malay nationalists term "Nusantara"—the Malay-speaking inhabitants of the archipelago of islands that stretch from Thailand to Java—and, second, the influence of the regional powers emanating from Indochina and India. The spread of Islam to the Malay Peninsula through Arab merchants, often protected by the Mughal dynasties of India in the fourteenth and fifteenth centuries, attests to these commercial and ideological exchanges.

The orthodox narrative of the island of Penang as a kind of tabula rasa for British colonial policies has also been challenged by a greater awareness of local political and economic issues that formed the backdrop of that period. So instead of the view that the Malay presence on the island consisted of little more than a few fishing villages, much more weight is being given to a view of the island as having a population comprising both migrants from Sumatra, Java, and the Philippines and refugees from the political turmoil in Kedah as well as having an embryonic trade in smelted tin and primitive wood oils.[9] Moreover, it is also clear that events in Europe, such as the defeat of Napoleon in 1815, and the dominance of Britain there allowed the East India Company and Britain to restrict the influence of the Dutch Empire, which had colonized much of Indonesia. As a result, in 1826 the British authorities made George Town the capital of the newly created Straits Settlements, which also included Malacca and Singapore (a precocious upstart in the eyes of the Penang mercantile class). George Town became a port that not only was closely connected to British-controlled Calcutta but also interacted closely with the wider Malay Archipelago to the south and west and with Indochina to the north. George Town was, in this way, not just a refueling station for ships on the way to China and Australasia but also a trading hub for the immediate hinterland. Migrants

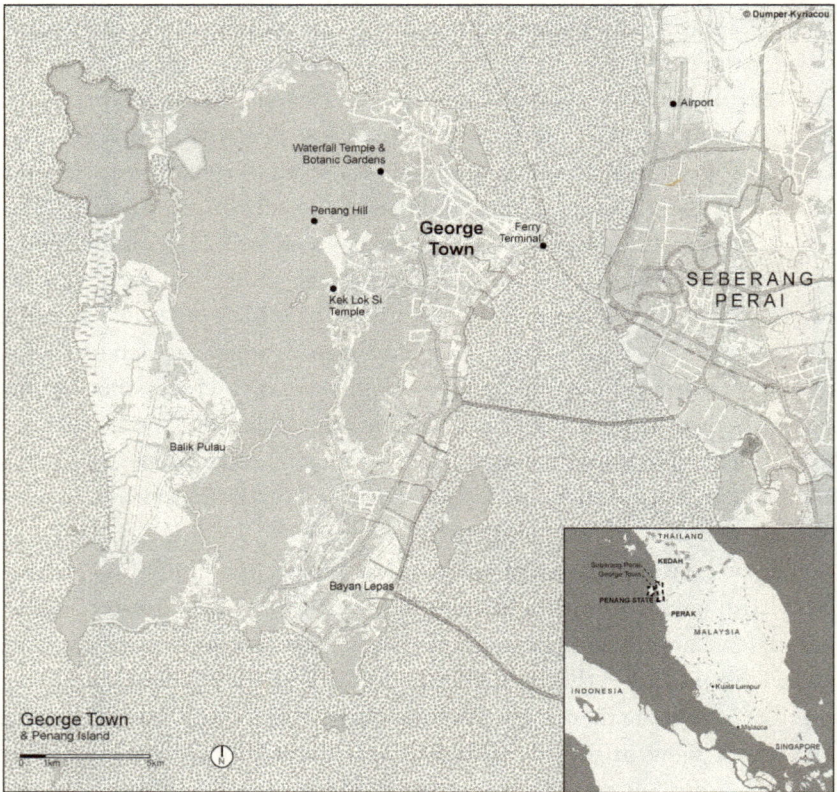

Map 5.1 George Town and Penang Island. (Map by Lefkos Kyriacou and Michael Dumper)

from all these locations were attracted to the British system of government, which took a laissez-faire approach toward the practice of religion and local customs. Thus, in George Town a unique conjunction of different religious and ethnic groups formed under a secular authority that refrained from intervening in the practices of these religions, from whence we get the origins of the prevailing discourse on a "culture of accommodation."

In terms of the urban development of the city, George Town is very much in keeping with other British, French, and Dutch colonial cities.[10] Attracting the most attention is the quasi-grid layout of the downtown area leading outward from Fort Cornwallis and its green open space, known as the Padang, with government and municipal buildings located in view of each other. What Westerners may not notice so easily is how the evolving design of the city was also influenced by non–British factors. Chinese settlement areas, whether of Taoist, Confucian, or Buddhist persuasion, tended to be determined by chi and guided by the principles of feng shui, in which the orientation of buildings, windows, and doors maximized positive chi. In this way, many of the classic large Chinese houses in George Town face the sea. Similarly, although there were very few renowned holy sites during the British colonial days, ancestor worship was important to the Chinese community, and the location of graveyards and their accessibility were often more important than straight roads and tidy, functional urban divisions.[11] The Hindu science of architecture, or *vastu shastra*, has also played a part in organizing the layout of the Indian community's residences and institutions.[12]

Despite these auspicious beginnings, George Town began to struggle to maintain its economic position under the later period of British rule. Following the acquisition of Singapore from the sultan of the Malay state of Johor in 1824, the British began to favor it at the expense of George Town, and by the end of the nineteenth century Singapore eclipsed George Town both as a port and as a city. George Town also became notorious for its part in the (legal) opium trade, which provided more than half of its revenue but also attracted the activities of Chinese secret societies, ultimately leading to clashes between them and with the British authorities. After World War II and the ravages of the Japanese occupation, George Town's economic situation did not improve markedly. In the first place, the postwar Federation of Malaya, which was a federation of the Malay sultanates on the Malay Peninsula and paved the way for the creation of Malaysia in 1963, incorporated Sarawak, Sabah, and, crucially,

Singapore, George Town's main rival. This incorporation diluted the influence of Penang's politicians on the new nation's economic policies. In the second place, despite Singapore leaving the federation two years later in an acrimonious divorce, Penang's status in the federation remained anomalous: it was, in contrast to nearly all the other states making up Malaysia, a state without a hereditary Malay sultan (it had a governor instead), and it was also a state whose population was dominated by both Chinese politicians and Chinese businesspeople. As we shall see later, under the new constitution of Malaysia, which privileged the Malay community, Penang was therefore at a disadvantage in the competition over the allocation of the state's resources.[13] Before looking at the impact that these developments had on the way George Town developed and the religious conflicts that may have arisen from the late twentieth century to the current period, we need first to understand some of the complexity of the city's demographic makeup.

Demography

Soon after the establishment of British rule in George Town in the late eighteenth century, the embryonic city quickly grew to approximately 10,000 people, mostly traders, settlers, and itinerant workers. One thousand of them were employees of the East India Company. By the 1850s, the population of the island had grown to more than 40,000, mostly Indians and Malays but also approximately 9,000 Chinese.[14] It was not until after the opening of the tin mines on the peninsula in the latter part of the nineteenth century that George Town was transformed from an entrepôt port into a major exporter of raw materials. One consequence of this change was the rapid rise in the city's Chinese population, which eventually overtook all the other ethnic groups combined. By 1911, the island's population had grown to 278,000, of which 41 percent were Malay, 40 percent were Chinese, and 16.7 percent were Indian. But the population of George Town, approximately 100,000, was 63 percent Chinese, 17.5 percent Indian, and 15.6 percent Malay.[15] This rural–urban divide on Penang, in which Malays and Muslims dominated the rural areas and the Chinese dominated the urban areas, has persisted until this day and is a key dynamic that continues to run through the politics and the sectarian relations in the city. Today, as Francis Loh observes, Penang is both the most densely populated state in Malaysia and the most urbanized one.[16] The census in 2010 revealed that the population of 1.471 million people for the whole state (comprising Penang island and Seberang Perai, a strip of land opposite the island that was formerly known as Province Wellesley) was almost equally split between Chinese and Malays.[17] At the same time, the census figures show that the Chinese outnumber Malays in the administrative district, which includes George Town, by three to one. Indians account for roughly 10 percent of the population in the city and 5 percent of the population on the rest of the island.[18]

For the purposes of this study, two observations need to be made about these figures. As is evident from the different sources, tracking the growth of the city's population is problematic. The figure for the city, which is expanding and incorporating larger and larger areas, is often subsumed into the figures for the island as a whole. In addition, the figures in the later censuses need to be distinguished from the figures that also include the population for the state of Penang, which incorporates the population of Seberang Perai on the mainland. A subcategory of population figures that relate to the areas within the UNESCO World Heritage Site are also highly relevant to this study, but because they are for a specific geographical area, they are different from the other figures mentioned and do not clarify the demographic picture significantly.

The second observation is that the figures refer to ethnicity and not to religious affiliation, which is the focus of this study. It should be emphasized that these ethnic and religious distinctions are particularly unclear in the George Town context. Not only do different ethnic communities in George Town share the same religion, but also, conversely, each religious community can comprise a number of ethnic communities and so is divided internally. As a local George Town historian observed in conversation, "People in the city have multiple identities, and ethnicity is not monolithic." Thus, the Chinese community, largely united by a common geographical origin in that the vast majority hail from southern China, is nevertheless highly fragmented into different religions, clan groups, linguistic groups, socioeconomic classes, and political parties. Chinese Penangites can be variously Muslim, Buddhist, Taoist, Confucian, and Christian—with each of these groups also divided into sects and denominations. They also speak a variety of languages: Hokkien, Cantonese, Hainanese, and Hakka, although Hokkien has emerged as the dominant lingua franca among the Chinese. Similarly, irrespective of religious beliefs, the Chinese community is also divided through allegiances to the numerous *kongsi*s, or clan organizations, which in the early days of settlement in Penang provided protection, political representation, and welfare to their members.[19] Finally, many of the early Chinese settlers adopted Malay cultural practices and created a hybrid subculture mixing Chinese and Malay traditions, known as "Straits Chinese" or "Peranakan" (or sometimes *nonya*). Although usually keeping the religion and name of the Chinese male line, members of the Straits Chinese community live a life very similar to Malays in dress, language, arts, music, and cuisine.

The Indian community is similarly fragmented by religion, language, and geographical origin. Indians on Penang come from different parts of the subcontinent: they are Malabaris, Chettiars from up the eastern coastline to Bengal, Bengalis, Gujeratis, Sindhis, as wells as Parsees (descendants of Zoroastrians) and Sikhs from the Punjab. They speak Tamil, Malayalam, Bengali, Urdu, and Hindi. Some are Theravadan Buddhists, some Hindus, some Christians, and although many were part of the large Muslim community in India, there are also many who were Hindus but converted to Malay Islam after their arrival in Penang. Nevertheless, the majority of the Hindus in George Town are South Indian and Dravidian in origin. Some scholars have argued that this origin may be significant in that they are more inclined to monotheism than Hindus from northern India. They are in this way more able to have a constructive dialogue with Muslims— whether Indian Muslims or Malay Muslims—on the questions of faith.[20]

For its part, the Malay community may appear to be the most cohesive of the main ethnic groups in George Town. But, putting aside a growing rural–urban divide among Malays that has been exacerbated by the emerging Malay middle class, the Malay identity is still quite complex. It is not a homogenous identity because it includes immigrants not only from the adjacent state of Kedah but also from Sumatra, Thailand (Kedah was formerly part of Thailand), and farther afield. The indigenous inhabitants of the peninsula, known as the *orang asli*, are also regarded as Malay, which is an elision of an identity for purely bureaucratic reasons. In addition, the privileged position accorded to Muslims by the Malaysian Constitution has blurred the edges of Malay identity. For example, all Malays are by law Muslim. At the same time, all Muslims who are not Malay are given some of the same privileges in law as all Malays. Therefore, the legal status of Chinese Muslims, Indian Muslims, Thai Muslims, Burmese Muslims, and so on gives them some advantages that non-Muslims do not have. Although in practice Malay Muslims may still be given priority in a range of fields that I cover later in this chapter, this ambiguous legal status erodes some of the social and cultural distinctions between the communities and makes it difficult to talk about the George Town population in terms of the ethnic and religious categories we are accustomed to use in discussions of other populations.

Taken together, these observations illustrate how identifying reliable figures for the religious affiliations of the population of the city of George Town is difficult. The 2010 census does not offer a breakdown by religion for the same administrative district as it does a breakdown by ethnicity. It is possible, however, to make some intelligent guesses. Francis Loh, a leading political scientist in Southeast Asian studies, contends that 100 percent of the Malays living in George Town are Muslim; approximately 80 percent of the Chinese residents are Buddhist; and approximately 80 percent of the Indians are Hindu.[21] A Universiti Sains Malaysia Survey in 1993 corroborates these figures to some extent and puts the Muslim and Hindu populations of the city at approximately 10 percent each of the total population.[22] Given the fact that the Chinese population is triple the Malay population, then the 2010 census suggests that because most of the city's Chinese are Buddhists, George Town is a predominantly Buddhist city.[23]

The Challenge of the Federal State

The ousting of the Barisan Nasional (BN, National Front) coalition from its position of dominance in the federal government in 2018 was a seismic electoral event, almost a "regime change" given the longevity of the coalition's tenure in government.[24] The BN comprised the three establishment parties representing the main ethnicities in Malaysia—the United Malays National Organization (UMNO), the Malaysian Chinese Association (MCA), and the Malaysian Indian Congress (MIC). Over time, the dominant and largest party, UMNO, increasingly pursued a Malay nationalist agenda, maintaining the support of its junior partners through a quasi-consociational process of co-optation and allocation of government positions. Penang, with its strong tradition of independent political action at the state level, was often seen as an impediment to the BN dominance and suffered from the federal government's antipathy. The elections of 2018 interrupted this dynamic. On one hand, the change of government at the federal level in 2018 ensured the continuity and the consolidation of the role of the incumbent Democratic Action Party (DAP) and Pakatan Harapan (PH) political leaders at the Penang state level. On the other hand, the weakening of the power of UMNO—still a significant political actor on the island—may have introduced a new dynamic into the politics of George Town and disturbed the delicate equilibrium between the ethnic and religious communities that has been maintained for several decades. In essence, since 2018 the Chinese leadership may or may not feel less constrained in their dealings with the Malay leadership, who run the bureaucracy and the police service on the island, now that they have sympathizers in Kuala Lumpur running the federal government.

A key partner in this victorious coalition was the DAP, whose electoral base was in Penang state and who had controlled the Penang state legislature since 2008. In addition, the deputy leader of the PH is the charismatic and former political prisoner Anwar Ibrahim, a native of Penang whose wife held a seat in the Penang state legislature while he was incarcerated. As a result of his status as a native Penangite, he has widespread support across all the ethnic groups on the island.[25] This turn of events appears to augur well for advancing Penang's and George Town's influence in the federal politics of Malaysia. Many Penangites on the night and the day after the election were celebrating in the streets of George Town and pinching themselves with disbelief as their leaders were swept into office on a wave of euphoria. Out of a possible forty seats in the Penang State Legislative Assembly, thirty-seven were won by the PH coalition, with only two held the UMNO and one by the Malaysian Islamic Party (PAS)—former parties of the BN coalition. At the same time, although George Town's prospects appear to have improved since the general election, the long history of attempts by central-government institutions to marginalize the city both politically and economically brought with it an awareness of not setting expectations too high. By examining some of the key political and economic issues confronting the city prior to the election in 2018, this subsection attempts to demonstrate that George Town has to a large extent encapsulated the challenges of multiethnicity, multiculturalism, and multiconfessionalism that have been inherent in Malaysian society and politics since independence. Such an examination allows us to appreciate and assess the unrelenting balancing act that political and religious leaders in George Town and Penang have had to perform. To what extent have they successfully navigated between the interests of the different communities, and has this task been embedded into the governance of the city? Can we say that the culture of accommodation is hardwired into the decision-making processes rather than being merely an exercise in name branding?

Even before the Federation of Malaya was established in 1957, some Chinese businesspeople and Straits Chinese leaders were concerned that George Town would lose its advantages by being incorporated into a federal government dominated by the Malay sultanates of the mainland. They tried to mobilize support to secede from the federation but were strongly opposed by the British, who, by being seen to side with Malay sentiment on this issue, were able to retain the support of the Malays against the incipient Communist military uprising.[26] Although secession petered out as a specific political goal by the early 1960s, Penang-centric politics still prevailed on the island and continued to permeate the interactions between federal and state levels of government. One example of this tussle between local and national political elites was the controversy over the status of George Town and the responsibilities of its municipal council. The council, established during the British colonial era, has in turn been suspended, reinstated, merged, and extended over the period of Penang's history as part of Malaysia. In 2008, the main opposition to the BN coalition at that time, the Pakatan Rakyat coalition, succeeded in taking over the Penang state legislature. It was not until then that relations between the Penang Island Municipal Council, which had inherited the powers of the George Town Municipal Council, and the Penang State Legislature became more cooperative.[27]

Similarly, the controversy over the official designation of George Town as a city is also part of this state–federal government rivalry. For many years, the federal government claimed that George Town's status as a city had been revoked, in part, it is thought, to prevent George Town from eclipsing Kuala Lumpur as the leading city of Malaysia. For their part, George Town residents have vociferously contested the government's position, and its status as a city was finally confirmed in 2014.[28] Part of this tussle concerning the governance of the city is the way in which George Town grew significantly both in population size and geographical area. It expanded to the south and eventually incorporated the satellite town of Bayan Lepas, near the island's airport and near the second bridge to the mainland. In this way, it was transformed from a city to a conurbation. In fact, it became the second largest conurbation in Malaysia. Ambitious plans are in place for projecting the city-conurbation and its hinterland as a regional trading hub and manufacturing base.[29] I describe these plans in more detail in the next section. The main point I wish to make here is that this acquisition of responsibility required reforms in the political decision-making process on the island, which has led to an ongoing struggle between political factions at both state and federal levels for control over the governance structures. It is almost as if George Town, as a conurbation, is almost too big for Penang as a state. The city-conurbation governance structures have emerged as a kind of cuckoo in the nest displacing the other state structures. Thus, the position of the chief minister—that is, the executive officer appointed to that position by virtue of being leader of the largest party in the state's Legislative Assembly—has become pivotal and has accrued many of the functions and responsibilities that in many other cities would fall to the mayor.

What gives this development an "edge" is that despite there being a slight majority of Malays in the state of Penang, the fact that the Chinese population dominates the George Town urban area has led to a unique situation in Malaysia wherein its chief minister has been an ethnic Chinese since the foundation of the country. One result of this delicate balance between ethnicity and political power is that the Penang state government is very keen not to be portrayed as anti-Muslim and is therefore alert to opportunities to cater to the concerns of the Malay Muslim community. For example, the Penang state government has been accused of trying to buy the Malay vote by setting aside state land for a sharia school and a sharia-compliant hospital when other needs may be more pressing.

In sum, we can see that in George Town the business and political elite have historically been in opposition to the federal government. As a reflection of the dominant role played by the Chinese population in the city, this opposition is a source of tension between them and the Malay population, who feel that their position in both the city and the state of Penang is not equivalent to that of other Malay citizens of Malaysia and that they are to some extent marginalized by virtue of their geographical location. At the same time, as a result of this demographic balance, it seems to be also the case that governance structures and political practices have emerged in Penang and George Town that reflect a more independent, multiethnic, multicultural, and multiconfessional agenda and that are necessary to accommodate the different social and religious customs and practices there. These deeper structural frameworks permit the narrative of transformative integration to emerge as the dominant narrative in both city and state.

At this point, I need to mention an earlier watershed in the political development of Malaysia that had a profound impact on intercommunal relations: a bout of extreme violence known as the May 1969 Riots, which Johan Saravanamuttu regards as "undoubtedly the most traumatic event of Malaysia's political history to date."[30] The catalyst for the riot was a succession of parades by opposition (mostly Chinese) and government supporters (mostly Malay) following an election in which the governing parties saw their dominant position eroded. Fighting between rival demonstrators spread and became generalized, leaving nearly 200 dead, hundreds wounded, widespread damage and arson, and more than 6,000 residents of Kuala Lumpur displaced and homeless (90 percent of whom were Chinese). The violence threatened to spread throughout Malaysia, so martial law was declared, a curfew established, and police were seen patrolling the streets of the main towns and cities.

Once the situation was brought under control, the government identified the lack of Malays' participation in the economy, business life, and civil service as the main reason why their grievances had come to the fore in such a violent manner. As a consequence, it embarked upon its New Economic Policy, which, in essence, was a program of positive discrimination to ensure that the Malays had access to higher education, to the higher reaches of government employment, and to the boardrooms of all private companies. In order to identify Malays eligible for these positions, legislation was passed to enshrine the enhanced rights of what is known as the *bumiputera*—that is, Muslim Malays and indigenous people. Targets were set, and to some extent there was a degree of success in that a new Malay middle class emerged with both the wealth and the skills to challenge the Chinese monopoly of the private sector. At the same time, one consequence of this success was to legitimize and mainstream the Malay supremacist discourse that hitherto had been lurking around the edges of Malaysian politics. To contain the PAS, which was channeling this discourse, UMNO fluctuated between either trying to defuse it or to outflank it with increasingly sectarian pronouncements and legislation.

The Economy of the City

In turning specifically to the economy of the city and of the state of Penang as a whole, we can see a gradual decline of George Town relative to its neighbors and how attempts to reverse that decline have been hampered in part as a result of the federal government's policies. It is ironic that after the secession of Singapore from Malaysia in 1965, which removed George Town's main urban rival from the national scene, a new threat to George Town emerged in the form of Kuala Lumpur, the country's capital. George Town had hitherto been the main urban center of Malaysia, but huge government investment in Kuala Lumpur, as would be expected for a capital city, meant that Kuala Lumpur raced ahead in terms of infrastructure, incentives for external investment, and support for construction. By the 1990s, new and well-connected satellite towns formed on the outskirts of the city to house high-tech manufacturing and information-technology businesses, and the full range of government offices and institutions were constructed in Cyberjaya and Putrajaya. It is envisaged that a conurbation stretching down the Klang Valley from Kuala Lumpur to Port Klang will eventually comprise a population of more than 10 million people by 2020.[31] In contrast, George Town was deprived of its free-port status in 1969, which had significant impact on its economy.[32] Starved of government and foreign investment, George Town also saw the beginning of a brain drain to Kuala Lumpur, Singapore, and cities farther afield.

The emergence of Penang state as the main location of the political opposition to the BN federal government, particularly after the opposition captured the Penang State Legislative Assembly in 2008, did not ease the situation, and there was increasing evidence that the federal government was using the withdrawal of federal funds to punish its opponents.[33] As a result, it was left to local agency—that is, Penang state institutions—to try and reverse this decline. This attempt led, in turn, to greater tension between the political elite in George Town and the federal government, which controlled much of the policy-implementation and delivery mechanisms. For example, the issue of efficient and well-maintained drainage is critical in urban areas with high rainfall and a monsoon season. In Penang, the local authorities are responsible for most of the drains, but the large monsoon drains and rivers are under the control of the federal Department of Irrigation and Drainage. Disputes over responsibility and maintenance have led to poor coordination and, as a consequence, to an annual and destructive wave of floods and landslides on the island.[34] We should bear in mind how these tensions between state and federal authorities are tinged with an ethnic coloring: UMNO trying to neutralize the electoral threat posed by the PAS and its Malay nationalism by pursuing a more strident

Islamic agenda, and Penang, predominantly Chinese, trying to neutralize the UMNO strategy by promoting a more inclusive and secular approach to Malaysian politics.

Nevertheless, the Penang state government's efforts did bear some fruit. Penang's political leaders began to realize that they were sitting on several unexploited assets. In the first place, advances in aviation and telecommunications freed it from needing to compete over sea-based trade and allowed it to rise above the constraints of its geographical proximity to both Kuala Lumpur and Singapore and directly link up with the emerging markets in China and India. But it was also the people who gave it an advantage. Overseas investors and companies may have been initially attracted by the brochures full of pictures of coconut-tree-lined beaches and romantic vistas across the Straits of Malacca over tree tops from Penang Hill and its colorful street markets, but they also valued Penang's multiethnic culture, good education (relative to other parts of Malaysia), and widespread use of English. So Penang state embarked upon an ambitious plan to reposition itself as the "Silicon Valley of the East." It succeeded in attracting well-known manufacturers of electronics and precision tooling to build industrial estates to the south of George Town.[35] A state government initiative known as the Creative and Technology Accelerator Zone is trying to capitalize on the vibrant and culturally diverse environment to encourage start-ups to choose the city for their production and administrative wings.[36] Some figures from 2014 bear out this relative success: for example, although Penang state has only 6 percent of the population of Malaysia, it has secured approximately 12 percent of foreign direct investment, and 14 percent of the country's manufacturing takes place there.[37]

As a consequence of these kinds of initiatives, unemployment in the state is lower than in most of the other federation states and several percentage points lower than the national average. One feature of divided cities is the lack of economic interdependence between the different sectors of the population. The accepted view of the overall pattern of economic activity in George Town is that the Chinese community dominates the private sector, the Malay community dominates the public sector and government service, and the Indian community provides a recognizable proportion of the professional class (legal and medical). This pattern is currently undergoing a transformation in Penang with the emergence of both a Malay middle class and a highly mixed voluntary and civil society sector. While economic prosperity continues, and while the state is able to support significant government expenditure and recruitment, this economic stratification appears to be continuing. The crunch will come when those conditions do not prevail, and the absence of mutually supporting economic activities may lead to greater competition over resources and state allocations.

In this context, the absence of low-cost housing is a growing problem in George Town. In part, this absence is due to the fact that the property market is driven by commercial developers who are exploiting the island's attractiveness as a high-end retail, retirement, and tourist location at the expense of affordable housing for factory workers. The huge air-conditioned shopping malls, expensive condominiums, and exclusive gated communities lining the sandy coastline of the island or peeking out between the tall jungle trees cladding the lower reaches of Penang Hill do, undoubtedly, bring wealth to the island. The price of condominiums on Penang island and in George Town is two or three times the price of similar housing on the mainland.[38] Yet the distribution of this wealth is limited, and much of it is channeled back to Singapore, Hong Kong, Taiwan, Japan, or wherever the investment originated.

Part of the problem for the Penang state authorities is the pattern of land-ownership and the limited tools at its disposal to influence the land's use. A breakdown of property ownership in George Town is difficult. Penang state owns only 12 percent of the total land area of the state, most of which lies across the channel from George Town in Seberang Perai. Most commentators concur that in addition to the state itself, the major property owners are a few seriously rich Chinese families, the five Chinese *kongsis* (clan organizations, of which the Khoo Kongsi has the most extensive holdings), the Muslim *waqf*, and the Chettiar Indian families.[39] The lifting of rent controls and other tenancy protections has led to a wave of tenant evictions, which in turn has added pressure on the low-cost housing market.[40] Contributing to the challenges posed by the housing market has been the inscription in 2008 of downtown George Town onto the UNESCO World Heritage Site list. The UNESCO inscription has been a source of great pride for the people of the city. It revitalized the downtown area, upgraded workmanship and construction skills, attracted additional investment, and incentivized key stakeholders and community leaders to ensure that social, economic, and religious problems are addressed and resolved. But it also resulted in a 70 percent increase in rents; the influx of highly cosmopolitanized shops, cafes, and boutique hotels; and, as night follows day, the eviction of long-standing tenants around whom much of the

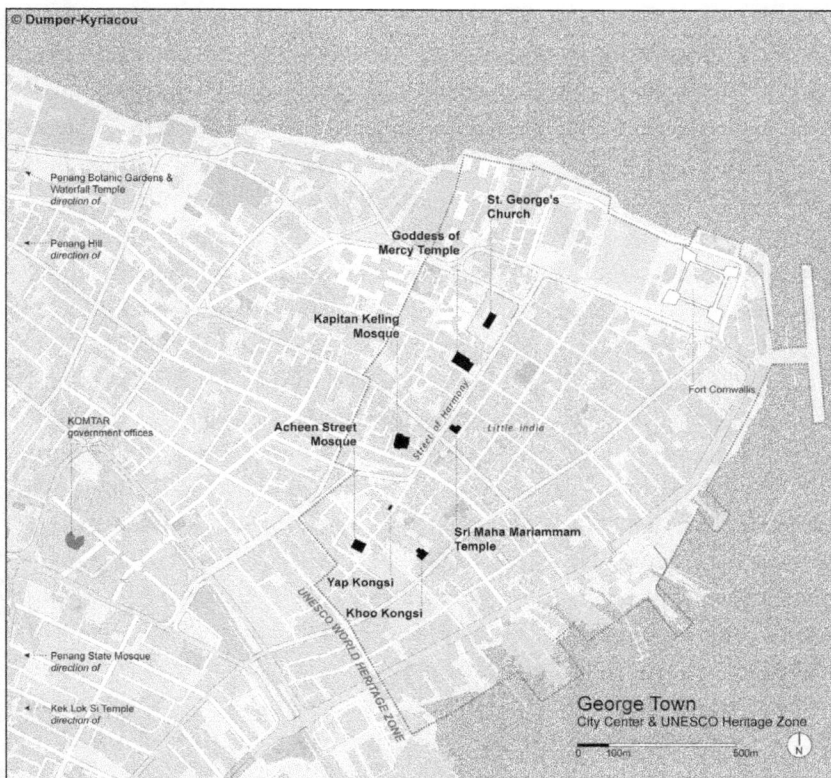

Map 5.2 George Town city center and UNESCO Heritage Zone. (Map by Lefkos Kyriacou and Michael Dumper)

traditional working practices and social relations of the downtown area revolved.[41] One effect has been the drastic reduction in population density: the Muslim population, both Indian and Malay, of central George Town has been reduced so much so that the Acheh Mosque (Malay) and the Kapitan Keling Mosque (Indian and Malay) hold Friday prayers on alternate weeks to ensure sufficient numbers of worshippers for the main midday service. Currently there is an acute realization that the gentrification of the heritage zone is not benefitting the poorer and more marginal residents.

Figures for a more precise breakdown of property ownership along ethnic and communal lines are not available, but there is considerable evidence to suggest that the real estate market is not ethnically driven. For example, there are no formal quotas for housing allocations. Unlike on the mainland, there is no land on the island reserved for the Malay community in accordance with the New Economic Policy positive-discrimination programs. Indeed, Malay-owned property in Balik Pulau, on the other side of the island from George Town, is being sold to non-Malays. In addition, predominantly Malay areas in the southern part of the city, such as Jelutong and Sungai Penang, have been increasingly transformed into high-rise housing for a mixed population. Similarly, a Khoo Kongsi development project of three hundred acres near Ayer Itam for more than 100,000 residents will also be a mixed-housing estate. At the same time, pockets of segregated housing do survive but usually on properties that have been historically connected to particular ethnic or religious communities. Malay Muslim *waqf* properties tend to have mostly Malays living in them, and properties owned by the Hindu Endowments Board are similarly tenanted mostly by Hindus.[42] But there is nothing like the extreme forms of residential segregation along ethnoreligious lines one finds in Jerusalem. Taken together, all this evidence suggests that difficulties over housing experienced by low-income George Town residents may be widespread but also that these difficulties are shared across the religious communities. However, although housing is not necessarily a cause of intercommunal tensions, the dissatisfaction and suffering experienced from housing difficulties can feed into other issues that have led to intercommunal tensions. James Anderson's research comparing conflicts in Belfast and Upper Silesia demonstrates that the lack of clear identity markers such as residential segregation is what precipitated extreme violence between communities. As Anderson emphasizes, it was because divisions were blurred or nonexistent in very "mixed" communities that extreme violence was deemed necessary by those wanting to create separate "German" and "Polish" communities in Upper Silesia.[43] This has not occurred in George Town.

The Culture of Accommodation

On the day after I left George Town in June 2017, a peaceful demonstration for interreligious communal harmony took place along Pitt Street in the center of the city. I have already mentioned Pitt Street as the thoroughfare along which or close to which some of the most religious sites in George Town can be found and which as a result has been branded the "Street of

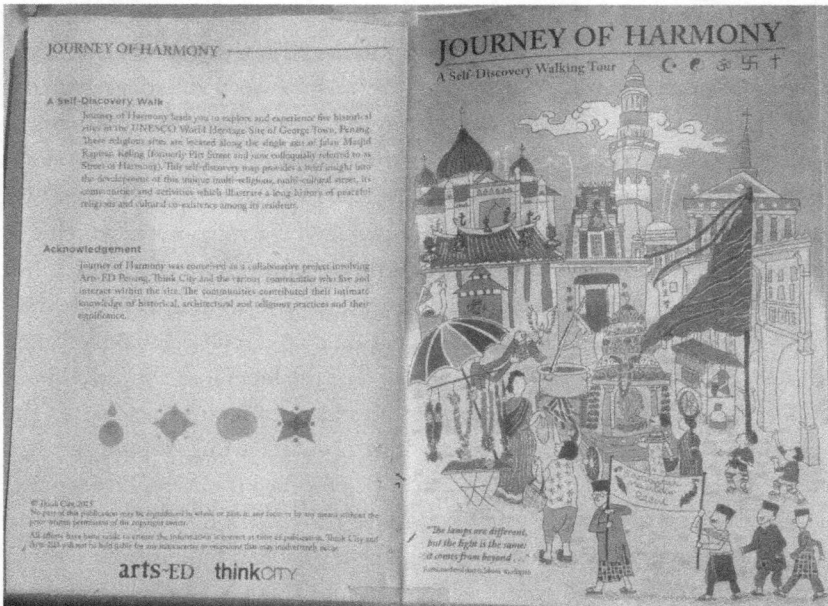

Figure 5.2 Leaflet for walking tour of the Street of Harmony, George Town, empha-sizing the common values of the different religious practices.

Harmony." As an affirmation of the culture of accommodation that prevails in George Town, the great and the good of George Town's religious com-munities took part in a walk along the street to visit the six main religious sites there in turn.[44] Starting with some prayers at St. George's Church at the northern end, they proceeded down the street and stopped at the Goddess of Mercy Temple, the Lord Ganesh shrine, the Sri Maha Mariammam Temple, the Kapitan Keling Mosque, and finally the Acheh Mosque. At each site, the participants joined in prayers, listened to the recital of some poetry, made offerings, conveyed expressions of goodwill, and were given some explanations of each institution's work. In front of the Gerak Budaya bookshop, a poem displayed outside in large print was read aloud. Entitled "The Great City of Harmony," it was written by the former president of India, the late A. P. J. Abdul Kalam, a Muslim, who had been inspired to write it in August 2008 after he had been invited by George Town com-munity leaders to walk down the street. At the Acheh Mosque, all the participants were invited to join in the *buka puasa*, or breaking of the Rama-dan fast (*'iftar* in Arabic).[45]

The Street of Harmony walk has emerged as an annual event and as a result has become gradually more formulaic and less resonant as an affirmation of interreligious cooperation, but in June 2017 it had a particular message to convey. In the weeks leading up to the event, increasing religious tensions had been stoked in part by radical Islamic youth organizations vociferously promoting a Malay Muslim agenda but also in part by a general climate of Islamization encouraged by the government, which was giving non-Muslim and non-Malay groups reasons to be concerned. For example, people recounted fearfully the intimidating and aggressive behavior of Perkasa, an Islamic youth organization associated with UMNO, and the apparent license to act with impunity that the federal and mostly Malay police force had given to it. In Penang, this issue came to a head when the chief minister of Penang State at the time, Lim Guan Eng, sought to reach out to Malays and Muslims at Ramadan by joining a traditional *buka puasa*. Radical Islamic groups protested against his participation as a non-Muslim, and at one demonstration a state government official attempting to remonstrate with the demonstrators was jostled and slapped before receiving police protection.[46]

In late May and June 2017, feelings in the city began to run high, and even as a visitor I became aware of a current of anxiety running through some of the informal conversations I was having. I found myself witness to some of the preliminary discussions regarding the organization of the Street of Harmony walk, so I was particularly disappointed when my travel budget ran out, and I was obliged to return to the United Kingdom before it could take place. But a number of key points in these discussions struck me.

First, there was a clear anxiety that the situation could get out of hand, that inflammatory language could lead to more violent displays of identity markers, and that it was correspondingly unclear to the organizers of the walk how strong the forces promoting religious exclusivity were. To my interlocutors, those voicing a "Malay Muslim First" nationalism and religiosity were not merely mavericks but had behind them an enthusiastic and volatile following as well. But how much support these Malay nationalists had from UMNO and from officials in the federal bureaucracy was at that time unknown. During some of these meetings, seated high up in the state government offices in the KOMTAR Tower, with its unparalleled views across the city and across the channel to Seberang Perai, I received the impression through these conversations that the uneasy equilibrium between the religious and ethnic communities in the city was indeed uneasy, verging on the fragile, much more so than I had originally thought.

Second, the proposed walk along the Street of Harmony was important. It was not just a branding exercise wheeled out to create a good atmosphere for the tourists. It was a serious endeavor to nip sectarianism in the bud and to forcefully frame the discourse of intercommunal relations in the city. The organizers were determined to prevent the "thugs" from taking over the street and from demolishing the good relations between the communities that had been fostered over the decades since the riots in 1969. In their minds, not taking this walk or some similar action would have serious consequences. It would mean ceding the public space to those with a different vision of a multiethnic and multiconfessional Penang and would be construed by the fundamentalist groups as a capitulation to their exclusivist position.

Finally, I could also observe from these meetings how, irrespective of the formal institutions and processes that the federal government has established for dialogue and reconciliation, it was the personal contacts and relationships that "saved the day." Despite the occasional muttered asides of exasperation with regard to an individual's foibles or perceived egotism, there was a degree of trust and respect among the people concerned that impressed me. These people had worked with each other on different occasions in the past and were honest about what they could achieve and the extent to which they could deliver their constituencies (and congregations). In one meeting held in a small boutique hotel lounge off Chulia Street, the warm heavy air of the long Ramadan afternoon moving only very grudgingly through the exertions of a ceiling fan, I sat with two Muslim leaders engaged in the organization of the walk. They were of quite contrasting persuasions and backgrounds but talked frankly with each other about what would work, what would not, who would need a particularly sensitive approach, and which group would require what level of reassurance. It was a master class in complex community activism by people who could draw on a deep well of experience. It also became clear to me that as important as the walk was, the preparation beforehand was equally important in reaffirming the links between key individuals and between their supporters. From these preparatory meetings, I could see that, yes, the day of the walk was important for conveying a critical public message, but equally crucial were the repair, consolidation, and reinvigoration of the bonds between the religious communities behind the scenes in the days beforehand.

With these impressions and reflections foremost, we can turn to examine more closely some of the religious disputes and conflicts that have arisen in George Town. But before we do so, we also need to look at the broader national context. The rest of this section offers a brief overview of the constitutional role of Islam in Malaysia in which I highlight some of the main issues that are confronting Malaysians in the religious sphere. While bearing in mind that Penang state and George Town are to some extent protected from the full force of the Malaysian government privileging of Islam, the national parameters have set both the legal framework and the popular discourse around the practice of religion.

As discussed earlier in this chapter, ethnic and religious categories and definitions in Malaysia overlap. This overlap causes a great deal of debate as to whether the distinguishing feature of a dispute is a religious one or an ethnic one. Anecdotally, at least in Penang, ethnicity appears to be paramount, with race defining daily conversation. For example, if there is a car accident, one of the first questions to be asked is which race the driver is. Yet at the same time it has to be reiterated that in the Malaysian Constitution religion and ethnicity are bundled together, particularly with reference to the Malay Muslim community. Although the Constitution declares support for the freedom of all citizens to practice their religion, it also declares Islam the religion of the federation (Article 3), placing it at the center of national life and other religions at the margin.[47] The federal government also administers a parallel legal system, with sharia courts being given jurisdiction over certain areas concerning Muslims, causing some confusion as to whether a non-Malay involved in a dispute with a Malay is subject to the sharia courts.

Two further important clauses privilege the Malay Muslim community above other ethnic and religious communities. First, Article 160 of the Constitution defines a Malay as "a Malaysian citizen born to a Malaysian citizen who professes the religion of Islam, habitually speaks the Malay language and conforms to Malay custom." Thus, if you speak like a Malay, live like a Malay, *and* are a Muslim, then you are a Malay as defined by the Constitution, even if you are, say, Indian by ethnicity. As Gwynn Jenkins observes, "Thus, there are two definitions of Malays—the constitutional definition and the 'ethnic' definition—and they are not necessarily the same. As a result, there are various 'Malay' cultural identities, influenced by both politics and ethnic origins."[48] The actual privileging of the Malay as Muslim takes place when this definition is added to the second important clause in the Constitution: under Article 153, Malays so defined under Article 160 are accorded *bumiputera* status, an official legal status that gives them a designated "special position" in the economic and political life of the country. *Bumiputera*s have access to reserved positions in the federal government service, to tertiary-education and university scholarships, and to business licenses. As we saw earlier, the New Economic Policy introduced by the federal government in 1970 set a target for the private sector to comprise 30 percent Malay employees. In the civil service, the target has been even higher. Since independence, civil service admissions for Malays have been increased until the current figure is estimated to be approximately 90 percent! Carolina Lopez sums up the situation baldly: "The existing legal regime places *bumiputera*—specifically Malays—as the default 'race,' creating a juxtaposition of 'us' and 'other' in which non-Malay Malaysian citizens constitute 'others.' Since Malays are constitutionally defined as Muslims, Islam becomes the default religion, with all other faith traditions juxtaposed as 'others.' "[49] It should also be noted that Malaysian citizens also have opportunities to "game" these definitions. For example, it is often observed rather acidly that the South Indian Malay Muslims are happy to be Indian in Little India (an area of downtown George Town) but will emphasize their Malay-ness when they visit the Penang state government offices in the KOMTAR Tower.

This privileging of the status of Malay Muslims occurs in several other fields: marriage laws, for example, state that a non-Muslim who marries a Malay has to convert to Islam for the marriage to be recognized; in laws regarding donations to charitable organizations, donors to Muslim religious organizations receive more tax relief than donors to non-Muslim organizations. Precedent is also given to sharia law in some cases, and in some states non-Muslims have no legal standing in sharia law. Successive federal governments have taken actions that, although not expressly supported by the Constitution, are nevertheless carried out as part of Malay Muslim dominance of the federation's institutions. For example, the government has restricted proselytization by non-Muslim religious groups, restricted the distribution of religious literature, prosecuted those critical of the government's policies on religion, and committed Muslims from non-Sunni sects to rehabilitation centers to ensure they adopt the government version of Islam. It also maintains an Islamic religious-enforcement division whose officers are authorized to raid private establishments suspected of violating Islamic codes on alcohol consumption, attire, and *khalwat* (the close proximity of a Muslim to a nonfamily member of the opposite sex). An egregious example of government intervention in proselytization was the banning of the distribution of the Malay-language translation of the Bible, a book that has been in existence since even before the British colonial period.[50] After independence, it was perhaps understandable that the new government would push back against both the powerful religion of its colonial past and, perhaps again, against the media-savvy missionary zeal of contemporary Christian evangelists. But more recent actions against the use of the name "Allah" in Christian literature written for Malay-speaking Christians in Sarawak and Sabah (known as the "Kalima Allah controversy") are less explicable.

In this context, it is worth remembering that non-Muslims constitute nearly 40 percent of the population of Malaysia. Furthermore, the distribution of Malays and non-Malays across the country is not even. In the eastern coast states of Kelantan and Terengganu, for example, the population is overwhelmingly Malay Muslim, particularly in the rural areas. In the states of Sabah and Sarawak, Christians predominate in both urban and rural areas. As noted earlier, in Penang state the split between Malay and non-Malay is about fifty–fifty, but in George Town non-Malays predominate. What this means is some areas of Malaysia, including George Town, have a population whose ethnicity and religion are officially marginalized if not discriminated against even though they constitute a majority. Non-Malay Malaysians, it is said, are tired of being regarded, sixty years after independence, as immigrants still. In addition, a new generation is emerging who no longer view such ethnic differences as making any sense. The fact that these restrictive definitions have not produced more tensions and more open conflict is quite remarkable and needs accounting for.

In the years preceding the general elections of 2018, UMNO, in coalition with PAS, ratcheted up the assertion of Islam as the dominant religion. Controversially, in an attempt to prevent its being outflanked by more radical Malay parties, it began to prepare legislation that would support the wish by Malay-controlled states to implement the Islamic penal code, or *hudud*.[51] Similarly, in 2013 the government-controlled judiciary reignited the issue concerning the use of the name "Allah" by non-Malays by reinstating a ban and arresting the editor of the Malaysian paper the *Catholic Herald*. This arrest was followed by raids on the Bible Society of Malaysia in 2014.[52] In this context, the rise of the Islamic youth organization Perkasa has been the cause of concern to many NGOs and human rights groups. Claiming to have approximately 420,000 members, Perkasa, meaning "Mighty Native Organization," is a right-wing "ultra Malay splinter group for Malay supremacy [*ketuanan*] whose symbol, tellingly, is a *keris* [Malay sword]."[53] It is also associated closely with UMNO, although not directly under UMNO, and has used violence to intimidate non-Malays, non-Muslims, and liberals, with a degree of impunity from prosecution that suggests tacit government support.[54] Some Perkasa activity is fueled by, on the one hand, the government's commitment to providing subsidized tertiary education for Malay students but, on the other hand, by the government's failure to provide government employment for all the Malay graduates coming onto the labor market. The result is a growing pool of young Malays who feel both entitled and let down by the government and are at the same time jobless.

Not all sectarian actions in Malaysia have been government initiated or directed solely against the Christian community. In the midst of the increasingly strident Malay nationalist tone coursing through the electoral politics before the elections in 2018, a conservative Islamic preacher, Zamihan Mat Zin, linked to the federal government's Department of Islamic Development and president of one of the largest Islamic NGOs in Malaysia, called for the segregation of laundrettes. As summarized by the human rights NGO Aliran, the reasons he gave are that "the Chinese apparently do not wash themselves after defecating, and are accordingly, almost naturally, dirty. Hence if Muslim clothes were washed in the same machines with non-Muslim ones, presto, the Muslims would get contaminated."[55] Although the government's silence in response was deafening, the demand went a step too far for the conservative but more moderate Malay Muslim sultans of the peninsular states, who intervened to curtail the preacher's activities.

Similarly, Hindus in Malaysia believe they are even more victimized and vulnerable to Muslim Malay dominance than other religious groups. They have neither the domestic commercial clout that Chinese Buddhist or Taoist groups have nor the active and powerful diasporic connections that the various Christian denominations can turn to, such as the Vatican, the World Council of Churches, and U.S. evangelical organizations. In 2001, violence broke out between Malaysian Hindus and Malays in Petaling Jaya, Selangor. Known as the "Kampong Medan Incident," this riot was triggered when preparations for a Muslim wedding ceremony apparently got in the way of preparations for a Hindu procession, and it led to at least six deaths and more than forty wounded.[56] Hindu activists also point to the widespread demolition of Hindu temples by the government on the grounds that the temples were unlicensed and inappropriately situated.[57] In 2006 alone, the popular temples Sri Siva Balamuniswara in Sepatak and Sri Kumaravel in Kampong Medan as well as two Muniswarar temples in Selangor and Negeri Sembilan were demolished.[58] As a result, the Hindu Rights Action Force was established and became successful in mobilizing working-class Hindus. Through large demonstrations, legal petitions, lobbying of external governments (the United Kingdom and India in particular), the use of media in print and online, the Hindu Rights Action Force has been able both to make advances in the protection of Hindus' religious practices and holy sites in Malaysia and to challenge their marginalized socioeconomic position.

Religious Disputes and Conflicts in George Town

In turning to George Town, we can see how, given this national context of privileging Malay Muslim interests, the potential for religious conflict in George Town is significant. In the first place, there is the sheer diversity of religious communities in the city, and the physical fact of their religious sites lying adjacent to each other could lead to conflicts over access and over religious festivities that coincide temporally and collide spatially. Second, there is a demographic split in the city in which no single ethnic and religious community is clearly dominant. Although in some respects there is a kind of balance of power that may prevent outrageous displays of sectarian domination, at the same time this "balance" is more like an unstable equilibrium between the Chinese and Malay communities. In addition, as Hayden has argued and as noted earlier, the historic evidence suggests that the lack of clear dominance by one community leads equal or subordinate communities to jockey for some kind of advantage over the others. Third, we have also seen in the cases presented in this book and discussed in the introduction how there is also a tendency for ethnic conflicts to spill over into religious conflicts, which are in turn more intractable and long term. The overlapping and multiple identities that are a feature in the life of George Town residents make this "spillover" even more likely to take place. Finally, as discussed earlier in this chapter, George Town's position as a trading city and geographically at the periphery of several cultural basins and archipelagos—Malay, Indian, Chinese, Thai, Arab, and Indochinese—is part of both its attractive cosmopolitanism and its permeability to outside influences. There is not enough space in this chapter to examine in more detail some contemporary influences—such as the impact of Islamic radicalism from the Middle East and the soft power of the Chinese state through its Belt and Road Initiative. Nevertheless, we should still note that, certainly, in very recent years the defeat and dispersal of the so-called Islamic State militants in the Middle East may have provided some impetus to the existing radicalism already present in some sections of the Malay Muslim community in George Town.

Despite all of these factors adding up to the likelihood of a propensity for conflict over religious issues, the fact remains that religious tension is minimal in George Town and has been for some time. Even during the Malay–Chinese riots in Kuala Lumpur in 1969, although George Town had some outbreaks of violence and experienced a great deal of fear, relative to the blood-letting in Kuala Lumpur, George Town remained peaceful. In the next section, I examine a number of points of tension in George Town that can be seen as primarily religious in nature, although class and ethnic issues also play an important part. The first involves a number of minor and general issues that I have drawn from discussions and personal observations. They constitute residents' "everyday life," which is often overlooked in favor of violent confrontations. They also provide examples of the "balance of power" between the different groups and the "probing sorties" that can characterize the uneasy equilibrium between groups, factions, and communities. I also explore the contention that a shared love of food in George Town is an important unifying dynamic, particularly in light of the various food prohibitions that exist in religious practice. A third point is what has become known as the "Kampong Rawa Temple-Mosque Incident," which in 1998 led to violence between Tamil Hindus and Malay Muslims. Then, in order to understand better a religious conflict in George Town that is not obviously ethnically based, I look at an intracommunal dispute between different Hindu groups over precedence at the festival of Thaipusam.

Everyday Life and Religion: Collisions and Sharings

When collating examples of how religious issues affect people's everyday lives in George Town, it is possible to group them around three main topics. The first topic concerns how the privileging of Malay Muslims in the Constitution plays out in George Town. For example, there is resentment of the degree to which mosques are often used as a platform to propagandize the federal government's message, with sermons expressing support for government policies and designating political parties, such as the DAP, as anti-Islam.[59] Equally, there is a perception that the five-times daily Islamic *azan*, call to prayer, is allowed to be excessively amplified and can be disruptive when it occurs during the ritual practices of other religious communities. It is also seen as discriminatory that proposals to build non-Muslim religious buildings that may exceed the height of the nearby mosques are not approved or are approved only if their heights are shortened. Increasingly it has become the case that when government officials visit, even in George Town, non-Muslims are expected to dress in certain ways, to cover their heads, and to refrain from shaking hands with women or to acquiesce when their hands are not shaken in greeting. Some Christians also observe that the legal requirement that children from marriages in which one of the couple is a Muslim be registered as a Muslim is patently inconsistent and hard to defend when it applies only to states in West Malaysia and not to Sabah and Sarawak, where there are many non-Muslim Malays. Many non-Malays speak of the fear of a gradual "Arabization" of Malaysian public life.

On the plus side, the federal Department of Islamic Development, which has become increasingly powerful on the Malay Peninsula, is less assertive in Penang state and George Town. This may be due to the balance of the population there, which, as we have seen, is mostly Buddhist, at least in the city, but it has also resulted in a greater tolerance and openness towards non-Sunni Islamic sects. For example, George Town still has a small Ahmadiyya community, whom the orthodox Islamic clergy regards as heretic, and although no openly professing Shi'a are known to be resident in George Town, the Shi'a cemetery remains and is undefaced, in contrast to Shi'a cemeteries on the peninsula.

The second topic that seems to arise frequently is that of different religions' festivities coinciding with each other or affecting the public urban space in ways that curtail other religious activities. To a degree, this issue is hardly surprising in a city where there are twenty-two annual public holidays, most of which are religious. That is almost one festival per fortnight! Such a proliferation of holidays interrupts and causes inconvenience to many (mostly Chinese) businesses but also to those who wish to have access to government and state services. During some festivals, roads are blocked to allow marquees to be erected on the streets when required for ceremonies or to allow processions to proceed between sites. Irrespective of the religious community organizing a festival, the festival includes the presence of police, who are in general Malay Muslim, which at times can cause some animosity. During the annual Hungry Ghost Festival held at the Temple of Mercy on Pitt Street, many of the surrounding roads are cut off, preventing vehicle access to offices, shops, and religious sites. Worshippers at St. George's Church, for example, who come from quite a wide area of George Town, are not able to drive into the church grounds during the course of the festival. Nevertheless, members of St. George's have learned to accept this inconvenience.

At the same time, many of the festivals are also partially a shared event. The Hindu Thaipusam festival in George Town has become not only a huge tourist event but also a very multicultural affair. The festival centerpiece is a large and flamboyant procession. Along the route, Chinese of many faiths watch, ritually smash coconuts before the chariot carrying Lord Murugan, the son of Shiva and Parvati, offer flowers and other token gifts, and spray the hot tarmac with water to cool the bare feet of those in the procession passing by.[60] Proceedings are coordinated with Malay Muslim police, and most of the workers cleaning up are likely to be Malay Muslim. This sharing, or perhaps a more neutral term would be *witnessing of*, religious festivities extends to other areas of George Town as well. In the shadow of Fort Cornwallis, close to the Victoria Memorial Clock Tower where Lebuh Light and Beach Street meet, lies a small but well-maintained Hindu shrine, the Sri Muniswarar Temple. It also doubles up as a Taoist shrine known as the Temple of Mercy (not the same Temple of Mercy located on Pitt Street), with statues and icons of both traditions sitting peacefully, contemplating each other. The site is maintained by Hindu devotees but receives support from a range of donors, including Chinese businessmen, a vineyard, and even a state government minister.[61] Another shared practice of religious faith is a tradition in which Chinese take their new cars to the Nattukotai Chettiar Temple near the Penang Botanical Gardens to be blessed by Hindu temple priests.

A Shared Love of Food

The preparation and consumption of food is among the most important markers of identity and purveyors of cultural traditions. You can walk through many ethnically diverse cities and tell by the smells seeping out of the kitchens and wafting down the street what the predominant culture is in that neighborhood. Ginger, garlic, cumin, coriander are giveaways of different cuisines generally. In George Town, in addition to these scents there is the particularly pungent reek of the ubiquitous *belachan* (rotting fish paste) and the pole-axing, suffocating pong of the durian fruit (thankfully for only a few weeks a year!).[62] Nevertheless, George Town celebrates its multiethnic cuisine. It has become world famous for its street food and hawker fare, with many promotional campaigns, books, and documentaries on the city making you salivate with hunger and desire. What makes the city quite unique is not only the diversity and quality of the food available but also the juxtaposition of cuisines. It is quite common to have a meal of Malay satay, Chinese noodles, and Indian sweets. This is despite the different religious prohibitions around beef, pork, shellfish and regarding the preparation or consumption of meat in general, which the residents of the city appear to navigate with aplomb. There is also a constantly evolving hybridity that reflects the city's cultural diversity without losing each dish's historical origins. One particular cuisine, the *nonya*, a mix of Malay and Straits Chinese, is not unique to Penang but is arguably one of its most celebrated.

The George Town middle classes commonly perceive the shared love of food and of each other's food as an important element in the glue that holds the city together. Sharing meals at home across the ethnic and religious divide may not be so common, but the prevalence of public eating malls—where hawkers representing the whole gamut of Asian cuisines line up their colorful stalls on the outer edges and seats and tables are provided for customers in the center—are very popular venues for both the simple daily lunch or the night out with family or friends. The ethnic mix in these food halls is a sight to behold, and the evident enjoyment being derived from the bowls in front of the punters even more so. Witnessing such scenes, one is tempted to make a Durkheimian ethnographic observation that the very sharing of meals in public in this way is in essence a religious activity.

However, even if one were to put to the side such an observation on the grounds that it is the *space* that is actually being shared and not the food itself, there is nevertheless a religious aspect to this collective feasting that is relevant to this book. In many public events at which there are receptions with a buffet, the range of different cultural traditions on offer is very evident and quite remarkable. During my visit in June 2017, I attended both a Ramadan *'iftar* presided over by the governor of Penang state and a post–Holy Communion parish breakfast at St. George's Church and was struck by the visual display of religious and cultural diversity on people's plates: sticky sweet rice *kueh*s sitting alongside samosas, curry puffs, *tauhu goreng*, and *pisang goreng*, while the quintessentially Malaysian dish *nasi lemak* and the Indian Muslim roadside snack *moma* were eaten by all and sundry, rich and poor.[63]

Such culinary eclecticism should not be overstated, though, because some red lines are drawn. Most Muslims, either Indian or Malay, will not patronize Chinese restaurants because most are not halal and cook pork, possibly contaminating all the other food in the kitchen. In fact, a prevailing view is that social interaction around food has become much more complex in recent years. Inviting a Malay colleague for a meal at a restaurant, for example, is more difficult than in the past. There had always been an understanding by non–Muslims on the avoidance of pork, but in recent years simply not ordering pork when sharing a meal is not enough; the restaurant should also be certified halal. Inviting a Malay friend to one's home is fraught with the possibility of faux pas because halal regulations require separate cooking utensils, crockery, and cutlery be used in the preparation and serving of food to Muslims. In this way, food as a social glue that transcends religious boundaries in George Town may not be as reliable a prop as it once was.

My own observations bear this out to some extent. One evening I walked from my hotel in Love Lane to the Medan Renong Satay food hall close to the Padang and beside the seashore. It was still Ramadan, and I rolled in about an hour before dusk to watch the sunset over the channel and to engage in my favorite pastime of people watching over a cold Tiger beer. The clientele was the usual Penangite mix of Malay, Chinese, and Indian families, with a few scattered pockets of Western tourists. The atmosphere was friendly, immensely busy, bustling, and noisy. Most people were busy ordering and tucking into their food, but I noticed quite a few tables where Indian and Malay Muslims were seated with their plates of food and drinks untouched. They were chatting away like everyone else, but as the light faded, a sense of expectancy grew, and their conversations tailed off. The food hall gradually began to get quieter. The music that had been pumping out over the PA system was turned down and then off. Tables with non-Muslims began to feel slightly self-conscious, making less noise with their chopsticks and cutlery, not quite falling silent but speaking a little more quietly, glancing in the direction of the Muslim tables, and refraining from going back and forth to the hawker stalls to get seconds.

Then, as the last ray of sunlight reflecting off the windows across the straits in Butterworth suddenly blinked off, the *azan* tunefully rose out from a radio that had been placed deliberately upon a high shelf. There was a burst of activity as the Muslims pulled their plates toward themselves and gave full rein to assuaging their hunger. Simultaneously, everyone else seemed to breathe out and to renew their chatting and tucking in with even greater vigor and noise. Soon the cacophony of sounds returned to its previous high levels. Food was being enjoyed. People were having fun. All was well. Observing this public breaking of the fast on a couple of other occasions in George Town, I found it quite hard to interpret. I would not say that I was witnessing an unambiguous sign of respect on the part of the non-Muslims for the breaking of the Muslim fast. "Antagonistic tolerance" (pace Hayden) would be too strong a phrase to describe it. They were expressing more a kind of tacit and collective deference, almost akin to when one feels obliged to stand up during the playing of another country's national anthem. There was an accommodation, for sure, and it was not a grudging one, but at the same time it did not seem to me to be strong evidence of social glue at work. Perhaps in the context of an "everyday" occurrence not much more should be expected. But what can be celebrated and welcomed unambiguously was the lack of intrusion into other people's lives and the absence of friction displayed.

The Kampong Rawa Temple-Mosque Incident, 1998

Religious tensions have occurred in the city, though, and this can be clearly illustrated by the Kampong Rawa Temple-Mosque Incident. Interethnic and interreligious violent conflicts in George Town are not unprecedented. As early as 1867, competition over the control over spices, opium, and prostitution between two Chinese *kongsi*s, each with different Malay allies (the so-called Red Flag and White Flag societies), led to violence and what became known as the Penang Riots.[64] Following independence, a series of conflicts flared up into riots—the Chingay riots in 1957, the Hartal riots in 1967, the Kuala Lumpur riots on May 13, 1969—which spilled over into and affected George Town.[65] The Kampong Rawa Incident of 1998 was not as widespread or destabilizing as the riots in 1969, but by all accounts the frightening experience of those earlier riots led to a great deal of fear and anxiety that the incident might escalate into a riot in the same way.[66]

Kampong Rawa is a low-lying suburb just south of the Penang River on the outskirts of George Town and susceptible to flooding. It is mainly a working-class area and made up mostly of Indian Muslims and Indian Hindus living cheek by jowl. The initial tension between Muslims and Hindus pitted Tamil-speaking Hindus and Tamil-speaking Indian Muslims residents against each other, but it later spread to include Malays and Indians from outside the area.[67] Both communities had their separate places of worship, and there had been little evidence of tensions between them up to this point. In the mid-1990s, the situation changed, which led to nearly two weeks of intercommunal fighting, casualties, incarcerations, and tensions that spilled over into the rest of the city and threatened to trigger a wider conflict like the riots of May 1969. The changed situation has been attributed in part to events not connected to Kampong Rawa. For example, the destruction of the Babri Masjid in Ayodhya, India, in 1992 and the Muslim–Hindu conflicts that surrounded it affected both Indian Muslim and Indian Hindu youths in George Town.[68] However, more internal and domestic reasons for the change have also been identified: Hindus' perceptions of government discrimination against them, the high unemployment rate among Hindus in George Town, and the resentment the Hindus felt with regard to the benefits accruing to their neighbors, Indian Muslims, who were eligible for the advantageous *bumiputera* status following Malaysian independence. In addition, as we also saw earlier, the government had carried out a wave of demolitions of Hindu temples, ostensibly on the grounds that they were illegal or breached building regulations or were inappropriately sited, but the working-class Hindus perceived the demolitions as direct attacks on their Hindu religion and South Indian culture. As Francis Loh observes,

Due to difficulties in acquiring Malaysian citizenship, a fair proportion of these Indian permanent residents in Malaysia remain Indian nationals. This group of transient Penang Indians, and indeed, the majority of Indians in Penang (and in Malaysia in general), are working-class and face various types of insecurity related to their employment, housing, educational opportunities for their children etc. In such an environment, frustrations have grown and tensions developed between Indian Hindus and Indian Muslims.[69]

Thus, even before we examine the particular circumstances inside the Kampong Rawa neighborhood that triggered the fighting, we can see there was a wider context of structural inequalities and dissatisfaction with the existing forms of representation and allocation of resources.

As Loh has pointed out, the official determination that the incident occurred as a result of the close proximity of the mosque and the temple in Kampong Rawa does not, on its own, cut much ice. Pitt Street in central George Town was already a testimony to the fact that proximity of religious sites was not a cause of sectarian tensions, even before it was rebranded as the Street of Harmony.[70] It is true that in Kampong Rawa the Sri Raja Mathiraiveeran Temple and the Masjid Kampong Rawa were only approximately thirty meters apart. However, the government-funded construction in 1996 of a new and larger mosque on the site of the old one fed into resentments regarding government discrimination against Hindus. The following year, the temple, which was in reality only a little bigger than a shrine, was extended, which brought it even closer to the enlarged mosque. In this way, proximity did begin to emerge as an issue when religious practices began to collide in ways they had not before, and the stage was set for a confrontation.

The incident can be divided into four main phases. The first phase began when mosque worshippers objected to the temple bells ringing during the course of the Muslim Friday prayers. By all accounts, the temple guardians assured the mosque guardians that this would not happen again. When the bells were rung during the next Friday prayers on March 20, 1998, it was seen as a deliberate provocation. Approximately 250 Muslim youths marched over to the temple to protest. This is an unusually large number of young people for a small local mosque, and their action suggests, rather than spontaneous response, both the degree of animosity that had been building up prior to March 20 and some degree of planning and preparation. Insults and stones were thrown, and at one point when it looked as if the Muslim youths were about to break into the temple, local police intervened to stop them. With backup by the riot police, the police cordoned off the temple and made ninety-four arrests, mostly, it should be noted, Indian Muslims, probably quite local to the area.[71] There were some injuries but no fatalities. Although the physical violence had been temporarily and effectively contained, this did not prevent the rumor mill from swinging into action, and George Town became awash with stories of destruction, death, and high drama. Working hard to resolve the issue before it flared up again at the next Friday's Muslim midday prayers, the chief minister of Penang and other political representatives persuaded the temple guardians that a relocated temple would regularize its status, enable them to construct a larger building, and allow the Hindus to practice their rituals undisturbed. With assurances that they would be able to reenter the current temple to de-consecrate it and remove statues and icons, the guardians agreed to the relocation and said that it would be carried out the day before the next Friday prayers, on Thursday, March 26.

The second phase began when the temple guardians were prevented from entering the temple to prepare for the relocation. This resulted in more than three hundred Hindus carrying out a protest outside the KOM-TAR Tower offices of the state government in the center of the city and closing down the streets in the vicinity, causing traffic jams, and igniting the rumor mill again. Although this hiccup in the proceedings was finally resolved, it created a suspicious and heated atmosphere, so that when on Thursday evening the deities were ceremoniously processed to their new home, the atmosphere was tense and ugly. The dedication ceremonies continued into the night, accompanied by crowds of Hindus coming from across George Town, but large numbers of Malay Muslim and Indian Muslims also turned up, stationing themselves beside the mosque grounds to ensure that no reprisals were carried out against it. I was not there in 1998, but based on my childhood memories of such night-time processions and my experience of tense stand-offs between Palestinians and Israeli Jews around holy sites in Jerusalem, I can picture the scene: darkness, intermittent shafts of light from torches, possibly even the smell of kerosene from flaming brands and lamps; crowds of excited devotees jostling, stumbling, pushing; the deities carried aloft and swaying amid singing and chanting, their painted faces illuminated by flickering candles; drums pounding and bells ringing; prayers being declaimed; sirens yowling; onlookers, some hostile, adding to the drama; and all the while in the background the small Hindu temple being urgently and quickly razed to the ground. All the ingredients for an explosive clash! The drama must have been palpable.

However, that night the police were on hand to prevent trouble, and more arrests were made to dissuade the more excitable elements in the crowds. At that point, it seemed that the dispute could be resolved.

The third phase began on Friday, March 27, when the dispute unfortunately began to escalate again. Overnight, the rumor mill had worked hard, and it was aided by the new technology of the internet. Two sets of pamphlets were quickly circulated digitally and physically through the city. One set warned the Muslim community that there might be reprisals by Hindus against the mosque in Kampong Rawa, while another set called on Hindus to be ready to deter any further Muslim encroachment on their faith and practices. As a precaution, the police not only cordoned off the Kampong Rawa area but also set up roadblocks on the Penang bridge and at the ferry terminals in an attempt to prevent outsiders from exacerbating the situation. They clearly failed in their efforts: an unprecedented large crowd of up to 7,000 worshippers turned up for Friday prayers! The mosque did not have the capacity to contain such numbers, and Muslims spilled out in the surrounding streets within view of the crowds of Hindus who had assembled, ostensibly to protect the new temple site. Although the police were positioned between the two opposing groups, the tense atmosphere was inflamed by the loud thudding of a police helicopter hovering just overhead. Insults, taunts, and stones were thrown, culminating in an attempt by the Muslim youths to break through the police cordon. Using water cannons and tear gas, the police responded by driving the worshippers and demonstrators back into the mosque grounds. There were scenes of panic, but the police gradually brought the situation under control, although it was still very tense. Another forty-three people were arrested, and petrol bombs and *parang*s (Malay-style machetes) were confiscated.[72]

It was also clear that many of the participants on both sides were not from Kampong Rawa but were outsiders who saw the dispute as part of a bigger contest over the position of Islam and Hinduism in Malaysian society and politics. The incident also presaged a worsening of relations between Indian Muslims and Indian Hindus in other mixed neighborhoods, especially iconic enclaves such as "Little India" in central George Town. As such, the prompt intervention by the UMNO deputy prime minister at that time, Anwar Ibrahim, was critical. Arriving in Kampong Rawa in the late afternoon of the same day, March 27, he was aware he had to head off any escalation of the dispute; otherwise, it would reverberate throughout

Malaysia and perhaps lead to even worse riots than in 1969. All the gains that Malaysia and the Malays had made since then would be under threat. As a Penangite, Anwar Ibrahim had high status in UMNO and in George Town, and he had the gravitas and external authority to bring about a public reconciliation. Following intense meetings with the guardians and committee members of both the mosque and the temple, he persuaded them to shake hands publicly in front of cameras. Film and photographs of the scene were quickly broadcast on the evening news, on the internet, and in the morning papers.

The fourth phase was the aftermath. Despite the public show of reconciliation in Kampong Rawa, the wider Hindu and Muslim communities in George Town had been roused, and there still remained the possibility that the unrest could still spread beyond Kampong Rawa. The same night, Friday, March 27, a number of Hindu shrines and temples were desecrated, a mosque's windows were broken, shops on Pitt Street (the Street of Harmony, no less!) and a few Indian Muslim eating stalls were attacked. George Town was still shaken by events. More police were shipped in; checkpoints were set up around the island; and many shops in the center of the city boarded up their windows as a precaution. There were some minor clashes, and more arrests were made (185 in total over the period), but gradually the threat of violence subsided.

In the short term, therefore, order was restored through a combination of high-profile political intervention and police decisiveness. It is relevant to note that none of the accounts I have read of the incident suggest that the predominantly Malay police force acted in an overtly partisan manner, despite some clear operational failings. Mistakes were made, but there have been no reports of excessive brutality or gratuitous anti-Hindu sentiments expressed by the police. Nevertheless, the incident left a legacy of mistrust and promoted a rise in radical and exclusivist sectarian activity. There is evidence to suggest that Indian Muslim and Indian Hindu relations in Little India in George Town worsened, and the unease caused by the incident accelerated the departure of Muslims from central George Town.[73] In addition, it is not a coincidence that, on the one hand, the Hindu Rights Action Force was formed soon after the incident and, on the other, Muslim radical groups increasingly drew attention to the proliferation of Hindu religious sites in Malaysia and to the discrimination of Muslims in India by Hindu-dominated Indian states and the Indian federal government.[74]

Intracommunal Disputes: The Thaipusam Procession

Not all disputes over religious matters are intercommunal. The sheer diversity of different sects within one religion means that internal disputes can occur and have occurred in the past. As in many other parts of the world, in George Town there have also been instances of intracommunal conflicts. In George Town, you will find not only scores of different Christian denominations, often reflecting the country of origin or the language of their early adherents, but also a wide range of Buddhist and Hindu sects—all with their own churches, temples, and shrines. As observed earlier, the Muslim community is perhaps the most homogenous of the different religious communities, largely because the Malaysian Constitution proscribes other non-Sunni Islamic sects, including all the varieties of Shi'ism and Sufism. Nevertheless, even in the Muslim community disagreements between Indian Muslims and Malay Muslims have resulted in the establishment of different mosques and the existence of Malay- and Tamil-speaking congregations. As I described in an earlier section, the Hindu community is also highly fragmented, with multiple subidentities derived from where they originated in India. Because the Hindu Indians lack the extensive civil, trade, and professional institutions that the Chinese have built up, disputes among them in Penang have often focused on religious matters. Sometimes intracommunal disputes break out onto the streets of George Town.

A recent example of such a dispute occurred during the annual Thaipusam Festival when the traditional Chettiar families who have organized the procession for more than one hundred years found their position usurped by a state government body, the Penang Hindu Endowments Board (PHEB).[75] In this dispute, we can see how the politics at both the federal and state levels regarding the Hindu community seeped into the organization of the festival's events. In addition, the dispute over who the organizer of the procession should be also reflects contestation within the Hindu community in George Town over who best represents the community to the state and to other religions. The procession traditionally leaves the Chettiar warehouse in Penang Street, where a silver chariot carrying the statue of Lord Murugan, the son of Shiva and Parvati, is housed. Pulled by two bullocks, the chariot is accompanied by priests and groups of men and women carrying *kavatis*, or sacred burdens, as a demonstration of their devotion or their penance. Crowds of devotees accompany the procession, and they are welcomed along the streets with crushed coconuts, flowers, fruit offerings, and the rhythmic chant "Vel-vel, vel-vel."[76] The spectacular nature of the highly decorated and ornate *karvatis* and the displays of self-mortification carried out by the devotees has put Thaipusam on the international circuit. Thousands of tourists attend to watch and film the skewering of cheeks and tongues by thin silver rods (serving as replica *vels*, or arrows) and the piercing of flesh by silver hooks, which are then attached by scores of strings to wooden chariots to pull them several miles along the streets of George Town. If this event were a film, it would be X rated.

However, in addition to the procession's traditional destination, the Chettiar-run Nattukotai Chettiar Temple near the entrance of the Penang Botanical Gardens, there is a second destination that tends to attract more working-class devotees: the Arulmigu Balathandayuthapani Temple, popularly known as the Waterfall Hilltop Temple, another half a mile up behind the Nattukotai Chettiar Temple and run by the PHEB. The Chettiars have a reputation for honesty, but as former moneylenders and as practitioners of endogamous marriage, they are a relatively closed community and so are viewed by other Indians with some suspicion.[77] Some of the Chettiar families are associated with the MIC, which has been part of the BN coalition with UNMO, in power from independence until the most recent general elections in 2018. But, as we have seen, the BN has not always been in power in George Town, Penang, losing control over the state government in 2008. In contrast, the PHEB is closely associated with what had been the long-standing opposition party, the DAP. Following the Penang state elections in 2008, which were won by a coalition headed by the DAP, the PHEB, which hitherto had been relatively moribund, was taken over by a new management, and its chairman, Professor Palanisamy Ramasamy, was also the DAP deputy chief minister of the Penang state government. One of the PHEB's main aims is to be more representative of the poorer working-class Hindus, who have been marginalized under the federal government's policies. To this end, ensuring that the benefits derived from the Thaipusam festival are directed toward this group has been important.

We should also recognize that Penang's Thaipusam has become an international festival attracting more than 700,000 people, not only devotees from Malaysia but also visitors and tourists from overseas.[78] The collection of hundreds of thousands of dollars in offerings and donations made to the Nattukotai Chettiar Temple during the course of Thaipusam has played no small part in the dispute. Frankly, the festival is a goldmine. Although the exact amount of income derived from the procession is not available, a back-of-an-envelope calculation suggests an income in the region of U.S.$3.5 million per annum.[79] The PHEB has raised concerns regarding the ultimate recipients of these funds and whether a significant proportion is being sent to the Chettiar areas in Tamil Nadu.[80] They point to the lack of transparency by the Chettiar trustees and the absence of charitable works in the Hindu community, which would show that the funds are being distributed locally to those most deserving.[81] In response to this criticism, the Chettiar trustees released details of their accounts in an attempt to resolve their differences with the PHEB. Nevertheless, the PHEB was not satisfied, and it has decided to build (at the cost of more than U.S.$3 million) a bigger, taller, and more spectacular temple on its Waterfall Temple site, with a capacity to welcome more than 800,000 people. Its promotional literature highlights that the new temple will be accessed by way of more steps than those that lead to the famous Batu Caves near Kuala Lumpur, the site of the largest Thaipusam temple in Southeast Asia (the more steps, the more penance and therefore the more merit for the person ascending the steps). It will also be the location of the tallest temple to Lord Murugan outside India.[82] To ensure that the devotees and tourists accompanying the chariot also visit the new temple, the PHEB announced that it would organize an alternative procession that would leave ninety minutes earlier than the Chettiar one and that it would be led by a golden chariot departing from the Sri Maha Mariammam Temple in central George Town, which is managed by the PHEB. In an interview with the Malaysian newspaper *The Star*, Professor Ramasamy argued that "the Board is the rightful organiser of Thaipusam. We introduced the golden chariot to address the long-standing grievance of Hindus who don't want Chettiars to monopolise the procession."[83] The dispute was not resolved, and, indeed, since 2016 two processions have taken place on the same day. But the Penang state authorities were able to ensure that the departure times and the stewarding of the processions were sufficiently coordinated to avoid any public disorder or conflict between the devotees of the different processions, so, despite the ongoing split in the Hindu community, the processions have proceeded without serious conflict.

We can see how religious practices such as processions, especially when they involve such high stakes, can be divisive. They act as an arena where a number of related disputes are drawn in. Control over Thaipusam in

Penang make the organizers major players in the Hindu community both in George Town and in Malaysia and possibly beyond. Thaipusam has attracted international attention and offers a lucrative stream of revenue to the organizers. It also reflects many of the changes taking place in Malaysian society and politics within the Hindu community. By unpacking the elements of the dispute, we can see a number of related issues: how new postindependence community institutions are challenging the older family-based networks; how the dispute over a religious festival reflects the political contest between the federal government and the Penang state government; and, finally, how the globalization of the religious event demands greater public accountability and scrutiny by the secular authorities and the wider Hindu community.

The politics of Penang state and of George Town frames the practice of religion there. To put it bluntly, by being seen as aligned too closely with the MIC, the Chettiar temple trustees backed the wrong horse. Change was gradually percolating through the politics of Malaysia, and the writing was already on the wall by the time of the elections in 2008. In the elections of 2018, the trustees' MIC protectors were swept away, and UMNO was replaced by a coalition that favored the PHEB. Although a compromise has been reached regarding the timing of the two processions, the dispute has not been settled. As the drastic political change brought about by the elections in 2018 unfolds, it is quite likely that the PHEB will capitalize on the presence of its new allies in government to further encroach onto previously established traditions and practices surrounding Thaipusam festivities in order to capture both the position of being Thaipusam's prime organizer and the lucrative revenues it accrues.

Mechanisms and Processes of Dialogue and Mediation

Anyone who has spent a short period of time in George Town cannot but help be impressed by the vibrancy of civil society in the city and across the island. Its annual flagship event, the George Town Festival, involves the participation of literally hundreds of associations and NGOs, ranging from sports and youth groups to parent–teacher associations and school boards; temple, church, and mosque committees; religious-welfare associations; old-boys clubs; occupational and trade organizations; language-based organizations; and even surname associations. To this we can add the human rights groups, environmental-protection groups, gender-equality groups, heritage-preservation groups, and various cultural, artistic, and literary associations.[84] In December 2016, Dr. Anwar Fazal, the embodiment of much of the civic action in George Town, delivered a speech entitled "The Spirit of Penang—Informing, Inspiring, and Igniting Change," in which he enumerated and celebrated the richness of civil society in Penang state and George Town and described the work of two dozen key associations.[85]

To some extent, this richness is derived from the oppositional culture that evolved in Penang as a result of the Chinese and Buddhist predominance, which diluted on the island the federal government's centralizing and Islamization tendencies of the federal government. Not receiving the degree of federal government support either politically or financially to satisfy their aspirations has precipitated a flowering of civil society to remedy this neglect and fill the vacuum.[86] A promising area of further research would be an exploration of the role of social capital in promoting a distinct George Town identity along the lines suggested by Robert Putnam.[87] Indeed, perhaps more relevant to this discussion would also be a look at the applicability of Ashutosh Varshney's hypothesis on how cross-communal associations mitigate the violent outcomes of sectarian conflict.[88] A focus on the ethnic and religious composition of business or occupational associations and trade unions in George Town, as he has done in India, would be very revealing.

Here I wish to outline a number of government programs and some national civil society initiatives that have promoted intercommunal understanding in Malaysia. Doing so will allow me to sketch out some tentative conclusions regarding the extent to which these activities have been essential and intrinsic to the maintenance of good relations between the different ethnic and religious groups in George Town. As I suggested at the beginning of the chapter, there is a perception that this period of relatively good relations prevailing in George Town may be fortuitous. Deeper structural issues, such as the lack of penetration of federal-level policies privileging the Malay Muslim community, have coincided with the presence of a cohort of charismatic religious and civic leaders who collectively experienced the postindependence state-building period and have built up a deep reservoir of conflict-resolution experience. It is their presence, rather than the effectiveness of formal mechanisms and processes for dialogue and mediation, that may account for the management of possible religious conflicts in George Town.

In 1968, one year before the riots in May 1969, the Malaysian federal government established the Department of National Unity and Integration, putting an office in each of the federation's thirteen states. Of all the government initiatives, this department is perhaps one of the most long-lasting even if it has not been as effective as intended. One of its key programs was Rukun Tetangga, a civil society organization that received government support. Rukun Tetangga initially was modelled on the United Kingdom's Neighbourhood Watch scheme, but beginning in the mid-1970s its main focus was to promote intercommunal harmony. To this end, it would carry out activities in community centers, housing estates, and schools in which different ethnic and religious groups would interact with each other.[89] The program also supported Unity kindergartens, which have the teaching of tolerance as part of their syllabus and provide training for mediation. In 2001, Rukun Tetangga was reorganized to focus more on community development; dialogue and mediation became increasingly a by-product of that work.[90] Following divisive elections in 2013, the federal government also set up the National Unity Consultative Council to kick-start enhanced reconciliation between the ethnic and religious groups in Malaysia. However, the focus of this body was the publication of a "blueprint" document to guide government bodies rather than a series of funded programs. Similarly, the Department of National Unity made a number of public pronouncements concerning projects aimed at building intercommunal harmony, such as Vision 2020 and its concept of an inclusive Malaysian identity known as "Bangsa Malaysia" (announced in 1991); Islam Hadhari, which sought to promote governance principles based on a moderate Islam; and, finally, 1Malaysia (unveiled in 2012), which sought to prioritize intercommunal harmony. However, as Lopez concludes in her survey of these federal-government initiatives:

> While these government initiatives strive to ensure peaceful inter-ethnic relations in the country, none of them examines, nor do they address, two core issues underlying and seemingly affecting intercommunal and interfaith relations: the privileged position of Islam vis-à-vis other religions practised in the country and the institutionalised privileges granted to a particular group of citizens based on "race"

and religion, to the distinct disadvantage of Malaysians from other religio-ethnic identity groups.[91]

In light of these comments, it is perhaps unsurprising that attempt by the Human Rights Commission of Malaysia in 2012 to set up an Interfaith Commission was unsuccessful. The commission was meant to foster dialogue between Islamic groups such as the Malaysian Ulama Association, the Malaysian Islamic Development Department, and the main non-Muslim coordinating group, the Malaysian Consultative Council for Buddhism, Christianity, Hinduism, Sikhism, and Taoism (MCCBCHST). Despite the backing of Prime Minister Abdullah Ahmad Badawi, an Islamic scholar, the commission was shelved due to strong opposition from the PAS, the main rival to UMNO for the Malay Muslim vote, and from others on the grounds that it would place Islam at the same level as other religions and erode its primacy as the country's religion.[92] What is revealing about this attempt in 2012 and underscores Lopez's comment is that it was the second time such an attempt had been made. The MCCBCHST (perhaps the longest acronym extant in the religious-dialogue field, which is infamous for its long acronyms!) had been established in 1983 to promote greater dialogue and collaboration between the religious communities in Malaysia. The initial steering committee comprised members of all faiths, including Muslims, but its foundational document was not satisfactory to the Muslim religious leaders, and so they declined to participate.

Other national nongovernmental initiatives have been made, including the Taiping Peace Initiative, its spin-off the Malaysian Interfaith Network, and the Nur Damai organization, based in Kuala Lumpur. I should also reiterate that not all Muslim groups are opposed to dialogue by any means. IKRAM, Sisters of Islam, and some members of PAS who broke off to form the Amanah Party have participated in dialogue and mediation activities. Datok Dr. Mujahid Rawa, formerly a member of Parliament with the PAS and now a member of the progressive Amanah Party and playing a leading role in the Acheh Mosque in George Town, is known for his engagement in dialogue work on the basis of a comparative approach. Regarding the "Kalima Allah" dispute, members of the Acheh Mosque, with the support of the mufti of Penang, entered into discussions with Christian leaders over it.[93]

In George Town, there seems to be the widespread view that these formal mechanisms and processes are not the main avenues for dialogue and mediation when disputes occur. They may play a part to the extent that individuals and groups become known to each other through participating in activities sponsored by such organizations, but, in the main, in George Town responses to disputes are formulated on an ad hoc basis and through the good offices of key individuals who are known to each other.[94] One view is that the formal mechanisms are usually dormant and are activated only when a dispute arises. In the Kampong Rawa Temple-Mosque Incident, we saw that when community leaders initially failed to resolve the differences, Penang state institutions stepped in, and when they too failed, the federal government stepped in through the deputy prime minister's intervention. Ultimately, though, once crowd behavior was controlled by the police, it was the members of the temple and mosque committees who resolved the problem by relocating the temple to a better and larger site.

Learning from the George Town Experience

In compiling this chapter, I can see that much more needs unpacking. Not only do we need to explore in more detail the correlations between demographic and economic change and the emergence of religious disputes, but we also need to establish a clearer idea of the positions taken by political parties and community leaders on the different areas of contestation. In addition, we also need to understand the impact of external actors on the city, whether it be through foreign direct investment and the soft power of the Chinese government's Belt and Road Initiative or through funds and ideology emanating from the Middle East, as well as, indeed, the impact of UNESCO's World Heritage Site inscription on both the city's urban development and its global profile.[95] A fuller study of this nature would allow us to identify some clearer elements and processes in the management of religious disputes in the city. At the same time, from the material presented it is possible to draw up a list of the significant features that make George Town relatively well placed to manage disputes and conflicts.

First, George Town is *not* a "holy city." Despite the large number of religious sites belonging to a wide range of faiths in George Town, they are not central sites to any of the major faiths. As Ron Hassner has argued, threats to such sites do not constitute, therefore, an existential threat to each faith as a whole. George Town has some important religious associations: it is the traditional departure point for Muslim haj pilgrims heading for Mecca; it has the oldest church in Southeast Asia, the Anglican St. George's Church; and it is the home of the largest reclining Buddha outside India, the Wat Chayamangkalaram of Lorong Burma. These sites are important to members of religious communities in George Town, but they are not on a par with sites in, say, Jerusalem as the most important city in Judaism, Christianity, and Islam or with sites in Banaras as the city of Shiva. This relatively peripheral characteristic of the religious sites in George Town is a significant element in keeping disputes between the different communities low key. It ensures that any disputes regarding these religious sites do not resonate much beyond the island itself and therefore can be addressed by local religious leaders and politicians. There is not a diaspora watching, hawklike, waiting to dive-bomb every minor infringement on or alteration to the sites' use, access, and practice.

Second, there is an absence of domineering clerical hierarchies and dominant religious institutions in the city. Partly due to the absence of religious sites of international significance, George Town is spared the presence of a powerful cadre of priests, imams, and other religious officials acting as a political force. In other cities with strong religious associations, the presence of such religious sites attracts revenues in the form of endowments, donations, and funds from large numbers of pilgrims. These revenues, in turn, offer the clergy the means to purchase and maintain properties, to recruit and provide employment for new clergy, and to carve out a degree of financial autonomy from the state. Although some temples, churches, and mosques in George Town are clearly well endowed and have wealthy supporters, they are not a dominating presence. In addition, external funding seems to be proportionate to the numbers of devotees and the number of sites. George Town is not a city where there has been huge investment in the construction of religious sites mainly for proselytizing and advertising purposes.[96] The only clerical hierarchy that could possibly act in the expansive and assertive manner described earlier is the Muslim clerical hierarchy. However, its power as an independent political force in George Town is constrained by two factors: first, it is fragmented by ethnicity, as demonstrated by the fact that the two main mosques in central George Town belong to the Tamil Muslim community (Masjid Kapitan Keling) and the Malay Muslim community (Masjid Melayu Lebuh Acheh); second, the Muslim religious leadership has largely been absorbed into the federal and state government structures to the extent that it does not act independently of the federal government and, as we have seen in Penang, is held in check to a certain degree by the state-level government.

A third reason why George Town has escaped the kinds of religious tensions often found in other religiously diverse cities is somewhat contradictory. Although religious and ethnic diversity provides ample scope for multiple points of friction, at the same time it can also dilute the flammability of those frictions. In George Town, we have seen not only that are there numerous ethnic communities but also that there are numerous religious communities that both straddle the ethnic communities and divide them. Thus, the Chinese community may be partially united by a common language, Hokkien, but it is also fragmented into different religions, clan groups, socioeconomic classes, and political parties. The Malay community may be the most cohesive, but its ability to act collectively is hampered by a rural–urban divide as well as by its close connections with non-Malay Muslims and its relations to the national ruling elite. In effect, and in contrast to Jerusalem and Lhasa, for example, there are no major binaries along ethnic or religious lines in George Town that would assist political mobilization around religious sites. Instead, similar to the situation in Banaras, there are both a weak "Us" and a weak "Them" as well as many "Us-es" and many "Thems."

A fourth reason is closely connected to the previous two reasons. Land and property ownership by religious communities in George Town does not drive residential or employment segregation along ethnic or religious lines. In Jerusalem, as I have described earlier, much of the city's land and property is owned by religious foundations (*waqfs*), by other trusts of the three faiths, and by the Israeli state, which, by its own statutes, can only lease land to Israeli Jews. This form of communal-based landownership has assisted in the creation of geographical areas in the city defined by the exclusive presence of one community at the expense of others. In George Town, we have seen that property ownership is highly fragmented: government- and Penang-state-owned land tends to be on the periphery and not associated with any religious sites; the majority of the property in George Town may be owned by large Chinese families and businesses and by *kongsi*s, but there is little appearance of segregation resulting from this ownership; there appear to be no major religious foundations holding land in order to promote sectarian interests. The only exception to this may be Muslim *waqf* property, but these holdings are not so extensive as to determine the ethnic or religious composition of large swathes of residential land. In George Town, therefore, the correlation between landownership and residential segregation based on religion is weak.

A fifth reason pertains to the strength and the resilience of the Malaysian state. Despite the existence of secessionist movements in Penang during the 1960s, the legitimacy of the Malaysian state itself is not contested in George Town. As we have seen, profound disagreements have arisen from the demographic and political differences between Penang island and state on the one side and the federation on the other. These differences include Penang's Chinese–Malay demographic parity, the absence of a Malay sultan in Penang, the control of the Penang state administration by opposition parties since 2008, and the perception that until the general elections of 2018 the government had been taken over by a corrupt national elite, which had led to a growing political "gangsterism." Even the growing push-back by non-Malays over the inequalities between the ethnic groups enshrined in the Constitution have not crystallized into opposition to and rejection of the Malaysian state itself. In cities such as Jerusalem, Belfast prior to the Good Friday Agreement, and parts of Beirut and Mostar, where the legitimacy of the state is contested, religious and other community leaders have taken on the role of political representatives and often function as power brokers in the allocation of resources. In these circumstances, religious sites become both symbols of community strength and community assets that need to be protected. This is not happening in George Town, where the political process, for all its faults, remains based on the negotiations between political parties. The "regime change" that took place as a result of the elections of 2018 was a remarkable demonstration of the viability of Malaysian federal institutions.

A sixth and final reason for the relative success of George Town in managing religious diversity is its long-standing culture of accommodation and mutual respect. This culture of accommodation flows from the unwritten social compact: that the religious communities will recognize the primacy of Islam and the privileging of Malay Muslim civil and religious rights in exchange for the federal government's nonintervention in the affairs of the non-Muslim religious communities. Despite the non-Malay communities' chaffing under the burden and restrictions of this compact, it is for the present holding. I described earlier some of the preparatory discussion for the Street of Harmony walk. These relationships are shaped by historical precedents and are embedded in both elite-level interactions and daily life. Similarly, there is widespread recognition that peaceful coexistence is to the mutual advantage of all communities. Personal links between religious leaders have been established for dispute resolution, and ad hoc processes seem to be more effective than formal mechanisms. The failure to establish the Interfaith Commission as a result of national-level political considerations points to the importance and acceptance of local initiatives that are rooted in the traditions of Penang.

In these six features, we can see that in George Town there is a unique combination of multiple religious identities and the fragmentation of power. Despite a federal constitution that privileges the Malay and Muslim community in Malaysia, in the city itself this discrimination is both dissipated and countered by historical precedents of cultural accommodation, demographic patterns that balance a Malay political dominance, dispersed property ownership, and a political and religious leadership that has avoided the temptations of an exclusivist ideology. Wrapping these elements into a package that can be replicated is, however, a very different matter.

CHAPTER VI

Religious Conflicts in Cities

The blue flag of the United Nations fluttering on the tops of buildings or a huge black "UN" painted on the side of passing white cars usually denotes a site of conflict and tension. And one paradoxically finds this organization dedicated to peace in the most unpeaceful of locations. In contrast to Cordoba, Banaras, Lhasa, and George Town, the presence of the UN in Jerusalem is quite striking. Whereas in these other cities the UN presence is confined largely to the work of UNESCO and to the UN Population Agency, there are almost two dozen UN agencies with active programs in and around East Jerusalem. Some of these agencies have only a small monitoring staff, but others, such as the UN Relief and Works Agency and the UN Development Program, have substantial budgets and a large bureaucracy that employs hundreds of people.[1] To Israel, this supersized UN presence in its self-declared capital is a grotesque affront. In the popular view, this presence puts Israel in the same bracket as, say, South Sudan or the Democratic Republic of Congo or Haiti, where government institutions are weak or where the rule of law has broken down and people live in fear of ambitious militia leaders or where services and infrastructure are minimal. But, more importantly, the prominent UN profile fundamentally questions Israel's presence in East Jerusalem and its claims to sovereignty over both sides of the city. How can the city's status as the self-proclaimed capital of Israel be settled if it requires so much international attention and monitoring? As a measure of the contested nature of a city, this "UN-ometer" places Jerusalem right at the top of the scale.

During the course of two decades of research into the city, I have had the opportunity to observe and engage in this UN presence in Jerusalem, and that experience has brought into sharp relief the opportunities and limitations of the role of international actors in resolving religious conflicts in cities.[2] A recent example of this engagement was in 2016–2017, when I was invited by the Office of the UN Special Coordinator of the Middle East Peace Process (UNSCO) to assist it in developing a strategy for coordinating UN activities in East Jerusalem. This UN initiative was prompted by two main considerations. By 2016, there was a clear consensus in the diplomatic community that all the efforts that had gone into implementing the Oslo Accords of 1993 had foundered and that a rethink was urgently required. On one hand, the Palestinians would not be satisfied with anything less than a fully-fledged independent state, and, on the other, the Israelis could not countenance either withdrawing from its main colonies in the occupied Palestinian territories (West Bank and East Jerusalem) or recognize any Palestinian entity that involved the participation of the Islamic group HAMAS. The momentum for a peace agreement had passed. The ensuing political impasse was simultaneously creating a vacuum in which hardliners on both sides could consolidate their positions and in which Israel, as the dominant party, could entrench itself in the West Bank and East Jerusalem. Without the prospect of a negotiated solution on the horizon, humanitarian agencies on the ground were looking for some UN guidance as to what the political goals would be in this new situation.

The second consideration was more concerned with the internal workings of the UN family of agencies in the city. These agencies had been mandated to deal with a variety of crises and to meet a variety of needs. For example, the UN Truce Supervisory Organization had been tasked with monitoring the Armistice Agreement of 1949 between Israel and Jordan; the UN Relief and Works Agency for Palestine Refugees with dealing with the refugee situation following the fighting in 1948 and 1967; UN-Habitat with addressing the poor housing conditions in the Palestinian areas of the city; UNESCO with advising and helping protect the cultural heritage of the city; and so on. Over time, these agencies' tasks overlapped; there was duplication and repetition of projects; there was competition over recruiting personnel, finding premises for office space, and raising project funds. More importantly, there was also a bewildering and sometimes contradictory array of responses regarding how to deal with the institutions of the Israeli state, from its military to the Jerusalem municipality. In the period 2013–2016, the UNSCO team estimated that the UN had embarked on 110 projects in East Jerusalem, with a budget of approximately $107 million. More than one-third of these projects were related to Palestinian access to health services. What was most revealing, however, is that these projects had no single sponsoring UN agency but were spread over a range of agencies, creating confusion as to which agency was taking the lead and ultimately resulting in unnecessary inefficiencies. The UN operation in East Jerusalem had been erected in an ad hoc and incremental manner and for a set of objectives that did not cohere and were no longer applicable in the same way. My task was to move forward the discussions taking place within and between the agencies as to how best to establish some common strategic goals and a coordination framework.

Among the different activities I was engaged in was the facilitation of workshops focusing on specific challenges in East Jerusalem that would benefit from a coherent UN response. One particular challenge was known as "the Gray Zone," and we pulled together a range of academic and practitioner experts to explore what the name meant, what conditions it related to, and what responses were possible. Gray Zones occur in many cities around the world and are in essence urban areas where there is such an absence of planning and resources that it constitutes a deliberate policy of controlling and colonizing minority groups in a city. The detrimental effect of such a policy is compounded by the legal and political ambiguity of these areas.[3] Yet as well as being areas of severe neglect, insecurity, and exclusion, Gray Zones are also areas of dynamism, opportunity, and grassroots community action. Interventions by donors and external bodies, such as the UN, can capitalize on that dynamism.

On a bright sunny day in May, we met at the St. George's Cathedral conference center on the Nablus Road in East Jerusalem. Heads of programs of all the major UN agencies came together to pool their experiences, and presentations by international, Palestinian, and Israeli urban planners, geographers, sociologists, legal experts, and political scientists were added to the agenda. Despite the jarring incongruity of discussing zones of deprivation and exclusion in the comfortable surroundings of St. George's, with its leafy courtyard trees throwing shade across the trickling fountain and flowerbeds, the workshop was tightly focused and productive. The challenges posed by these Gray Zones for the UN in

Jerusalem are mainly practical and operational. In legal terms, East Jerusalem is occupied, and Israel remains the occupying power and is therefore responsible for the provision of services to the Palestinians of East Jerusalem and its Gray Zones. But because Israel was not meeting this responsibility, the UN agencies were confronted with a dilemma: Do the political costs of replacing the Israeli municipality and other Israeli institutions in the provision of services outweigh the political and welfare gains in doing so? The workshop delineated a range of options and priorities that the agencies would need to discuss with their own staff, but a framework for joint action on this topic was in the making. Amid the hurly-burly of raising funds, writing reports and assessments, searching and evaluating partners from Palestinian civil society, recruiting, navigating access to premises and project sites, sorting divergent priorities, and so on, some sort of coordination and coherence appeared to be gradually emerging. *Progress* may be too strong or too optimistic a word to use for this stage, but certainly a "pathway to progress" was being cleared. Then in December 2017 the U.S. government announced it was recognizing Israeli sovereignty over Jerusalem and moving its embassy from Tel Aviv to Jerusalem, and the whole process screeched to an abrupt halt. If the future of Jerusalem was no longer on the negotiating table by dint of this U.S. action in support of Israel's position, then the Oslo framework was definitely dead beyond resuscitating. In the light of such a rupture of the international consensus on Jerusalem, the UN Country Team in the occupied territories needed to take stock and reassess its options.

The purpose of referring to this UN activity on Gray Zones is not merely to highlight the value of comparative study in formulating policy and designing programs—although such comparisons are also important. Despite the pitfalls in trying to replicate policies and solutions based on certain set of circumstances, I remain convinced of the value of comparative study.[4] Learning for oneself and informing policy makers of the combinations of factors that are likely either to ameliorate or inflame a conflicted situation as well as delineating the key dynamics inherent in different kinds of cities—whether they be frontier cities, holy cities, port cities, capital cities, or cities in economic decline—provide academics and policy makers with useful and appropriate tools to fashion an effective response to conflicts in cities. Nevertheless, the purpose of highlighting this UN activity lies more in bringing the discussion back to the beginning—back, that is, to the city of Jerusalem. Given the ongoing and seemingly intractable dispute about the future of this city, has the examination of Cordoba, Banaras, Lhasa, and George Town provided us with a new approach to the conflict over Jerusalem, and does that approach have any relevance to the other cities covered in this book and to other cities not covered in such depth? The problems of Jerusalem set the bar for policy transfer very high. As the progress of the UNSCO East Jerusalem strategy initiative amply illustrates, attempts at conflict resolution and management in this city are easily blown off course by extraneous factors that relate less to the conflicts being generated in the city and more to the high politics of international relations, in which the city is reduced to the status of a pawn (well, given the topic, maybe a bishop) in a complex and fast-moving chess game. Although the solution to Jerusalem's problems may be beyond the assistance that can be brought to bear from an examination of conflicts in other cities with strong religious associations, nevertheless that comparison will certainly contribute to managing expectations of what can be achieved and thus provide a realistic basis for formulating policy responses.

The "findings" of this project can be loosely grouped under two main headings, which I have touched upon in different ways in the conclusions of the preceding chapters but draw together here more schematically: the impact of religiosity and the role of the state and systems of governance.

The Impact of Religiosity

A recurring theme in the cities studied has been the implications of the "centrality" of holy sites in the faiths of their populations. Ron Hassner's argument that this is a key issue and a cause of both religious conflict and the intractability of religious conflict has been a useful contribution to the debate but has also been criticized by anthropologists and ethnographers alike. The more central to the faith a site may be, the less likelihood there is that a compromise over access and use of that site can be agreed upon. This argument has particular relevance to sites that are jointly used, "shared," or jointly claimed by two or more religions, such as the Haram al-Sharif in Jerusalem and the Gyan Vapi Mosque in Banaras. Prominent critics such as Elazar Barkan and Karen Barkey point to the lack of clarity regarding how one defines "centrality" and "marginality" and to the uncertainty over the objectivity of those who may make such a definition.[5]

Indeed, such a characterization does not stand the test of time as sites can move in and out of such a central role. The Mezquita in Cordoba is a good example of such a role changing over time, and who knows what grand status may be foisted upon the Waterfall Temple beside the Penang Botanical Gardens once the Penang Hindu Endowments Board's plans come to fruition. Moreover, the notion of centrality is contingent on accepting an essentialist view of religion, when for many this view would be a misreading of the data.[6]

For political scientists, in particular those involved in the policy world, however, the notion has some merit. Political scientists tend to have a meso- or macrolevel perspective in contrast to the more microlevel perspective of anthropologists and ethnographers, and they require greater generalization to delineate patterns and processes. Anthropologists are bound to emphasize fluidity, the personal and the contingent nature of ritual and religious arrangements, but political scientists, for their part, will be looking for the shape of power structures at any given moment and the way they may continue. Thus, I have not ruled out Hassner. With clarifying caveats, his ideas have proved useful in identifying key actors, trends, and processes that allow for some predictive discussion. It seems pretty conclusive to me, for example, that the contemporary lack of centrality of the Mezquita in Islam in Cordoba or of the mosaic of religious sites in George Town is an important factor in managing conflict around those sites. If those situations were to change—if, for example, a large and prosperous Spanish Muslim community emerged in Cordoba or if the Kek Lok Si Temple outside George Town continues to be a magnet for wealthy expatriate Chinese donors—then these sites' "centrality" will undoubtedly increase in the internal discourse of their respective religions and, in turn, will spill over into their prominence in the political world.

This research has also confirmed Francis Peters's identification of the important role played by powerful religious hierarchies and their associated institutions. It is an important corrective to the focus on conflict around buildings and sites. In fact, on the basis of my study I would go further. I would add that the actions of supporting religious personnel are as much, if not more, of a factor than the centrality of a holy site in managing or exacerbating religious conflicts in cities. As we saw in George Town and to a lesser extent in Banaras, maintaining a degree of religious coexistence and the "culture of accommodation" requires personal commitment by the religious leadership in those cities. In Cordoba, this commitment was not forthcoming, and one can speculate that the Roman Catholic authorities there are lucky there is not a strong Muslim community residing in the city because if there were, they would need to change their approach in order to avoid an escalating conflict over non-Christian access to the Mezquita. In Lhasa, the role of the Tibetan Buddhist religious hierarchy is a fundamental threat to the occupying Chinese state, and the Chinese authorities have dealt with it ruthlessly. Yet what is remarkable and significant is that after seventy years of repression, surveillance, and close administrative control, those authorities have not been able to remove that threat. This points to how much an issue of national identity is being manifested by the religious leadership. In Lhasa, so long as you have Tibetans, you are going to have Tibetan Buddhists, who will throw up a leadership that is Buddhist. In Jerusalem, so long as you have Muslim Palestinians in the city, Israel will have a Muslim religious leadership to contend with, and the more that Jewishness is asserted as the sole Israeli identity, the less likely it is that Palestinian Muslims can be absorbed into an Israeli-dominated city.

Another important issue emerging in this research is also closely related to religion and identity. What exacerbates the conflict between the secular Chinese state and Tibetan Buddhism is the simple binary that exists in Lhasa—there are the Han Chinese, who comprise most of the ruling elite and all of the new settlers, and there are the indigenous Tibetans. This binary provides the main area of conflict and contestation over urban space and religious sites. This situation can be contrasted with George Town, where religious and ethnic diversity has resulted in the dilution of tensions over religious practices and holy sites. Where one would expect that the sheer diversity of religious communities would provide many points of possible friction between the religious communities that might lead to violent conflict—from religious sites lying adjacent to each other to religious festivities coinciding both spatially and temporally—this has not occurred in practice largely because the religious leadership operates within the particular political configuration of Malaysian state–federal tensions. In Banaras, what appears to be a simple binary at the root of the tension between Muslims and Hindus over their holy sites is also, on deeper examination, much more nuanced and complex. In essence, Hinduism is both very accommodating and very diverse; it has scores of sects, castes, and philosophical schools, and its believers speak a range of languages and come from a wide geographical area. As a consequence, Banaras is a magnet for all kinds of Hindus and "Hinduisms." This heterodoxy may not be exactly matched by a similar patchwork of Muslim beliefs and identities, but it does exist to the extent that tensions are not always polarized around religious issues. One likely consequence of the way in which religiosity and spirituality have infused the city's daily life is that the material rewards that politicians offer to their voters cannot really compete with the rewards offered by the spiritual realm. In this way, we can see how the vitality of a religious system in a city does not necessarily translate into a political movement that can be mobilized aggressively against another religious community.

The Role of the State and Systems of Governance

The legitimacy of the state authority is absolutely a key factor in the ability to resolve or manage religious conflicts in cities. When that legitimacy is contested, there seems little possibility of avoiding the phenomenon of either religious conflicts spilling over into political ones or, if there has been colonization, interethnic conflicts spilling over into religious ones. Jerusalem is a somewhat extreme case of legitimacy being contested, and this contestation over legitimacy provides a trigger for almost every conflict over religion that takes place in the city. Every action by Israel that impinges upon a religious site or a religious practice is seen as an assertion of its illegitimate authority in the city. From a Palestinian perspective, the situation is a zero-sum game. Any action by Israel that is uncontested is Israel's "gain," so every Israeli action must be resisted lest it set a precedent and establish a new status quo. In Lhasa, the legitimacy of the Chinese authorities in the city is also contested by its Tibetan inhabitants. Yet unlike the Palestinians of Jerusalem, the Tibetans do not have a body of international law, the panoply of UN agencies, and the overwhelming majority of the international community on their side over this matter. This relative lack of international intervention allows the Chinese authorities to act with a degree of impunity in the city that the Israeli government can only envy. At the same time, the fact that the Chinese authorities are not seeking to take over Tibetan Buddhist holy sites for religious purposes—that is, to replace one religion with another—removes some of the heat from the situation. The exercise is more a naked quest for control rather than replacement of one religious system by another. Desecrations have taken place in Lhasa, but they could be considered less inflammatory than, for example, replacing a statue of Buddha with some other religious icon. What this suggests, then, is that the religious element in the ethnonational contest over space and territory in Jerusalem is more incendiary, that it will engender greater political costs to Israel, and, therefore, that it is a prime reason why Israel stays its hand.

As we also have seen, interventions by external actors can take other forms and constrain the state's actions in different ways. Diasporic connections provide channels for overseas religious communities to lobby on behalf of their coreligionists in locations where their religious practices are being disrupted or their sites encroached upon. In many respects, this feature is most clearly seen in Jerusalem, where the wider Christian community and the Islamic world can muster considerable diplomatic clout to hold Israel's more expansionist tendencies in check. In Lhasa and Cordoba, these channels are not so strong and do not play a significant role beyond ensuring that key historical and religious sites are maintained to a high standard. In Banaras and George Town, such external interventions are complex. Although there is evidence of funds being directed toward Muslim and Christian educational establishments from the Arab states of the Persian Gulf and from Europe and North America, respectively, such interventions have not led to significant influence over government or municipal policies. Nor have they led to a significant increase in militancy. Fears, for example, of the impetus that the defeat and subsequent dispersal of the so-called Islamic State in the Middle East may have on the existing radicalism of some sections of the Muslim community in Banaras and the Malay Muslim community in George Town have proved so far to be unfounded.

In these two cities, what appears to have greater impact is the government's federal structure. In Banaras, in addition to the fact that the Indian Constitution formally protects the religious and civil rights of minorities, the division of functions and responsibilities between the municipal, state, and federal levels of government has opened up a space that allows local agency to push back against the ethnonationalist polices of a resurgent Hindutva movement. In George Town, although the Malaysian Constitution privileges the indigenous Malay Muslim population, the state-level government is able to act as a buffer and neutralize some of the more egregious aspects of that privileging. Again, this allows space for local agency to resolve differences without conflicts being mapped out onto a national tableau. An important and more generally applicable pattern that this research has confirmed, however, is the way that the projection of ethnonationalism into the governance of a city comprises some contradictory dynamics. As I argued in the introduction to this book, because cities are inherently cosmopolitan, and cities that are religiously diverse are also largely multiethnic, ethnonationalist policies that promote the interests of one ethnic or religious community over the interests of others create responses that undermine those ethnonationalist policies. I termed this process the "paradox of ethnonationalist urban governance." If a religious community is deprived of resources and representation and is discriminated against in other ways, it will seek support from its coreligionists and political sympathizers from outside the city and outside the state, harnessing external political forces to its cause, as in the case of the Palestinians in Jerusalem.

A similar pattern associated with the role of the state and city governance is less a "finding" of this project in that data were not collected specifically for it and more a possible avenue for further research that emerged from observations and reflections following fieldwork. This pattern involves the way cities have adopted or have been obliged to adopt a neoliberal model of the small state, where the provision of services, policing and security, and infrastructure is made by nonstate actors. This pattern opens up cities with strong religious associations to a new set of dynamics that need further examination and discussion. For example, the provision of some city services may be contracted out to the private sector but might also be taken up by welfare organizations that have a religious basis. In the absence of state provision, temples, mosques, and churches often step in with outreach programs to fill the needs for basic care of the elderly, low-cost housing, schooling, and economic support. In East Jerusalem and in George Town, the role of religious and civil society in these service areas is quite pronounced. In Lhasa, the intervention of civil society is, to all intents and purposes, forbidden. In Cordoba, the Muslim community serves this role on a small scale, but the majority Christian (Roman Catholic) community serves it more extensively and mostly but not entirely as a supplement to state provision. In Banaras, this option may more be prompted by financial constraints, the lack of resources, and weak institutional capacity on the part of state institutions as much as by ideological design. But here the paucity of the resources available to all communities appears to have an unexpected result: the struggle against poverty is a shared experience that unites poor Hindus and Muslims in their search for sources of support. Nevertheless, the general point to be made is that if the state is not involved in some form of equitable allocation of resources, then religious organizations and external supporters are likely to step in to supply those needs, in part out of compassion for their coreligionists and in part possibly to further an explicit religious or political agenda. Dependencies and organizational loyalties are easily constructed on the basis of the distribution of needed resources, providing the basis for mobilizing groups and firming up identities. So an important finding of this project is that in cities where religious conflicts are close to the surface, the absence of state provision can fuel the flames of antagonism between religious communities.

In this connection, a city's economy plays a critical part in defusing or fanning the flames of religious conflict. In the introduction, I highlighted how both mobility and specialization are key characteristics of a city and that without them a city's prosperity, cosmopolitanism, and high culture would be absent. Economic interactions between different population groups in the city allow skills, the knowledge base, labor, and capital to flow between them, leading to the creation of both mass-production and high-quality production, whether it be in industry, learning, or culture. I contended that despite rivalries and grievances that may occur, in cities where economic interdependence between different ethnic and religious communities has emerged, both labor and capital will be loath to disrupt the smooth functioning of the agreements and contracts that provide employment and, for some, wealth. We see this most clearly in Banaras, where economic interdependence between the Muslim and Hindu communities in the silk industry, the largest employment sector in the city, has acted as a deterrent to religious conflict. Leaders of both communities are well aware that a breakdown in public order would adversely affect both of them, and so they work at preempting disruption through public displays of cooperation. In the case of George Town, the picture is more confused. Although there is some anecdotal evidence of employment differentiation along sectarian lines—Malay Muslims in the public sector, Chinese of all religions in the private sector, and Indians of all religions occupying positions from the professions to manual labor—it is language rather than religion that is the salient factor for employment in one field or the other. Certainly, the end result is one where employment cuts across the important cleavages of ethnicity and religion.

In contrast to George Town, the cases of Lhasa and Jerusalem are illustrative of how economic cleavages have fed the ethnonational and religious divisions. Despite the overwhelming power of the Chinese Communist Party over the functioning of Lhasa, and despite the dominance of

Chinese settlers in many sectors of the economy, the Tibetan population's capacity to interrupt the burgeoning tourist trade—the single largest generator of wealth in the city—is striking. One wonders if the Chinese state has taken note. In contrast to its brutal polices of the 1950s and 1960s, the Chinese state has in recent years acted with greater caution toward the sensitive area of religion in Lhasa. It is incontestable that reducing the size of the Tibetan-dominated Barkor quarter and carrying out renovations that have destroyed much of the cultural uniqueness of the older parts of Lhasa have been painful blows to Tibetan Lhasans and their nationalist aspirations. But razing the iconic holy sites, the very places where the flame of Tibetan nationalism continues to steadily flicker, is not on the cards. The state has instead attempted a more oblique approach by co-opting the Tibetan middle classes and allowing Tibetan religious culture a degree of freedom of expression, however superficial and constrained it is, in order to safeguard the income that tourism brings to the city's coffers.

The capacity for Palestinians, largely Muslims, to disrupt the tourist trade in Jerusalem is also significant. The problem for those Palestinians who would consider this action as a means of advancing their political and religious claims in Jerusalem is that such disruption would proportionately affect their own community more than any other. Apart from the tourist trade, the "Palestinian economy" of East Jerusalem is tiny, akin to the economy of any small town in the United Kingdom.[7] Most of the non-tourist-sector economy is characterized by dependency, not interdependency. Palestinian laborers trudge daily over to Israeli West Jerusalem or to the Israeli colonies in and around East Jerusalem to work in construction, retail, hospitality, and the lower levels of municipal and government service. There is almost no reciprocity taking place in that very, very few Israeli Jews, if any, work in Palestinian enterprises. This one-sidedness offers further evidence of how the absence of such mutually supporting ties leads to intercommunal conflicts, which in the case of Jerusalem is further exacerbated by Israeli government policies that seek to extend Israeli dominance in East Jerusalem.

A final area touches on a number of related issues regarding the organization of urban space that can contribute significantly to religious conflicts, including demographic change, land ownership, residential segregation, and economic interdependence. As noted earlier, the demographic composition of a city can lead to polarization between communities and provide a catalyst for religious conflict. Changes in that composition, whether an increase in one community and a decrease in another, will result in the flexing of muscles by the communities' leadership that can be manifested in the ways public space is used in religious practice. The stand-off between the Israeli state and Palestinian Muslim worshippers over access to the Haram al-Sharif is a good example of this muscle-flexing exercise. Property ownership will also affect the spatial arrangement of housing. In Banaras and George Town, the dispersed, fragmented, and multiple agencies involved in property ownership lessen the use of ownership for political ends. In Lhasa and Jerusalem, the opposite is the case.

One way of summing up all these points is to organize them into a kind of policy "tool kit." In this Religious Conflict in Cities Resolution Tool Kit, I would include seven essential tools. In no specific order of importance (which is open to discussion), they are:

1. The legitimacy of state institutions to arbitrate conflicts and execute legal decisions
2. An ethnonationalist dominance that is moderated by a commitment to some inclusivity
3. A culture of accommodation that both recognizes and celebrates difference
4. A respect for the centrality or importance of key religious sites to a religious community and a willingness of the leadership to envisage alternative arrangements
5. A mobility framework that fosters economic interdependence between different religious communities
6. A fragmented and dispersed land-ownership system that discourages residential segregation
7. An informal monitoring role for external actors that, on the one hand, can constrain excessive zealotry but, on the other hand, can allow space for local agency.

Clearly, these "tools" form a fairly abstract framework and would need to be filled out with more specific policies—for example, around educational curricula, the management of festivities, and the training of religious personnel, police, and government officials. However, the distillation of this research to seven main factors affecting religious conflicts in cities is offered here as a starting point for any discussions in the process of policy formation.

Return to Jerusalem

How do these findings help us think of ways to resolve or manage the situation in Jerusalem? And if this situation cannot be resolved or adequately managed, what is the prognosis? At the outset, I should bluntly state that what this project has helped me see is that the search for peace in this city is a futile search for fool's gold. Unless the tectonic plates of the current balance of power between Israel and the PLO shift dramatically, I see little change in the ongoing unbalanced dynamic: Israel gradually encroaches upon non-Jewish holy sites, and the Palestinian population is either gradually squeezed out of the eastern part of the city or absorbed as second-class residents of the city. As a consequence, the prognosis is that there will be continuing tensions, which every now and then will break out into spasms of violence when a new threshold is approached, probed, or crossed. The reason for this constant low-level conflict is that although Israel can take incremental steps to advance its interests with relative impunity, it is not in so strong a position as to be able to take any bigger or more drastic steps. Unless it acts with even greater ruthlessness than the Chinese have done in Lhasa—for example, by expelling the Palestinians from the city and dismantling the religious institutions that constitute the Islamic presence in the city, a step that Israel is very, very unlikely to take or to be able to carry out—then I cannot envisage the city experiencing any semblance of a negotiated agreement in the near to medium term—that is, in the next five to fifteen years. The contrasting prospect of Israel recognizing Palestinian sovereignty over East Jerusalem and abandoning the land and property it has acquired there since 1967 is equally very remote.

In this scenario, Israel will continue to slowly encircle the Haram al-Sharif by acquiring more properties and implanting increasing numbers of settlers in the Old City; it will continue to regulate and reduce the number of Muslim worshippers entering the city, the Old City, and the Haram enclosure; it will gradually starve the Waqf Administration of the funds required for maintenance, for restoration, and for housing—social and welfare activities that give the Muslim community in the city some of its vitality. It could also ratchet up its marginalization of the Palestinians in the city, imposing higher property taxes and housing construction costs; continue to break up concentrations of Palestinian housing with new colonies; and impose greater restrictions on movement, on education, on health services, on education, and on employment. The burden of being a Palestinian in Jerusalem will become increasingly high, precipitating a brain drain and ultimately leading to a tipping point where the population declines and only the aged and very young remain. At the same time, Israel will refrain from taking the most significant step that the many Israeli nationalists want their government to take: the demolition of the al-Aqsa Mosque and Dome of the Rock in the Haram al-Sharif. This would be a step too far. The constellation of political forces in Israel, in the region, in the UN, and in the countries of the world that Israel counts on as its allies or its main trading partners is too strong for it to take such a drastic step: the political costs for the country would be too high. As a result, there is and will be for the foreseeable future a kind of impasse, with the Palestinians and their supporters still being able to resist but not being strong enough to prevent the erosion of their position. In sum: the scenario will be one of continuing low-level conflict.

A final word. Reviewing the factors that contribute to religious conflicts in cities, from the absence of the state authority's legitimacy to the role of external actors to the presence of strong religious institutions and leadership to property ownership and changes in demography, spatial organization, and economic prosperity, one can see that the solution to such conflicts is multifaceted and multileveled. A simple formula will not be enough, and each city has a particular dynamic that needs to be closely read before any intervention can take place. Although on a more general level cities with strong religious associations conform to a range of similar features, directing one's attentions to specific conflicts within a city can lead one to study its specific features and dynamics. One pattern, however, that remains pretty constant can be drawn from the study of the Mezquita in Cordoba: what we are witnessing now in the cities studied is but an episode in an unfolding story, a snapshot of the historical trajectory, and whatever arrangements have been agreed upon by the parties concerned, they are not permanent and will be subject to change and new configurations.

Glossary

JERUSALEM

AZAN the Muslim call to prayer

MIKVE Jewish ritual bath (plural: *mikva'ot*)

MURABITAAT female defenders of the Haram al-Sharif

MURABITYYN male defenders of the Haram al-Sharif

QIBLA Muslim direction of prayer (toward Mecca)

WAQF Islamic endowment (plural: *awqaf*)

CORDOBA

HALAL food production in accordance with Muslim tradition

MIHRAB niche in mosque wall designating the *qibla*

MOZARABES Christian converts to Islam prior to the Reconquista

MORISCOS Muslims who were forced to convert to Christianity but who kept
many Islamic practices

MUDEJAR Muslims living under Christian rule

BANARAS

AARTI/ARATI Hindu evening prayers

BHAI-BHAI brotherhood (Urdu)

BHAIACHARA brotherhood (Hindi)

GANGA JAMUNI TAHZEB shared culture of the Ganges plain (Urdu)

HINDUTVA "Hindu-ness," meaning Hindu nationalism

KARSEVAK Hindu temple priest, often hereditary

LINGA a sign or emblem, often a phallic-shaped stone, representing the divine
energy of Shiva

MAHANT chief priest of a Hindu temple

MUFTI senior Muslim cleric, often the acknowledged spokesperson of
the Muslim community

MUHARRAM first month in the Islamic calendar; Muharram 10 is a Shiʿa festival marking the
martyrdom of Ali, the grandson of the prophet Muhammed

PURANA a collection of stories that preserve Hindu traditions, myths, and rites

RAMLILA Hindu festival based on the recitation of the epic poem and religious
text the Ramayana

SALAFI a fundamentalist interpretation of Islam whose most famous proponent is the
Saudi Arabian–influenced movement Wahhabism

SANSKRITI shared culture of the Ganges plain

TANA BANA warp and weft (Hindi), meaning interconnectedness of cultures

TANZEEM civic and political organization of the Muslim community

YATRA a pilgrimage or pilgrimage route

LHASA

DENSA an elite monastery in Lhasa, referring to either the Sera or Drepang or
Ganden monastery

FENPEI Chinese government policy of guaranteeing public-sector employment
for graduates

LAMA title given to a monk of particularly high spiritual attainment

KORA ritual circumambulation of a religious site in Tibet Buddhism

GEORGE TOWN

BUKA PUASA Malay term for breaking the Ramadan fast; ʿiftar in Arabic

BUMIPUTERA privileged status accorded to Muslim Malays in the Malaysian Constitution

CHI Chinese term for energy

FENG SHUI Chinese geomancy based on Taoist principles

KHALWAT close proximity of nonfamily members of the opposite sex, forbidden in most
traditions of Islam

KONGSI Chinese clan-based protection and welfare organization

ORANG ASLI indigenous tribes of the Malay Peninsula

NONYA cultural hybrid of Chinese and Malays traditions, sometimes known as "Straits
Chinese" or, more currently, *peranakan*

VASTU SHASTRA Indian science of architecture

VEL mythical arrows in Hinduism, representations of which are used in the
Thaipusam processions

Notes

Acknowledgments

1. Power, Piety and People: The Politics of Holy Cities in the 21st Century, Leverhulme Trust, MRF-2014-098.

Introduction

1. International Crisis Group, *The Status of the Status Quo at Jerusalem's Holy Esplanade*, Middle East Report no. 159 (Brussels: International Crisis Group, June 30, 2015); Ofer Zalzberg, "Jerusalem's Crumbling Status Quo," *Today's Zaman*, October 26, 2015, https://www.crisisgroup.org/middle-east-north-africa/eastern-mediterranean /israelpalestine/jerusalem-s-crumbling-status-quo; Michael Dumper, "*The Status of the Status Quo at Jerusalem's Holy Esplanade*: A Critique," *Jerusalem Quarterly* 63–64 (Autumn–Winter 2015): 120–41.
2. Power, Piety, and People: The Politics of Holy Cities in the 21st Century, Leverhulme Trust, MRF-2014-098.
3. United Nations, Department of Economic and Social Affairs, Population Division, *World Urbanization Prospects: 2014 Revision* (New York: United Nations, 2014), https://esa.un.org/unpd/wup/Publications/Files/WUP2014-Highlights.pdf.
4. See, for example, Vincent Bernard, "War in Cities: The Spectre of Total War" (editorial), *International Review of the Red Cross* 98, no. 1 (April 2017), https://www.icrc.org /en/international-review/article/editorial-war-cities-spectre-total-war; Martin Coward, *Urbicide: The Politics of Urban Destruction* (London: Routledge, 2009); Michael Evans, *City Without Joy: Urban Military Operations Into the 21st Century*, Occasional

Paper no. 2 (Canberra: Australian Defence College, 2007), 2, http://www.defence .gov.au/ADC/publications/Occasional/PublcnsOccasional_310310_Citywithout Joy.pdf; Stephen Graham, *Cities Under Siege: The New Military Urbanism* (London: Verso, 2011); David Kilcullen, *Out of the Mountains: The Coming Age of the Urban Guerrilla* (London: Hurst, 2013); World Bank, *Violence in the City: Understanding and Supporting Community Responses to Urban Violence* (Washington, DC: Social Development Department, Conflict, Crime, and Violence Team, World Bank, 2011).

5. Pew Research Center, "The Changing Global Religious Landscape," April 5, 2017, http://www.pewforum.org/2017/04/05/the-changing-global-religious-landscape/.

6. Ron E. Hassner, "'To Halve and to Hold': Conflicts Over Sacred Space and the Problem of Indivisibility," *Security Studies* 12, no. 4 (Summer 2003): 1–33; Isak Svensson, "Fighting with Faith: Religion and Conflict Resolution in Civil Wars," *Journal of Conflict Resolution* 51, no. 6 (2007): 930–49.

7. See, for example, John Bowker, *Problems of Suffering in Religions of the World* (Cambridge: Cambridge University Press, 1970), and John Hick, *Evil and the God of Love* (London: Palgrave Macmillan, 1985).

8. Francis E. Peters, *Jerusalem and Mecca: The Typology of the Holy City in the Near East* (New York: New York University Press, 1986).

9. Conflict in Cities and the Contested State: Everyday Life and the Possibilities of Transformation in Belfast, Jerusalem, and Other Divided Cities, ESRC Large Grant, RES-060-25-0015.

10. Ron E. Hassner, *War on Sacred Grounds* (Ithaca, NY: Cornell University Press, 2013); Robert M. Hayden, "Intersecting Religioscapes and Antagonistic Tolerance: Trajectories of Competition and Sharing of Religious Spaces in the Balkans," *Space and Polity* 17, no. 3 (2013): 320–34.

11. For the three books, see Michael Dumper, *Jerusalem Unbound: Geography, History, and the Future of the Holy City* (New York: Columbia University Press, 2014); *The Politics of Sacred Space: The Old City of Jerusalem in the Middle East Conflict, 1967–2000* (Boulder, CO: Lynne Rienner, 2002); and *The Politics of Jerusalem Since 1967* (New York: Columbia University Press, 1997).

12. Lewis Mumford, *The City in History: Its Origins, Its Transformations, and Its Prospects* (London: Secker and Warburg, 1961).

13. Mumford, *The City in History*, 48, 95.

14. Mumford, *The City in History*, 268.

15. Mumford, *The City in History*, 276–77.

16. See, for example, Scott Bollens, *On Narrow Ground: Urban Policy and Ethnic Conflict in Jerusalem and Belfast* (Albany: State University of New York Press, 2000); Saskia Sassen, "On Concentration and Centrality in the Global City," in *World Cities in a World System*, ed. Paul L. Knox and Peter J. Taylor (Cambridge: Cambridge University Press, 1995), 63–78; Richard Sennett, *The Uses of Disorder: Personal Identity and City Life* (New York: Norton, 1970).

17. These issues are explored to a limited extent in Bollens, *On Narrow Ground*; Sassen, "On Concentration and Centrality in the Global City"; and Sennett, *The Uses of Disorder*.

18. Khaldoun Samman, *Cities of God and Nationalism: Rome, Mecca, and Jerusalem as Contested Sacred World Cities* (London: Routledge, 2007); Nezar AlSayyad and Mejgan Massoumi, eds., *The Fundamentalist City? Religiosity and the Remaking of Urban Space* (London: Routledge, 2011); Elazar Barkan and Karen Barkey, eds., *Choreographies of Shared Sacred Sites: Religion, Politics, and Conflict Resolution* (New York: Columbia University Press, 2015); Dionigi Albera and Maria Couroucli, *Sharing Sacred Spaces in the Mediterranean: Christians, Muslims, and Jews at Shrines and Sanctuaries* (Bloomington: Indiana University Press, 2012); Glenn Bowman, *Sharing the Sacra: The Politics and Pragmatics of Intercommunal Relations Around Holy Places* (Oxford: Berghahn, 2015); Marshall J. Breger, Yitzhak Reiter, and Leonard Hammer, eds., *Holy Places in the Israeli–Palestinian Conflict: Confrontation and Co-existence* (London: Routledge, 2010); Hassner, "'To Halve and to Hold'"; Hassner, *War on Sacred Grounds*; Robert M. Hayden and Timothy D. Walker, "Intersecting Religioscapes: A Comparative Approach to Trajectories of Change, Scale, and Competitive Sharing of Religious Spaces," *Journal of the American Academy of Religion* 81, no. 2 (2013): 320–426; Hayden, "Intersecting Religioscapes and Antagonistic Tolerance."

19. Ashutosh Varshney, *Ethnic Conflict and Civic Life: Hindus and Muslims in India* (New Haven, CN: Yale University Press, 2002), 71.

20. James Anderson, "Religious and Ethno-national Conflict in Divided Cities: How Do Cities Shape Conflicts?" in *Contested Holy Cities: The Urban Dimension of Religious Conflict*, ed. Michael Dumper (London: Routledge, 2019), 22–43.

21. Francis Kok Wah Loh, "Managing Conflict Amidst Development and Developmentalism: George Town, Penang," in *Contested Holy Cities*, ed. Dumper, 81.

22. Madhuri Desai, *Banaras Reconstructed: Architecture and Sacred Space in a Hindu Holy City* (Seattle: University of Washington Press, 2017).

23. See, for example, Hannah Arendt, *On Violence* (Orlando, FL: Harcourt Books, 1969); Graham, *Cities Under Siege*; Kilcullen, *Out of the Mountains*; and Mark Kurlansky, *Nonviolence: The History of a Dangerous Idea* (New York: Random House, 2006).

24. See, for example, Derek Gregory, *Colonial Present: Afghanistan, Palestine, and Iraq* (Oxford: Blackwell, 2006); Fiona McConnell, Nick Megoran, and Philippa Williams, eds., *Geographies of Peace: New Approaches to Boundaries, Diplomacy, and Conflict Resolution* (London: I. B. Tauris, 2014); Rachel Pain and Susan Smith, *Fear: Critical Geopolitics and Everyday Life* (Aldershot, U.K.: Ashgate, 2008); Philippa Williams, *Everyday Peace? Politics, Citizenships, and Muslim Lives in India* (Oxford: Wiley, 2015); Oren Yiftachel, *Ethnocracy: Land and the Politics of Identity in Israel/Palestine* (Philadelphia: University of Pennsylvania Press, 2006).

25. Hayden, "Intersecting Religioscapes and Antagonistic Tolerance."

26. Hayden and Walker, "Intersecting Religioscapes."

27. Michael Dumper, "The Study of Religious Conflicts in Cities," in *Contested Holy Cities*, ed. Dumper, 13.

28. James Anderson, "Imperial Ethnocracy and Demography: Foundations of Ethnonational Conflict in Belfast and Jerusalem," in *Locating Urban Conflicts: Ethnicity, Nationalism, and the Everyday*, ed. Wendy Pullan and Britt Baillie (Basingstoke, U.K.: Palgrave MacMillan, 2013), 195–213.

29. This is a much-debated topic, but the heterodoxy of "Hinduism" is summed up in Ninian Smart, *The Religious Experience of Mankind* (Glasgow: Collins, 1971), 184–85. Some scholars of the religions of India see Hinduism as an invented colonial idea.

30. Mayfair Mei-hui Yang, *Chinese Religiosities: Affliction of Modernity and State Formation* (Berkeley: University of California Press, 2008), 1–40.

31. Yang, *Chinese Religiosities*, 13.

1. Jerusalem

1. The cause of the conflict between Israel and the Palestinians is well researched and well covered by many publications. See, for example, Tom Segev, *One Palestine, Complete: Jews and Arabs Under the British Mandate* (New York: Metropolitan Books, 2000); Baruch Kimmerling and Joel S. Migdal, *The Palestinian People: A History* (Cambridge, MA: Harvard University Press, 2003); and Charles D. Smith, *Palestine and the Arab–Israeli Conflict: A History with Documents* (Boston: Bedford/St. Martin's, 2007).

2. FATAH is the translation of an Arabic reverse acronym meaning the Movement for the Liberation of Palestine. FATAH is the largest of the factions inside the PLO. See Yezid Sayigh, *Armed Struggle and the Search for State: The Palestinian National Movement, 1949–1993* (Oxford: Oxford University Press, 1997).

3. For further reading on the Oslo process, see Joel Peters and David Newman, *The Routledge Handbook on the Israeli–Palestinian Conflict* (New York: Routledge, 2013); Jeremy Pressman, "Visions in Collision: What Happened at Camp David and Taba?" *International Security* 28, no. 2 (2003): 5–43; and Henry Siegman, "The Great Middle East Peace Process Scam," *London Review of Books* 29, no. 16 (2007): 6–7.

4. Ron Hassner, *War on Sacred Grounds* (Ithaca, NY: Cornell Paperbacks, 2013).

5. Robert M. Hayden, "Intersecting Religioscapes and Antagonistic Tolerance: Trajectories of Competition and Sharing of Religious Spaces in the Balkans," *Space and Polity* 17, no. 3 (2013): 320–34.

6. This question of tourism induced by the World Heritage List is a large subdiscipline that I return to in chapter 5. For further details, see Anna Leask and Alan Fyall, *Managing World Heritage Sites* (Oxford: Elsevier, 2006), and David Harrison and Michael Hitchcock, eds., *The Politics of World Heritage: Negotiating Tourism and Conservation* (Toronto: Channel View, 2005).

7. See, for example, Liam O'Dowd and Martina McKnight, eds., *Religion, Violence, and Cities* (London: Routledge, 2013).

8. Dale Eickelman, "Is There an Islamic City? The Making of a Quarter in a Moroccan Town," *International Journal of Middle East Studies* 5 (1974): 274–94.

9. Janet Abu-Lughod, "Islamic City: Historical Myth, Islamic Essence, and Contemporary Relevance," *International Journal of Middle East Studies* 19 (1987): 155–76.

10. Francis Peters, *Jerusalem and Mecca: The Typology of the Holy City in the Near East* (New York: New York University Press, 1986).

11. Hayden, "Intersecting Religioscapes and Antagonistic Tolerance."

12. Michael Dumper, *Jerusalem Unbound: Geography, History, and the Future of the Holy City* (New York: Columbia University Press, 2014), 99.

13. Other actors besides the State of Israel and the PLO also wish to be consulted over the future governance of the city: the Vatican, the councils of various Protestant denominations, Jordan, and Saudi Arabia. Unlike Israel and the PLO, however, they do not wish to claim sovereignty. For a summary of these various claims, see Larry Kletter, "The Sovereignty of Jerusalem under International Law," *Columbia Journal of Transnational Law* 20 (1981): 319–56.

14. At night, when the traffic is light, it is possible to drive from the Wall on the eastern edge to the western suburbs in less than fifteen minutes. Jerusalem has a population of less than one million people.

15. See Shmuel Berkowitz, "The Holy Places in Jerusalem: Legal Aspects," *Justice* 11 (1996): 6. Berkowitz also makes the point that of the thirty most important holy places in Jerusalem, only three are situated in the western half of the city—that is, the Israeli half.

16. Yitzhak Reiter, Marlen Eordegian, and Marwan Abu Khallaf, "Between Divine and Human: The Complexity of Holy Places in Jerusalem," in *Jerusalem: Points of Friction—and Beyond*, ed. Moshe Maoz and Sami Nusseibeh (The Hague: Kluwer Law International, 2000), appendix 1, 155–59.

17. Simone Ricca, *Reinventing Jerusalem: Israel's Reconstruction of the Jewish Quarter After 1967* (London: I. B. Tauris, 2007), 22, 103–6. For a more detailed discussion of these events, see Michael Dumper, *The Politics of Sacred Space: The Old City of Jerusalem in the Middle East Conflict, 1967–2000* (Boulder, CO: Lynne Rienner, 2002), 175. More than a thousand properties, housing 6,000 Palestinians, were expropriated, and the Buraq and Afdali Mosques were destroyed to create a new plaza for Jewish worship and prayer. In this context, archaeological excavations in the post-1967 period became crucial for reimagining and reclaiming Israel's past. See Amos Elon, "Politics and Archaeology," *New York Review of Books* 41 (1994): 14–20.

18. Amnon Ramon, "Delicate Balances at the Temple Mount, 1967–1999," in *Jerusalem: A City and Its Future*, ed. Marshall J. Breger and Ora Ahimeir (Syracuse, NY: Syracuse University Press, 2002), 296–332.

19. Dumper, *The Politics of Sacred Space*, ix, 185; Yitzhak Reiter, "Jewish–Muslim Modus Vivendi at the Temple Mount/al-Haram al-Sharif Since 1967," in *Jerusalem*, ed. Breger and Ahimeir, 269–95.

20. For a more detailed exposition of this dual-administration system, see Michael Dumper, "Security and the Holy Places in Jerusalem: An Israeli Policy of Incremental Control—'Hebronisation'?," in *Locating Urban Conflicts: Ethnicity, Nationalism, and the Everyday*, ed. Wendy Pullan and Britt Baillie (Basingstoke, U.K.: Palgrave MacMillan, 2013), 76–90; Reiter, "Jewish–Muslim Modus Vivendi at the Temple Mount"; Ramon, "Delicate Balances at the Temple Mount"; Gideon Avni and Jon Seligman, *The Temple Mount 1917–2001: Documentation, Research, and Inspection of Antiquities*, Israeli Antiquities Authority (Jerusalem: Keter Press Enterprises, 2001).

21. For example, in August 1969 a Christian tourist set fire to Salah-ed Din's pulpit in the al-Aqsa Mosque; during the 1970s and 1980s, Jewish terrorist groups plotted to

blow up sites in the Haram, and Palestinians carried out stabbings of tourists and a Jewish worshipper; in 1986, a Palestinian resistance cell carried out a grenade attack on an Israeli military ceremony beside the Wailing Wall; in the 1980s and 1990s, the Waqf Administration clashed with Israeli settler groups such as Ataret Cohanim over their tunneling under the Haram (Dumper, "Security and the Holy Places in Jerusalem," 80).

22. By 1994, the PLO and its executive body in the Palestinian National Authority were functioning openly on the outskirts of Jerusalem and influencing the conduct of Palestinian affairs in the city. An indication of the PLO's role in the management of the holy sites was the appointment of the former director-general of the Jordanian-controlled Waqf Administration, Shaykh Hassan Tahbuub, as the Palestinian National Authority minister of endowments and religious affairs, with an office close to the Haram al-Sharif. See Menachem Klein, "The Islamic Holy Places as a Political Bargaining Card (1993–1995)," *Catholic University Law Review* 45, no. 3 (1996): 745–64, and Sami Musallem, *The Struggle for Jerusalem* (Jerusalem: PASSIA, 1996).

23. Further details on this change can be found in Michael Dumper, "Israeli Settlement in the Old City of Jerusalem," *Journal of Palestine Studies* 21 (1992): 32–53, and Wendy Pullan and Maximillian Gwiazda, "The Biblical Present in Jerusalem's 'City of David,'" in *Memory, Culture, and the Contemporary City: Building Sites*, ed. Andrew Webber, Uta Staiger, and Henriette Steiner (London: Palgrave Macmillan, 2009), 106–25.

24. This securitized culture is offset in part by the emergence of the Palestinian Muslims from inside Israel as a political actor in the struggle over the control of the holy sites. As Israeli citizens, they have more freedom to maneuver in the city and have exploited this freedom to buttress the Palestinian position as well as to step into the political vacuum created by Israeli policies to marginalize the PLO and the Jordanians in the city. See Michael Dumper, "Jerusalem's Troublesome Sheikh," *The Guardian*, October 7, 2009, and Michael Dumper and Craig Larkin, "In Defence of al-Aqsa: The Islamic Movement Inside Israel and Battle for Jerusalem," *Middle East Journal* 66, no. 1 (2012): 31–52.

25. Ramon, "Delicate Balances at the Temple Mount." See also Yizhar Be'er, *Targeting the Temple Mount: A Current Look at Threats to the Temple Mount by Extremist and Messianic Groups* (Jerusalem: Centre for the Protection of Democracy in Israel—Keshev, January 2001).

26. Josef W. Meri, *The Cult of Saints Among Muslims and Jews in Medieval Syria* (Oxford: Oxford University Press, 2002); Aliaa Ezzeldin Ismail El Sandouby, *The Ahl al-Bayt in Cairo and Damascus: The Dynamics of Making Shrines for the Family of the Prophet* (N.p.: ProQuest, 2008); Edith Szanto, "Sayyida Zaynab in the State of Exception: Shi'i Sainthood as 'Qualified Life' in Contemporary Syria," *International Journal of Middle East Studies* 44, no. 2 (2012): 285–99.

27. East Jerusalem Heads of Mission, European Union, *Annual Report* (Brussels: European Union, 2014), http://www.eccpalestine.org/eu-diplomats-warn-of-regional-conflagration-over-temple-mount/. See also Peter Beaumont, "Jerusalem at Boiling Point of Polarisation and Violence—EU Report," *The Guardian*, March 20, 2015, https://www

.theguardian.com/world/2015/mar/20/jerusalem-at-boiling-point-of-polarisation
-and-violence-eu-report.

28. Jerusalem Institute for Israeli Studies, *Statistical Yearbook of Jerusalem* (Jerusalem: Jerusalem Institute for Israel Studies, 2018), chap. 3, "Population," http://www.jerusalem
institute.org.il/.upload/yearbook/2018/shnaton_C0918.pdf.

29. International Crisis Group, *Extreme Makeover? (I): Israel's Politics of Land and Faith in
East Jerusalem*, Middle East Report no. 134 (Brussels: International Crisis Group, 2012), 4.

30. Jerusalem Institute for Israeli Studies, *Statistical Yearbook of Jerusalem*, chap. 3, "Population."

31. Hassner, *War on Sacred Grounds*.

32. No more than 20 percent of eligible Palestinian voters have participated in Israeli Jerusalem Municipality elections, and that portion consists mostly of employees of the
municipality. See Moshe Amirav, *Jerusalem Syndrome: The Palestinian Israeli Battle for
the Holy City* (Sussex, U.K.: Sussex Academic Press, 2009), 13.

33. HAMAS is the acronym for Harakat al-Muqawamah al-ʿIslamiyyah, or Islamic
Resistance Movement.

34. Michael Dumper, *Islam and Israel: Muslim Religious Endowments and the Jewish State*
(Washington, DC: Institute for Palestine Studies, 1994), 14.

35. Dumper, *Jerusalem Unbound*, 231. The figures given here were supplied by an Israeli
security adviser to the Israeli Jerusalem Municipality during discussions organized
by the Canadian-sponsored project Jerusalem Old City Initiative.

36. Kenny Schmitt, "Living Islam in Jerusalem: Faith, Conflict, and the Disruption of
Religious Practice," PhD diss., University of Exeter, 2018, 219.

37. Wael Salaymeh, "In Pictures: Ramadan's Holiest Night," *Al Jazeera*, August 5, 2013,
http://www.aljazeera.com/indepth/inpictures/2013/08/2013851380381790.html.

38. *Haaretz*, "Some 400,000 Muslims Attend Overnight Prayers at al-Aqsa Mosque in
Jerusalem," July 2, 2016, http://www.haaretz.com/israel-news/1.728438.

39. International Crisis Group, *The Status of the Status Quo at Jerusalem's Holy Esplanade*,
Middle East Report no. 159 (Brussels: International Crisis Group, 2015), 2. See also
Ben Hartman and Daniel K. Eisenbud, "Massive West Bank Clashes Leave Palestinian
Dead," *Jerusalem Post*, July 25, 2014, http://www.jpost.com/National-News/Clashes
-break-out-in-West-Bank-reportedly-leaving-a-Palestinian-dead-368864.

40. Schmitt, "Living Islam in Jerusalem," 221.

41. For more details, see Yitzhak Reiter, "Contest or Cohabitation in Shared Holy
Places? The Cave of the Patriarchs and Samuel's Tomb," in *Holy Places in the Israeli–
Palestinian Conflict: Confrontation and Co-existence*, ed. Marshall J. Breger, Yitzhak
Reiter, and Leonard Hammer (London: Routledge, 2010), 158–77.

42. A small subdiscipline in urban studies has emerged to consider the impacts of these
kinds of urban configurations on social and political relations in highly congested
cities. See, for example, Caroline Melly, *Bottleneck: Moving, Building, and Belonging in
an African City.* (Chicago: University of Chicago Press, 2017), cited in Kenny Schmitt,
"Jerusalem's Ramadan Fridays: Pilgrimage Through Bottlenecks of Occupation," in
Contested Holy Cities: The Urban Dimension of Religious Conflict, ed. Michael Dumper
(London: Routledge, 2019), 103.

43. See Conflict in Cities and the Contested State: Everyday Life and the Possibilities of Transformation in Belfast, Jerusalem, and Other Divided Cities, ESRC Large Grant, RES-060-25-0015.

44. The Israeli government presented its proposals to rebuild the Maghrabi Ascent as "preventive archaeology." See Israeli National Commission, *Report of the Israeli National Commission for UNESCO* (Paris: UNESCO, February 28, 2007), cited in Michael Dumper and Craig Larkin, "The Politics of Heritage and the Limitations of International Agency in Divided Cities: The Role of UNESCO in Jerusalem's Old City," *Review of International Studies* 38, no. 1 (January 2012): 25–52.

45. UNESCO, *Report of the Technical Mission to the Old City of Jerusalem (27 February–2 March 2007)* (Paris: UNESCO, March 12, 2007), http://www.unesco.org/bpi/pdf/jerusalem_report_en.pdf. See also Dumper, *Jerusalem Unbound*, 168–69.

46. See also Daniel Seidemann, *The Events Surrounding the Mugrabi Gate—2007: A Case Study Jerusalem* (Windsor, U.K.: University of Windsor, 2007).

47. The tour is recorded in a video. See Temple Institute, *Tisha B'Av, 5775: Return to the Temple Mount*, July 27, 2015, https://www.youtube.com/watch?v=vESctNnkyvo.

48. For a breakdown of the categories of police and security forces operating in Jerusalem, see Michael Dumper, "Policing Divided Cities: Stabilisation and Law Enforcement in Palestinian East Jerusalem," *International Affairs* 89, no. 5 (September 2013): 1247–64.

49. Temple Institute, *Tisha B'Av, 5775*; International Crisis Group, *Jerusalem's Holy Esplanade Reveals the Limits of Israeli Counter-Terrorism* (Brussels: International Crisis Group, May 14, 2018), https://www.crisisgroup.org/middle-east-north-africa/eastern-mediterranean/israelpalestine/jerusalems-holy-esplanade-reveals-limits-israeli-counter-terrorism#; International Crisis Group, *How to Preserve the Fragile Calm at Jerusalem's Holy Esplanade*, Middle East Briefing no. 48 (Brussels: International Crisis Group, 2016), 1–19; International Crisis Group, *The Status of the Status Quo at Jerusalem's Holy Esplanade*.

50. *BBC Panorama*, "A Train That Divides Jerusalem," July 20, 2015, http://mediacenter.tveyes.com/downloadgateway.aspx?UserID=195235&MDID=3802334&MDSeed=9122&Type=Media.

51. See discussion in Schmitt, "Living Islam in Jerusalem."

52. Exceptions include Robert Shepherd, "UNESCO and the Politics of Cultural Heritage in Tibet," *Journal of Contemporary Asia* 36, no. 2 (2006): 243–57; John Pendlebury, Michael Short, and Aidan While, "Urban World Heritage Sites and the Problem of Authenticity," *Cities* 26, no. 6 (2009): 349–58; Graeme Evans, "Living in a World Heritage City: Stakeholders in the Dialectic of the Universal and Particular," *International Journal for Heritage Studies* 8, no. 2 (2002): 117–35.

53. U.S. Congress, Jerusalem Embassy Act, 104th Cong., 1st sess., October 23, 1995, http://www.gpo.gov/fdsys/pkg/BILLS-104s1322es/pdf/BILLS-104s1322es.pdf. See also Walid Khalidi, "The Ownership of the US Embassy Site in Jerusalem," *Journal of Palestine Studies* 29, no. 4 (2000): 80–101.

54. International Crisis Group, "Has President Trump Endorsed Israel's Position on the Status of Jerusalem?," December 7, 2017, https://www.crisisgroup.org/middle-east

-north-africa/eastern-mediterranean/israelpalestine/counting-costs-us-recognition
-jerusalem-israels-capital.

55. Ron Hassner, "'To Halve and to Hold': Conflicts Over Sacred Space and the Problem of Indivisibility," *Security Studies* 12, no. 4 (Summer 2003): 1–33; see also Isak Svensson, "Fighting with Faith: Religion and Conflict Resolution in Civil Wars," *Journal of Conflict Resolution* 51, no. 6 (2007): 930–49.

2. The Politics of Regionalism

1. There is some evidence that during the period of the Arab and Muslim expansion in the seventh and eighth centuries, smaller churches were commonly demolished or taken over completely following the conquest of major cities. It was also common practice that the principle church was partitioned and shared between Muslims and Christians. Damascus is an example. See Albert F. Calvert and Walter M. Gallichan, *Cordova: A City of the Moors* (London: John Lane, Bodley Head, 1907), 99.

2. The Córdoba España, the city's official tourist agency, writes on its website that the Arab conquerors *paid* the Visigothic Christians for the "rights to move the musalla [the primitive prayer area outside the city walls] to the Visigoth basilica of San Vicente, thus forming the beginnings of the Great Mosque which still survives to this day" (Córdoba España, "Muslim Cordoba," 2017, http://english.turismodecordoba.org/muslim-cordoba.cfm).

3. Nuha Khoury, "The Meaning of the Great Mosque of Cordoba in the Tenth Century," *Muqarnas* 13 (1996): 83–86; for references on this debate, see also Michele Lamprakos, "Memento Mauri: The Mosque-Cathedral of Cordoba," *Aggregate*, 2016, 21–24, 23–32, http://we-aggregate.org/piece/memento-mauri-the-mosque-cathedral-of-cordoba. The UNESCO World Heritage Center website states that "the Great Mosque, with its juxtaposition of cultures and architectural styles, has retained its material integrity. It was built in the 8th century, over the remains of the Visigoth Basilica of San Vicente" (UNESCO, "The Historic Centre of Cordoba," n.d. (date of inscription: 1984), http://whc.unesco.org/en/list/313). D. Fairchild Ruggles writes that "archaeological excavations carried out in the 1920s by Ricardo Velazquez Bosco and in 1931–1936 by Felix Hernandez Gimenez and expanded in recent years under the direction of Pedro Marfil *unequivocally* confirm the presence of a much older and smaller church under the present site of the Cathedral-Mosque" ("The Stratigraphy of Forgetting: The Great Mosque of Cordoba and Its Contested Legacy," in *Contested Cultural Heritage: Religion, Nationalism, Erasure, and Exclusion in a Global World*, ed. Helaine Silverman [New York: Springer, 2011], 56, emphasis added). For others, whatever the merits of the archaeological evidence, the highlighting of the Visigothic remains diminishes the importance of the architectural achievements of the Islamic period (for example, Manuel Torres Aguilar, UNESCO Chair in Conflict Resolution, University of Cordoba, interviewed by the author, November 9, 2016, Cordoba, Spain).

4. Al-Himyari, quoted in Brenda D. Schildgen, *Heritage or Heresy: Preservation and Destruction of Religious Art and Architecture in Europe* (New York: Palgrave Macmillan, 2008), 87.

5. Spanish sources frequently use the term *bosques de columnas* to describe the columns. See Lamprakos, "Memento Mauri," 4.

6. Lamprakos, "Memento Mauri," 4.

7. The *qibla* was, very unusually, fixed to the south and not to the east, which would be in the approximate direction of Mecca. This peculiarity was unique to the Mezquita and much vaunted by the Muslim community there. For Hakam II's support for this peculiarity, see Khoury, "The Meaning of the Great Mosque," 83. Other ritualistic and liturgical practices were also unique to the Islam of Cordoba, including carrying the Qur'an around the mosque behind a lit candle before reading it, a practice with strong suggestions of Christian influences. See Schildgen, *Heritage or Heresy*, 86.

8. In 732 CE, Arab–Berber forces under Abd al-Rahman al-Ghafiqi were defeated by the French king Charles Martel in the vicinity of Tours (James O'Callaghan, *A History of Medieval Spain* [Ithaca, NY: Cornell University Press, 1975], 98). Although this campaign preceded the ʿUmayyad dynasty's takeover in Cordoba, it nonetheless marked the northernmost point of Arab penetration into France.

9. Muslim Cordoba "probably had a population in excess of 100,000 people, though some writers have greatly inflated that figure" ("Cordoba," in *International Dictionary of Historic Places: Southern Europe*, ed. Trudy Ring [London: Fitzroy Dearborn, 1994], 3:155).

10. Thomas F. Glick, *Islamic and Christian Spain in the Early Middle Ages* (Princeton, NJ: Princeton University Press, 1979), 20, 40–41.

11. Glick, *Islamic and Christian Spain in the Early Middle Ages*, 41.

12. Khoury forcefully argues this shift in power in a rather convoluted way in "The Meaning of the Great Mosque," 80–82.

13. Américo Castro, *The Structure of Spanish History* (Princeton, NJ: Princeton University Press, 1954), 147, 158–60.

14. Glick, *Islamic and Christian Spain in the Early Middle Ages*, 41–42. See also Castro, *The Structure of Spanish History*, 157.

15. The exercise was reciprocated when Ferdinand III removed the bells from the Mezquita and returned them to Santiago de Compostela using Muslim prisoners. See Julie Harris, "Mosque to Church Conversions in the Spanish Reconquest," *Medieval Encounters* 3, no. 2 (1997): 161, https://www.academia.edu/1162610/Mosque_to_Church_Conversions_in_the_Iberian_Reconquest?auto=download, and Robert Hodum, *Pilgrims' Steps: A Search for Spain's Santiago and an Examination of His Way* (Bloomington, IN: iUniverse, 2012), 53–54.

16. Schildgen, *Heritage or Heresy*, 87.

17. See Glick's discussion of Bulliet's conversion curve, which suggests that by 1100 CE Muslims outnumbered Christians (*Islamic and Christian Spain in the Early Middle Ages*, 33–35).

18. John Edwards, *Christian Cordoba: The City and Its Region in the Late Middle Ages* (Cambridge: Cambridge University Press, 1982), 7–8, 178. Edwards discusses the difficulty

in trying to ascertain the number of Muslim residents who remained in Cordoba after the transfer of power due to the paucity of the evidence available. One indication that significant numbers were allowed back was the relatively unsuccessful efforts in trying to attract new Christian settlers from the North.

19. See references in Schildgen, *Heritage or Heresy*, 87 n. 59.

20. Heather Ecker, "The Great Mosque of Cordoba in the 12th and Thirteenth Centuries," *Muqarnas* 20 (2003): 117–18; Lamprakos, "Memento Mauri," 6.

21. Jerrilyn Dodds, one of the foremost scholars of the Mezquita, comments that "the Christians who conquered Cordoba understood that there was much more power to be gained from appropriating this extraordinary metaphor of their conquest than from destroying it" (quoted in Ruggles, "The Stratigraphy of Forgetting," 54).

22. Robert Burns, *The Crusader Kingdom of Valencia: Reconstruction on a Thirteenth-Century Frontier*, vol. 2 (Cambridge, MA: Harvard University Press, 1967).

23. Schildgen, *Heritage or Heresy*, 90.

24. Edwards, *Christian Cordoba*, 7.

25. Edwards, *Christian Cordoba*, 180. Edwards also highlights the "elaborate structures for dealing efficiently with problems such as the exchange of prisoners, theft and kidnapping" (180).

26. See discussion in Edwards, *Christian Cordoba*, 166. See also Ecker, "The Great Mosque of Cordoba," 120–25.

27. At the same time, it is also clear that such revenues extracted from visitors and pilgrims were insufficient for the upkeep of and alterations planned for the cathedral. New endowments and targeted forms of taxes were introduced to raise additional funds. See Ecker, "The Great Mosque of Cordoba," 119–22.

28. Jeronimo, *Descriptio Cordovbae*, possibly 1456, quoted in Lamprakos, "Memento Mauri," 7 n. 15.

29. We should also note that the position of the Jewish community, which for many years forged strong connections with the higher Christian nobility in Cordoba and received some protection from the Crown, deteriorated dramatically after attacks against it in 1391, culminating in the Jews' expulsion in 1483—eighteen years before that of the Muslims. Even those who converted, the *conversos*, were strongly discriminated against. See Edwards, *Christian Cordoba*, 182.

30. Edwards, *Christian Cordoba*, 7.

31. Ecker, "The Great Mosque of Cordoba," 126.

32. Glick, *Islamic and Christian Spain in the Early Middle Ages*, 50.

33. Schildgen, *Heritage or Heresy*, 96.

34. Charles V, quoted in Lamprakos, "Memento Mauri," 8, emphasis added.

35. Lamprakos, "Memento Mauri," 11.

36. A good example of this view of an interfaith period is a renowned speech by President Barack Obama in Cairo on June 4, 2002, in which he celebrated Islam's "proud tradition of tolerance" exemplified by the history of Cordoba (quoted in Elena Arigita, "'The Cordoba Paradigm': Memory and Silence Around Europe's Islamic Past," in *Islam and the Politics of Culture in Europe: Memory, Aesthetics, Art*, ed. Peter Frank, Sarah Dornhof, and Elena Arigita [Bielefeld, Germany: Transcript, 2013], 23 n. 5).

37. Lamprakos, "Memento Mauri," 11.
38. Schildgen, *Heritage or Heresy*, 97.
39. Lamprakos, "Memento Mauri," 14–15; Schildgen, *Heritage or Heresy*, 97.
40. One of the main differences between Spain and other federal entities is that for historic political reasons some regional governments have more powers and responsibilities than others. In addition, there was no attempt to create some parity in geographic size, demography, or wealth when delineating federal regions, which has created an impediment to a representative federal electoral system. The Spanish Socialist Party in Catalan refers to the Spanish system as "asymmetric federalism." See Christopher Ross, Bill Richardson, and Begona Sangrador-Vegas, *Contemporary Spain*, 4th ed. (London: Routledge, 2016), 37.
41. "Cordoba," in *International Dictionary of Historic Places*, ed. Ring, 3:158.
42. Yves Cabannes, "Participatory Budgeting: A Significant Contribution to Participatory Democracy," *Environment and Urbanisation* 16, no. 1 (2004): 27–46. Cabannes writes that Cordoba was "one of the first Spanish cities which established a normative framework for citizen participation on the local level through the Regulations on Citizen Participation." These regulations, enacted in 1981, were the first of their kind in Spain and were accompanied by the creation of a regional government department for citizens' participation. See Enrique Ortega de Miguel and Andrés Sanz Mulas, "Water Management in Cordoba (Spain): A Participative Efficient and Effective Public Model," in *Reclaiming Public Water: Achievements, Struggles, and Visions from Around the World* (Amsterdam: Transnational Institute, 2005), https://www.tni.org /files/waterspain.pdf.
43. Stephen Burgen, "In Andalucía, the Poor and Jobless Have Little Faith in a Better Mañana," *The Guardian*, April 27, 2014, https://www.theguardian.com/world/2014 /apr/27/spain-andalucia-financial-crisis-unemployment.
44. Stephen Burgen, "Spain's Population Set to Drop 11% by 2050," *The Guardian*, October 20, 2016, https://www.theguardian.com/world/2016/oct/20/spain-population -drop-by-2050-trends-low-birth-high-life-elderly-singles. According to a report released by the National Statistics Office of Spain in 2016, Spain is facing a serious demographic crisis because of low birth rates and high life expectancy: by 2050, those older than sixty-five will account for 34.6 percent of the population. Conversely, the young population is also declining: in 1975, close to 30 percent of the population was younger than fifteen, but by 2015 this percentage was halved to only 15 percent (William Chislett, "Spain 40 Years After General Franco: Change of a Nation," Real Instituto El Cano, November 16, 2015, http://www.realinstitutoel cano.org/wps/portal/rielcano_en/contenido?WCM_GLOBAL_CONTEXT =/elcano/elcano_in/zonas_in/ari66-2015-chislett-spain-40-years-after-franco- change-nation).
45. "Cordoba," in *International Dictionary of Historic Places*, ed. Ring, 3:158.
46. Thomas Brinkhoff, "Population of Cordoba and Spain," City Populations Database, 2017, https://www.quandl.com/data/CITYPOP/CITY_CORDOBAANDSPAIN. The province and city follow the same trends in terms of changes to family units, with the average number of children also falling.

47. Burgen, "In Andalucía, the Poor and Jobless Have Little Faith in a Better Mañana."

48. Eric Calderwood, "The Reconquista of the Mosque of Cordoba," *Foreign Policy*, April 10, 2015, https://foreignpolicy.com/2015/04/10/the-reconquista-of-the-mosque-of-cordoba-spain-catholic-church-islam/.

49. Alfonso Alba, "La Cordoba halal aspira a recibar 200.000 turistas musulmanes mas al año," *Cordopolis*, January 13, 2015, http://cordopolis.es/2015/01/13/la-cordoba-halal-aspira-a-recibir-200-000-turistas-musulmanes-mas-al-ano/.

50. Ismael Nafria, "Interactive: Religious Beliefs and Practices in Spain," *La Vanguardia* April 3, 2015, http://www.lavanguardia.com/vangdata/20150402/54429637154/interactivo-creencias-y-practicas-religiosas-en-espana.html. The Centre for Sociological Investigation report with slightly lower figures is cited in U.S. Department of State, Bureau of Democracy, Human Rights, and Labor, *International Religious Freedom Report 2015* (Washington, DC: U.S. Department of State, 2015), https://www.state.gov/j/drl/rls/irf/2015/index.htm.

51. Centre for Sociological Investigation report, cited in U.S. Department of State, *International Religious Freedom Report 2015*.

52. U.S. Department of State, Bureau of Democracy, Human Rights, and Labor, *International Religious Freedom Report 2005* (Washington, DC: U.S. Department of State, 2005), https://www.state.gov/j/drl/rls/irf/2005/51582.htm.

53. U.S. Department of State, *International Religious Freedom Report 2015*. According to the most recent census of Spain's Muslim population, 1,858,409 Muslims are currently living in Spain. Of this number, nearly 800,000 are Moroccan citizens (Union de Comunidades Islamicas de Espana [UCIDE], *Estudio demografico de la poblacion musulmana*" (N.p.: UCIDE, 2015), http://ucide.org/es/content/estudio-demogr%C3%A1fico-de-la-poblaci%C3%B3n-musulmana-2). One explanation of this apparent discrepancy in totals is that nonforeign Muslims (i.e., Spanish nationals who have converted to Islam) are not enumerated systematically in the various censi and independent surveys. For further discussion of this issue, see Ana Contreras Planet, "Spain," in *The Oxford Handbook of European Islam*, ed. Jocelyn Cesari (Oxford: Oxford University Press, 2014), 311–49.

54. In 2005, an estimated 13.7 percent of the 3.7 million immigrants in Spain were from Morocco. There were "386,958 Moroccans living in the country legally and as many as 120,000 illegal Moroccan immigrants" at this time (U.S. Department of State, *International Religious Freedom Report 2005*). See also Samuel Loewenberg, "As Spaniards Lose Their Religion, Church Leaders Struggle to Hold On," *New York Times*, June 26, 2005, http://www.nytimes.com/2005/06/26/weekinreview/as-spaniards-lose-their-religion-church-leaders-struggle-to.html).

55. Two examples of this extrication are the legalization of abortion and divorce in the decades following Franco's death.

56. Geoff Pingree, "Secular Drive Challenges Spain's Catholic Identity," *Christian Science Monitor*, October 1, 2004, https://www.csmonitor.com/2004/1001/p07s02-woeu.html. Article 16 of the Constitution of 1979 also states that although "no religion shall have a state character . . . public authorities shall take into account the religious beliefs of Spanish society and consequently maintain appropriate cooperative

relations with the Catholic Church" and other denominations (quoted in U.S. Department of State, *International Religious Freedom Report 2015*, 2). This is an interesting formulation. The article could have referred more generally to Christian values drawn from the Bible, in the same way as many Arab states refer to the Qur'an and sharia law as inspirations for and guides to their constitutions. The specification of a particular institution, the Roman Catholic Church, in practice formalizes that relationship and elevates the church to a position of *primes inter pares*.

57. For a good summary of the twists and turns of this story of the Catholic Church's relationship with the Spanish state, see John Hooper, *The New Spaniards* (London: Penguin, 2006), 96–99. See also U.S. Department of State, *International Religious Freedom Report 2015*, 4.

58. Hooper, *The New Spaniards*, 95.

59. Part of the anger stems from the lack of transparency in the process of registration. The church has not publicly disclosed the number of properties it has obtained because the law does not oblige it to declare them.

60. Other important but lessor concerns for the Association of Muslims in Cordoba are Muslims' right to practice their religion when incarcerated and the extent to which religious instruction in schools, which is normally Catholic, is obligatory.

61. The Junta Islámica was established in 1989 and comprises largely converts and indigenous Spanish Muslims. Its main focus is publication of research on Spanish Muslim identity, Muslim feminism, and the promotion of interfaith dialogue. Its funding is independent of the Spanish government or any other state, coming mainly from the fees accruing to the Halal Institute. The Halal Institute is one of its most active and successful initiatives in Spain and is responsible for the supervision of food production according to Islamic halal principles for certification. See the websites for Junta Islámica (http://www.juntaislamica.org) and the Halal Institute (http://www.institutohalal.com).

62. Aside from the Mezquita, some of the most famous Catholic churches in Cordoba are the Basilica del Juramento de San Rafael and the Royal Collegiate Church of Saint Hippolytus. With regard to the non–Roman Catholic Christian churches, at the beginning of the 1960s there was just one Protestant church in Cordoba, and Andalucia was "recognized as one of the least evangelized provinces in the whole country." After the death of General Franco, more Baptist, Independent, Pentecostal, and Apostolic churches emerged. The pastors of these churches formed the Fraternidad Ministerial Evangélica de Córdoba. During the late 1980s and early 1990s, the group began working on a project called "2000/30," which at its core had a view to build thirty congregations in the province of Cordoba by the year 2000, which it succeeded in doing. See Jim Memory, "Collaboratice Church Planting in Cordoba—a Model for Europe," *Evangelical Focus*, 2015, http://evangelicalfocus.com/blogs/1018/Collaborative_church_planting_in_Cordobaa_model_for_Europe.

63. Arigita, "'The Cordoba Paradigm,'" 33–34.

64. Lyra D. Monteiro, "The Mezquita of Cordoba Is Made of More Than Bricks: Towards a Broader Definition of the 'Heritage' Protected at UNESCO World Heritage Sites,"

Archaeologies 7, no. 2 (August 2011): 319–20; Arigita, "'The Cordoba Paradigm,'" 33–34.

65. Arigita, "'The Cordoba Paradigm,'" 33–34.

66. See Monteiro, "The Mezquita of Cordoba," 325 n. 10; Arigita, "'The Cordoba Paradigm,'" 33–34. Activists belonging to the La Platforma de la Mezquita-Catedral suspect that some corporate functions hosted by the diocese in the Mezquita include wealthy Muslims, who are allowed to pray, because the corporate rates charged are extremely lucrative.

67. See Escudero's account of these overtures in Sheikh Mansour Abdussalaam Escudero, "The Mezquita-Cathedral of Cordoba: A Shared Space for Prayer," speech at the First Junta Islámica University Seminar on Religious Freedom and Shared Spaces: The Mezquita-Cathedral of Cordoba, July 4, 2012, https://www.webislam.com/articles/72210-the_mezquitacathedral_of_cordoba_a_shared_space_for_prayer.html.

68. Bishop Juan José Asenjo, quoted in Escudero, "The Mezquita-Cathedral of Cordoba."

69. Geoff Pingree and Liza Abend, "Spain's New Muslims; Converts Have Become the Agreeable Face of Spanish Islam," *Walrus Magazine*, August 15, 2007, https://thewalrus.ca/2007-09-religion/. See also Ruggles, "The Stratigraphy of Forgetting," 56.

70. *El Mundo*, 1, 3, 22, cited in Emerson Vermaat, "The Rapid Re-Islamization of Southern Spain," *Militant Islam Monitor*, August 4, 2008, http://www.militantislammonitor.org/article/id/3558.

71. Arigita, "'The Cordoba Paradigm,'" 35–36; Monteiro, "The Mezquita of Cordoba," 315.

72. The judge's sentence and declaration can be found at *Europa Press*, "El juez absuelve a los ocho musulmanes que rezaron en la Mezquita de Córdoba en 2010," February 7, 2013, http://www.europapress.es/nacional/noticia-amp-juez-absuelve-ocho-musulmanes-rezaron-mezquita-cordoba-2010-20130207155419.html. For a right-wing version of the events, see *El Mundo*, "Prestan declaración los vigilantes agredidos en la Mezquita por musulmanes," April 2, 2010, http://www.elmundo.es/elmundo/2010/04/02/andalucia/1270205072.html.

73. See Monteiro, "The Mezquita of Cordoba," 315, which lists several of these protests; see also Video Dos Acciones, https://vime+o.com/41763684.

74. Uniformed guards employed by private security firms have been deployed in the Mezquita, but their absence during my site visits may indicate a change of policy by the diocese in an attempt to be less confrontational. For a photograph of such deployments, see Brian Roisa and Jaime Jover-Baez, "Contested Urban Heritage: Discourse of Meaning and Ownership of the Mosque-Cathedral of Cordoba, Spain," *Journal of Urban Cultural Studies* 4, nos. 1–2 (2017): 146.

75. Calderwood, "The Reconquista of the Mosque of Cordoba," 1–3. See also Antonio [*sic*], "La Mezquita de Córdoba desaparece de Google Maps," *Andaluces Diario*, November 23, 2014, http://www.andalucesdiario.es/ciudadanxs/la-mezquita-de-cordoba-desaparece-de-google-maps/. The actual conflict over the name started in 2010. See Rachel Donadio, "Name Debate Echoes an Old Clash of Faiths," *New York Times*, November 5, 2010, https://www.nytimes.com/2010/11/05/world/europe/05cordoba.html.

76. Lamprakos, "Memento Mauri," 15. Others put the date of the change at 2010.

77. *The Cathedral of Cordoba: A Live Witness to Our History* (no publication information), leaflet available for tourists on entering the Mezquita, acquired November 2015, in author's files. Monteiro deconstructs the language and design of the leaflet in more detail in "The Mezquita of Cordoba," 320. Her version of the leaflet is similar but not identical to the one I acquired.

78. *Monumental Site: The Mosque-Cathedral of Cordoba* (no publication information), leaflet available for tourists on entering the Mezquita, acquired November 2016, in author's files.

79. Up to 2011, Cordoba city had been ruled by the traditional leftist-Communist party Izquierda Unida, but in 2014 the mayor was drawn from the Spanish right-wing Popular Party. He absented himself from the debate. Podemos, a new left-wing and green party, made the "public ownership" of the Mosque-Cathedral and the Giralda of Seville part of its electoral program. See *El Mundo*, "Podemos propone que la Mezquita de Cordoba o la Giralda pasen a tener titularidad publica," March 12, 2015, http://www.elmundo.es/andalucia/2015/03/12/550161ad22601d563f8b456e.html, and *ABC News*, "Las elecciones, o el guión de la campaña por la Mezquita-Catedral," November 18, 2015, http://sevilla.abc.es/andalucia/cordoba/sevi-elecciones-o-guion -campana-mezquita-catedral-201511180810_noticia.html.

80. Among the public figures supporting La Platforma were Federico Mayor Zaragoza, director of UNESCO between 1987 and 1999 and president of Fundación Cultural de Paz.

81. See also "Let's Save the Mosque of Córdoba—for a Mosque-Cathedral for All," https://www.change.org/p/salvemos-la-mezquita-de-c%C3%B3rdoba-por-una -mezquita-catedral-de-todos.

82. *El País*, "La Iglesia inscribió 4.500 propiedades sin publicidad y sin pagar impuestos," May 6, 2013.

83. *El País*, "Guerra laica por el patrimonio," May 26, 2016, http://politica.elpais.com /politica/2016/05/20/actualidad/1463762572_434761.html.

84. In Navarre, the church registered 1,087 properties, but a well-organized citizen movement has had some traction in reversing cases, leading to the return of property to state administration (*El País*, "Guerra laica por el patrimonio").

85. *El País*, "Guerra laica por el patrimonio."

86. The cost of entrance in 2016 was eight euros per person, and official figures show that there are 1.1 to 1.5 million visitors a year.

87. See Ruggles, "The Stratigraphy of Forgetting," 56.

88. According to La Platforma, the regional government of Andalusia was responsible for all restoration work in the Mezquita, but this task was ceded to the diocese in 1994.

89. *Andaluces Diario*, "Ni IBI, ni IVA, ni sociedades: La Iglesia no paga impuestos por la Mezquita de Córdoba," July 20, 2013, http://www.andalucesdiario.es/ciudadanxs/ni -ibi-ni-iva-ni-sociedades-la-iglesia-no-paga-impuestos-por-la-mezquita-de-cordoba/.

90. Ruggles makes an interesting but not entirely persuasive point that it is the actual form of prayer in Islam that is considered unacceptable because it is "intrusive." She

contends that it is not the individual worship that is controversial but the collective, public, and orchestrated bowing and prostrations that accentuate Islam's difference with Christian practice and make it impossible to accommodate Islam ("The Stratigraphy of Forgetting," 61).

91. Mansur Escudero, quoted in Pingree and Abend, "Spain's New Muslims." See also Escudero, "The Mezquita-Cathedral of Cordoba," where Escudero states, "Among Spanish Muslims today, there is no desire to replicate the past, nor are we impelled by a romantic vision of a new Umayyad period in our city." See also Arigita, "'The Cordoba Paradigm,'" 34–35, and Ruggles, "The Stratigraphy of Forgetting," 57.

92. The Association of Muslims in Cordoba has taken the position that the demand for prayer and shared space is unrealistic and provocative. See also Arigita, "'The Cordoba Paradigm,'" 34–35.

3. Hindu–Muslim Rivalries in Banaras

1. The exact number of fatalities from the combined explosions differs in the sources, ranging from twenty-three to twenty-eight. See *Times of India*, March 8, 2006, cited in Philippa Williams, "Hindu–Muslim Brotherhood: Exploring the Dynamics of Communal Relations in Varanasi, North India," *Journal of South Asian Development* 2, no. 2 (2007), http://journals.sagepub.com/doi/abs/10.1177/097317410700200201; Sharat Pradhan, "Ancient Varanasi Keeps Its Peace, Proves Its Mettle," *Combating Communalism* 12, no. 114 (March 9, 2006), http://www.sabrang.com/cc/archive/2006/mar06/varanasi/media1.html; and Prinyanka Upadhyaya, "Communal Peace in India: Lessons from Multicultural Banaras," in *Religion and Security in South and Central Asia*, ed. K. Warikoo (London: Routledge, 2010), 83–95.

2. Philippa Williams, however, highlights how her key Hindu interviewees were cautious in attributing blame to any specific community, preferring to talk about the activities of outsiders (*Everyday Peace? Politics, Citizenships, and Muslim Lives in India* [Oxford: Wiley, 2015], 70).

3. "Mapping Militant Organizations, Lashkar-e-Taiba," Stanford University, January 30, 2016, http://web.stanford.edu/group/mappingmilitants/cgi-bin/groups/view/79.

4. The number of fatalities and casualties in the attack in October 2005 was exceeded on November 26, 2008, when Lashkar-e-Taiba carried out a series of coordinated attacks on multiple targets in Mumbai, killing 170 and wounding 300.

5. Williams, *Everyday Peace?*, 72.

6. Praveen Swami, "Roads to Perdition? The Politics and Practice of Islamist Terrorism in India," in *Religion and Security in South and Central Asia*, ed. Warikoo, 52–66.

7. Pradhan, "Ancient Varanasi Keeps Its Peace, Proves Its Mettle."

8. Upadhyaya, "Communal Peace in India," 89. Following the death of Veer Bhadra Mishra, his son Vishambhar Nath Mishra succeeded him. Vishambhar Mishra is also a renowned hydrologist concerned with the pollution of the Ganges River.

9. Williams, "Hindu–Muslim Brotherhood," 156–57.

10. Upadhyaya, "Communal Peace in India," 90.

11. Upadhyaya, "Communal Peace in India," 93–94. It should be recognized that given the very small numbers of Christians, Jains, and Buddhists living in Banaras, these dialogues are confined to religious elites, and it is unlikely that they have popular currency and a significant effect on intercommunal relations at the street level. Nevertheless, at the very least they contribute to and consolidate the public discourse concerning the uniqueness of Baranasi intercommunal relations.

12. Meera Vohra, "Sonu Nigam & Javed Akhtar Felicitated at Sankat Mochan Music Festival in Varanasi," *Times of India*, April 8, 2018, https://timesofindia.indiatimes.com /entertainment/hindi/music/sonu-nigam-javed-akhtar-felicitated-at-sankat-mochan -music-festival-in-varanasi/articleshow/63656860.cms.

13. Upadhyaya, "Communal Peace in India," 89. See also Williams, *Everyday Peace?*, 85. The idea here is that Muslim–Hindu relations resemble the warp and weft of the woven traditional silk fabric that is a proud product of Banaras.

14. Williams, *Everyday Peace?*, 68–73. The term *tahzeb* is Urdu for "manners" or "way of life," and *sanskriti* is Hindi for "culture." As Williams writes, "More broadly this narrative [of inclusion and shared cultural life] referred to a history of cultural collaboration between Muslims and Hindus with regard to their artistic, literary and musical production in the region" (71). See also the discussion in Upadhyaya, "Communal Peace in India," 86–87.

15. There are many names for this temple, which sows some confusion because similarly named temples serve as replacement or alternative sites. Another popular name is "Kashi Vishvanath Temple," which needs to be distinguished from the Adi Vishvanath Temple, built nearby as a substitute when the earlier temple was destroyed by Aurangzeb. For this reason, in this chapter I use the name "Vishweshwur Temple" simply because it is easier to distinguish from the Adi Vishvanath Temple.

16. Madhuri Desai, *Banaras Reconstructed: Architecture and Sacred Space in a Hindu Holy City* (Seattle: University of Washington Press, 2017), 51. The actual date of construction is unclear, but according to Desai the temple was in existence by 1781 (Madhuri Desai to the author, personal correspondence, November 30, 2018).

17. A note of caution: these comparisons are for illustrative purposes only. Jerusalem, Mecca, and Rome are central to their faiths for many different reasons—location of a primary temple, site of death and burial of a founder, site of the first direction of prayer, location of highest clerical authority, and so on. They are not exact parallels.

18. Ellen Barry and Raj Suhasini, "Firebrand Hindu Cleric Ascends India's Political Ladder," *New York Times*, July 12, 2017, https://www.nytimes.com/2017/07/12/world/asia /india-yogi-adityanath-bjp-modi.html.

19. Taking place on the day after the eighteenth anniversary of the demolition of the Babri Masjid in Ayodhya, this bombing on the steps of the Shitala Ghat killed three people and wounded thirty-eight (*The Economist*, "Bombing in Varanasi: Grim Anniversary," December 10, 2010, https://www.economist.com/blogs/banyan/2010/12/bombing _varanasi; see also Rana P. B. Singh, "Politics and Pilgrimage in North India: Varanasi Between Communitas and Contestation," *Tourism Review* 59 [2011]: 294).

20. The Rapid Action Force is a unit of the Central Reserve Police Force trained especially in crowd control. For further details, see AllGov India, "Rapid Action Force," n.d.,

http://www.allgov.com/india/departments/ministry-of-home-affairs/rapid-action
-force?agencyid=7604.

21. Siddharthya Roy, "Varanasi on Edge as Tradition—and Politics—Clash with Mission
to Clean Ganga," *The Wire*, October 10, 2010, https://thewire.in/culture/violence
-in-varanasi-after-tradition-clashes-with-governments-clean-ganges-mission. See
also *Hindustan Times*, "Varanasi Curfew Lifted; Schools, Colleges to Remain Closed
Tomorrow," October 5, 2015, http://www.hindustantimes.com/india/varanasi
-violence-vehicles-set-ablaze-curfew-imposed-in-3-areas/story-lvEh4sjfqkPpSupJPg
Tl8I.html.

22. See Nandini Gooptu, *The Politics of the Urban Poor in Early Twentieth-Century India*
(Cambridge: Cambridge University Press, 2001), 222.

23. Musirul Hasan, *Legacy of a Divided Nation: India's Muslims Since Independence* (London:
Hurst, 1997). It should also be noted that because of its sizeable Muslim minority,
India is the most populous Muslim state in the world. Indonesia, which has a Mus-
lim majority, comes second.

24. Varshney, *Ethnic Conflict and Civic Life*, 57.

25. See discussions in Niraja Gopal Jayal, "The Transformation of Citizenship in India
in 1990s and Beyond," in *Understanding India's New Political Economy: A Great Transformation?*, ed. Sanjay Ruparelia, Sanjay Reddy, John Hariss, and Stuart Corbridge (London: Routledge, 2011), 141–56, and Arjun Appadurai, *Fear of Small Numbers: An
Essay on the Geography of Anger* (Durham, NC: Duke University Press, 2006).

26. Varshney, *Ethnic Conflict and Civic Life*, 68.

27. So extensive have these disturbances been that the study of Muslim–Indian "riots"
has become a minor subdiscipline in South Asian social sciences. For example, see
Paul Brass, *The Production of Hindu–Muslim Violence in Contemporary India* (New Delhi:
Oxford University Press, 2003), 377–79. See also the discussion in Williams, *Everyday Peace?*, 74–75, and the citations in note 25.

28. Rupal Oza, "The Geography of Right Wing Violence in India," in *Violent Geographies: Fear, Terror, and Political Violence*, ed. Derek Gregory and Allan Pred (London:
Routledge, 2006), 153–74; Peter van de Veer, *Religious Nationalism: Hindu and Muslims in India* (Berkeley: University of California Press, 1994).

29. Government of India, "Varanasi (Varanasi) District: Census 2011 Data," Census 2011,
https://www.census2011.co.in/census/district/568-varanasi.html.

30. Government of India, "Varanasi (Varanasi) District."

31. United Nations Children's Fund, "India Development Indicators Revised," 2012,
https://knoema.com/atlas/india/varanasi-district. The population density of Banaras
is nearly three times the average of the state of Uttar Pradesh, at 829 persons per
square kilometer; see Government of India, Directorate of Census Operations in
Uttar Pradesh, "2011 Census, Uttar Pradesh," Census 2011, https://www.census2011
.co.in/questions/1/state-density/density-per-sq-km-of-uttar-pradesh-census-2011
.html.

32. A recent estimate by the doyen of geographic and heritage studies on Banaras, Rana
Singh of the Banaras Hindu University, estimates the proportion of Muslims in the city
in 2013 to have been approximately 33.7 percent ("Muslim Shrines and Multi-religious

Visitations in Hindus' City of Banaras, India: Co-existential Scenario," in *Pilgrims and Pilgrimages as Peacemakers in Christianity, Judaism, and Islam*, ed. Antón M. Pazos [Farnham, U.K.: Ashgate, 2013], 127–59).

33. It is interesting to note that despite offering some of the most popular educational establishments in the city, the various Christian denominations account for just 0.34 percent of Banaras's population, compared to the national average of 2.3 percent of India's population.

34. See, for instance, Singh, "Muslim Shrines and Multi-religious Visitations," 128. For a revealing range of narratives of this early settlement, see Mary Searle-Chatterjee, "Religious Division and the Mythology of the Past," in *Living Banaras: Hindu Religion in Cultural Context*, ed. Bradley R. Hertel and Cynthia A. Humes (Albany: State University of New York Press, 1998), 145–58. Madhuri Desai places an established Muslim presence in northern India at a later date, to the time of the Ghurid rulers in the late twelfth century (Desai to the author, personal communication, November 30, 2018).

35. Desai, *Banaras Reconstructed*, 35.

36. The lower house includes one minister, nominated to represent the Anglo-Indian community. For further details, see Election Commission of India, *Statistical Report on General Election 2012* (New Delhi: Government of India, 2012), http://uttarpradesh congress.com/english/wp-content/uploads/2013/11/2012.pdf.

37. Uttar Pradesh Congress Committee, "About Us," website, 2017, http://uttarpradesh congress.com/english/introduction/ideology.

38. Narendra Modi, "Varanasi Constituency," Narendra Modi website, 2017, http://www.narendramodi.in/varanasi#MediaCoverage, emphasis in original.

39. Varshney, *Ethnic Conflict and Civic Life*, 83.

40. Williams, *Everyday Peace?*, 79, 98–100.

41. Williams, *Everyday Peace?*, 100.

42. Jawaharlal Nehru National Urban Renewal Mission (JNNURM), "City Development Plan for Varanasi," *Feedback Ventures*, August 2006, http://www.indiaenvironment portal.org.in/files/file/varanasi%20city%20development%20plan.pdf. Large manufacturing companies include the Diesel Locomotive Works and Bharat Heavy Electricals Limited, a large power-equipment manufacturer (JNNURM, "City Development Plan for Varanasi").

43. Government of Uttar Pradesh, "Banaras Hindu University," Uttar Pradesh Tourism, 2015, http://uptourism.gov.in/pages/top/explore/top-explore-varanasi—sarnath /banaras-hindu-university.

44. See Nita Kumar, "Work and Leisure in the Formation of Identity: Muslim Weavers in a Hindu City," in *Culture and Power in Banaras: Community, Performance, and Environment, 1800–1980*, ed. Sandra B. Freitag (Berkeley: University of California Press, 1992), 147–70; Vesudev Shefalee, "The Banaras Bind," *LiveMint Ground Report*, November 23, 2013, https://www.livemint.com/Leisure/5h1lnyORjhtn9ProZ4wiXL /Ground-Report—The-Banaras-bind.html; Williams, *Everyday Peace?*, 50.

45. Singh, "Muslim Shrines and Multi-religious Visitations," 130.

46. See Shefalee, "The Banaras Bind," which cites the 2011 census as saying the sari industry employs 51 percent of the population. As a proportion of the workforce, the percentage would be much higher, but I found no figures for the workforce.
47. Williams, *Everyday Peace?*, 52–53.
48. Richard H. Davis, "The Iconography of Rama's Chariot," in *Making India Hindu: Religion, Community, and the Politics of Democracy in India*, ed. David Ludden (Oxford: Oxford University Press, 2007), 27–54.
49. Williams, *Everyday Peace?*, 53–54.
50. A traditional sari can take up to fifteen days to weave, and handloom weavers can rarely make more than two saris a month, so the decline in demand for the saris has a significant effect on individual weavers.
51. Williams, *Everyday Peace?*, 53, 151.
52. Rajeev Dikshit, "Sari Industry in Fix Over CSB Move," *Times of India*, January 23, 2015, https://timesofindia.indiatimes.com/city/varanasi/Sari-industry-in-fix-over-CSB-move/articleshow/45984891.cms; Asgar Qadri, "In India, Fashion Has Become a Nationalist Cause," *New York Times*, November 12, 2017, https://www.nytimes.com/2017/11/12/fashion/india-nationalism-sari.html; Shefalee, "The Banaras Bind."
53. Williams, *Everyday Peace?*, 55. According to Mary Searle-Chatterjee, the conversion to Wahhabism is a way to distinguish one's status from both that of the old Muslim elites and that of the poorer weavers (cited in Williams, *Everyday Peace?*, 56).
54. For further details on the drift toward Salafism, see Christophe Jaffrelot and Laurence Louër, eds., *Pan-Islamic Connections: Transnational Networks Between South Asia and the Gulf* (London: Hurst, 2017). See also James Dorsey, "Indian Muslims: A Rich Hunting Ground for Middle Eastern Rivals," Global Village, January 5, 2019, https://www.globalvillagespace.com/indian-muslims-a-rich-hunting-ground-for-middle-eastern-rivals-james-m-dorsey/.
55. Williams, *Everyday Peace?*, 58; Gooptu, *The Politics of the Urban Poor*, 261.
56. Williams, *Everyday Peace?*, 58.
57. Gooptu deconstructs this phenomenon persuasively for the interwar period of the twentieth century (*The Politics of the Urban Poor*, 244–320).
58. Singh, "Muslim Shrines and Multi-religious Visitations," 130.
59. Raman Sunil, "The New Threat to Islam in India: Hardline Wahabis and Salafis Are Attracting New Converts," *The Diplomat*, February 4, 2016, https://thediplomat.com/2016/02/the-new-threat-to-islam-in-india/. A breakdown of Arab Gulf-funded mosques specifically for Banaras is not available. See also Christophe Jaffrelot and Laurence Louër, "Conclusion," in *Pan-Islamic Connections*, ed. Jaffrelot and Louër, 238–41.
60. Singh, "Muslim Shrines and Multi-religious Visitations," 130.
61. Desai, *Banaras Reconstructed*, 18.
62. I also observed a truly ferocious game of cricket being played along the uneven steps and confined space at the very gates of the mosque. A hard cricket ball was bowled at the speed of a missile at the batsmen in bare feet and shorts and no head protection. The pitch was a stairwell, with the wicket at the top of one flight of steps and the

bowler up another. In order to make a run, the batsman had to aim the hurtling ball down a number of small alleyways leading off from this junction in front of the mosque, then run down and up the steps before the crowd of zealous teenagers, who, having miraculously dodged the driven ball, could gather it and return it to the keeper with equal ferocity. I pity the English cricket team if this is their Indian opponents' early training. I was so absorbed by the drama before my eyes that I forgot to make a note of whether the crowd was Muslim or Hindu.

63. Anna Bigelow, "The Monumental and the Mundane: Navigating the Sharing of Sacred Sites in India and Turkey," paper presented at the seminar "The Urban Dimensions of Religious Conflict," Power, Piety, People, Leverhulme Project, March 5–10, 2018, Tourtour, France.

64. Singh, "Muslim Shrines and Multi-religious Visitations," 137.

65. Williams, *Everyday Peace?*, 49, 71–80. Ustad Bismillah Khan (1916–2006) was one of the most renowned *shehnai* (classical Indian horn) players in India. His uncle, the late Ali Baksh "Vilayatu," was the *shehnai* player in the Vishwanath Temple.

66. *The Hindu*, April 20, 2006, cited in Williams, *Everyday Peace?*, 89.

67. The figure 3,000 is taken from Singh, "Proposing Varanasi as a Heritage City."

68. I demurred from the option of jumping in the soupy river, let alone washing myself, my clothes, or my teeth in it, as the true believers do.

69. The classic and most cited description of Banaras and its role in Hinduism can be found in Diana Eck, *Banaras: City of Light* (New York: Columbia University Press, 1999). Later scholars have queried Eck's reliance on medieval scriptures as sources of historical fact without contextualizing the purposes for which they were written.

70. Wilbert Gesler and Margaret Pierce, "Hindu Varanasi," *Geographical Review* 90, no. 2 (2000): 224.

71. Surinder Mohan Bhardwaj holds a slightly contrary view. He points out that in the earlier Vedic texts, such as the Mahabharata, the city of Pashkara had greater prominence than Banaras: "The space devoted to eulogizing the merits of Pashkara far exceeds that given to Varanasi. Furthermore, the merit of visiting Pashkara is considered in the epic to be equal to ten asvamedha yajxas, that is ten horse sacrifices. On the other hand, the merit of visiting Varanasi was merely a rajasu yajna—a normal ceremony of kingship and concomitant sacrifice much inferior to the horse sacrifice" (*Hindu Places of Pilgrimage in India: A Study in Cultural Geography* [Berkeley: University of California Press, 1983], 41).

72. Eck, *Banaras*, 31.

73. For a full discussion of the practice and meaning of cremation rituals that are carried out on the banks of the river Ganges in Banaras, see John Parry, *Death in Banaras* (Cambridge: Cambridge University Press, 1994).

74. Kashi Kanda, verse 3, quoted and translated in Parry, *Death in Banaras*, 31.

75. Eck, *Banaras*, 28–29.

76. Eck, *Banaras*, 50, 118. Modern urban developments have of course both polluted the river's "clear and pure water" and natural course during the rainy season.

77. Eck, *Banaras*, 285.

78. The official Vishweshwur Temple website gives a detailed day-by-day itinerary of the *panchakroshi yatra* route and the religious sites that a pilgrim should visit along the way. See Shri Kashi Vishvanath Mandir Trust, official website, https://www.shrikashivish wanath.org/PanchKroshiyatra.aspx.

79. Shri Kashi Vishvanath Mandir Trust, official website.

80. Mark Twain, *Following the Equator: A Journey Around the World* (1904; reprint, New York: Dover, 1989), 480.

81. Desai, *Banaras Reconstructed*, 154.

82. In a wonderfully understated conclusion, Desai sums up the gap between text and archaeology thus: "Textual imaginations of the city were always more extensive and complex than their manifestations on the ground" (*Banaras Reconstructed*, 72).

83. Desai, *Banaras Reconstructed*, 24.

84. See Eck, *Banaras*, 112–16, for a description of locating the different temples.

85. Eck, *Banaras*, 120, 129. Eck's description and history are extraordinarily confusing, moving from rhetorical storytelling to historical fact.

86. Desai, *Banaras Reconstructed*, 69.

87. Desai, *Banaras Reconstructed*, 58, 82.

88. Eck, *Banaras*, 135.

89. Desai, *Banaras Reconstructed*, 83, 162.

90. Eck, *Banaras*, 120.

91. In 2016 alone, for example, donations amounted to 97 million rupees, approximately U.S.$14.5 million. See the financial page of the Shri Kashi Vishvanath Mandir Trust official website, https://www.shrikashivishwanath.org/financials.aspx.

92. On paper, this varied board membership should offer the checks and balances required to ensure that experience and continuity are drawn from the members who are closely associated with the temple and to ensure accountability in the form of public officeholders, but in practice either many of the ex officio members are poor attendees of trustee meetings, or there is little capacity in the legal system to enforce compliance in the light of transgressions. For a detailed example of the temple's inner administrative workings, see Deonnie Moodie, *The Making of a Modern Temple and a Hindu City: Kalighat and Kolkata* (New York: Oxford University Press, 2018), chap. 2.

93. Uttar Pradesh Sri Kashi Vishwanath Temple Act of 1983, photocopy of legislation in author's files.

94. Gooptu, *The Politics of the Urban Poor*, 307.

95. Gooptu, *The Politics of the Urban Poor*, 307.

96. Williams, *Everyday Peace?*, 48.

97. Varshney, *Ethnic Conflict and Civic Life*, 104.

98. Paul R. Brass, *Theft of an Idol: Text and Context in the Representation of Collective Violence* (Princeton, NJ: Princeton University Press, 1997), 49.

99. Williams, *Everyday Peace?*, 60.

100. The goddess Durga is held to be a fierce protector of Banaras and of a temple for residents of largely Bengali origins, which is located close to the Sangkat Mochan Temple

in the south of the city and was built by a Bengali queen. For further details, see Hillary Rodrigues, *Ritual Worship of the Great Goddess: The Liturgy of the Durga Puja with Interpretations* (Albany: State University of New York Press, 2003).

101. Williams, *Everyday Peace?*, 57.

102. Williams, *Everyday Peace?*, 72, 76.

103. See Hasan, *Legacy of a Divided Nation*, 302–3.

104. Williams, *Everyday Peace?*, 176–77.

105. This renaming of Ayodhya would be the equivalent of, say, the Yeovil Town Council in the United Kingdom deciding to rename their town "Camelot" so that it would be more closely associated with the Arthurian legend and so that over time residents and visitors alike would believe that indeed it was the site of King Arthur's government. See Reinhard Bernbeck and Susan Pollock, "Ayodhya, Archaeology, and Identity," in "Anthropology in Public," special issue of *Current Anthropology* 37, no. 1 (1996): 139–40.

106. Davis, "The Iconography of Rama's Chariot," 35. VHP chose to promote the god Rama rather than Krishna (birthplace Mathura) or Shiva (residence in Banaras) because he has wider popular appeal. Hence, the choice of Ayodhya, the believed birthplace of Rama.

107. John M. Lundquist, *The Temple of Jerusalem: Past, Present, and Future* (Westport, CN: Praeger, 2008), 46.

108. Varshney, *Ethnic Conflict and Civic Life*, 82.

109. Davis, "The Iconography of Rama's Chariot," 38.

110. Varshney, *Ethnic Conflict and Civic Life*, 80–81.

111. Davis, "The Iconography of Rama's Chariot," 40–41.

112. See *BBC News*, "Mob Rips Apart Mosque in Ayodhya," December 6, 1992, http://news.bbc.co.uk/onthisday/hi/dates/stories/december/6/newsid_3712000/3712777.stm.

113. Varshney, *Ethnic Conflict and Civic Life*, 302. This figure excludes loss of trading revenue, exports, and taxes.

114. Barry and Suhasini, "Firebrand Hindu Cleric Ascends India's Political Ladder."

115. Two of the mosques are big and well used, the Masjid Begum and the Masjid Salman, but the rest are smaller or are in poor condition and not used. Two are for the Shiʿa community. Most of the imams for the mosques come from the local region, although one or two come from farther away.

116. Michael Safi, "India, Home of the World's Tallest Statue, Announces Plan to Build a Taller One," *The Guardian*, November 26, 2018, https://www.theguardian.com/world/2018/nov/26/india-worlds-tallest-statue-plan-to-build-a-taller-one-uttar-pradesh-hindu-go-ram.

117. Williams, *Everyday Peace?*, 69; Hasan, *Legacy of a Divided Nation*, 302.

118. The Samajwadi Party lost control over Banaras at the most recent mayoral elections, owing largely to Muslim dissatisfaction with the party, which resulted in a number of Independents being fielded instead.

119. Williams, *Everyday Peace?*, 85. Gooptu points out that the Sangkat Mochan Temple is dedicated to Hanuman, who, although a lesser deity, is revered particularly by the *shudra* castes, which have traditionally provided much of the activists and energy in the Hindutva movement (*The Politics of the Urban Poor*, 208–11).

120. Williams, *Everyday Peace?*, 49.

121. Bigelow, "The Monumental and the Mundane."

122. Singh, "Muslim Shrines and Multi-religious Visitations"; Sandra B. Freitag, "State and Community: Symbolic Popular Protests in Banaras's Public Arenas," in *Culture and Power in Banaras*, ed. Freitag, 203–28.

123. See the fascinating and informative chapter "Civic Space: Playing with Peace and Insecurity," in Williams, *Everyday Peace?*, 109–37.

124. Abhishek Srivastava, "Is BJP Planning an Ayodhya 2.0 in Varanasi?," *India National Herald*, March 24, 2018, https://www.nationalheraldindia.com/news/is-the-bjp-plann ing-an-ayodha-2-in-varanasi-gyanvapi-masjid-stands-in-way-of-connecting-kashi -vishwanath-with-ganga-ghats5.317.

125. It is also unclear what the implications of this plan are for the numerous smaller temples, deities, and pilgrimage routes between them that exist in the vicinity of the Vishweshwur Temple.

126. Faisal Fareed, "In Varanasi, a Plan to Build Corridor from Kashi Vishwanath Temple to River Ganga Sparks Anger," *Reuters*, February 10, 2018, https://scroll.in /article/868178/destruction-not-development-plan-for-varanasis-kashi-vishwanath -temple-sparks-protests.

127. Bishwanath Ghosh, "Beautification Plan Destroys Oldest Neighbourhoods in Varanasi," *The Hindu*, December 9, 2018, https://www.thehindu.com/news/national /other-states/beautification-plan-destroys-oldest-neighbourhoods-in-varanasi /article25704389.ece; A. Srivathsan, "Varanasi and the Politics of Change," *Hindu Sunday Magazine*, March 24, 2019.

4. A Very Secular Occupation

1. Jason Burke, "One Tibetan Woman's Tragic Path to Self-Immolation," *The Guardian*, March 27, 2018, https://www.theguardian.com/world/2012/mar/26/nomad -path-self-immolation.

2. There is some evidence that Tsering Kyi's act was a protest against Chinese government educational reforms that would limit the use of Tibetan-medium instruction. See Clémence Henry, "The Chinese Education System as a Source of Conflict in Tibetan Areas," in *Ethnic Conflict and Protest in Tibet and Xinjiang: Unrest in China's West*, ed. Ben Hillman and Gray Tuttle (New York: Columbia University Press, 2016), 112–14; David M. Crowe, "The 'Tibet Question': Tibetan, Chinese, and Western Perspectives," *Nationalities Papers: Journal of Nationalism and Ethnicity* 41, no. 6 (2013): 1123.

3. Of the 144 self-immolations, 127 were reportedly fatal. For further details, see U.S. Congressional-Executive Commission on China, *Annual Report* (Washington, DC: U.S. Government Publication Office, 2017), https://www.cecc.gov/sites/chinacom mission.house.gov/files/documents/AR17%20Tibet_final.pdf.

4. John Powers, *The Buddha Party: How the People's Republic of China Works to Define and Control Tibetan Buddhism* (New York: Oxford University Press, 2017), 82–86.

5. John Whalen-Bridge, *Tibet on Fire: Buddhism, Protest, and the Rhetoric of Self-Immolation* (London: Palgrave Macmillan, 2015), 11; see also U.S. Congressional-Executive Commission on China, *Special Report: Tibetan Self-Immolation—Rising Frequency, Wider Spread, Greater Diversity* (Washington, DC: U.S. Government Publication Office, August 22, 2012).

6. Lhasa Public Security Bureau, "Notice of the Tibet Autonomous Region Public Security Department on Reporting Leads on Crimes and Violations by Underworld Forces," February 7, 2018, cited in Human Rights Watch, *China's Crackdown on Tibetan Social Groups* (New York: Human Rights Watch, 2018), https://www.hrw.org/report /2018/07/30/illegal-organizations/chinas-crackdown-tibetan-social-groups.

7. Robert Barnett, *Lhasa: Streets with Memories* (New York: Columbia University Press, 2010); Emily T. Yeh, *Taming Tibet: Landscape Transformation and the Gift of Chinese Development* (Ithaca, NY: Cornell University Press, 2013); Powers, *The Buddha Party*.

8. Amund Sinding-Larsen, "Lhasa Community, World Heritage, and Human Rights," in *World Heritage Management and Human Rights*, ed. Stener Ekern, William Logan, Birgitte Sauge, and Amund Sinding-Larsen (New York: Routledge, 2015), 85–94; Qing Li, *The Evolution and Preservation of the Old City of Lhasa* (Singapore: Springer Nature and Social Sciences Academic Press, 2018).

9. Yeh, *Taming Tibet*, 228–29.

10. Michael Dumper, *Jerusalem Unbound: Geography, History, and the Future of the Holy City* (New York: Columbia University Press, 2014), 234.

11. Barnett, *Lhasa*, xxxvi.

12. Barnett, *Lhasa*, 195, 198.

13. Yeh, *Taming Tibet*, 18.

14. Duo Chu, Yili Zhang, Ciran Bianba, and Linshan Liu, "Land Use Dynamics in Lhasa Area, Tibetan Plateau," *Journal of Geographical Sciences* 20, no. 6 (2010): 899–912.

15. Yeh, *Taming Tibet*, 18. The Tibetan word for "goat," *ra*, is etymologically connected to the original name for Lhasa, "Ra Sa."

16. The first iteration of the temple was laid out by King Gampo's Nepalese wife, Bhri-kuti, and has a Nepal-facing orientation as opposed to the usual east–west orientation of Buddhist temples. His Chinese wife's, Princess Wencheng's, Buddha was originally housed in another important temple, the Ramoche Temple, but was transferred at a later date to the Jokhang Temple as well.

17. The Jokhang Temple was, for example, desecrated by Maoist Red Guards and was reputedly used as a pig sty during the Maoist Cultural Revolution in the 1960s.

18. Unlike the Jokhang Temple, the Potala Palace was spared the ravages of the Cultural Revolution, although it was shelled during the Tibetan uprising against Chinese rule in 1959. It is now, with the Jokhang Temple and the Norbulingka Palace, a UNESCO World Heritage Site.

19. See the colorful description regarding the fall of Chamdo in Bradley Mayhew and Robert Kelly, *Tibet* (Singapore: Lonely Planet, 2015), 260.

20. The Chinese leader Mao Zedong is reputed to have remarked after the signing of this agreement, "Welcome back to the motherland."

21. Seventeen-Point Agreement on Measures for the Peaceful Liberation of Tibet, 1951, in Chenqing Ying, *Tibetan History* (Beijing: China Intercontinental Press, 2003), appendix.

22. See, for example, Mikel Dunham, *Buddha's Warriors: The Story of the CIA-Backed Tibetan Freedom Fighters, the Chinese Invasion, and the Ultimate Fall of Tibet* (London: Penguin Books, 2004), 61–64. The controversial authors Jung Chang and Jon Halliday also make these points in their highly critical biography of Mao Zedong, *Mao: The Unknown Story* (London: Vintage, 2006), 473–75.

23. Jianglin Li and Susan Wilf, *Tibet in Agony: Lhasa 1959* (Cambridge, MA: Harvard University Press, 2016). For an official Chinese view of these events, see Ying, *Tibetan History*, 164–74.

24. June Teufel Dreyer, *China's Political System: Modernization and Tradition* (New York: Pearson Education, 2006), 290.

25. Chenqing Ying asserts that Mao Zedong gave orders to allow the Dalai Lama to flee, which explains why he was not pursued by the PLA (*Tibetan History*, 174). However, Ying also refers to the Dalai Lama as being "kidnapped" by Tibetan rebels; if that is the case, it would have prompted a pursuit or rescue attempt by the PLA.

26. Mayhew and Kelly, *Tibet*, 261.

27. This party perspective can be clearly seen in Ying, *Tibetan History*.

28. The Dalai Lama made this claim of "cultural genocide" in a statement to Voice of America, quoted in Andrew Fischer, " 'Population Transfer' Versus Urban Exclusion in the Tibetan Areas of Western China," *Population and Development Review* 34, no. 4 (2008): 631 n. 3. See also Jose Ignacio Cabezon, "State Control of Tibetan Buddhist Monasticism in the People's Republic of China," in *Chinese Religiosities: Affliction of Modernity and State Formation*, ed. Mayfair Mei-hui Yang (Berkeley: University of California Press, 2008), 262.

29. The most strident exposition of this position was seen during the Cultural Revolution between 1966 and 1975, when the rallying cry "The nationalities problem is in essence a class problem!" was promoted. See Dreyer, *China's Political System*, 291.

30. Jeffrey Hays, "Minorities in China," Facts and Details, People's Republic of China, 2015, http://factsanddetails.com/china/cat5/sub29/item192.html.

31. Figures for the Mongols are: 0.4488 percent of the total population of the People's Republic of China, 4,806,849 in 1990, 5,827,808 in 2000, and 5,981,840 in 2010 (Hays, "Minorities in China").

32. Hays, "Minorities in China."

33. Most of the details and ideas in this section are derived from Dreyer, *China's Political System*, 279–303.

34. Claude Arpi, "China's Leadership Change and Its Tibet Policy," *Strategic Analysis* 37, no. 5 (2013): 540. It is also worth noting that India's desire both under Nehru and leading up to Chinese incursion into India in 1962 overlooked the fact that an independent Tibet had offered India a buffer zone against China.

35. A major plank in the Shanghai Cooperation Organization's work is that it will combat "the Three Evils": terrorism, separatism, and extremism. See Eleanor Albert,

Shanghai Cooperation Organisation: Backgrounder (Washington, DC: Council for Foreign Relations, October 14, 2015), https://www.cfr.org/backgrounder/shanghai-cooperation-organization.

36. Dreyer, *China's Political System*, 279.
37. Central Tibetan Administration, *Environment and Development Issues: Introduction* (N.p.: Central Tibetan Administration, 2018), http://tibet.net/important-issues/tibets-environment-and-development-issues/. One section of this report also states that "Tibet has deposits of about 132 different minerals accounting for a significant share of the entire world's reserves of gold, chromite, copper, borax and iron. Recent research findings revealed that there is a huge reserve of lithium and rare earth elements in certain parts of Tibet. It was also reported by the former Chinese Communist Party Chair, Yin Fatang, that the world's largest supply of uranium was locked in to the Himalayan region of Tibet" (Central Tibetan Administration, *Environment Overview* [N.p.: Central Tibetan Administration, 2018], http://tibet.net/important-issues/tibets-environment-and-development-issues/#codeoslide1).
38. Dreyer, *China's Political System*, 281.
39. Dreyer, *China's Political System*, 294–96. A frequent example cited concerns the foreign-investment schemes in which Saudi Arabian and Malaysian businesspeople are supporting projects to assist their Muslim coreligionists.
40. Dreyer, *China's Political System*, 281.
41. Dreyer, *China's Political System*, 285–88. One striking example of such accommodation was to allow the minority group known as the Yi, whose areas straddle the Sichuan and Yunnan provincial borders, to continue owning slaves!
42. Dreyer, *China's Political System*, 295.
43. Ben Hillman, "Unrest in Tibet and the Limits of Regional Autonomy" in *Ethnic Conflict and Protest in Tibet and Xinjiang*, ed. Hillman and Tuttle, 19.
44. Sichuan province, for example, comprises 21 prefectures, 181 counties, and 5,114 townships. I was unable to locate a clear exposition of local government in China, but the *Wikipedia* entry "Administrative Divisions of China" (https://en.wikipedia.org/wiki/Administrative_divisions_of_China) gives a flavor of its complexity.
45. In addition to the TAR, Tibetan "autonomous" local government includes eight Tibetan autonomous prefectures in Qinghai, Gansu, Yunnan, and Sichuan provinces and two Tibetan autonomous counties in Gansu and Sichuan provinces. See Hillman, "Unrest in Tibet," 19 n. 4.
46. Hillman, "Unrest in Tibet," 20, provides examples of exemptions and discretionary initiatives obtained by local government officials in Tibetan areas.
47. Dreyer, *China's Political System*, 301.
48. Dreyer, *China's Political System*, 301.
49. Yeh, *Taming Tibet*, 19.
50. There is traditionally a third *kora*, which is a circuit within the walls of the Jokhang Temple. A fourth *kora* is equally popular and runs around the foot of the Potala Palace.
51. For a comparison of a series of maps of Lhasa drawn between 1935 and 2002, see Ma Rong, *Population and Society in Contemporary Tibet* (Hong Kong: Hong Long University Press, 2011), 349–50.

52. Wei Tang, Tiancai Zhou, Jian Sun, Yurui Li, and Weipeng Li, "Accelerated Urban Expansion in Lhasa City and the Implications for Sustainable Development in a Plateau City," *Sustainability* 9, no. 49 (2017): 1–19.
53. Clare Harris, "Potala Palace: Remembering to Forget in Contemporary Tibet," in "Afterlives of Monuments," special issue of *South Asian Studies* 29, no. 1 (2013): 61–75.
54. Barnett, *Lhasa*, xxix.
55. A helpful summary of China's residency registration system can be found in Rong, *Population and Society in Contemporary Tibet*, 332–33.
56. Rong, *Population and Society in Contemporary Tibet*, 334–35.
57. Some sources specify that the figures do include the monastic population; others are not clear.
58. Fischer, "'Population Transfer' Versus Urban Exclusion," 647–48. See also the discussion of these Lhasa population figures in Yeh, *Taming Tibet*, 103–5.
59. Fischer, "'Population Transfer' Versus Urban Exclusion." See also Yeh, *Taming Tibet*, 99.
60. Fischer, "'Population Transfer' Versus Urban Exclusion," 642.
61. Yeh, *Taming Tibet*, 98. Yeh quotes a sociologist from Sichuan saying, "Going to Lhasa it feels like you haven't left Sichuan. Everywhere you go you can hear Sichuan dialect."
62. Yeh, *Taming Tibet*, 103–5.
63. This estimate is drawn from the Lhasa Public Security Bureau, which issues temporary residency certificates to temporary migrants (Yeh, *Taming Tibet*, 103).
64. Author's Lhasa fieldwork notes, May 2018.
65. Fischer, "'Population Transfer' Versus Urban Exclusion," 650.
66. Yeh, *Taming Tibet*, 107.
67. Andrew Fischer and Adrian Zenz, "The Limits to Buying Stability in Tibet: Tibetan Representation and Preferentiality in China's Contemporary Public Employment System," *China Quarterly* 234 (2018): 535.
68. Fischer and Zenz, "The Limits to Buying Stability in Tibet," 536.
69. Fischer and Zenz, "The Limits to Buying Stability in Tibet," 535.
70. Fischer and Zenz, "The Limits to Buying Stability in Tibet," 536. Fischer and Zenz speculate that Communist Party officials increasingly recognized that providing jobs for the rising number of Tibetan graduates was unsustainable and that alternative means of creating employment would need to be sought.
71. Fischer and Zenz also speculate that the transfer of the leading party official in the TAR, Chen Quanguo, who was the key driver behind this policy, to Xinjiang may be an explanation for the loss of impetus ("The Limits to Buying Stability in Tibet," 536).
72. See Dumper, *Jerusalem Unbound*, 154–55, 160–70.
73. Robert Shepherd, "UNESCO and the Politics of Cultural Heritage in Tibet," *Journal of Contemporary Asia* 36, no. 2 (2006): 243–57.
74. Fischer, "'Population Transfer' Versus Urban Exclusion," 647.
75. Tang et al., "Accelerated Urban Expansion in Lhasa City," 11. A higher estimate of 15 million for 2014 can be found in Jeffrey Hays, "Tourism in Tibet," Facts and Details, 2018, http://factsanddetails.com/china/cat6/sub37/item2846.html.

76. Tang et al., "Accelerated Urban Expansion in Lhasa City," 11.

77. See Simone Ricca, *Reinventing Jerusalem: Israel's Reconstruction of the Jewish Quarter After 1967* (New York: I. B. Tauris, 2007).

78. The literature on the impact of tourism on religious sites is extensive. See, for example, Myra Shackley, *Managing Sacred Sites* (Andover, MA: Cengage Learning EMEA, 2012); Michael Stausberg, *Religion and Tourism: Crossroads, Destinations, and Encounters* (Abingdon, U.K.: Routledge, 2011); Bernard Feilden and Jukka Jokilehto, *Management Guidelines for World Cultural Heritage Sites* (Rome: ICCROM, UNESCO, and ICOMOS, 1993).

79. Sinding-Larsen, "Lhasa Community," 88.

80. Harris, "Potala Palace"; Robert Bevan, *The Destruction of Memory: Architecture at War* (London: Reaktion Books, 2016), 133–34.

81. Other examples include the renovation of the protected Tromsikhang Palace, which led to the resettlement of the forty families living there to outside Lhasa, and the construction of the Barkor Shopping Mall, which led to the relocation of the former residents in the area to Tolung Dechen, a distant suburb west of Lhasa. The mall was designed to house 1,117 vehicles in an underground carpark. See Michael Sheridan, "Ancient Tibet Shrivels Before China's Sprawl," *Sunday Times* (London), May 26, 2013, https://www.thetimes.co.uk/article/ancient-tibet-shrivels-before-chinas-sprawl-nfmnmfbz3lp.

82. Harris, "Potala Palace."

83. Jamyang Norbu, "Lhasa: The Eternal City (2)," blog, Rangzen Alliance, June 23, 2013, http://www.rangzen.net/2013/06/03/lhasa-eternal-city-2/.

84. Harris, "Potala Palace."

85. Clare Harris, *The Museum on the Roof of the World: Art, Politics, and the Representation of Tibet* (Chicago: University of Chicago Press, 2012), 4–5.

86. Shepherd, "UNESCO and the Politics of Cultural Heritage in Tibet." A more effective institution was the Tibet Heritage Fund, which was created in 1996 with the encouragement of the Lhasa municipality and received funds from well-established European and North American foundations, such as the Trace Foundation, the Heinrich Boll Foundation, the German Catholic Bishops' Organisation for Development Cooperation, and the Rubin Foundation. It was effective in persuading local officials to issue protection orders for vernacular architecture and secular buildings of historic value and in mobilizing and retraining an entire generation of local craftsmen. The Tibet Heritage Fund was, as a well-known analyst of Lhasa concludes, "one of the extremely few foreign NGOs in Tibet to have significant, measurable impact, and was banned from Tibet almost as soon as its achievements became clear" (Robert Barnett to the author, email, November 26, 2019).

87. Shepherd, "UNESCO and the Politics of Cultural Heritage in Tibet." Another criticism leveled at UNESCO is that its work is concentrated on religious sites, neglecting almost 90 percent of the city's historical architecture, which is secular.

88. Shepherd, "UNESCO and the Politics of Cultural Heritage in Tibet," 251.

89. Sheridan, "Ancient Tibet Shrivels Before China's Sprawl."

90. See Norbu, "Lhasa." Jamyang Norbu writes: "In 1985, alcohol consumption in the Tibet Autonomous Region had already reached *fifteen times* the average alcohol consumption in China, according to the 1990 China Statistical Yearbook" (emphasis in original). He also cites Tibet Information Network Briefing Paper no. 31, *Social Evils: Prostitution and Pornography in Lhasa*, which details incidences of alcoholism in the city. I was not able to trace this document, and the Tibet Information Network website has closed down.

91. Yeh, *Taming Tibet*, 14. See also Yeh's discussion of Han perceptions of Tibetans as being backward (116). Mao Zedong is supposed to have lamented the adverse effects of Han chauvinisms on Sino-Tibetan relations (Crowe, "The 'Tibet Question,'" 1128).

92. The Religious Affairs Bureau was superseded in 1998 by the State Administration of Religious Affairs and given increased administrative responsibilities. See Fenggang Yang, *Religion in China: Survival and Revival Under Communist Rule* (Oxford: Oxford University Press, 2011), 13–14.

93. F. Yang, *Religion in China*, 5.

94. The Four Olds are old customs, old culture, old habits, and old ideas (F. Yang, *Religion in China*, 8).

95. Mayfair Meh-hui Yang, introduction to *Chinese Religiosities: Affliction of Modernity and State Formation*, ed. Mayfair Meh-hui Yang (Berkeley: University of California Press, 2008), 27.

96. Fenggang Yang provides a useful periodization of the different phases in Chinese government and Communist Party policy toward religion (*Religion in China*, 1–2). It is more detailed than necessary for my purpose here, which is focused more on the situation in Tibetan areas, but it nonetheless conveys the disconnect between religious policy and economic policies that have become more open.

97. F. Yang, *Religion in China*, 11.

98. F. Yang, *Religion in China*, 11.

99. For a detailed exposition of the close state monitoring of that revival, see M. Yang, *Chinese Religiosities*.

100. M. Yang, introduction to *Chinese Religiosities*, ed. M. Yang, 29.

101. Cabezon, "State Control of Tibetan Buddhist Monasticism in the People's Republic of China," 261.

102. Mayhew and Kelly, *Tibet*, 84.

103. According to Bradley Mayhew and Robert Kelly, "In 1950, on the eve of the Chinese invasion, it was estimated that as much as a quarter of the entire population of Tibet were monks" (*Tibet*, 284). Compare this proportion to a figure of between one and two percent of the population being monks in Buddhist Thailand (Crowe, "The 'Tibet Question,'" 1109).

104. Yeh, *Taming Tibet*, 31.

105. Yeh, *Taming Tibet*, 31.

106. Dunham, *Buddha's Warriors*, 267.

107. Cabezon, "State Control of Tibetan Buddhist Monasticism in the People's Republic of China," 262.

108. Cabezon, "State Control of Tibetan Buddhist Monasticism in the People's Republic of China," 266; Mayhew and Kelly, *Tibet*, 84.
109. Mao Zedong, quoted in F. Yang, *Religion in China*, 6.
110. Hillman and Tuttle, *Ethnic Conflict and Protest in Tibet and Xinjiang*.
111. Ninian Smart, *The Religious Experience of Mankind* (Glasgow: Collins, 1971), 149.
112. Cabezon, "State Control of Tibetan Buddhist Monasticism in the People's Republic of China," 273.
113. Powers, *The Buddha Party*, 69.
114. Cabezon, "State Control of Tibetan Buddhist Monasticism in the People's Republic of China," 273. Cabezon's essay provides more details on the workings of subcommittees of the Democratic Management Committee in Sera monastery.
115. Cabezon, "State Control of Tibetan Buddhist Monasticism in the People's Republic of China," 274.
116. At the time John Powers did his study (published in 2017), some monks and nuns endured classes that ran from 9:00 a.m. to 6:30 p.m., with a break between 1:00 and 3:00 p.m. for lunch and prayers, for six or seven days a week. See Powers, *The Buddha Party*, 71.
117. Powers describes these lectures on Buddhist beliefs in full in *The Buddha Party*, 163.
118. Cabezon, "State Control of Tibetan Buddhist Monasticism in the People's Republic of China," 274–77.
119. Mayhew and Kelly, *Tibet*, 262. These numbers refer to the TAR only. A report by the Tibetan government in exile reported on the destruction of 6,254 monasteries and nunneries in all Tibetan areas (Mayhew and Kelly, *Tibet*, 263).
120. Cabezon, "State Control of Tibetan Buddhist Monasticism in the People's Republic of China," 284.
121. See Powers, *The Buddha Party*, 58, 70; Cabezon, "State Control of Tibetan Buddhist Monasticism in the People's Republic of China," 287; F. Yang, *Religion in China*, 17.
122. Powers, *The Buddha Party*, 77, 86.
123. Barnett, *Lhasa*; Powers, *The Buddha Party*, 19.
124. Barnett, *Lhasa*; Mayhew and Kelly, *Tibet*, 262. In Dunham, *Buddha's Warriors*, see the recollections of a *tulku*, or reincarnated lama, Dr. Lobsang Tensing, who was present at the scene (401–3).
125. Powers, *The Buddha Party*, 24, 80–81.
126. Cabezon, "State Control of Tibetan Buddhist Monasticism in the People's Republic of China," 287.
127. Cabezon, "State Control of Tibetan Buddhist Monasticism in the People's Republic of China," 285.
128. Powers, *The Buddha Party*, 21–27.
129. *The Economist*, "Lhasa Under Siege," March 17, 2018, https://www.economist.com/node/10871821.
130. Powers, *The Buddha Party*, 24.
131. Powers, *The Buddha Party*, 34. Citing the Tibetan Centre for Human Rights and Democracy, Powers states that 6,500 Tibetans were arrested (45).

132. *The Economist*, "Lhasa Under Siege."

133. *Tibet Daily*, June 2, 2008, quoted in Powers, *The Buddha Party*, 47.

134. Ben Hillman, "Introduction: Understanding the Current Wave of Conflict and Protest in Tibet and Xinjiang," in *Ethnic Conflict and Protest in Tibet and Xinjiang*, ed. Hillman and Tuttle, 8.

135. Fiona McConnell and Tenzin Tsering, "Lhakar: Proud to Be Tibetan," *Open Democracy*, January 2013, https://www.opendemocracy.net/fiona-mcconnell-tenzin-tsering /lhakar-proud-to-be-tibetan; the Lhakar (White Wednesday) Pledge can be seen at https://lhakardiaries.com/. See also Powers, *The Buddha Party*, 80.

136. Powers, *The Buddha Party*, 81.

137. Hillman, "Introduction," 12. Hillman adds that "China's total spending on domestic security now exceeds total spending on external defence!" (exclamation point in the original).

138. U.S. Congressional-Executive Commission on China, *Annual Report*.

139. Hillman, "Unrest in Tibet."

140. Details of the fire in the Jokhang Temple in 2018 can be found at Robert Barnett's Twitter account, https://twitter.com/RobbieBarnett?ref_src=twsrc%5Etfw&ref_url =https%3A%2F%2Fwww.theguardian.com%2Fworld%2F2018%2Ffeb%2F18%2Fjokh ang-temple-fire-engulfs-ancient-heart-of-tibetan-buddhism.

141. There is only one time zone throughout all of China.

142. Crowe, "The 'Tibet Question,'" 1128–29. The Tibetan government in exile's first prime minister, Lobsang Sangay, a Harvard-educated lawyer, has continued the Dalai Lama's "middle way" of calling for "genuine autonomy for Tibet within the People Republic of China," to be achieved through peaceful means (Crowe, "The 'Tibet Question,'" 1126–27).

143. Arpi, "China's Leadership Change and Its Tibet Policy."

144. Mayhew and Kelly, *Tibet*, 96, 140.

5. Branding Religious Coexistence

1. This discussion is also explored in more detail in Michael Dumper, "The Study of Religious Conflicts in Cities," in *Contested Holy Cities: The Urban Dimension of Religious Conflict*, ed. Michael Dumper (London: Routledge, 2019), 3–21.

2. The name "Pitt Street" was officially replaced with the Malay name "Jalan Masjid Kapitan Keling," but "Pitt Street" is used more often colloquially.

3. An overview of the Kek Lok Si Temple's early history can be found in Ooi Lee Tan, *The Making of Modern Buddhism: Chinese Buddhist Revitalization in Malaysia* (N.p.: ScholarBank@NUS Repository, 2013), 37–40.

4. Known as the Ten Thousand Buddhas Pagoda, it is the largest Buddhist temple in Malaysia. See also the entry on it in *Encyclopaedia Britannica* (2017 ed.).

5. Twenty thousand Chinese lanterns and tens of thousands of LED and neon lights are installed and lit by twenty full-time employees during this month. See Edmund Lee,

"Kek Lok Si Temple to Continue with Lighting Ceremony," *Sun Daily*, February 8, 2018.

6. Jean DeBernardi, *Penang: Rites of Belonging in a Malaysian Chinese Community* (Singapore: National University of Singapore Press, 2009), 143. Opposition to the statue was also based on the false rumor that Muslims in the state mosque would end up praying in its direction because that was the direction of Mecca, which it was not. See also Gaik Cheng Khoo, *Reclaiming Adat: Contemporary Malaysian Film and Literature* (Vancouver: University of British Columbia, 2006), 227.

7. For an exposition of this theme, see Ooi, *The Making of Modern Buddhism.*

8. Ahmad Hassan and Shaiful Yahaya, *Architecture and Heritage Buildings in George Town, Penang* (N.p.: Penerbit Universiti Sains Malaysia, 2012).

9. A good overview of the historiography of early Penang can be found in Judith Nagata, "Heritage as History: Plural Narratives on Penang Malays," Asia Research Institute Working Paper Series no. 173, 2012, http://www.ari.nus.edu.sg/wps/wps12_173.pdf.

10. See, for example, Nezar AlSayyad, ed., *Forms of Dominance: On the Architecture and Urbanism of the Colonial Enterprise* (Aldershot, U.K.: Ashgate, 1992); Anthony King, *Urbanism, Colonialism, and the World Economy* (London: Routledge, 1990); Zeynep Celik, *Urban Forms and Colonial Confrontations: Algiers Under French Rule* (Berkeley: University of California Press, 1997); Brenda S. A. Yeoh, *Contesting Space in Colonial Singapore Power Relations and the Built Environment* (Singapore: Singapore University Press, 2003); Nihal Perera, *Society and Space: Colonialism, Nationalism, and Postcolonial Identity in Sri Lanka* (Boulder, CO: Westview Press, 1998).

11. DeBernardi, *Penang*, 131–33. See also the discussion of the influence of native styles on the urban design of George Town in Gwynn Jenkins, *Contested Space: Cultural Heritage and Identity Reconstructions: Conservation Strategies Within a Developing Asian City* (Wien, Germany: Lit, 2008), 52–56.

12. Jenkins, *Contested Space*, 190.

13. We should note that the state of Penang also comprises a strip of land on the peninsula mainland known initially as Province Wellesley, with an important harbor in Butterworth that complemented the one in George Town. Nowadays this area is known as Seberang Perai.

14. Jenkins, *Contested Space*, 41. A good overview of the complex mix that constituted the early settlers in Penang can be found in Jenkins, *Contested Space*, 36–45.

15. Francis Kok Wah Loh, "Managing Conflict Amidst Development and Developmentalism: George Town, Penang," in *Contested Holy Cities*, ed. Dumper, 81–99.

16. Loh, "Managing Conflict Amidst Development and Developmentalism." See also World Bank, "Malaysia Among Most Urbanized Countries in East Asia," *World Bank News*, January 26, 2015, http://www.worldbank.org/en/news/feature/2015/01/26/malaysia-among-most-urbanized-countries-in-east-asia.

17. See also Malaysia Department of Statistics, *Population and Housing Census of Malaysia: 2010 Census* (Kuala Lumpur: Malaysia Department of Statistics, 2010), https://web.archive.org/web/20150301154300/http://www.statistics.gov.my/portal/download_Population/files/census2010/Taburan_Penduduk_dan_Ciri-ciri_Asas_Demografi.pdf.

18. Loh, "Managing Conflict Amidst Development and Developmentalism." See also Malaysia Department of Statistics, *Population and Housing Census of Malaysia.*

19. In George Town, there are five major *kongsis*, known as the Goh Tai Seh, Five Big Clans, serving the Hokkien Chinese community alone. See Jenkins, *Contested Space,* 42; Leong San Tong Khoo Kongsi Publication Committee, *Leong San Tong Khoo Kongsi: The History and Architecture* (Penang, Malaysia: Trustees of Leong San Tong Khoo Kongsi, 2004), 1.

20. Many South Indian Hindus do not recognize either the term *Hinduism* or the term *Hindutva* because they see them as inspired by foreign ideas. In South India historically, Hindu–Muslim tensions are less heightened than in North India, and the Hindu–Muslim riots after, for example, the demolition of the Babri Masjid Mosque in Ayodhya were confined largely to the North. This relatively benign experience of Hindu–Muslim coexistence also permeates the discourse and relations in George Town.

21. Loh, "Managing Conflict Amidst Development and Developmentalism," 84–85.

22. Universiti Sains Malaysia Survey, 1993, cited in Jenkins, *Contested Space,* 166. An important caveat should be borne in mind with this survey: it is unlikely that the area surveyed corresponds exactly to the administrative district of the 2010 census and is likely to be much smaller.

23. Malaysia Department of Statistics, *Population and Housing Census of Malaysia.*

24. Francis Loh and Anil Netto, eds., *Regime Change in Malaysia: GE14 and the End of UMNO-BN's 60-Year Rule* (Petaling Jaya, Malaysia: SIRD and Aliran, 2018).

25. *The Guardian,* "Anwar Ibrahim Returns to Malaysian Politics with Landslide by Election Victory," October 13, 2018, https://www.theguardian.com/world/2018/oct/13/anwar-ibrahim-returns-to-malaysian-politics.

26. Loh, "Managing Conflict Amidst Development and Developmentalism."

27. Ooi Kee Bang, "George Town—from City to Municipality to Culture Centre," *Penang Monthly,* January 2015, https://penangmonthly.com/article.aspx?pageid=2698&name=george_town_from_city_to_municipality_to_culture_centre.

28. Royce Tan, "Penang Island Gets City Status," *The Star Online* (Malaysia), December 18, 2014, https://www.thestar.com.my/news/nation/2014/12/18/penang-island-gets-city-status-mbpp-set-to-take-over-as-new-city-council/.

29. ThinkCity, *George Town Conurbation: Spatial Strategy 2013* (George Town, Malaysia: Geographia, 2013).

30. Johan Saravanamuttu, "Conflict and Compromise in Inter-religious Issues in Malaysia," in "Intercivilizational Conflict: Can It Be Moderated?," special issue of *Israel Journal of Conflict Resolution* 1, no. 1 (Spring 2009), http://pconfl.biu.ac.il/files/pconfl/shared/final_full_text_0.pdf#page=89.

31. Malaysian National Physical Plan 2, 2010, cited in ThinkCity, *George Town Conurbation,* 28, table 2.3.

32. Daniel P. S. Goh, "Between History and Heritage: Post-colonialism, Globalisation, and the Remaking of Malacca, Penang, and Singapore," *TRaNS: Trans-Regional and -National Studies of Southeast Asia* 2 (2014): 92; Francis Hutchinson, "Situating Penang in Asia and Malaysia," in *Catching the Wind: Penang in a Rising Asia,* ed. Francis

Hutchinson and Johan Saravanamuttu (Singapore: Institute of South East Asian Studies; George Town, Malaysia: Penang Institute, 2012), 6.

33. Suresh Narayanan, Lim Mah Hui, and Ong Wooi Leng, "Re-examining State Finances and Governance: The Challenge for Penang," in *Pilot Studies for a New Penang*, ed. Ooi Kee Beng and Goh Ban Lee (Singapore: Institute of Southeast Asian Studies, 2010), 189, 205.

34. Ooi Kee Beng and Goh Ban Lee, "Tweaking the State Delivery Mechanism: The Case of the MPP," in *Pilot Studies for a New Penang*, ed. Ooi and Goh, 228–34. There is a similar tension in the area of solid-waste management.

35. The presence of multinational companies such as Advanced Micro Devices, Agilent Technologies (formerly Hewlett-Packard), Clarion, Fairchild Semiconductor (formerly N. S. Electronics), Renesas (formerly Hitachi), Intel, Osram (formerly Litronix), and Robert Bosch is a key indicator of Penang's success. See the Penang government website Invest Penang, "Why Penang?," n.d., http://www.investpenang.gov .my/why-penang.php?pid=1. One prestigious "catch" was the aerospace instrumentation arm of the U.S. multinational Honeywell. One-third of Malaysia's revenue from medical tourism comes through Penang-based institutions. Another area of potential growth is the halal retail trade, which is being incentivized in Penang.

36. Invest Penang, "Why Penang?"; *Tech in Asia*, "Connecting Asia's Startup Ecosystem," June 11, 2015, https://www.techinasia.com/penang-silicon-valley-of-east-iot.

37. Figures from *Penang Monthly*, January 2015.

38. Lim Chee Han, "The Housing Market in Penang Today," *Penang Monthly*, January 2015. Table 3 in the article gives a breakdown of the most expensive types of properties.

39. Much of Pitt Street is owned by the Indian–Muslim *waqf* based round the Kapitan Kling Mosque. Muslim *waqf*s in George Town fall under the aegis of the Majlis Agama Islam, a federal body. With regard to private family ownership, one family is reputed to own at least two hundred properties in George Town.

40. In 1999, the Khoo Kongsi evicted a swathe of tenants who were unable to meet the demand for higher rents.

41. For dull details of these developments, see chapters 5 and 6 in Jenkins, *Contested Space*.

42. A list of Muslim *waqf* properties can be found in the leaflet by the Academy of Socioeconomic Research and Analysis, *Muslim Heritage in George Town* (George Town, Malaysia: George Town World Heritage, 2013).

43. James Anderson, "Religious and Ethno-national Conflict in Divided Cities: How Do Cities Shape Conflicts?" in *Contested Holy Cities*, ed. Dumper, 22–43.

44. The individuals who participated in the walk included the vicar of St. George's Church, Bishop Charles Samuel; the Roman Catholic bishop of Penang, Reverend Datuk Sebastian Francis; College General Seminary father Gerard Theraviam; Cheah Kongsi representative Cheah Swee Huat; Sikh community representative Sukhindarpal Singh; State Chinese (Penang) Association vice president Lillian Tong; Acheen Street Mosque Committee chairman Datuk Dr. Mujahid Yusof; and Penang Gandhi Peace Centre chairman Datuk Dr. Anwar Fazal.

45. For more details and some remarkable photographs of the walk, see N. Trisha, "A Walk for Unity on Street of Harmony," *The Star Online* (Malaysia), June 24, 2017,https://www.thestar.com.my/news/nation/2017/06/24/a-walk-for-unity-on -street-of-harmony-religious-leaders-join-hands-in-a-show-of-strength-to-defy -big/#6kJD20F7xJ7fhQZ6.99; Predeep Nambiar, "Imams, Bishops, and Faith Leaders in Walk of Hope in Penang," *Free Malaysia Today*, June 23, 2017, http://www .freemalaysiatoday.com/category/nation/2017/06/23/imams-bishops-and-faith -leaders-in-walk-of-hope-in-penang/; Anil Netto, "Historic Interfaith Solidarity at Breaking of Fast at Mosque in Penang," *Aliran*, June 22, 2017, https://aliran.com /events/historic-interfaith-solidarity-breaking-fast-mosque-penang/.

46. Predeep Nambiar, "Group Draws the Line for Non-Muslims at *Buka Puasa* Events," *Free Malaysia Today*, June 2, 2017, https://www.freemalaysiatoday.com/category /nation/2017/06/02/group-draws-the-line-for-non-muslims-at-buka-puasa-events/.

47. See also U.S. Department of State, *Report on International Religious Freedom: Malaysia* (Washington, DC: U.S. Department of State, 2015).

48. Jenkins, *Contested Space*, 27.

49. Carolina Lopez, "Interfaith Relations in Malaysia: Moving Beyond Muslim Versus 'Others,' " in *Routledge Handbook of Contemporary Malaysia*, ed. Meredith L. Weiss (London: Taylor and Francis, 2014), 327.

50. Lopez, "Interfaith Relations in Malaysia," 329–30.

51. U.S. Department of State, *Report on International Religious Freedom: Malaysia*, 6.

52. Lopez, "Interfaith Relations in Malaysia," 330.

53. Nagata, "Heritage as History," 26.

54. Royce Tan, "Perkasa Poised for a New Role," *The Star Online* (Malaysia), January 5, 2014, http://www.thestar.com.my/opinion/columnists/analysis/2014/01/05/perkasa -poised-for-a-new-role/. These policies are reminiscent of the Chinese government's *fenpei* system, whose abolition contributed to Tibetan resistance to the Chinese presence in Lhasa. See chapter 4.

55. Zamihan Mat Zin's reasons are summarized in Francis Loh, "Religious Extemism and Bigotry in Our Midst," *Aliran e-Newsletter*, October 23, 2017, https://aliran.com /newsletters/2017-newsletters/religious-extremism-bigotry-midst/.

56. Lopez, "Interfaith Relations in Malaysia," 328.

57. One claim made is that in Malaysia a Hindu temple is demolished every three weeks. See Farish A. Noor, *The Hindu Rights Action Force (Hindraf) of Malaysia: Communitarianism Across Borders?* (Singapore: Rajaratnam School of International Studies, July 2008); Francis Kok Wah Loh, "The Marginalisation of the Indians in Malaysia: Contesting Explanations and the Search for Alternatives," in *Southeast Asia Over Three Generations*, ed. James T. Siegel and Audrey R. Kahin (New York: Southeast Asia Program Publications, 2003), 223–44.

58. Noor, *The Hindu Rights Action Force*, 3.

59. U.S. Department of State, *Report on International Religious Freedom: Malaysia*, 6.

60. Further details of the Hindu Thaipusam festival can be found in Alexandra Kent, "Transcendence and Tolerance: Cultural Diversity in the Tamil Celebration of

Taipūcam in Penang, Malaysia," *International Journal of Hindu Studies* 8, no. 1 (2004): 81–105.

61. In 2000, the land adjacent to the Sri Muniswarar Temple was purchased for development as a marina for wealthy yacht owners, but the marina would have blocked the temple's access to the sea, which was one of the purposes of its location, and interrupt the Taoist temple's feng shui. The story goes that a curse was leveled against the marina, and it has never been completed!

62. Durian is the only fruit I know of that in public buildings warrants "Forbidden" signs with a picture of the fruit and a red line through it!

63. The interest in food and the awareness that money can be made out of it has spawned a relatively new phenomenon in Malaysia to attract Muslim customers: Chinese halal restaurants.

64. Jenkins, *Contested Space*, 43.

65. The Chingay riots between Malays and Chinese were triggered when a Chinese banner parade clashed with watching Malay youths. The riots lasted ten days, requiring the imposition of a curfew, and five people were killed. The Hartal riots occurred as a result of an economic boycott by the predominantly Chinese and socialist Labour Party but descended into an interethnic conflict and spread from George Town to neighboring states (Loh, "Managing Conflict Amidst Development and Developmentalism").

66. Saravanamuttu, "Conflict and Compromise." A detailed account of the unfolding of the Kampong Rawa Incident is contained in Loh, "The Marginalisation of the Indians in Malaysia."

67. Loh, "The Marginalisation of the Indians in Malaysia," 225–26.

68. Four Penangite Indian Muslims were detained in the Indian state of Tamil Nadu for participating in the Hindu–Muslim clashes in February 1998, one month before the Kampong Rawa Incident. See Loh, "The Marginalisation of the Indians in Malaysia," 229.

69. Loh, "The Marginalisation of the Indians in Malaysia," 229.

70. This narration of the incident is drawn manly from Loh, "The Marginalisation of the Indians in Malaysia," 225–30. However, an engaged commentary on the events is also available on the Indian-Malaysian Online website, which supplies a pro-Hindu perspective. See Indian-Malaysian Online, "Dispute Over a Shrine," n.d., https://www.indianmalaysian.com/demolition.htm.

71. Malaysian riot-control police are a paramilitary unit known as the Federal Reserve Unit.

72. Loh, "The Marginalisation of the Indians in Malaysia," 228.

73. Loh, "The Marginalisation of the Indians in Malaysia," 228.

74. See comments in Johan Abdullah, "The Slide in Ethnic Relations," *Aliran*, October 7, 2006, https://aliran.com/aliran-monthly/2006/2006-6/the-slide-in-ethnic-relations/.

75. For further details on the PHEB, see Jeffrey Hardy Quah, "The Remarkable Resurgence of Penang's Hindu Endowment Board," *Penang Monthly*, June 2016,

https://penangmonthly.com/article.aspx?pageid=2360&name=the_remarkable_resurgence_of_penangs_hindu_endowment_board.

76. A *vel* is the lance of wisdom Parvati gave to Lord Murugan to vanquish his enemies.

77. Kent, "Transcendence and Tolerance," 88.

78. See the Penang Hindu Endowments Board website, http://hebpenang.gov.my/waterfall-road-temple/.

79. This figure is based on the simple calculation that if 700,000 people attend the festival, each making an offering of around U.S.$5, the total would be $3.5 million.

80. Predeep Nambiar, "Chettiars Strike Back Over State Hindu Body Claims," *Free Malaysia Today*, January 16, 2017, https://www.freemalaysiatoday.com/category/nation/2017/01/16/chettiars-strike-back-over-state-hindu-body-claims/; *Just Read Online*, "Penang Chettiars Reveal Thaipusam Accounts," January 19, 2017, https://www.justreadonline.com/2017/01/19/penang-chettiars-reveal-thaipusam-accounts/.

81. K. Suthakar and T. Logeiswary, "'Battle of the Chariots' in Penang," *The Star Online* (Malaysia), December 31, 2016, http://www.thestar.com.my/news/nation/2016/12/31/battle-of-the-chariots-in-penang-the-thaipusam-chariot-war-between-the-chettiars-and-the-hindu-endow/.

82. Further details of the plans for the PHEB's Waterfall Hilltop Temple can be found on its website at https://hebpenang.gov.my/waterfall-road-temple/Assets/Temples/SriArulmigu BalathandayuthapaniTemple.

83. Palanisamy Ramasamy, quoted in Suthakar and Logeiswary, "'Battle of the Chariots' in Penang."

84. See W. Edward Cheng and Ma Shu-Yun, "A City's Status and Its Civil Society," *Penang Monthly*, January 2015.

85. Anwar Fazal, "The Spirit of Penang—Informing, Inspiring, and Igniting Change," Inaugural Lecture of the Penang Story, George Town, Penang, Malaysia, December 10, 2016, copy in author's files.

86. There is much debate among scholars of Malaysia and Southeast Asia regarding this topic. See, for example, the essays in Francis Kok Wah Loh, ed., *Building Bridges, Crossing Boundaries: Everyday Forms of Inter-ethnic Peacebuilding* (Petaling Jaya: Malaysian Social Science Council and Ford Foundation, 2010).

87. Robert Putnam, *Bowling Alone: The Collapse and Revival of American Community* (New York: Simon and Schuster, 2000).

88. Ashutosh Varshney, *Ethnic Conflict and Civic Life: Hindus and Muslims in India* (New Haven, CN: Yale University Press, 2002).

89. Lopez, "Interfaith Relations in Malaysia," 333.

90. See Ask Questions About Malaysia, "What Is *Rukun Tetangga* and What Is It For?" October 28, 2015, http://ask.my/malaysia/what-is-rukun-tetangga-and-what-is-it-for.html.

91. Lopez, "Interfaith Relations in Malaysia," 335. Similar views are also expressed in Saravanamuttu, "Conflict and Compromise in Inter-religious Issues in Malaysia."

92. For further details on the Interfaith Commission, see S. Hadi Abdullah and K. S. Sieh, *The Initiative for the Formation of a Malaysian Interfaith Commission: A Documentation*

(Kuala Lumpur, Malaysia: Konrad Adenauer Foundation, 2007). This fascinating publication charts the twists and turns of this failed initiative. It reveals not only the hidden agendas, petty grouses, and paranoias of the various actors involved but also the vision and resilience of others in the attempt to try and make the initiative work. See also the discussion in Saravanamuttu, "Conflict and Compromise in Inter-religious Issues in Malaysia," 96–98.

93. See *AsiaNews.IT*, "Bishop of Penang: Great Enthusiasm for Easter, Faith Flourishes in Dialogue with Muslims," March 23, 2016, http://www.asianews.it/news-en /Bishop-of-Penang:-Great-enthusiasm-for-Easter,-faith-flourishes-in-dialogue-wit h-Muslims-37027.html.

94. Such individuals include Father Sebastian, Roman Catholic bishop; Dr. Anwar Fazal, mufti of Penang; Wan Salim; and Dr. Mujahid Rawa, member of Parliament.

95. Christophe Jaffrelot and Laurence Louër, eds., *Pan-Islamic Connections: Transnational Networks Between South Asia and the Gulf* (London: Hurst, 2017).

96. Possible exceptions are the additions to the Buddhist Kek Lok Si Temple and the huge statue of Kuan Yin mentioned at the beginning of this chapter.

6. Religious Conflicts in Cities

1. A full picture of the role of the UN in the Arab–Israeli conflict can be found in Karim Makdisi and Vijay Prashad, eds., *Land of Blue Helmets: The United Nations and the Arab World* (Oakland: University of California Press, 2017). For Jerusalem specifically, see Michael Dumper, *Jerusalem Unbound: Geography, History, and the Future of the Holy City* (New York: Columbia University Press, 2014), 160–70.

2. See, for example, Michael Dumper and Craig Larkin, "The Politics of Heritage and the Limitations of International Agency in Divided Cities: The Role of UNESCO in Jerusalem's Old City," *Review of International Studies* 38, no. 1 (January 2012): 25–52.

3. On Gray Zones, see, for example, Nufar Avni and Ofen Yiftachel, "The New Divided City? Planning and 'Gray Space' Between Global North-west and South-east," in *The Routledge Handbook on Cities of the Global South*, ed. Susan Parnell and Sophie Oldfield (London: Routledge, 2014), 487–505.

4. See arguments concerning the problems with "policy transfer" in, for example, David Dolowitz and David Marsh, "Learning from Abroad: The Role of Policy Transfer in Contemporary Policy-Making," *Governance* 13, no. 1 (2000): 5–24, as well as Oliver James and Martin Lodge, "The Limitations of Policy Transfer and Lesson Drawing for Public Policy," *Political Studies Review* 1 (2003): 179–93.

5. Elazar Barkan and Karen Barkey, introduction to *Choreographies of Shared Sacred Sites: Religion, Politics, and Conflict Resolution*, ed. Elazar Barkan and Karen Barkey (New York: Columbia University Press, 2015), 12–13.

6. Karen Barkey, "Religious Pluralism, Shared Sacred Sites, and the Ottoman Empire," in *Choreographies of Shared Sacred Sites*, ed. Barkan and Barkey, 45–46.

7. Very little hard data are available regarding the Palestinian economy in East Jerusalem, but a UN report has pulled together sufficient data to make this claim. See United Nations Conference on Trade and Development (UNCTD), *The Palestinian Economy in East Jerusalem: Enduring Annexation, Isolation, and Disintegration* (New York: UNCTD).

Bibliography

ABC News. "Las elecciones, o el guión de la campaña por la Mezquita-Catedral." November 18, 2015. http://sevilla.abc.es/andalucia/cordoba/sevi-elecciones-o-guion-campana -mezquita-catedral-201511180810_noticia.html.

Abdullah, Johan. "The Slide in Ethnic Relations." *Aliran*, October 7, 2006. https://aliran .com/aliran-monthly/2006/2006-6/the-slide-in-ethnic-relations/.

Abdullah, S. Hadi, and K. S. Sieh, eds. *The Initiative for the Formation of a Malaysian Interfaith Commission: A Documentation.* Kuala Lumpur: Konrad Adenauer Foundation, 2007.

Abu-Lughod, Janet. "Islamic City: Historical Myth, Islamic Essence, and Contemporary Relevance." *International Journal of Middle East Studies* 19 (1987): 155–76.

Abuzayda, Sufyan. "Continuity and Change in Israeli Policy over Jerusalem Before and After the Establishment of the Israeli State." PhD diss., University of Exeter, 2005.

Academy of Socio-economic Research and Analysis. *Muslim Heritage in George Town.* Leaflet. George Town, Malaysia: George Town World Heritage, 2013.

Agier, Michel, and David Fernbach. *Managing the Undesirables: Refugee Camps and Humanitarian Government.* Cambridge, U.K.: Polity, 2011.

Ahmed, Nazeer. "The Fall of Cordoba." *History of Islam: An Encyclopedia of Islamic History,* n.d. https://historyofislam.com/cordoba-the-fall-of/.

Alba, Alfonso. "La Cordoba halal aspira a recibar 200.000 turistas musulmanes mas al año." *Cordopolis*, January 13, 2015. http://cordopolis.es/2015/01/13/la-cordoba-halal-aspira-a -recibir-200-000-turistas-musulmanes-mas-al-ano/.

Albera, Dionigi, and Maria Couroucli. *Sharing Sacred Spaces in the Mediterranean: Christians, Muslims, and Jews at Shrines and Sanctuaries.* Bloomington: Indiana University Press, 2012.

Albert, Eleanor. *Shanghai Cooperation Organisation: Backgrounder.* Washington, DC: Council for Foreign Relations, October 14, 2015. https://www.cfr.org/backgrounder/shanghai -cooperation-organization.

AllGov India. "Rapid Action Force." N.d. http://www.allgov.com/india/departments/ministry-of-home-affairs/rapid-action-force?agencyid=7604.

AlSayyad, Nezar, ed. *Forms of Dominance: On the Architecture and Urbanism of the Colonial Enterprise*. Aldershot, U.K.: Ashgate, 1992.

AlSayyad, Nezar, and Mejgan Massoumi, eds. *The Fundamentalist City? Religiosity and the Remaking of Urban Space*. London: Routledge, 2011.

Amirav, Moshe. *Jerusalem Syndrome: The Palestinian Israeli Battle for the Holy City*. Sussex, U.K.: Sussex Academic Press, 2009.

Andaluces Diario. "Ni IBI, ni IVA, ni sociedades: La Iglesia no paga impuestos por la Mezquita de Córdoba." July 20, 2013. http://www.andalucesdiario.es/ciudadanxs/ni-ibi-ni-iva-ni-sociedades-la-iglesia-no-paga-impuestos-por-la-mezquita-de-cordoba/.

Anderson, James. "Imperial Ethnocracy and Demography: Foundations of Ethno-national Conflict in Belfast and Jerusalem." In *Locating Urban Conflicts: Ethnicity, Nationalism, and the Everyday*, ed. Wendy Pullan and Britt Baillie, 195–213. Basingstoke, U.K.: Palgrave Macmillan, 2013.

——. "Religious and Ethno-national Conflict in Divided Cities: How Do Cities Shape Conflicts?" In *Contested Holy Cities: The Urban Dimension of Religious Conflict*, ed. Michael Dumper, 22–43. London: Routledge, 2019.

Antonio [sic]. "La Mezquita de Córdoba desaparece de Google Maps." *Andaluces Diario*, November 23, 2014. http://www.andalucesdiario.es/ciudadanxs/la-mezquita-de-cordoba-desaparece-de-google-maps/.

Appadurai, Arjun. *Fear of Small Numbers: An Essay on the Geography of Anger*. Durham, NC: Duke University Press, 2006.

Appleby, R. Scott. *Religious Fundamentalism and Global Conflict*. New York: Foreign Policy Association, 1994.

Arendt, Hannah. *On Violence*. Orlando, FL: Harcourt Books, 1969.

Arezki, Rabah, Reda Cherif, and John Piotrowski. *Tourism Specialization and Economic Development: Evidence from the UNESCO World Heritage List*. Washington, DC: International Monetary Fund, 2009.

Arigita, Elena. "'The Cordoba Paradigm': Memory and Silence Around Europe's Islamic Past." In *Islam and the Politics of Culture in Europe: Memory, Aesthetics, Art*, ed. Peter Frank, Sarah Dornhof, and Elena Arigita, 21–40. Bielefeld, Germany: Transcript, 2013.

Arpi, Claude. "China's Leadership Change and Its Tibet Policy." *Strategic Analysis* 37, no. 5 (2013): 539–57.

AsiaNews.IT. "Bishop of Penang: Great Enthusiasm for Easter, Faith Flourishes in Dialogue with Muslims." March 23, 2016. http://www.asianews.it/news-en/Bishop-of-Penang:-Great-enthusiasm-for-Easter,-faith-flourishes-in-dialogue-with-Muslims-37027.html.

Ask Questions About Malaysia. "What Is *Rukun Tengga* and What Is It For?" October 28, 2015. http://ask.my/malaysia/what-is-rukun-tetangga-and-what-is-it-for.htm.

Avineri, Shlomo. *The Making of Modern Zionism: The Intellectual Origins of the Jewish State*. London: Weidenfeld and Nicolson, 1981.

Avni, Gideon, and Jon Seligman. *The Temple Mount 1917–2001: Documentation, Research, and Inspection of Antiquities*. Israeli Antiquities Authority. Jerusalem: Keter Press Enterprises, 2001.

Avni, Nufar, and Oren Yiftachel. "The New Divided City? Planning and 'Gray Space' Between Global North-west and South-east." In *The Routledge Handbook on Cities of the Global South*, ed. Susan Parnell and Sophie Oldfield, 487–505. London: Routledge, 2014.

Barkan, Elazar, and Karen Barkey, eds. *Choreographies of Shared Sacred Sites: Religion, Politics, and Conflict Resolution*. New York: Columbia University Press, 2015.

——. Introduction to *Choreographies of Shared Sacred Sites: Religion, Politics, and Conflict Resolution*, ed. Elazar Barkan and Karen Barkey, 1–31. New York: Columbia University Press, 2015.

Barkey, Karen. "Religious Pluralism, Shared Sacred Sites, and the Ottoman Empire." In *Choreographies of Shared Sacred Sites: Religion, Politics, and Conflict Resolution*, ed. Elazar Barkan and Karen Barkey, 33–65. New York: Columbia University Press, 2015.

Barnett, Robert. *Lhasa: Streets with Memories*. New York: Columbia University Press, 2010.

Barry, Ellen, and Raj Suhasini. "Firebrand Hindu Cleric Ascends India's Political Ladder." *New York Times*, July 12, 2017. https://www.nytimes.com/2017/07/12/world/asia/india -yogi-adityanath-bjp-modi.html.

BBC News. "Mob Rips Apart Mosque in Ayodhya." December 6, 1992. http://news.bbc .co.uk/onthisday/hi/dates/stories/december/6/newsid_3712000/3712777.stm.

BBC Panorama. "A Train That Divides Jerusalem." July 20, 2015. http://mediacenter.tveyes .com/downloadgateway.aspx?UserID=195235&MDID=3802334&MDSeed=9122&Ty pe=Media.

Beaumont, Peter. "Jerusalem at Boiling Point of Polarisation and Violence—EU Report." *The Guardian*, March 20, 2015. https://www.theguardian.com/world/2015/mar/20 /jerusalem-at-boiling-point-of-polarisation-and-violence-eu-report.

Be'er, Yizhar. *Targeting the Temple Mount: A Current Look at Threats to the Temple Mount by Extremist and Messianic Groups*. Jerusalem: Center for the Protection of Democracy in Israel—Keshev, January 2001.

Berkowitz, Shmuel. "The Holy Places in Jerusalem: Legal Aspects." *Justice* 11 (1996).

Bernard, Vincent. "War in Cities: The Spectre of Total War" (editorial). *International Review of the Red Cross* 98, no. 1 (April 2017). https://www.icrc.org/en/international-review /article/editorial-war-cities-spectre-total-war.

Bernbeck, Reinhard, and Susan Pollock. "Ayodhya, Archaeology, and Identity." In "Anthropology in Public," special issue of *Current Anthropology* 37, no. 1 (February 1996): 138–42.

Bevan, Robert. *The Destruction of Memory: Architecture at War*. London: Reaktion Books, 2016.

Bhardwaj, Surinder Mohan. *Hindu Places of Pilgrimage in India: A Study in Cultural Geography*. Berkeley: University of California Press, 1983.

Bigelow, Anna. "The Monumental and the Mundane: Navigating the Sharing of Sacred Sites in India and Turkey." Paper presented at the seminar "The Urban Dimensions of Religious Conflict," Power, Piety, People Leverhulme Project, March 5–10, 2018, Tourtour, France.

Bollens, Scott. *Cities, Nationalism, and Democratization*. London: Routledge, 2007.

——. *City and Soul in Divided Societies*. London: Routledge, 2012.

——. *On Narrow Ground: Urban Policy and Ethnic Conflict in Jerusalem and Belfast.* Albany: State University of New York Press, 2000.

Bowker, John. *Problems of Suffering in Religions of the World.* Cambridge: Cambridge University Press, 1970.

Bowman, Glenn. *Sharing the Sacra: The Politics and Pragmatics of Intercommunal Relations Around Holy Places.* Oxford: Berghahn, 2015.

Brass, Paul R. *The Production of Hindu–Muslim Violence in Contemporary India.* New Delhi: Oxford University Press, 2003.

——. *Theft of an Idol: Text and Context in the Representation of Collective Violence.* Princeton, NJ: Princeton University Press, 1997.

Breger, Marshall J., Yitzhak Reiter, and Leonard Hammer, eds. *Holy Places in the Israeli–Palestinian Conflict: Confrontation and Co-existence.* London: Routledge, 2010.

Brinkhoff, Thomas. "Population of Cordoba and Spain." City Populations Database, 2017. https://www.quandl.com/data/CITYPOP/CITY_CORDOBAANDSPAIN.

Burgen, Stephen. "In Andalucía, the Poor and Jobless Have Little Faith in a Better Mañana." *The Guardian*, April 27, 2014. https://www.theguardian.com/world/2014/apr/27/spain-andalucia-financial-crisis-unemployment.

——. "Spain's Population Set to Drop 11% by 2050." *The Guardian*, October 20, 2016. https://www.theguardian.com/world/2016/oct/20/spain-population-drop-by-2050-trends-low-birth-high-life-elderly-singles.

Burgoyne, Michael. *Mamluk Jerusalem: An Architectural Study.* London: World of Islam Trust, 1987.

Burke, Jason. "One Tibetan Woman's Tragic Path to Self-Immolation." *The Guardian*, March 26, 2018. https://www.theguardian.com/world/2012/mar/26/nomad-path-self-immolation.

Burns, Robert. *The Crusader Kingdom of Valencia: Reconstruction on a Thirteenth-Century Frontier.* Vol. 2. Cambridge, MA: Harvard University Press, 1967.

Cabannes, Yves. "Participatory Budgeting: A Significant Contribution to Participatory Democracy." *Environment and Urbanisation* 16, no. 1 (2004): 27–46.

Cabezon, Jose Ignacio. "State Control of Tibetan Buddhist Monasticism in the People's Republic of China." In *Chinese Religiosities: Affliction of Modernity and State Formation*, ed. Mayfair Mei-hui Yang, 261–92. Berkeley: University of California Press, 2008.

Calderwood, Eric. "The Reconquista of the Mosque of Cordoba." *Foreign Policy*, April 10, 2015. http://foreignpolicy.com/2015/04/10/the-reconquista-of-the-mosque-of-cordoba-spain-catholic-church-islam/.

Calvert, Albert F., and Walter. M. Gallichan. *Cordova: A City of the Moors.* London: John Lane, Bodley Head, 1907.

Capitel, Antón. "La Catedral de Córdoba: Transformación cristiana de la Mezquita." *Arquitectura* 256 (1985): 37–46.

Castro, Américo. *The Structure of Spanish History.* Princeton, NJ: Princeton University Press, 1954.

The Cathedral of Cordoba: A Live Witness to Our History. No publication information given. Leaflet available for tourists on entering the Mezquita. Acquired November 2015, in author's files.

Celik, Zeynep. *Urban Forms and Colonial Confrontations: Algiers Under French Rule*. Berkeley: University of California Press, 1997.

Central Tibetan Administration. *Environment and Development Issues: Introduction*. N.p.: Central Tibetan Administration. 2018. http://tibet.net/important-issues/tibets-environment-and-development-issues/.

———. *Environment Overview*. Lhasa: Central Tibetan Administration, 2018. http://tibet.net/important-issues/tibets-environment-and-development-issues/#codeoslide1.

Chang, Jung, and Jon Halliday. *Mao: The Unknown Story*. London: Vintage, 2006.

Cheng, W. Edward, and Ma Shu-Yun. "A City's Status and Its Civil Society." *Penang Monthly*, January 2015.

Chislett, William. "Spain 40 Years After General Franco: Change of a Nation." Real Instituto El Cano, November 16, 2015. http://www.realinstitutoelcano.org/wps/portal/rielcano_en/contenido?WCM_GLOBAL_CONTEXT=/elcano/elcano_in/zonas_in/ari66-2015-chislett-spain-40-years-after-franco-change-nation.

Chu, Duo, Yili Zhang, Ciran Bianba, and Linshan Liu. "Land Use Dynamics in Lhasa Area, Tibetan Plateau." *Journal of Geographical Sciences* 20, no. 6 (2010): 899–912.

Collier, David. "New Perspectives on the Comparative Method." In *Comparative Political Dynamics: Global Research Perspectives*, ed. Dankwart A. Rustow and Kenneth P. Erikson, 7–31. New York: Harper Collins,1991.

"Cordoba (City, Spain)." In *The Columbia Encyclopaedia*, 6th ed. New York: Columbia University Press, 2000. http://www.encyclopedia.com/places/spain-portugal-italy-greece-and-balkans/spanish-and-portuguese-political-geography/cordoba.

Córdoba España. "Muslim Cordoba." 2017. http://english.turismodecordoba.org/muslim-cordoba.cfm.

Coward, Martin. *Urbicide: The Politics of Urban Destruction*. London: Routledge, 2009.

Crowe, David M. "The 'Tibet Question': Tibetan, Chinese, and Western Perspectives." *Nationalities Papers: Journal of Nationalism and Ethnicity* 41, no. 6 (2013): 1100–1135.

Davis, Richard H. "The Iconography of Rama's Chariot." In *Making India Hindu: Religion, Community, and the Politics of Democracy in India*, ed. David Ludden, 27–54. Oxford: Oxford University Press, 2007.

DeBernardi, Jean. *Penang: Rites of Belonging in a Malaysian Chinese Community*. Singapore: National University of Singapore Press, 2009.

Desai, Madhuri. *Banaras Reconstructed: Architecture and Sacred Space in a Hindu Holy City*. Seattle: University of Washington Press, 2017.

Diker, Dan. "The Expulsion of the Palestinian Authority from Jerusalem and the Temple Mount." *Jerusalem Centre for Public Affairs* 3, no. 51 (2004). https://jcpa.org/article/the-expulsion-of-the-palestinian-authority-from-jerusalem-and-the-temple-mount/.

Dikshit, Rajeev. "Sari Industry in Fix Over CSB Move." *Times of India*, January 23, 2015. https://timesofindia.indiatimes.com/city/varanasi/Sari-industry-in-fix-over-CSB-move/articleshow/45984891.cms.

Dolowitz, David, and David Marsh. "Learning from Abroad: The Role of Policy Transfer in Contemporary Policy-Making." *Governance* 13, no. 1 (2000): 5–24.

Donadio, Rachel. "Name Debate Echoes an Old Clash of Faiths." *New York Times*, November 5, 2010. https://www.nytimes.com/2010/11/05/world/europe/05cordoba.html.

Dorsey, James, "Indian Muslims: A Rich Hunting Ground for Middle Eastern Rivals." *Global Village*, January 5, 2019. https://www.globalvillagespace.com/indian-muslims-a-rich-hunting-ground-for-middle-eastern-rivals-james-m-dorsey/.

Dreyer, June Teufel. *China's Political System: Modernization and Tradition*. New York: Pearson Education, 2006.

Dumper, Michael, ed. *Contested Holy Cities: The Urban Dimension of Religious Conflict*. London: Routledge, 2019.

——. *Islam and Israel: Muslim Religious Endowments and the Jewish State*. Washington, DC: Institute for Palestine Studies, 1994.

——. "Israeli Settlement in the Old City of Jerusalem." *Journal of Palestine Studies* 21 (1992): 32–53.

——. "Jerusalem's Troublesome Sheikh." *The Guardian*, October 7, 2009.

——. *Jerusalem Unbound: Geography, History, and the Future of the Holy City*. New York: Columbia University Press, 2014.

——. "Policing Divided Cities: Stabilisation and Law Enforcement in Palestinian East Jerusalem." *International Affairs* 89, no. 5 (September 2013): 1247–64.

——. *The Politics of Jerusalem Since 1967*. New York: Columbia University Press, 1997.

——. *The Politics of Sacred Space: The Old City of Jerusalem in the Middle East Conflict, 1967–2000*. Boulder, CO: Lynne Rienner, 2002.

——. "Security and the Holy Places in Jerusalem: An Israeli Policy of Incremental Control—'Hebronisation'?" In *Locating Urban Conflicts: Ethnicity, Nationalism, and the Everyday*, ed. Wendy Pullan and Britt Baillie, 76–90. Basingstoke, U.K.: Palgrave MacMillan, 2013.

——. "The Status of the Status Quo at Jerusalem's Holy Esplanade: A Critique." *Jerusalem Quarterly* 63–64 (Autumn–Winter 2015): 120–41.

——. "The Study of Religious Conflicts in Cities." In *Contested Holy Cities: The Urban Dimension of Religious Conflict*, ed. Michael Dumper, 3–21. London: Routledge, 2019.

Dumper, Michael, and Craig Larkin. "In Defence of al-Aqsa: The Islamic Movement Inside Israel and the Battle for Jerusalem." *Middle East Journal* 66, no. 1 (2012): 31–52.

——. "The Politics of Heritage and the Limitations of International Agency in Divided Cities: The Role of UNESCO in Jerusalem's Old City." *Review of International Studies* 38, no. 1 (January 2012): 25–52.

Dumper, Michael, and Wendy Pullan. *Jerusalem: The Cost of Failure*. Briefing paper. London: Chatham House, 2010. http://www.chathamhouse.org.uk/publications/papers/view/-/id/835/.

Dunham, Mikel. *Buddha's Warriors: The Story of the CIA-Backed Tibetan Freedom Fighters, the Chinese Invasion, and the Ultimate Fall of Tibet*. London: Penguin Books, 2004.

East Jerusalem Heads of Mission, European Union. *Annual Report*. Brussels: European Union, 2014. http://www.eccpalestine.org/eu-diplomats-warn-of-regional-conflagration-over-temple-mount/.

Eck, Diana L. *Banaras: City of Light*. New York: Columbia University Press, 1999.

Ecker, Heather. "The Great Mosque of Cordoba in the 12th and Thirteenth Centuries." *Muqarnas* 20 (2003): 113–41.

The Economist. "Bombing in Varanasi: Grim Anniversary." December 10, 2010. https://www
.economist.com/blogs/banyan/2010/12/bombing_varanasi.

——. "The Golden Urn: Even China Accepts That Only the Dalai Lama Can Legitimise Its
Rule in Tibet." March 19, 2015. https://www.economist.com/china/2015/03/19/the
-golden-urn?zid=309&ah=80dcf288b8561b012f603b9fd9577f0e.

——. "Lhasa Under Siege." March 17, 2018. https://www.economist.com/node/10871821.

Edwards, John. *Christian Cordoba: The City and Its Region in the Late Middle Ages.* Cambridge:
Cambridge University Press, 1982.

Eickelman, Dale. "Is There an Islamic City? The Making of a Quarter in a Moroccan
Town." *International Journal of Middle East Studies* 5 (1974): 274–94.

Election Commission of India. *Statistical Report on General Election, 2012.* New Delhi: Government of India, 2012. http://uttarpradeshcongress.com/english/wp-content/uploads
/2013/11/2012.pdf.

Elon, Amos. "Politics and Archaeology." *New York Review of Books* 41 (1994): 14–20.

El Sandouby, Aliaa Ezzeldin Ismail. *The Ahl al-Bayt in Cairo and Damascus: The Dynamics of
Making Shrines for the Family of the Prophet.* N.p.: ProQuest, 2008.

Escudero, Sheikh Mansour Abdussalaam. "The Mezquita-Cathedral of Cordoba: A Shared
Space for Prayer." Speech at the First Junta Islámica University Seminar on Religious
Freedom and Shared Spaces: The Mezquita-Cathedral of Cordoba, July 4, 2012.
https://www.webislam.com/articles/72210-the_mezquitacathedral_of_cordoba_a
_shared_space_for_prayer.html.

Europa Press. "El juez absuelve a los ocho musulmanes que rezaron en la Mezquita de Córdoba en 2010." February 7, 2013. http://www.europapress.es/nacional/noticia-amp-juez
-absuelve-ocho-musulmanes-rezaron-mezquita-cordoba-2010-20130207155419.html.

European Commission. "Eurobarometre 69: Values of Europeans." 2008. http://ec.europa
.eu/commfrontoffice/publicopinion/archives/eb/eb69/eb69_values_en.pdf .

Evans, Graeme. "Living in a World Heritage City: Stakeholders in the Dialectic of the Universal and Particular." *International Journal for Heritage Studies* 8, no. 2 (2002): 117–35.

Evans, Michael. *City Without Joy: Urban Military Operations Into the 21st Century.* Occasional
Paper no. 2. Canberra: Australian Defence College. http://www.defence.gov.au/ADC
/publications/Occasional/PublcnsOccasional_310310_CitywithoutJoy.pdf.

Fareed, Faisal. "In Varanasi, a Plan to Build Corridor from Kashi Vishwanath Temple to
River Ganga Sparks Anger." Reuters, February 10, 2018. https://scroll.in/article/868178
/destruction-not-development-plan-for-varanasis-kashi-vishwanath-temple-sparks
-protests.

Fazal, Anwar. "The Spirit of Penang—Informing, Inspiring, and Igniting Change." Inaugural lecture of the Penang Story, George Town, Penang, Malaysia, December 10,
2016. Copy in author's files.

Feilden, Bernard, and Jukka Jokilehto. *Management Guidelines for World Cultural Heritage Sites.*
Rome: ICCROM, UNESCO, and ICOMOS, 1993.

Fischer, Andrew. "'Population Transfer' Versus Urban Exclusion in the Tibetan Areas
of Western China." *Population and Development Review* 34, no. 4 (December 2008):
631–62.

Fischer, Andrew, and Adrian Zenz. "The Limits to Buying Stability in Tibet: Tibetan Representation and Preferentiality in China's Contemporary Public Employment System." *China Quarterly* 234 (2018): 527–51.

Fletcher, Richard. *Moorish Spain*. London: Weidenfield, 1994.

Freitag, Sandra B., ed. *Culture and Power in Banaras: Community, Performance, and Environment, 1800–1980*. Berkeley: University of California Press, 1992.

——. "State and Community: Symbolic Popular Protests in Banaras's Public Arenas." In *Culture and Power in Banaras: Community, Performance, and Environment, 1800–1980*, ed. Sandra B. Freitag, 203–28. Berkeley: University of California Press, 1992.

Fuchs, Dale. "Mass Versus Minarets: The Cordoba Controversy." *Independent*, October 15, 2010.

Gesler, Wilbert, and Margaret Pierce. "Hindu Varanasi." *Geographical Review* 90, no. 2 (2000): 222–37.

Ghosh, Bishwanath. "Beautification Plan Destroys Oldest Neighbourhoods in Varanasi." *The Hindu*, December 9, 2018. https://www.thehindu.com/news/national/other-states/beautification-plan-destroys-oldest-neighbourhoods-in-varanasi/article25704389.ece.

Glick, Thomas. *Islamic and Christian Spain in the Early Middle Ages*. Princeton, NJ: Princeton University Press, 1979.

Goh, Daniel P. S. "Between History and Heritage: Post-colonialism, Globalisation, and the Remaking of Malacca, Penang, and Singapore." *TRaNS: Trans-Regional and -National Studies of Southeast Asia* 2 (2014): 79–101.

Gomez, Terence E., and Hsin-Huang Michael Hsiao, eds. *Chinese Business in Southeast Asia: Contesting Cultural Explanations, Understanding Entrepreneurship*. London: Curzon Press, 2001.

Gooptu, Nandini. *The Politics of the Urban Poor in Early Twentieth-Century India*. Cambridge: Cambridge University Press, 2001.

Government of India. "Religion Census 2011." 2011. https://www.census2011.co.in/religion.php.

——. "Varanasi (Varanasi) District: Census 2011 Data." Census 2011. https://www.census2011.co.in/census/district/568-varanasi.html.

Government of India, Directorate of Census Operations in Uttar Pradesh. "2011 Census: Religion." 2011. https://www.census2011.co.in/religion.php.

——. "2011 Census, Uttar Pradesh." 2011. https://www.census2011.co.in/questions/1/state-density/density-per-sq-km-of-uttar-pradesh-census-2011.html.

——. "Varanasi City." 2011. https://www.census2011.co.in/census/city/153-varanasi.html.

Government of India, Office of the Registrar General and Census Commissioner. "Census Data 2001." 2001. http://www.censusindia.gov.in/2011-common/census_data_2001.html.

Government of Uttar Pradesh. "Banaras Hindu University." Uttar Pradesh Tourism, 2015. http://uptourism.gov.in/pages/top/explore/top-explore-varanasi—sarnath/banaras-hindu-university.

——. *Human Development Report*. Lucknow: Government of Uttar Pradesh, 2007. http://hdr.undp.org/sites/default/files/india_uttar_pradesh_2007.pdf.

Graham, Stephen. *Cities Under Siege: The New Military Urbanism*. London: Verso, 2011.

Gregory, Derek. *Colonial Present: Afghanistan, Palestine, and Iraq*. Oxford: Blackwell, 2006.

The Guardian. "Anwar Ibrahim Returns to Malaysian Politics with Landslide by Election Victory." October 13, 2018. https://www.theguardian.com/world/2018/oct/13/anwar -ibrahim-returns-to-malaysian-politics.

Guia, Aitana. "Completing the Religious Transition? Catholics and Muslims Navigate Secularism in Democratic Spain." *New Diversities* 17, no. 1 (2015): 95–108.

Guinn, David E. *Protecting Jerusalem's Holy Sites: A Strategy for Negotiating a Sacred Peace*. Cambridge: Cambridge University Press, 2006.

Haaretz. "Some 400,000 Muslims Attend Overnight Prayers at al-Aqsa Mosque in Jerusalem." July 2, 2016. http://www.haaretz.com/israel-news/1.728438.

Han, Enze, and Christopher Paik. "Dynamics of Political Resistance in Tibet: Religious Repression and Controversies of Demographic Change." *China Quarterly* 217 (2014): 69–98.

Hancox, Dan. "Spain's Communist Model Village." *The Guardian*, October 20, 2013. https://www.theguardian.com/world/2013/oct/20/marinaleda-spanish-communist -village-utopia.

Hansen, Thomas B. "Recuperating Masculinity: Hindu Nationalism, Violence, and the Exorcism of the Muslim 'Other.'" *Critique of Anthropology* 16, no. 2 (1996): 137–72.

——. *Wages of Violence: Naming and Identity in Postcolonial Bombay*. Princeton, NJ: Princeton University Press, 2001.

Harris, Clare. *The Museum on the Roof of the World: Art, Politics, and the Representation of Tibet*. Chicago: University of Chicago Press, 2012.

——. "Potala Palace: Remembering to Forget in Contemporary Tibet." In "Afterlives of Monuments," special issue of *South Asian Studies* 29, no. 1 (2013): 61–75.

Harris, Julie. "Mosque to Church Conversions in the Spanish Reconquest." *Medieval Encounters* 3, no. 2 (1997): 158–73. https://www.academia.edu/1162610/Mosque_to _Church_Conversions_in_the_Iberian_Reconquest?auto=download.

Harrison, David, and Michael Hitchcock, eds. *The Politics of World Heritage: Negotiating Tourism and Conservation*. Toronto: Channel View, 2005.

Hartman, Ben, and Daniel K. Eisenbud. "Massive West Bank Clashes Leave Palestinian Dead." *Jerusalem Post*, July 25, 2014. http://www.jpost.com/National-News/Clashes -break-out-in-West-Bank-reportedly-leaving-a-Palestinian-dead-368864.

Hasan, Musirul. *Legacy of a Divided Nation: India's Muslims Since Independence*. London: Hurst, 1997.

Hassan, Ahmad, and Shaiful Yahaya. *Architecture and Heritage Buildings in George Town, Penang*. N.p.: Penerbit Universiti Sains Malaysia, 2012.

Hassner, Ron E. "'To Halve and to Hold': Conflicts Over Sacred Space and the Problem of Indivisibility." *Security Studies* 12, no. 4 (Summer 2003): 1–33.

——. *War on Sacred Grounds*. Ithaca, NY: Cornell Paperbacks, 2013.

(I,1)Hayden, Robert M. "Intersecting Religioscapes and Antagonistic Tolerance: Trajectories of Competition and Sharing of Religious Spaces in the Balkans." *Space and Polity* 17, no. 3 (2013): 320–34.

Hayden, Robert, and Timothy D. Walker. "Intersecting Religioscapes: A Comparative Approach to Trajectories of Change, Scale, and Competitive Sharing of Religious Spaces." *Journal of the American Academy of Religion* 81, no. 2 (2013): 320–426.

Hays, Jeffrey. "Minorities in China." Facts and Details, People's Republic of China, 2015. http://factsanddetails.com/china/cat5/sub29/item192.html.

——. "Tourism in Tibet." Facts and Details, 2018. http://factsanddetails.com/china/cat6/sub37/item2846.html.

Henry, Clémence. "The Chinese Education System as a Source of Conflict in Tibetan Areas." In *Ethnic Conflict and Protest in Tibet and Xinjiang: Unrest in China's West*, ed. Ben Hillman and Gray Tuttle, 97–121. New York: Columbia University Press, 2016.

Hepburn, A. C. *Contested Cities in the Modern West*. London: Palgrave Macmillan, 2004.

Heyd, Uriel. *Ottoman Documents on Palestine, 1552–1615*. London: Oxford University Press, 1960.

Hick, John. *Evil and the God of Love*. London: Palgrave Macmillan, 1985.

Hillman, Ben. "Introduction: Understanding the Current Wave of Conflict and Protest in Tibet and Xinjiang." In *Ethnic Conflict and Protest in Tibet and Xinjiang: Unrest in China's West*, ed. Ben Hillman and Gray Tuttle, 1–17. New York: Columbia University Press, 2016.

——. "Unrest in Tibet and the Limits of Regional Autonomy." In *Ethnic Conflict and Protest in Tibet and Xinjiang: Unrest in China's West*, ed. Ben Hillman and Gray Tuttle, 18–39. New York: Columbia University Press 2016.

Hindustan Times. "Varanasi Curfew Lifted; Schools, Colleges to Remain Closed Tomorrow." October 5, 2015. http://www.hindustantimes.com/india/varanasi-violence-vehicles-set-ablaze-curfew-imposed-in-3-areas/story-lvEh4sjfqkPpSupJPgTl8I.html.

Hodum, Robert. *Pilgrims' Steps: A Search for Spain's Santiago and an Examination of His Way*. Bloomington, IN: iUniverse, 2012.

Hooper, John. *The New Spaniards*. London: Penguin, 2006.

Huang, Chia-Hui, Tsaur Jen-Ruez, and Chih-Hail Yang. "Does World Heritage List Really Induce More Tourists? Evidence from Macau." *Tourism Management* 33, no. 6 (2012): 1450–57.

Human Rights Watch. *China's Crackdown on Tibetan Social Groups*. New York: Human Rights Watch, July 2018. https://www.hrw.org/report/2018/07/30/illegal-organizations/chinas-crackdown-tibetan-social-groups.

Hutchinson, Francis. "Situating Penang in Asia and Malaysia." In *Catching the Wind: Penang in a Rising Asia*, ed. Francis Hutchinson and Johan Saravanamuttu, 1–19. Singapore: Institute of South East Asian Studies; Penang, Malaysia: Penang Institute, 2012.

Hutchinson, Francis, and Johan Saravanamuttu, eds. *Catching the Wind: Penang in a Rising Asia*. Singapore: Institute of South East Asian Studies; George Town, Malaysia: Penang Institute, 2012.

Illume. "Interfaith Lessons from Southern Spain." 2015. http://www.travelillume.com/bibliography/interfaith-spain.

Indian-Malaysian Online. "Dispute Over a Shrine." N.d. https://www.indianmalaysian.com/demolition.htm.

Indian Express. "Varanasi Violence: Ajay Rai Held, Congress Says Ploy to Save VHP, Bajrang Dal." October 7, 2015. http://indianexpress.com/article/india/india-news -india/congress-mla-arrested-for-his-alleged-role-in-varanasi-violence/.

IndiKosh. "Varanasi Municipal Corporation." All About India, 2018. https://indikosh .com/city/223156/Varanasi.

Instituto Nacional de Estadistica. "The Electoral Census." 2018. http://www.ine.es/ss /Satellite?L=en_GB&c=Page&cid=1254735788994&p=1254735788994&pagename=Ce nsoElectoral%2FINELayout.

International Crisis Group. *Extreme Makeover? : Israel's Politics of Land and Faith in East Jeru- salem.* Middle East Report no. 134. Brussels: International Crisis Group, 2012.

——. *How to Preserve the Fragile Calm at Jerusalem's Holy Esplanade.* Middle East Briefing no. 48. Brussels: International Crisis Group, April 2016.

——. *Jerusalem's Holy Esplanade Reveals the Limits of Israeli Counter-Terrorism.* Brussels: Inter- national Crisis Group, May 14, 2018. https://www.crisisgroup.org/middle-east-north -africa/eastern-mediterranean/israelpalestine/jerusalems-holy-esplanade-reveals-limits -israeli-counter-terrorism#

——. *The Status of the Status Quo at Jerusalem's Holy Esplanade.* Middle East Report no. 159. Brussels: International Crisis Group, June 30, 2015.

Invest Penang. "Why Penang?" n.d. http://www.investpenang.gov.my/why-penang .php?pid=1.

Ismail, Sumarni., Yahaya, and Hasniyati Hamzah. "Heritage Conservation for City Market- ing: The Imaging of the Historic City of Georgetown, Penang." *Journal of Design and Built Environment* 4, no. 1 (2008): 27–40.

Israeli National Commission. *Report of the Israeli National Commission for UNESCO.* Paris: UNESCO, February 28, 2007.

Jacobs, Andrew. "Tibetan Self-Immolations Rise as China Tightens Grip." *New York Times,* March 22, 2012.

Jaffrelot, Christophe. *Hindu Nationalist Movement, 1925–1992: Social and Political Strategies.* London: Hurst, 1996.

Jaffrelot, Christophe, and Laurence Louër. "Conclusion." In *Pan-Islamic Connections: Trans- national Networks Between South Asia and the Gulf,* ed. Christophe Jaffrelot and Laurence Louër, 233–44. London: Hurst, 2017.

——, eds. *Pan-Islamic Connections: Transnational Networks Between South Asia and the Gulf.* London: Hurst, 2017.

James, Oliver, and Martin Lodge. "The Limitations of Policy Transfer and Lesson Draw- ing for Public Policy." *Political Studies Review* 1 (2003): 179–93.

Jawaharlal Nehru National Urban Renewal Mission. "City Development Plan for Vara- nasi." *Feedback Ventures,* August 2006. http://www.indiaenvironmentportal.org.in/files /file/varanasi%20city%20development%20plan.pdf.

Jayal, Niraja Gopal. "The Transformation of Citizenship in India in 1990s and Beyond." In *Understanding India's New Political Economy: A Great Transformation?* ed. Sanjay Rupare- lia, Sanjay Reddy, John Hariss, and Stuart Corbridge, 141–56. London: Routledge, 2011.

Jenkins, Gwynn. *Contested Space: Cultural Heritage and Identity Reconstructions: Conservation Strategies Within a Developing Asian City*. Wien, Germany: Lit, 2008.

Jerusalem Institute for Israeli Studies. *Statistical Yearbook of Jerusalem*. Jerusalem: Jerusalem Institute for Israel Studies, 2018. http://www.jerusaleminstitute.org.il/.upload/yearbook/2018/shnaton_C0918.pdf.

Just Read Online. "Penang Chettiars Reveal Thaipusam Accounts." January 19, 2017. https://www.justreadonline.com/2017/01/19/penang-chettiars-reveal-thaipusam-accounts/.

Kent, Alexandra. "Transcendence and Tolerance: Cultural Diversity in the Tamil Celebration of Taipūcam in Penang, Malaysia." *International Journal of Hindu Studies* 8, no. 1 (2004): 81–105.

Kern, Soeren. "Ban Remains on Muslim Prayer in Spanish Cathedral." Gatestone Institute, 2013. https://www.gatestoneinstitute.org/3589/cordoba-cathedral-muslim-prayer.

Khalidi, Walid. "The Ownership of the US Embassy Site in Jerusalem." *Journal of Palestine Studies* 29, no. 4 (2000): 80–101.

Khoo, Gaik Cheng. *Reclaiming Adat: Contemporary Malaysian Film and Literature*. Vancouver: University of British Columbia, 2006.

Khoury, Nuha. "The Meaning of the Great Mosque of Cordoba in the Tenth Century." *Muqarnas* 13 (1996): 80–98.

Kilcullen, David. *Out of the Mountains: The Coming Age of the Urban Guerrilla*. London: Hurst, 2013.

Kimmerling, Baruch, and Joel S. Migdal. *The Palestinian People: A History*. Cambridge, MA: Harvard University Press, 2003.

King, Anthony. *Urbanism, Colonialism, and the World Economy*. London: Routledge, 1990.

Klein, Menachem. "The Islamic Holy Places as a Political Bargaining Card (1993–1995)." *Catholic University Law Review* 45, no. 3 (1996): 745–64.

Kletter, Larry. "The Sovereignty of Jerusalem Under International Law." *Columbia Journal of Transnational Law* 20 (1981): 319–56.

Kumar, Nita. "Work and Leisure in the Formation of Identity: Muslim Weavers in a Hindu City." In *Culture and Power in Banaras: Community, Performance, and Environment, 1800–1980*, ed. Sandra B. Freitag, 147–70. Berkeley: University of California Press, 1992.

Kurlansky, Mark. *Nonviolence: The History of a Dangerous Idea*. New York: Random House, 2006.

Lamprakos, Michele. "Memento Mauri: The Mosque–Cathedral of Cordoba." Aggregate, 2016. http://we-aggregate.org/piece/memento-mauri-the-mosque-cathedral-of-cordoba.

Lancaster, John. "Temple, Station Attacked in India." *Washington Post Foreign Service*, last updated March 8, 2006. http://www.washingtonpost.com/wp-dyn/content/article/2006/03/07/AR2006030700961.html.

Landman, Todd. *Issues and Methods in Comparative Politics: An Introduction*. London: Routledge, 2003.

Leask, Anna, and Alan Fyall. *Managing World Heritage Sites*. Oxford: Elsevier, 2006.

Lee, Edmund. "Kek Lok Si Temple to Continue with Lighting Ceremony." *Sun Daily*, February 8, 2018.

Lee, Julian C. H. *Islamization and Activism in Malaysia*. Singapore: Institute of South-East Asian Studies, 2010.

Leong San Tong Khoo Kongsi Publication Committee. *Leong San Tong Khoo Kongsi: The History and Architecture*. Penang, Malaysia: Trustees of Leong San Tong Khoo Kongsi, 2004.

Lhasa Public Security Bureau, People's Republic of China. "Notice of the Tibet Autonomous Region Public Security Department on Reporting Leads on Crimes and Violations by Underworld Forces." February 7, 2018.

Li, Jianglin, and Susan Wilf. *Tibet in Agony: Lhasa 1959*. Cambridge, MA: Harvard University Press, 2016.

Li, Qing. *The Evolution and Preservation of the Old City of Lhasa*. Singapore: Springer Nature and Social Sciences Academic Press, 2018.

Lim Chee Han. "The Housing Market in Penang Today." *Penang Monthly*, January 2015.

Loewenberg, Samuel. "As Spaniards Lose Their Religion, Church Leaders Struggle to Hold On." *New York Times*, June 26, 2005. http://www.nytimes.com/2005/06/26/weekinreview/as-spaniards-lose-their-religion-church-leaders-struggle-to.html.

Loh, Francis Kok Wah. "BRI and Spike in Chinese Investments in Malaysia: What Are the Implications for Malaysia's Politics and Sovereignty?" *Aliran*, September 2017. https://aliran.com/aliran-csi/aliran-csi-2017/bri-spike-chinese-investments-malaysia-implications-malaysias-politics-sovereignty/.

——, ed. *Building Bridges, Crossing Boundaries: Everyday Forms of Inter-ethnic Peacebuilding*. Petaling Jaya: Malaysian Social Science Council and Ford Foundation, 2010.

——. "Managing Conflict Amidst Development and Developmentalism: George Town, Penang." In *Contested Holy Cities: The Urban Dimension of Religious Conflict*, ed. Michael Dumper, 81–99. London: Routledge, 2019.

——. "The Marginalisation of the Indians in Malaysia: Contesting Explanations and the Search for Alternatives." In *Southeast Asia Over Three Generations*, ed. James T. Siegel and Audrey R. Kahin, 223–43. Ithaca, NY: Southeast Asia Program Publications, 2003.

——. "Religious Extemism and Bigotry in Our Midst." *Aliran e-Newsletter*, October 23, 2017. https://aliran.com/newsletters/2017-newsletters/religious-extremism-bigotry-midst/.

Loh, Francis, and Anil Netto, eds. *Regime Change in Malaysia: GE14 and the End of UMNO-BN's 60-Year Rule*. Petaling Jaya, Malaysia: SIRD and Aliran, 2018.

Lopez, Avila. *Modern Spain: Understanding Modern Nations*. Santa Barbara, CA: ABC-CLIO, 2016.

Lopez, Carolina. "Interfaith Relations in Malaysia: Moving Beyond Muslim Versus 'Others.'" In *Routledge Handbook of Contemporary Malaysia*, ed. Meredith L. Weiss, 324–36. London: Taylor and Francis, 2014.

Lowney, Chris. *A Vanished World: Muslims, Christians, and Jews in Medieval Spain*. Oxford: Oxford University Press, 2006.

Ludden, David, ed. *Making India Hindu: Religion, Community, and the Politics of Democracy in India*. Oxford: Oxford University Press, 2007.

Lundquist, John M. *The Temple of Jerusalem: Past, Present, and Future*. Westport, CN: Praeger, 2008.

Makdisi, Karim, and Vijay Prashad, eds. *Land of Blue Helmets: The United Nations and the Arab World*. Oakland: University of California Press, 2017.

Malaysia Department of Statistics. *Population and Housing Census of Malaysia: 2010 Census*. Kuala Lumpur: Malaysia Department of Statistics, 2012. https://web.archive.org/web/20150301154300/http://www.statistics.gov.my/portal/download_Population/files/census2010/Taburan_Penduduk_dan_Ciri-ciri_Asas_Demografi.pdf.

"Mapping Militant Organizations, Lashkar e-Taiba." Stanford University, 2016. http://web.stanford.edu/group/mappingmilitants/cgi-bin/groups/view/79.

Mayhew, Bradley, and Robert Kelly. *Tibet*. Singapore: Lonely Planet, 2015.

McConnell, Fiona, Nick Megoran, and Philippa Williams, eds. *Geographies of Peace: New Approaches to Boundaries, Diplomacy, and Conflict Resolution*. London: I. B. Tauris, 2014.

McConnell, Fiona, and Tenzin Tsering. "Lhakar: Proud to Be Tibetan." *Open Democracy*, January 2013. https://www.opendemocracy.net/fiona-mcconnell-tenzin-tsering/lhakar-proud-to-be-tibetan.

Melly, Caroline. *Bottleneck: Moving, Building, and Belonging in an African City*. Chicago: University of Chicago Press, 2017.

Memory, Jim. "Collaboratice Church Planting in Cordoba—a Model for Europe." *Evangelical Focus*, 2015. http://evangelicalfocus.com/blogs/1018/Collaborative_church_planting_in_Cordobaa_model_for_Europe.

Meri, Josef W. *The Cult of Saints Among Muslims and Jews in Medieval Syria*. Oxford: Oxford University Press, 2002.

Milton-Edwards, Beverley. *The Israeli–Palestinian Conflict: A People's War*. New York: Routledge, 2009.

Modi, Narendra. "Varanasi Constituency." Narendra Modi website, 2017. http://www.narendramodi.in/varanasi#MediaCoverage.

Monteiro, Lyra. "The Mezquita of Cordoba Is Made of More Than Bricks: Towards a Broader Definition of the 'Heritage' Protected at UNESCO World Heritage Sites." *Archaeologies* 7, no. 2 (August 2011): 312–28.

Monumental Site: The Mosque-Cathedral of Cordoba. No publication information given. Leaflet available for tourists on entering the Mezquita. Acquired November 2016, in author's files.

Moodie, Deonnie. *The Making of a Modern Temple and a Hindu City: Kalighat and Kolkata*. New York: Oxford University Press, 2018.

Mumford, Lewis. *The City in History: Its Origins, Its Transformations, and Its Prospects*. London: Secker and Warburg, 1961.

El Mundo. "Podemos propone que la Mezquita de Cordoba o la Giralda pasen a tener titularidad publica." March 12, 2015. http://www.elmundo.es/andalucia/2015/03/12/5501 61ad22601d563f8b456e.html.

——. "Prestan declaración los vigilantes agredidos en la Mezquita por musulmanes." April 2, 2010. http://www.elmundo.es/elmundo/2010/04/02/andalucia/1270205072.html.

Muqaddasi. *Description of Syria Including Palestine*. Trans. G. Le Strange. Pilgrims Text Society no. 3. New York: AMS Press, 1971.

Murakami, Haruki. *1Q84*. London: Secker Harville, 2011.

Musallem, Sami. *The Struggle for Jerusalem*. Jerusalem: PASSIA, 1996.

Nafria, Ismael. "Interactive: Religious Beliefs and Practices in Spain." *La Vanguardia*, April 3, 2015. http://www.lavanguardia.com/vangdata/20150402/54429637154/interactivo-creen cias-y-practicas-religiosas-en-espana.html.

Nagata, Judith. "Heritage as History: Plural Narratives on Penang Malays." Asia Research Institute Working Paper Series no. 173, 2012. http://www.ari.nus.edu.sg/wps/wps12_173 .pdf.

Nambiar, Predeep. "Chettiars Strike Back Over State Hindu Body Claims." *Free Malaysia Today*, January16, 2017. https://www.freemalaysiatoday.com/category/nation/2017/01 /16/chettiars-strike-back-over-state-hindu-body-claims/.

——. "Group Draws the Line for Non-Muslims at *Buka Puasa* Events." *Free Malaysia Today*, June 2, 2017. https://www.freemalaysiatoday.com/category/nation/2017/06 /02/group-draws-the-line-for-non-muslims-at-buka-puasa-events/.

——. "Imams, Bishops, and Faith Leaders in Walk of Hope in Penang." *Free Malaysia Today*, June 23, 2017. http://www.freemalaysiatoday.com/category/nation/2017/06 /23/imams-bishops-and-faith-leaders-in-walk-of-hope-in-penang/.

——. "Thaipusam in Penang—'a Clash of Chariots.'" *Free Malaysia Today*, January 12, 2017. https://www.freemalaysiatoday.com/category/nation/2017/01/12/thaipusam-in -penang-a-clash-of-chariots/.

Narayanan, Suresh, Lim Mah Hui, and Ong Wooi Leng. "Re-examining State Finances and Governance: The Challenge for Penang." In *Pilot Studies for a New Penang*, ed. O. K. Beng and G. B. Lee, 189–222. Singapore: Institute of Southeast Asian Studies, 2010.

Nash, Elizabeth. *Seville, Cordoba, and Granada: A Cultural History*. London: Oxford University Press, 2005.

Netto, Anil. "Historic Interfaith Solidarity at Breaking of Fast at Mosque in Penang." *Ali-ran*, June 22, 2017. https://aliran.com/events/historic-interfaith-solidarity-breaking -fast-mosque-penang/.

Nieto, Manuel. *La Catedral de Córdoba*. Cordoba, Spain: Publicaciones Obra Social y Cultural Caja Sur, 1998.

Nonini, Donald. *"Getting By": Class and State Formation Among Chinese in Malaysia*. Ithaca, NY: Cornell University Press, 2015. http://0-search.ebscohost.com.lib.exeter.ac.uk /login.aspx?direct=true&db=edsebk&AN=972418&site=eds-live.

Noor, Farish A. *The Hindu Rights Action Force (Hindraf) of Malaysia: Communitarianism Across Borders?* Singapore: Rajaratnam School of International Studies, July 4, 2008. https:// www.loc.gov/item/2013341896/.

Norbu, Jamyang. "Lhasa: The Eternal City ." Rangzen Alliance, June 23, 2013. http://www .rangzen.net/2013/06/03/lhasa-eternal-city-2/.

O'Callaghan, James. *A History of Medieval Spain*. Ithaca, NY: Cornell University Press,1975.

——. *Reconquest and Crusade in Medieval Spain*. Philadelphia: University of Pennsylvania Press, 2003.

O'Connor, Karl. *Public Administration in Contested Societies*. Basingstoke, U.K.: Palgrave Macmillan, 2014.

O'Dowd, Liam, and Martina McKnight, eds. *Religion, Violence, and Cities*. London: Routledge, 2013.

Ooi Kee Beng. "George Town—from City to Municipality to Culture Centre." *Penang Monthly*, January 2015. https://penangmonthly.com/article.aspx?pageid=2698&name =george_town_from_city_to_municipality_to_culture_centre.

——. "In 60 Years, the Art of Dismantling Cultural Pluralism." *Malaysia Insight*, August 31, 2017. https://www.themalaysianinsight.com/s/12954/.

Ooi Kee Beng and Goh Ban Lee, eds. *Pilot Studies for a New Penang*. Singapore: Institute of Southeast Asian Studies, 2010.

——. "Tweaking the State Delivery Mechanism: The Case of the MPP." In *Pilot Studies for a New Penang*, ed. Ooi Kee Beng and Goh Ban Lee, 228–34. Singapore: Institute of Southeast Asian Studies, 2010.

Ooi Lee Tan. *The Making of Modern Buddhism: Chinese Buddhist Revitalization in Malaysia*. N.p.: ScholarBank NUS Repository, 2013.

Organization for Economic Cooperation and Development (OECD). *The OECD Handbook on Security Sector Reform (SSR)*. Paris: OECD, 2007. http://www.oecd.org/dataoecd /43/25/38406485.pdf.

Ortega de Miguel, Enrique, and Andrés Sanz Mulas. "Water Management in Cordoba (Spain): A Participative Efficient and Effective Public Model." In *Reclaiming Public Water: Achievements, Struggles, and Visions from Around the World*, ed. Belén Balanyá, Brid Brennan, Olivier Hoedeman, Satoko Kishimoto, and Philipp Terhorst. Amsterdam: Transnational Institution, 2005. https://www.tni.org/files/waterspain.pdf.

Oza, Rupal. "The Geography of Right-Wing Violence in India." In *Violent Geographies: Fear, Terror, and Political Violence*, ed. Derek Gregory and Allan Pred, 153–74. London: Routledge, 2006.

Pain, Rachel, and Susan J. Smith, eds. *Fear: Critical Geopolitics and Everyday Life*. Aldershot, U.K.: Ashgate, 2008.

El País. "Elecciones autonomicas." January 14, 2015. http://resultados.elpais.com/elecciones /2015/autonomicas/01/14.html.

——. "Guerra laica por el patrimonio." May 26, 2016. http://politica.elpais.com/politica /2016/05/20/actualidad/1463762572_434761.html.

——. "La Iglesia inscribió 4.500 propiedades sin publicidad y sin pagar impuestos." May 6, 2013.

Pappé, Ilan. *A History of Modern Palestine: One Land, Two Peoples*. 2nd ed. Cambridge: Cambridge University Press, 2006.

Parry, John. *Death in Banaras*. Cambridge: Cambridge University Press, 1994.

Pendlebury, John, Michael Short, and Aidan While. "Urban World Heritage Sites and the Problem of Authenticity." *Cities* 26, no. 6 (2009): 349–58.

Perera, Nihal. *Society and Space: Colonialism, Nationalism, and Postcolonial Identity in Sri Lanka*. Boulder, CO: Westview Press, 1998.

Peri, O. "The Waqf as an Instrument to Increase and Consolidate Political Power: The Case of Khasseki Sultan Waqf in Late Eighteenth-Century Ottoman Jerusalem." In *Studies in Islamic Society: Contributions in Memory of Gabriel Baer*, ed. Gad G. Gilbar and Gabriel J. Warburg, 48–49. Haifa: Haifa University Press, 1984.

Peters, Francis E. *Jerusalem*. Princeton, NJ: Princeton University Press, 1985.

———. *Jerusalem and Mecca: The Typology of the Holy City in the Near East.* New York: New York University Press, 1986.

Peters, Joel, and David Newman, eds. *The Routledge Handbook on the Israeli–Palestinian Conflict.* New York: Routledge, 2013.

Pew Research Center. "The Changing Global Religious Landscape." April 5, 2017. http://www.pewforum.org/2017/04/05/the-changing-global-religious-landscape/.

Pingree, Geoff. "Secular Drive Challenges Spain's Catholic Identity." *Christian Science Monitor*, October 1, 2004. https://www.csmonitor.com/2004/1001/p07s02-woeu.html.

Pingree, Geoff, and Liza Abend. "Spain's New Muslims: Converts Have Become the Agreeable Face of Spanish Islam." *Walrus Magazine*, August 15, 2007. https://thewalrus.ca/2007-09-religion/.

Planet, Ana Contreras. "Spain." In *The Oxford Handbook of European Islam*, ed. Jocelyn Cesari, 311–49. Oxford: Oxford University Press, 2014.

Platzdasch, Bernhard, and Johan Saravanamuttu, eds. *Religious Diversity in Muslim-Majority States in South-East Asia: Areas of Toleration and Conflict.* Singapore: Institute of South-East Asian Studies, 2014.

Powers, John. *The Buddha Party: How the People's Republic of China Works to Define and Control Tibetan Buddhism.* New York: Oxford University Press, 2017.

Pradhan, Sharat. "Ancient Varanasi Keeps Its Peace, Proves Its Mettle." *Combating Communalism* 12, no. 114 (March 9, 2006). http://www.sabrang.com/cc/archive/2006/mar06/varanasi/media1.html.

Pressman, Jeremy. "Visions in Collision: What Happened at Camp David and Taba?" *International Security* 28, no. 2 (2003): 5–43.

Preston, Paul. "Spain Feels Franco's Legacy 40 Years After His Death." *BBC News,* November 20, 2015. http://www.bbc.co.uk/news/world-europe-34844939.

Pullan, Wendy, and Maximillian Gwiazda. "The Biblical Present in Jerusalem's 'City of David.'" In *Memory, Culture, and the Contemporary City: Building Sites*, ed. Andrew Webber, Uta Staiger, and Henriette Steiner, 106–25. London: Palgrave Macmillan, 2009.

Pullan, Wendy, Maximillian Sternberg, Lefkos Kyriacou, Craig Larkin, and Michael Dumper. *The Struggle for Jerusalem's Holy Places.* London: Routledge, 2013.

Putnam, Robert. *Bowling Alone: The Collapse and Revival of American Community.* New York: Simon and Schuster, 2000.

Qadri, Asgar. "In India, Fashion Has Become a Nationalist Cause." *New York Times*, November 12, 2017. https://www.nytimes.com/2017/11/12/fashion/india-nationalism-sari.html.

Quah, Jeffrey Hardy. "The Remarkable Resurgence of Penang's Hindu Endowment Board." *Penang Monthly*, June 2016. https://penangmonthly.com/article.aspx?pageid=2360&name=the_remarkable_resurgence_of_penangs_hindu_endowment_board.

Ramon, Amnon. "Delicate Balances at the Temple Mount, 1967–1999." In *Jerusalem: A City and Its Future*, ed. Marshall J. Breger and Ora Ahimeir, 296–332. Syracuse, NY: Syracuse University Press, 2002.

Reiter, Yitzhak. "Contest or Cohabitation in Shared Holy Places? The Cave of the Patriarchs and Samuel's Tomb." In *Holy Places in the Israeli–Palestinian Conflict: Confrontation and Co-existence*, ed. Marshall J. Breger, Yitzhak Reiter, and Leonard Hammer, 158–77. London: Routledge, 2010.

——. "Jewish–Muslim Modus Vivendi at the Temple Mount/al-Haram al-Sharif Since 1967." In *Jerusalem: A City and Its Future*, ed. Marshall J. Breger and Ora Ahimeir, 269–95. Syracuse, NY: Syracuse University Press, 2002.

Reiter, Yitzhak, Marlen Eordegian, and Marwan Abu Khallaf. "Between Divine and Human: The Complexity of Holy Places in Jerusalem." In *Jerusalem: Points of Friction—and Beyond*, ed. Moshe Maoz and Sami Nusseibeh, 95–153. The Hague: Kluwer Law International, 2000.

Religion & Ethics News Weekly. "Catholicism in Spain." PBS, aired July 7, 2006. http://www.pbs.org/wnet/religionandethics/2006/07/07/july-7-2006-catholicism-in-spain/19937/.

Ricca, Simone. *Reinventing Jerusalem: Israel's Reconstruction of the Jewish Quarter After 1967.* London: I. B. Tauris, 2007.

Ring, Trudy, ed. *International Dictionary of Historic Places: Southern Europe.* Vol. 3. London: Fitzroy Dearborn, 1994.

Rodrigues, Hillary. *Ritual Worship of the Great Goddess: The Liturgy of the Durga Puja with Interpretations.* Albany: State University of New York Press, 2003.

Rodrigues, Pedro. "Andalucia Poorest Region in Spain." *Olive Press*, October 18, 2013. http://www.theolivepress.es/spain-news/2013/10/18/andalucia-poorest-region-in-spain/.

Roisa, Brian, and Jaime Jover-Baez. "Contested Urban Heritage: Discourse of Meaning and Ownership of the Mosque-Cathedral of Cordoba, Spain." *Journal of Urban Cultural Studies* 4, nos. 1–2 (2017): 127–54.

Rong, Ma. *Population and Society in Contemporary Tibet.* Hong Kong: Hong Kong University Press, 2011.

Rong, Ma, and Tanzen Lhundup. "Temporary Migrants in Lhasa in 2005." *Journal of the International Association of Tibetan Studies*, no. 4 (December 2008): 1–42.

Rose, Richard. *Lesson Drawing in Public Policy.* Chatham NJ: Chatham House, 1993.

Ross, Christopher, Bill Richardson, and Begona Sangrador-Vegas. *Contemporary Spain.* 4th ed. London: Routledge, 2016.

Roy, Siddharthya. "Varanasi on Edge as Tradition—and Politics—Clash with Mission to Clean Ganga." *The Wire*, October 10, 2010. https://thewire.in/culture/violence-in-varanasi-after-tradition-clashes-with-governments-clean-ganges-mission.

Ruggles, D. Fairchild. "The Stratigraphy of Forgetting: The Great Mosque of Cordoba and Its Contested Legacy." In *Contested Cultural Heritage: Religion, Nationalism, Erasure, and Exclusion in a Global World*, ed. Helaine Silverman, 51–68. New York: Springer, 2011.

Safi, Michael. "India, Home of the World's Tallest Statue, Announces Plan to Build a Taller One." *The Guardian*, November 26, 2018. https://www.theguardian.com/world/2018/nov/26/india-worlds-tallest-statue-plan-to-build-a-taller-one-uttar-pradesh-hindu-go-ram.

Salaymeh, Wael. "In Pictures: Ramadan's Holiest Night." *Al Jazeera*, August 5, 2013. http://www.aljazeera.com/indepth/inpictures/2013/08/2013851380381790.html.

Samman, Khaldoun. *Cities of God and Nationalism: Rome, Mecca, and Jerusalem as Contested Sacred World Cities.* London: Routledge, 2007.

Saravanamuttu, Johan. "Conflict and Compromise in Inter-religious Issues in Malaysia." In "Intercivilizational Conflict: Can It Be Moderated?" special issue of *Israel Journal of Conflict Resolution* 1, no. 1 (Spring 2009). http://pconfl.biu.ac.il/files/pconfl/shared/final_full_text_0.pdf#page=89.

Sassen, Saskia. "On Concentration and Centrality in the Global City." In *World Cities in a World System*, ed. Paul L. Knox and Peter J. Taylor, 63–76. Cambridge: Cambridge University Press, 1995.

Satellite View of Kashi Vishwanath Temple and Gyan Vapi Mosque in Varanasi, Every Hindu Should Watch. YouTube, Cityscapes and Infrastructure, April 13, 2017. https://www.youtube.com/watch?v=yDV9xwRZDAg.

Sayigh, Yezid. *Armed Struggle and the Search for State: The Palestinian National Movement, 1949–1993*. Oxford: Oxford University Press, 1997.

Schildgen, Brenda D. *Heritage or Heresy: Preservation and Destruction of Religious Art and Architecture in Europe*. New York: Palgrave Macmillan, 2008.

Schmitt, Kenny. "Living Islam in Jerusalem: Faith, Conflict, and the Disruption of Religious Practice." PhD diss., University of Exeter, 2018.

Searle-Chatterjee, Mary. "Religious Division and the Mythology of the Past." In *Living Banaras: Hindu Religion in Cultural Context*, ed. Bradley R. Hertel and Cynthia A. Humes, 145–58. Albany: State University of New York Press, 1998.

Segev, Tom. *One Palestine, Complete: Jews and Arabs Under the British Mandate*. New York: Metropolitan Books, 2000.

Seidemann, Daniel. *The Events Surrounding the Mugrabi Gate—2007: A Case Study Jerusalem*. Windsor, U.K.: University of Windsor, June 2007.

Sennett, Richard. *The Uses of Disorder: Personal Identity and City Life*. New York: Norton, 1970.

Shackley, Myra. *Managing Sacred Sites*. Andover, MA: Cengage Learning EMEA, 2012.

Shefalee, Vesudev. "The Banaras Bind." *LiveMint Ground Report*, November 23, 2013. https://www.livemint.com/Leisure/5h1lnyORjhtn9ProZ4wiXL/Ground-Report—The-Banaras-bind.html.

Shepherd, Robert. "UNESCO and the Politics of Cultural Heritage in Tibet." *Journal of Contemporary Asia* 36, no. 2 (2006): 243–57.

Sheridan, Michael. "Ancient Tibet Shrivels Before China's Sprawl." *Sunday Times* (London), May 26, 2013. https://www.thetimes.co.uk/article/ancient-tibet-shrivels-before-chinas-sprawl-nfmnmfbz3lp.

Siegman, Henry. "The Great Middle East Peace Process Scam." *London Review of Books* 29, no. 16 (2007): 6–7.

Sinding-Larsen, Amund. "Lhasa Community, World Heritage, and Human Rights." In *World Heritage Management and Human Rights*, ed. Stener Ekern, William Logan, Birgitte Sauge, and Amund Sinding-Larsen, 85–94. New York: Routledge, 2015.

Singh, Rana P. B. "Muslim Shrines and Multi-religious Visitations in Hindus' City of Banaras, India: Co-existential Scenario." In *Pilgrims and Pilgrimages as Peacemakers in Christianity, Judaism, and Islam*, Compostela International Studies in Pilgrimage History and Culture, ed. Antón M. Pazos, 127–59. Farnham, U.K.: Ashgate, 2013.

——. "Politics and Pilgrimage in North India: Varanasi Between Communitas and Contestation." *Tourism Review* 59 (2011). http://hrcak.srce.hr/74034.

———. "Proposing Varanasi as a Heritage City for Inclusion in the UNESCO World Heritage List." N.d. Draft approved by Manoj Kumar, divisional commissioner, Society of Heritage Planning and Environmental Health and Vrinda Dar-Kautilya Society, Varanasi. Copy in author's files.

Smart, Ninian. *The Religious Experience of Mankind.* Glasgow: Collins, 1971.

Smith, C., and S. Fletcher. "Cordoba Participatory Budget." *Participedia,* 2016. http://participedia.net/en/cases/cordoba-participatory-budget.

Smith, Charles D. *Palestine and the Arab–Israeli Conflict: A History with Documents.* Boston: Bedford/St. Martin's, 2007.

Solsten, Eric, and Sandra Meditz. "Social Values and Attitudes." In *Spain: A Country Study.* Washington, DC: U.S. Government Publication Office for the Library of Congress, 1988. http://countrystudies.us/spain/43.htm.

Sontheimer, Gunterh-Dietz, and Hermann Kulke, eds. *Hinduism Reconsidered.* Delhi: Manohar, 1989.

Soong, Kua Kia. "Why Migrants Lives Matter." *Malaysiakini,* November 3, 2017. https://www.malaysiakini.com/letters/400582

Spain Then and Now. "Cordoba: Historical Overview." 2009. http://www.spainthenandnow.com/spanish-history/cordoba-historical-overview/default_41.aspx.

Srivastava, Abhishek. "Is BJP Planning an Ayodhya 2.0 in Varanasi?" *India National Herald,* March 24, 2018. https://www.nationalheraldindia.com/news/is-the-bjp-planning-an-ayodha-2-in-varanasi-gyanvapi-masjid-stands-in-way-of-connecting-kashi-vishwanath-with-ganga-ghats5.317.

Srivathsan, A. "Varanasi and the Politics of Change." *Hindu Sunday Magazine,* March 24, 2019.

The Statesman's Yearbook 2017: The Politics, Cultures, and Economies of the World. London: Palgrave Macmillan, 2016.

Stausberg, Michael. *Religion and Tourism: Crossroads, Destinations, and Encounters.* Abingdon, U.K.: Routledge, 2011.

Stephan, S. H. "An Endowment Deed of Khasski el-Sultan, Dated 24th May, 1922." *Quarterly of the Department of Antiquities in Palestine* 10 (1944): 170–94.

Sunil, Raman. "The New Threat to Islam in India: Hardline Wahabis and Salafis Are Attracting New Converts." *The Diplomat,* February 4, 2016. https://thediplomat.com/2016/02/the-new-threat-to-islam-in-india/.

Suthakar, K., and T. Logeiswary. "'Battle of the Chariots' in Penang." *The Star Online* (Malaysia), December 31, 2016. http://www.thestar.com.my/news/nation/2016/12/31/battle-of-the-chariots-in-penang-the-thaipusam-chariot-war-between-the-chettiars-and-the-hindu-endow/.

Svensson, Isak. "Fighting with Faith: Religion and Conflict Resolution in Civil Wars." *Journal of Conflict Resolution* 51, no. 6 (2007): 930–49.

Swami, Praveen. "Roads to Perdition? The Politics and Practice of Islamist Terrorism in India." In *Religion and Security in South and Central Asia,* ed. K. Warikoo, 52–66. London: Routledge, 2010.

Szanto, Edith. "Sayyida Zaynab in the State of Exception: Shiʿi Sainthood as 'Qualified Life' in Contemporary Syria." *International Journal of Middle East Studies* 44, no. 2 (2012): 285–99.

Tan, Royce. "Penang Island Gets City Status." *The Star Online* (Malaysia), December 18, 2014. https://www.thestar.com.my/news/nation/2014/12/18/penang-island-gets-city-status-mbpp-set-to-take-over-as-new-city-council/.

———. "Perkasa Poised for a New Role." *The Star Online* (Malaysia), January 5, 2014. http://www.thestar.com.my/opinion/columnists/analysis/2014/01/05/perkasa-poised-for-a-new-role/.

Tang, Wei, Tiancai Zhou, Jian Sun, Yurui Li, and Weipeng Li. "Accelerated Urban Expansion in Lhasa City and the Implications for Sustainable Development in a Plateau City." *Sustainability* 9, no. 49 (2017): 1–19.

Tech in Asia. "Connecting Asia's Startup Ecosystem." June 11, 2015. https://www.techinasia.com/penang-silicon-valley-of-east-iot.

Telegraph. "Serial Blasts in Varanasi." March 8, 2006. https://www.telegraphindia.com/1060308/asp/frontpage/story_5941755.asp.

Temple Institute. *Tisha B'Av, 5775: Return to the Temple Mount.* Video, July 27, 2015. https://www.youtube.com/watch?v=vESctNnkyvo.

ThinkCity. *George Town Conurbation: Spatial Strategy.* George Town, Malaysia: ThinkCity, 2013.

———. *George Town World Heritage Site: Population and Land Use Change, 2009–2013.* George Town, Malaysia: Think City, 2014.

Trisha, N. "A Walk for Unity on Street of Harmony." *The Star Online* (Malaysia), June 24, 2017. https://www.thestar.com.my/news/nation/2017/06/24/a-walk-for-unity-on-street-of-harmony-religious-leaders-join-hands-in-a-show-of-strength-to-defy-big/#6kJD20F7xJ7fhQZ6.99.

Tsur, Jacob. *Zionism: National Liberation Movement.* Jerusalem: Israel Government Printing Press, 1969.

Twain, Mark. *Following the Equator: A Journey Around the World.* 1904. Reprint. New York: Dover, 1989.

Union de Comunidades Islamicas de Espana (UCIDE). *Estudio demografico de la poblacion musulmana.* N.p.: UCIDE, 2015. http://ucide.org/es/content/estudio-demogr%C3%A1fico-de-la-poblaci%C3%B3n-musulmana-2.

United Nations Children's Fund. "India Development Indicators Revised." 2010. https://knoema.com/atlas/india/varanasi-district.

United Nations Conference on Trade and Development (UNCTD). *The Palestinian Economy in East Jerusalem: Enduring Annexation, Isolation, and Disintegration.* New York: UNCTD.

United Nations, Department of Economic and Social Affairs, Population Division. *World Urbanization Prospects, the 2014 Revision.* New York: United Nations, 2014. https://esa.un.org/unpd/wup/Publications/Files/WUP2014-Highlights.pdf.

United Nations Educational, Scientific, and Cultural Organization (UNESCO). "The Historic Centre of Cordoba." N.d. (date of inscription: 1984). http://whc.unesco.org/en/list/313.

———. *Report of the Technical Mission to the Old City of Jerusalem (27 February–2 March 2007).* Paris: UNESCO, March 12, 2007. http://www.unesco.org/bpi/pdf/jerusalem_report_en.pdf.

United Nations Habitat. *Cities and Climate Change—Global Report on Human Settlements*. New York: United Nations, 2011. http://www.unhabitat.org/content.asp?typeid=19 &catid=555&cid=9272.

United Nations Office on Drugs and Crime (UNODC). *Introductory Handbook on Policing Urban Space*. New York: United Nations, 2011.

United Nations and World Bank. 2018. *Pathways for Peace: Inclusive Approaches to Preventing Violent Conflict*. Washington, DC: World Bank. doi:10.1596/978-1-4648-1162-3.

Upadhyaya, Pradhan. "Communal Peace in India: Lessons from Multicultural Banaras." In *Religion and Security in South and Central Asia*, ed. K. Warikoo, 83–95. London: Routledge, 2010.

U.S. Congressional-Executive Commission on China. *Annual Report*. Washington, DC: U.S. Government Publication Office, 2017. https://www.cecc.gov/sites/chinacommission .house.gov/files/documents/AR17%20Tibet_final.pdf.

———. *Special Report: Tibetan Self-Immolation—Rising Frequency, Wider Spread, Greater Diversity*. Washington, DC: U.S. Government Publication Office, August 22, 2012. https://www .cecc.gov/publications/issue-papers/special-report-tibetan-self-immolation-rising-fre quency-wider-spread.

U.S. Department of State. *Report on International Religious Freedom: Malaysia*. Washington, DC: U.S. Department of State, 2015.

U.S. Department of State, Bureau of Democracy, Human Rights, and Labor. *International Religious Freedom Report 2005*. Washington, DC: U.S. Department of State, 2005. https:// www.state.gov/j/drl/rls/irf/2005/51582.htm.

———. *International Religious Freedom Report 2015*. Washington, DC: U.S. Department of State, 2015. https://www.state.gov/j/drl/rls/irf/2015/index.htm.

Uttar Pradesh Congress Committee. "About Us." Website, 2017. http://uttarpradesh congress.com/english/introduction/ideology.

Van de Veer, Peter. *Religious Nationalism: Hindu and Muslims in India*. Berkeley: University of California Press, 1994.

Varadarajan, Siddharth. *Gujarat: The Making of a Tragedy*. New Delhi: Penguin Books, 2002.

Varshney, Ashutosh. *Ethnic Conflict and Civic Life: Hindus and Muslims in India*. New Haven, CN: Yale University Press, 2002.

Vermaat, Emerson. "The Rapid Re-Islamization of Southern Spain." *Militant Islam Monitor*, August 4, 2008. http://www.militantislammonitor.org/article/id/3558.

Vohra, Meera. "Sonu Nigam & Javed Akhtar Felicitated at Sankat Mochan Music Festival in Varanasi." *Times of India*, April 8, 2018. https://timesofindia.indiatimes.com/entertain ment/hindi/music/sonu-nigam-javed-akhtar-felicitated-at-sankat-mochan-music -festival-in-varanasi/articleshow/63656860.cms.

Whalen-Bridge, John. *Tibet on Fire: Buddhism, Protest, and the Rhetoric of Self-Immolation*. London: Palgrave Macmillan, 2015.

Williams, Philippa. *Everyday Peace? Politics, Citizenships, and Muslim Lives in India*. Oxford: Wiley, 2015.

———. "Hindu–Muslim Brotherhood: Exploring the Dynamics of Communal Relations in Varanasi, North India." *Journal of South Asian Development* 2, no. 2 (2007). http://journals .sagepub.com/doi/abs/10.1177/097317410700200201.

World Bank. "Malaysia Among Most Urbanized Countries in East Asia." *World Bank News*, January 26, 2015. http://www.worldbank.org/en/news/feature/2015/01/26/malaysia-among -most-urbanized-countries-in-east-asia.

——. *Violence in the City: Understanding and Supporting Community Responses to Urban Violence*. Washington, DC: Social Development Department, Conflict, Crime, and Violence Team, World Bank, 2011.

Yang, Fenggang. *Religion in China: Survival and Revival Under Communist Rule*. Oxford: Oxford University Press, 2011.

Yang, Mayfair Mei-hui, ed. *Chinese Religiosities: Affliction of Modernity and State Formation*. Berkeley: University of California Press, 2008.

——. Introduction to *Chinese Religiosities: Affliction of Modernity and State Formation*, ed. Mayfair Mei-hui Yang, 1–42. Berkeley: University of California Press, 2008.

Yeh, Emily T. *Taming Tibet: Landscape Transformation and the Gift of Chinese Development*. Ithaca, NY: Cornell University Press, 2013.

Yeoh, Brenda S. A. *Contesting Space in Colonial Singapore Power Relations and the Built Environment*. Singapore: Singapore University Press, 2003.

Yiftachel, Oren. *Ethnocracy: Land and the Politics of Identity in Israel/Palestine*. Philadelphia: University of Pennsylvania Press, 2006.

Ying, Chenqing. *Tibetan History*. Beijing: China Intercontinental Press, 2003.

Zaimeche, Salah. *Islam and Science*. Manchester, U.K.: Foundation for Science Technology and Civilisation, 2002.

Zalzberg, Ofer. "Jerusalem's Crumbling Status Quo." *Today's Zaman*, October 26, 2015. https://www.crisisgroup.org/middle-east-north-africa/eastern-mediterranean/israel palestine/jerusalem-s-crumbling-status-quo.

Grants

Conflict in Cities and the Contested State: Everyday Life and the Possibilities of Transformation in Belfast, Jerusalem, and Other Divided Cities. ESRC Large Grant, RES-060-25-0015.

Power, Piety, and People: The Politics of Holy Cities in the 21st Century. Leverhulme Trust, MRF-2014-098.

Index

China (*continued*)

Chinese Catholic Patriotic Movement, 188; Christians in, 189; and conquests, 160, 164–65; and Cultural Revolution, 185, 188, 193; and Dalai Lama, 154, 163, 165–67, 203; demography of, 168; dress in, 170; economy of, 169, 170–71, 189, 198, 203; education in 171, 190; Falun Gong cult in, 181; and *fenpei*, 180–81, 197; geography of, 168; governance of, 154–55, 171–73, 188–89, 193–94, 203–4; and Great Leap Forward, 166; and investment, 167, 171, 176, 203, 214, 226, 239, 257; and Jokhang Palace, 157, 166; and language, 171; and martial law, 183, 197; and media, 181; and migration, 13, 155, 157, 170–72; minorities in, 161, 164, 167–69, 170–72, 183; National Daoist Association, 188; Olympic Games in, 181, 197–98; Patriotic Education Program, 197; People's Liberation Army, 165–66; People's University, 190; photography in, 171; propaganda in, 170; Qing dynasty of, 163–64; Red Guards, 188–89; reeducation programs in, 154, 166, 196; Regulations in Religious Affairs, 189; and religions, 26, 188–90; Religious Affairs Bureau, 188, 193, 194; repression by, 154–55, 165–66, 172, 188–89, 193–95, 197–99, 268; secularism in, 13, 154, 189–90, 268; and Sichuan, 154, 160–61, 166, 189, 199, 201; Smash the Four Olds Campaign, 188; Strike Hard Campaign, 197; Three-Self Patriotic Movement, 188; tourism in, 170, 190; university graduates in, 182. *See also* Communist Party (China)

China Islamic Association, 188

Chinese: in George Town, 217–24, 227, 228, 241, 259, 267, 272; in Malaysia, 225; in Penang, 254; in Straits Settlements, 220, 223

Chinese Catholic Patriotic Movement, 188

Chinese New Year, 213

Christians, 25–26; in Banaras, 107; in China, 189; demography of, 6; in George Town, 240, 241, 258; in Jerusalem, 38, 45, 47; and Kalima Allah controversy, 236, 256; in Malaysia, 236–37

Church of the Holy Sepulcher (Jerusalem), 38, 52

cities: comparisons between, 11–12, 265–66; and Conflict in Cities project, 10, 55; and data collection, 14, 271; demography of, 18, 273–74; and Dumper, 17–19; economy of, 272–73; literature review of, 19–20; religious conflict in, 5–7, 10, 12–14, 36, 41, 46, 50; and urbanization, 26, 210; violence in, 5–7, 23, 36. *See also* holy cities

civil society, 209, 227, 253, 254, 255, 265, 271

climate, 161

Cluny Abbey (France), 76

coexistence. *See* tolerance

Commission on National Affairs (Lhasa), 193

Communist Party (China), 85, 165, 197, 200, 204, 272; and Buddhism, 196, 210; and conquests, 160; and Document 19, 189; and education, 190; and employment, 182; and economy, 158, 189, 198; and minorities, 161, 167, 169, 170–72; and monasteries, 166–67, 192–94,

199; and monks and nuns, 167, 192; and reeducation programs, 154; and religions, 188, 190; and secularism, 13; United Front Work Department, 193. *See also* China

Communist Party (Spain), 83

Communist Uprising (Malaysia), 223

concrete, 169

Conflict in Cities and Contested States Project, 10, 55

Congressional Committee on China (United States), 153, 200

Congress Party (India), 112, 117, 118

conquests, 21, 69, 73–76, 160

constitutions: India, 149, 220; Malaysia, 158, 212, 214, 218, 220, 234–35, 250, 260, 261, 270

conversion (religious), 72, 74, 89, 135, 235

Cordoba (Spain): Association of Muslims in Cordoba, 88, 89–90; cemeteries in, 89; Communist Party in, 83; conquest of, 73–74; demography of, 71, 84–85; and Diocese of Cordoba, 75, 91, 94–95, 96–98, 99–102, 108, 211; dress in, 89, 92; economy of, 85–86, 89; elections in, 95; governance of, 83–84; and halal food, 95; history of, 67–68, 69–78; as holy city, 12–13; Islamic scholars in, 72; Jews in, 72, 289n29; Junta Islámica in, 91, 101, 292n61; mayors of, 83, 95; migration to, 84–85, 89, 90, 98, 102; mosques in, 73, 89; Muslims in, 88–92, 95, 101, 271; public space in, 89; religious economy of, 75, 97; religious revenues in, 75, 97; Romans in, 69; and tolerance, 74, 77, 81, 83, 91, 100, 267–68; tourism in, 86, 90, 93, 94, 95, 97; Umayyads in, 69–73; United Left in, 89; Visigoths in, 69. *See also*

Diocese of Cordoba; Mezquita-Cathedral of Cordoba

Cordoba Cathedral. *See* Mezquita-Cathedral of Cordoba

corruption, 84, 260

Creative and Technology Accelerator Zone (George Town), 227

crowds, 52–53, 54–55, 127, 147

cultural genocide, 167, 179

cultural identity: in George Town, 219–20; in Lhasa, 174, 185–87, 191, 194, 199, 202, 206; in Tibet, 174, 185–87, 191, 194, 199, 202, 206, 268, 270, 272

Cultural Revolution (China), 185, 188, 193

Dalai Lama: fifth, 162–63; seventh, 163; thirteenth, 160, 164; fourteenth, 160, 165, 203; and China, 154, 163, 165–67, 203; and India, 166–67, 191–92, 211; and Mongolia, 169; and Potala Palace, 162, 185; and resistance, 165, 196–97; and the Seventeen-Point Agreement, 165, 167

Dalit community (India), 150

Damascus, 42

Daoism. *See* Taoism

Das, Baba Khalil, 135

Das, Tulsi, 143

data collection, 14–15, 271

Democratic Action Party (Malaysia), 222, 240, 251

Democratic Management Committees (China), 194

Democratic Republic of Congo, 262

demography, 6, 18, 31, 44; in Banaras, 115–16, 122, 142, 150; in China, 168; in cities, 18, 173–74; in Cordoba, 71, 84–85; in George Town, 212, 214, 218–21, 223, 229, 236; in India, 6, 113; in Jerusalem, 45, 63; in Lhasa, 166,

demography (*continued*)
173, 178–80, 192; in Penang, 215,
218–21; in Spain, 84, 86–87, 100,
290n44; in Tibet, 162, 179

demonstrations, 57; in Banaras, 106, 135;
in George Town, 230; in India, 114;
in Jerusalem, 53; in Lhasa, 197–98,
200; in Penang 232

Deng, Xiaoping, 171

Department of Islamic Development
(Malaysia), 237, 240, 256

Department of National Unity and
Integration (Malaysia), 255

Desai, Madhuri, 116–17, 128, 129, 130,
132

Dharamsala (India), 167

diaspora communities, 7, 34, 270

Diocese of Cordoba, 75, 91, 94–95,
96–98, 99–102, 108, 211. *See also*
Roman Catholic Church

dob-dobs (Buddhist monks), 192

Document 19 (China), 189

Dome of the Rock (Jerusalem), 2, 38,
49–51, 276

drainage, 226

Drepung Monastery (Lhasa), 154, 190,
191, 197, 198

dress, 194; in Banaras, 107; in China,
170; in Cordoba 89, 92; in George
Town, 240; in Malaysia, 238, 240; in
Tibet, 197, 199

Dreyer, Jane, 170–71, 172

dual administration (Jerusalem), 39, 65

Dumper, Michael: and American
Academy of Arts and Sciences, 36;
background, 8–9, 207; on cities,
17–19; and data collection, 14–15,
271; and fieldwork, 15, and
Jerusalem, 9, 55–56, 263; and
literature review, 19–20, 22–23; and
Leverhulme Major Research

Fellowship, 5; and London Track,
27–29; in Malaysia, 8, 207; and
methodology, 14–15, 20–36; and
NGOs, 9; and religious belief, 9,
25–26; and United Nations, 263

Dunham, Mikel, 191

Durga Puja (Hindu festival), 135

East India Company, 127, 215–16, 218

Eck, Diana, 125, 126–27, 129–30, 133

economic interdependence, 120, 150,
152, 227, 272–74

economy: of Banaras, 108–9, 118–20,
123, 272; of China, 169, 170–71, 189,
198, 203; of cities, 272–73; and
Communist Party (China), 158, 189,
198; of Cordoba, 85–86, 89; of
George Town, 226–30; of Jerusalem,
273; of Malaysia, 225, 230, 235; of
monasteries, 192; and New
Economic Order, 230, 235; and
Tibet, 154–55, 158, 167

education, 274; in Banaras, 270; in
China, 171, 190; and Communist
Party (China), 171, 192; in Lhasa,
180; and monasteries, 193–95; in
Spain, 87; in Tibet, 176, 180–82,
193–95

Edwards, John, 74

elections: in Banaras, 117, 142; in
Cordoba, 95; in George Town,
221–22; in India, 118; in Jerusalem,
46; in Malaysia, 225, 237, 255, 260; in
monasteries, 194; in Penang, 221–22,
251–52; in Uttar Pradesh, 117, 149

embassies, 60–62, 64–65, 265

empires, 24, 215

employment, 180–82, 227, 272–73

enclaves, 7, 210

endowments, 48; in George Town, 228,
230, 250, 260; in Jerusalem, 48–49,

Gooptu, Nardini, 135

governance: in Banaras, 117, 151–52; in China, 154–55, 171–73, 188–89, 193–94, 203–4; in Cordoba, 83–84; of Mezquita-Cathedral of Cordoba, 101

Granada (Spain), 74

graveyards. See cemeteries

Gray Zones, 264–65

Great Britain: and George Town, 215–17; and India, 109, 112, 117; and Jerusalem, 38; and Malaysia, 215–17; and Tibet, 163–64, 165. See also East India Company

Great Leap Forward (China), 166

Great Prayer Festival (Buddhism). See Monlam

Greek Orthodox Patriarchate (Jerusalem), 99

Guatemala, 65

guerrillas, 166, 191

Gujarat, 106, 114, 139

Gyan Vapi Mosque (Banaras), 109–10, 122, 128, 132–33, 136, 142–48, 266

Haiti, 262

al-Hakam II, Umayyad ruler, 71

halal food, 85, 243

HAMAS (Palestinian political movement), 47, 263

Haram al-Sharif (Jerusalem): and Abdallah, King of Jordan, 2–3; conference on, 1–3; and Israel, 2–3, 4, 39–41, 48–49, 56–59, 273; and Jordan, 2–3, 39, 56; in media, 2; compared to Mezquita-Cathedral of Cordoba, 4–5; and *murabit*, 58–59; and Muslims, 41, 52–59; and Netanyahu, 2–3; and November 2015 incident, 55–59; and Palestinians, 2, 39, 43, 53, 56–59, 274; photography of, 49–51; police in, 2, 49–51, 52, 58;

prayers in, 4, 52–59; and religious conflict, 53–59, 274–75; and religious festivals, 52–57; and religious revenues, 49; and United States, 2–3. *See also* al-Aqsa Mosque; Dome of the Rock; Maghrabi Ascent; Western Wall

Harris, Clare, 186

Hassner, Ron, 10, 20, 45, 62, 258, 266–67

Hastings, Warren, 117

Hayden, Robert, 10, 20, 23, 33, 208, 238, 243

healthcare, 176, 264

Hebron (West Bank), 54

Hernán Ruiz I, architect, 77

Hick, John, 89

Higher Islamic Council (Jerusalem), 39

Hillman, Ben, 171, 201

al-Himyari, Arab historian, 69–70

Hindu Endowment Board (George Town), 230

Hinduism, 133–34; and Ayodhya 137–38; and Banaras 125–28, 132–33, 149, 268; and Brahmins, 132, 133, 150

Hindu Rights Action Force, 238, 249

Hindus, 313n20; and Ayodhya, 4, 106, 108, 109, 111, 114, 136–42; and Babri Mosque, 4, 106, 108, 109, 111, 114, 136–42; in Banaras, 13, 99, 105–11, 115–16, 119, 123–24, 128–35, 142–52, 268–69; demography of, 6; in India, 112–14; in Malaysia, 237, 238, 249

Hindutva (Hindu nationalism), 24, 113–14; in Banaras, 107, 134–35, 136, 145–46, 211, 270; in India, 109, 158; in Uttar Pradesh, 149

history: of Cordoba, 67–68, 69–78; of George Town, 215–18; of Lhasa, 162–67; of Penang, 215–18; of Tibet, 162–67

Hizb at-Tahrir (Islamic organization), 47

Holi (Hindu festival), 104

Holkar, Ahilyabai, 132–33

holy cities, 10–13; Banaras as, 13, 22, 23, 32; Cordoba as, 12–13; definition of, 29–36; Jerusalem as, 12, 22, 29, 33–34, 37–41; and literature review, 19–20, 22–23; and methodology, 14–15, 20–26; and religious conflict, 36

holy sites, 7, 12, 30–31, 59–60, 62–63, 68, 209, 211, 260, 270, 274; and George Town, 13, 217, 257–58; and Jerusalem, 2–4, 37–41, 205, 275–76; and Lhasa, 155–57, 159, 184–85, 191, 205–6, 269, 273; and Malaysia, 249; and methodology, 14, 266–67; and urbanization, 30, 32

Hong Kong, 172, 214, 228

hospitals, 118

housing, 18; in Banaras, 147–48; in George Town, 217, 228–29, 259; in Jerusalem, 42, 263, 275–76, 283n17; in Lhasa, 155, 158, 176–78, 184, 204–5. *See also* land use; urbanization

hudud (Islamic punishments), 236

Human Rights Commission (Malaysia), 256

Hungry Ghost Festival (Buddhism), 241

Hussein, Faisal, 27

Ibn Hazm, 72

Ibn Rushd, 72

Ibrahim, Anwar, 148–49, 222

al-Ibrahimi Mosque (Hebron), 54

identity. *See* cultural identity

IKRAM (Malaysian organization), 256

immigration. *See* migration

India, 215; Bharatiya Janata Party in, 106, 117, 118, 140, 144, 158; Buddhism in, 193; Congress Party in, 112, 117, 118; constitution of, 149, 220; and Dalai Lama, 166–67, 191–92, 211; Dalit

Community in, 150; demography of, 6, 113; demonstrations in, 114; elections in, 118; and Great Britain, 109, 112, 117; Hindutva in, 109, 158; law in, 138, 140, 149; monasteries in, 193; monks and nuns in, 167; Mughal dynasty in, 109, 112, 116–17, 128–32, 193; Muslims in, 112–14, 118, 120, 135–42, 249; Rapid Action Force in, 110, 111, 144–45; Rashtriya Swayamsevak Sangh in, 140, 142; religious conflict in, 105, 112–14, 135–42; riots in, 139; Samajwadi Party in, 117, 142; and Shah Bano affair, 138; terrorism in, 104–6; and Tibet, 161, 162, 165, 166, 167, 169, 196; violence in, 139; Vishna Hindu Parishad in, 136, 138–39, 142. *See also* Ayodhya; Banaras

Indian Mujahideen, 111

Indian National Congress, 112, 118

Indians: in George Town, 218–21, 227, 228, 235, 245–46, 258–59, 272

Indochina, 215, 216

Indonesia, 216

Inner Mongolia Autonomous Region (China), 172

Interfaith Commission (Malaysia), 256, 261

International Commission on Monuments and Sites, 82–83

International Crisis Group, 61

internationalization: in Banaras, 152; in Jerusalem, 63–65, 152, 159, 183, 204, 269–70, 275–76; in Lhasa, 159, 183, 204, 211, 269–70

interreligious harmony. *See* tolerance

investment: by China, 167, 171, 176, 203, 214, 226, 239, 257; in George Town, 226, 257

Ipoh (Malaysia), 8, 207

in, 154, 190, 191, 197, 198; education
in, 180; employment in, 180–82;
ethnonationalism in, 64, 158, 204,
270–71, 274; Ganden Monastery in,
154, 191, 198; gated communities in,
158, 178; geography of, 161–62;
history of, 162–67; as holy site,
155–57, 159, 184–85, 191, 205–6, 269,
273; housing in, 155, 158, 176–78,
184, 204–5; internationalization of,
159, 183, 204, 211, 269–70; Jokhang
Temple in, 157, 159, 162, 166, 173,
174, 186, 187, 196, 197, 201, 206; and
kora, 173, 174, 175, 184, 191, 196, 197,
199; land use in, 156, 166, 174,
176–77, 184–87, 203, 205; and *The
Lhasa Atlas*, 184; and Lhasa
Development Plan, 184; Loseling
College in, 170; migration to, 13,
155, 156, 172, 174, 178–80, 184, 268,
272–73; monasteries in, 13, 154, 166,
184–85, 190, 191–99, 206;
Norbulingka Palace in, 159, 166, 173,
186, 206; pilgrimage to, 156–57, 162,
184; plazas in, 185; police in, 194,
196–98, 202; Potala Palace in, 157,
159, 163, 166, 173, 174, 185–86, 201,
206; prostitution in, 184; Public
Security Bureau in, 187, 193, 194;
public space in, 210; railway stations
in, 155; religious conflict in, 155–57,
166, 191, 204; religious leaders in,
204; religious property in, 184–85;
riots in, 154, 158, 182, 197; roads in,
176, 184; security in, 177–78, 182,
192, 200, 202; Sera Monastery in,
154, 166, 191, 194, 195, 196, 197, 198;
Shol in, 185; shopping malls in,
306n37; Tibet Museum in, 185–86;
tourism in, 176, 179–80, 183–84, 186,
195, 198, 201, 273; urbanization of,

156, 173–78, 184–87, 203; violence in,
154, 166, 196, 198; as World Heritage
Site, 159, 186–87, 204; youth in, 189,
198, 201–2
Lhasa Atlas, The 184
Lhasa Development Plan, 184
Light, Sir Francis, 215
lighting, 77
Lim, Gua Eng, 232
literature review, 19–20, 22–23
Lithang Monastery (Kham, Tibet), 166
Loh, Francis, 218–19, 221, 245–46
London Track (peace negotiations),
27–29, 36
Lopez, Carolina, 235, 255–56
Lord Ganesh Shrine (George Town), 230
Lord Murugan (Hindu deity), 241, 250,
251
Lorong Burma (George Town), 258
Loseling College (Lhasa), 190
Lourdes (France), 12, 32
Lucknow (India), 106, 140
Lundquist, John, 137–38

Machu (Tibet), 153
Madrid, 1, 3
Maghrabi Ascent (Jerusalem), 56–57
Mahmud al-Ghaznawi (Muslim ruler),
116
Maimonides. *See* Moshe ben Maimon
Maitri Bhavan (Banaras), 107
Malacca (Malaysia), 215, 216
Malays: in George Town, 218–24, 227,
259, 270, 272; in Malaysia, 225, 230,
234–38, 241, 254
Malaysia: Aliran in, 232; Amanah Party
in, 256; and Bangsa Malaysia, 255;
Barisan National in, 221, 226, 251;
Buddhism in, 8, 237; *bumiputera* in,
74, 225, 235, 245; Chinese in, 225;
Christians in, 236–37; civil society

Malaysia (*continued*)

in, 255; communist uprising in, 223; constitution of, 158, 212, 214, 218, 220, 234–35, 250, 260, 261, 270; Democratic Action Party in, 222, 240, 251; Department of Islamic Development in, 232, 240, 256; Department of National Unity and Integration in, 255; dress in, 238, 240; Dumper in, 8, 207; economy of, 225, 230, 235; elections in, 225, 237, 255, 260; ethnicity in, 234–38; and Federation of Malaya, 217; freedom of religion in, 234; and Great Britain, 215–17; Hindu Rights Action Force in, 238, 249; Hindus in, 237, 238, 249; holy sites in, 249; Human Rights Commission in, 256; IKRAM in, 256; Interfaith Commission in, 256, 261; Islam Hadhari in, 255; Islamic law in, 234–37; Kampong Medan incident in, 238; Malays in, 225, 230, 234–35, 241, 254; Malaysian Chinese Association in, 221; Malaysian Consultative Commission for Buddhism, Christianity, Hinduism, Sikhism and Taoism in, 256; Malaysian Indian Congress in, 221, 251–52; Malaysian Interfaith Network in, 256; Malaysian Islamic Party in, 222, 225, 226, 236, 256; Malaysian Ulama Association in, 256; marriage in, 235; martial law in, 225; middle classes in, 220, 225; mining in, 218; monasteries in, 8; monks and nuns in, 8; Muslims in, 212, 214, 215, 217, 234–38; National Unity Consultative Council in, 255; New Economic Policy in, 225, 230, 235; NGOs in, 237; Nur Damai in, 256; One Malaysia in, 255; Pakatan Harapan in, 222; Pakatan Rakyat in, 223; Perkasa in, 232, 237; police in, 225; politics in, 225–26, 260; religions in, 217, 219–21, 235–38; religious leaders in, 256; riots in, 225, 239, 244–45, 255, 316n65; Rukun Tetangga in, 255; and Singapore, 217, 228; Sisters of Islam in, 256; and sultans, 218, 223, 237, 260; Taipei Peace Initiative in, 256; tolerance in, 255–56; unemployment in, 237; United Malays National Organization in, 221–22, 225, 226–27, 232, 236–37, 248–49, 251–52, 256; and United States, 237; Unity kindergartens in, 255; violence in, 237–38; Vision 2020 in, 255. *See also* George Town; Penang

Malaysian Chinese Association, 221

Malaysian Consultative Commission for Buddhism, Christianity, Hinduism, Sikhism and Taoism, 256

Malaysian Indian Congress, 221, 251–52

Malaysian Interfaith Network, 256

Malaysian Islamic Development Department. *See* Department of Islamic Development (Malaysia)

Malaysian Islamic Party (PAS), 222, 225, 226, 236, 256

Malaysian Ulama Association, 256

Manchu (ethnic group), 168

Manikarnika Ghat (Banaras), 127

al-Mansur, Umayyad ruler, 69, 71, 72, 73

manufacturing, 227. *See also* weaving industry

Mao, Zedong, 165, 171, 189, 192

marriage, 104, 162, 235, 240

martial law, 183, 197, 225

masses (religious service), 93

mayors, 83, 95, 224

Mecca, 12, 30, 32, 59, 109, 129, 142, 258

media, 2, 64, 152, 181, 183, 187,
   197–98
Mendelsohn, Everett, 36
methodology, 14–15, 20–26
Mezquita-Cathedral of Cordoba:
   architecture of, 3, 70–71;
   Christianization of, 77–80, 82, 83,
   94; construction of new cathedral,
   73–77; demolition of old cathedral,
   72; governance of, 101; compared to
   Haram al-Sharif, 4–5; and
   International Commission on
   Monuments and Sites, 82–83;
   lighting in, 77; masses in, 93, *mihrab*
   in, 70–71, 76, 82, 91, 92; and
   Muslims, 4, 68, 75–76, 90–92, 100–2,
   267–68; naming of, 94–95;
   photography in, 93; Platforma de la
   Mezquita-Catedral, 84, 95, 97, 101;
   police in, 92; prayers in, 4, 66,
   90–92, 98, 100–1; publicity for,
   94–95, 97; *qibla* in, 70, 288n7;
   religious conflict in, 91–92; and
   religious property, 96–98; and
   religious revenues, 45, 75, 96–97;
   security in, 92–94; symbolic role of,
   71–72; and tourism, 93, 94–95, 97; as
   World Heritage Site, 82–83, 85, 91,
   93. *See also* Diocese of Cordoba
middle classes: in George Town, 230,
   242; in Malaysia, 220, 225; in
   Penang, 227; in Tibet, 155, 176,
   180–81, 273
migration, 84; to Banaras, 116, 123, 136,
   150; and China, 13, 155, 157, 170–72;
   to George Town, 215, 216–17; to
   Lhasa, 13, 155, 156, 172, 174, 178–80,
   184, 269, 272–73; to Spain, 84
mihrab (prayer niche), 70–71, 76, 82, 91,
   92
Mill, John Stuart, 11

mining, 169, 218
minorities: in China, 161, 164, 167–69,
   170–72, 183
Mishra, Veer Bhadra, 107
mobility, 19, 35
Modi, Narendra, 118
moksha (liberation from death), 109, 126,
   134, 149
monasteries and nunneries (Buddhist),
   203; and Buddhism, 13, 154, 256, 161,
   181, 184–85, 190–99, 206; colleges in,
   190, 192; and Communist Party
   (China), 166–67, 192–94, 199; and
   Democratic Management
   Committee, 194; Drepung
   Monastery, 154, 190, 191, 197, 198;
   economy of, 192; and education,
   193–95; Ganden Monastery, 154, 191,
   198; in George Town, 212; in India,
   193; in Lhasa, 13, 154, 166, 184–85,
   190, 191–99, 206; Lithang Monastery,
   166; in Malaysia, 8; organization of,
   192; and regional identity, 192; Sera
   Monastery, 154, 166, 191, 194, 195,
   196, 197, 198; in Sichuan, 201; in
   Tibet, 166, 181, 184–85, 190, 191–99,
   206
Mongolia, 169
Mongols (ethnic group), 168
monks and nuns (Buddhist), 13; *dob-dobs*,
   192; Gelugpa monastic order, 162; in
   India, 167; in Lhasa, 154, 189–90,
   190–92, 192–99; in Penang, 8; and
   self-immolation, 154; in Tibet, 13,
   162, 167, 168, 181, 190–92, 192–99
Monlam (Buddhist festival), 191
Moriscos (Muslim converts in Spain),
   82, 92
Morocco, 87
Mortgage Act (Spain), 96
Moshe ben Maimon, 72

Mosque-Cathedral of Cordoba. *See* Mezquita-Cathedral of Cordoba

Mosques (general): in Banaras, 121–22, 130–32; in Cordoba, 73, 89; in George Town, 208, 229, 231, 240, 244–49, 256, 258–59; in Penang, 213–14. *See also* the names of individual mosques

Mostar (Bosnia-Herzegovina), 260

Moussa, Amr, 92

Mozárabes (Christians under Muslim rule in Spain), 69

Mozarabic liturgy, 76

Muammar Gaddhafi, 91

mudejar (Muslims under Christian rule in Spain), 76, 82

Mughal dynasty, 109, 112, 116–17, 128–32, 193, 215

Muhammad Iqbal, 91

Mumbai, 114

Mumford, Lewis, 15–17

municipal councils: in George Town, 209, 223; in Jerusalem, 46; in Penang, 223

murabit (Muslim religious activist), 58–59

museumification, 173, 183

music, 124, 125

Muslims: in Andalusia, 87; in Ayodhya, 136–142; and Babri Mosque, 136–42; in Banaras, 13, 47, 99, 105–11, 115–17, 119–24, 128–32, 135–36, 142–52, 268–69, 270; and demography, 6; expulsion from Cordoba, 75; in George Town, 208, 220–21, 229, 240, 245–49, 254, 258–59, 270; and Haram al-Sharif, 41, 52–59; in India, 112–14, 118, 120, 135–42, 249; in Jerusalem, 4, 45, 47, 63, 268, 275; in Malaysia, 212, 214, 215, 217, 234–38; and Mezquita-Cathedral of Cordoba, 4, 66, 68, 75–76, 90–92, 100–2, 267–68; in Spain, 86–90

Najaf (Iraq), 12, 66

National Daoist Association (China), 188

nationalism, 24, 64, 155, 232. *See also bumiputera;* ethnonationalism; Hindutva; Zionism

National Unity Consultative Council (Malaysia), 255

Native Americans, 194, 195

Nattukotai Chettiar Temple (George Town), 241, 251–52

natural resources, 169, 306n37

Netanyahu, Benjamin, 2–3

New Delhi, 106

New Economic Policy (Malaysia), 225, 230, 235

New Year Festival (Judaism), 52

Ngaba (Tibet), 161

Nobel Peace Prize, 197

nomadism, 160, 162

Nomani, Abdul Batin, 107

non-governmental organizations (NGOs), 9, 183, 204, 237

nonya (Straits Chinese), 220

Noor Fatima, 107

Norbulingka Palace (Lhasa), 159, 166, 173, 186, 206

Northern Ireland, 210. *See also* Belfast

November 2015 incident (Jerusalem), 24, 58–59

Nur Damai (Malaysian organization), 256

Nusantara, 215

Oberammergau (Germany), 12

offensive behaviour, 57

Old City (Jerusalem), 28, 38, 39, 40, 52–57, 275

Olympic Games (2008), 181, 197–98

One Malaysia (Malaysian organization), 255

opium trade, 217

142–52; and Buddhism, 162–167, 173, 190–92; and cities, 5–7, 10, 12–14, 36, 41, 46, 50; data collection for, 14–15; in George Town, 212, 214, 232, 238, 244–49, 250–52, 257–61; and Haram al-Sharif, 53–59, 274–75; and holy cities, 36; in India, 105, 113–14, 135–42; in Jerusalem, 53–57, 63–64, 274–75; in Lhasa, 155–57, 166, 191, 274–75; and methodology, 14–15, 22–26; in Mezquita-Cathedral of Cordoba, 91–92; and urbanization, 5–7

Religious Conflict in Cities Resolution Tool Kit, 26, 154, 274–75

religious economy, 6–7, 12, 14, 34, 47–49; in Cordoba, 75, 97. *See also* religious revenues

religious festivals, 12, 33, 44–45; in Banaras, 104, 107, 111, 121, 135–36, 146–47, 210; in George Town, 213–14, 238, 241, 247, 250–52; in Jerusalem, 52–53. *See also* religious rituals

religious leaders, 6, 31, 34, 46, 48, 209–10, 260, 267–69; in Banaras, 106, 107, 135, 272; in George Town, 231–33, 254–55, 257, 258–59, 261; in Lhasa, 204; in Malaysia, 256; and methodology, 14

religious property, 33, 34, 38, 46, 52, 55, 210; in George Town, 259–60; in Jerusalem, 99, 151; in Lhasa, 184–85; and Mezquita-Cathedral of Cordoba, 96–98; in Spain, 87–88, 95–96

religious revenues, 6–7, 12, 34, 47, 48–49; in Cordoba, 75, 97; in George Town, 252, 258; and Haram al-Sharif, 49; and methodology, 14; and Mezquita-Cathedral of Cordoba, 45, 75, 96–97. *See also* religious economy

religious rituals, 7, 12, 33, 44–45, 52, 210; in Banaras, 121–23, 135; and

methodology, 14. *See also* religious festivals

religious sites. *See* holy sites

rents, 228

repression by China, 154–55, 165–66, 172, 188–89, 193–95, 197–99, 268

resistance, 210–11; in Tibet, 13, 154–55, 161, 165–66, 191, 196–99, 205–6

riots: in India, 139; in Lhasa, 154, 158, 182, 197; in Malaysia, 225, 239, 244–45, 255, 316n65; in Penang, 244–45. *See also* violence

rivers, 169–70

roads, 165, 176, 184, 217, 241

Roman Catholic Church in Spain, 4, 66, 80–81, 86–88, 94–102, 211. *See also* Diocese of Cordoba

Romans, 69

Rome, 12, 30, 109

Rukun Tetangga (Malaysian organization), 255

Russia, 163

Sabah (Malaysia), 217, 236, 240

Saddam Hussein, 91

Saint George's Cathedral (Jerusalem), 264

Saint George's Church (George Town), 208, 231, 241, 258

Salafism, 120, 122

Salt Lake City (United States), 12

Samajwadi Party (India), 117, 142

Sangkat Mochan Temple (Banaras), 104, 106–7, 124, 142–43

Santiago de Compostela (Spain), 35, 71

Sarajevo (Bosnia-Herzegovina), 12, 86, 209

Saravanamuttu, Johan, 225

Sarawak (Malaysia), 217, 236, 240

saris, 119–120. *See also* weaving industry

Sarnath (Banaras), 128

Street of Harmony (George Town), 208, 230–33, 246, 249, 261, 314n44. *See also* Pitt Street (George Town)

Strike Hard campaign (China), 197

suicide. *See* self-immolation

sultans: in Malaysia, 218, 223, 237, 260

Sumatra, 215, 220

Taiping Peace Initiative (Malaysia), 256

Taiwan, 214, 228

Taj Mahal (India), 112, 133

Tanzeem (Indian organization), 135

Taoism, 189, 237, 241

Tariq al-Wad (Jerusalem), 55–56

Tashlich (Jewish festival), 52

Tel Aviv (Israel), 60, 265

Temple Institute (Israel), 58

Temple Mount (Jerusalem), 37–28, 41, 58, 205, 209–10

Terengganu (Malaysia), 236

terrorism: in Banaras, 104–5, 111, 136, 143; in India, 104–6; in Jerusalem, 283–84n21; in Spain, 89, 98, 102

Thailand, 215, 220

Thaipusam (Hindu festival), 48, 214, 239, 241, 250–52

Three-Self Patriotic Movement (China), 188

Tibet; alcoholism in, 187; borders of, 200; Buddhism in, 162–67, 190–91, 268; conquest of, 160, 164–165; and cultural genocide, 167, 179; and cultural identity, 174, 185–87, 191, 194, 199, 202, 206, 268, 270, 272; demography of, 162, 179; dress in, 197, 199; economy of, 154–55, 158, 167; education in, 176, 180–82, 193–95; employment in, 180–82; geography of, 169; and Great Britain,

163–64, 165; healthcare in, 176; history of, 162–67; and India, 161, 162, 165, 166, 167, 169, 196; law in, 160; middle-classes in, 155, 176, 180–81, 273; mining in, 169; monasteries and nunneries in, 166, 181, 184–85, 190, 191–99, 206; monks and nuns in, 13, 162, 167, 168, 181, 190–92, 192–99; natural resources of, 169, 306n37; police in, 200; railways in, 1790, 179, 180; resistance in, 13, 154–55, 161, 165–66, 191, 196–99, 205–6; rivers in, 169–70; and Russia, 163; self-immolation in, 153–54, 160, 174, 182, 199, 201; tourism in, 183, 194; and United Nations, 165; and United States, 165; and university graduates, 180–82; violence in, 166, 191, 196, 198; welfare services in, 155

Tibetan Autonomous Region (TAR), 153–55, 160, 172, 179, 182–83, 193, 200–201

Tibet Museum (Lhasa), 185–86

tolerance, 210, 274, 313n20; in Banaras, 99, 107–8, 111, 117, 121, 124, 146–47, 267–68; in Cordoba, 74, 77, 81, 83, 91, 100, 267–68; in George Town, 208–9, 214, 217, 222–24, 230–34, 240–44, 254–55, 257–61, 267, 314n44; in Malaysia, 255–58. *See also* equilibrium

tool kits. *See* Religious Conflict in Cities Resolution Tool Kit

tourism: in Banaras, 118–19, 127, 147; in China, 170, 190; in Cordoba, 86, 90, 93, 94, 95, 97; in George Town, 212, 228, 233, 243, 251–52; in Jerusalem, 54–55, 273; in Lhasa, 176, 179–80, 183–84, 186, 195, 198, 201, 273; in Tibet, 183, 194

Track Two Negotiations, 65

trade: and George Town, 215–17, 223–24, 227, 239. *See also* opium trade; silk trade

transformative integration, 21–22, 81, 107–8, 145, 211–12

transition zones, 55

tsampa (Tibetan barley flour), 197

Tsering Kyi, Tibetan schoolgirl, 153

Twain, Mark, 128

Uighurs (ethnic group), 193

Umayyads (Islamic dynasty), 69, 71–73

unemployment, 227, 237, 245

UNESCO, 31, 39, 56–57, 60, 262–63. *See also* World Heritage Sites

United First Work Department (Communist Party of China), 193

United Kingdom. *See* Great Britain

United Left (Cordoba), 89

United Malays National Organization (UNMO) (Malaysia), 221–22, 225, 226–27, 232, 236–37, 248–49, 251–252, 256

United Nations, 152, 160, 183, 211, 269; and Dumper, 263; and Jerusalem, 63–64, 262–64, 276; and Tibet, 165

United Nations Development Program (UNDP), 262

United Nations Habitat, 263

United Nations Population Agency, 262

United Nations Relief and Works Agency (UNRWA), 262, 263

United Nations Special Coordinator of the Middle East Peace Process (UNSCO), 263, 264–66

United Nations Truce Supervisory Organization, 263

United States: and Haram al-Sharif, 2, 3; and embassy in Israel, 60–62, 64–65, 265; and Malaysia, 237; and Native Americans, 194, 195; and Tibet, 165

Unity kindergartens (Malaysia), 255

universities, 119. *See also* Banaras Hindu University; People's University

Universiti Sains Malaysia survey, 221

university graduates, 180–82

Upper Silesia (Poland and Czech Republic), 230

urbanization: and cities, 36, 210; and George Town, 215, 217, 223; and holy cities, 30, 32; and Kuala Lumpur, 226; and Lhasa, 156, 173–78, 184–87, 204; and religious conflict, 5–7. *See also* housing; land use

Uttar Pradesh (India), 115, 117–18, 134–35, 149

Varanasi (India). *See* Banaras (India)

Varanasi Cantonment Railway Station (Banaras), 104–5, 107

Varanasi Development Authority (Banaras), 147

Varshney, Ashutosh, 113–14, 118, 135, 138, 254

vastu shastra (Hindu architecture), 217

Vatican, 188, 231

Via Dolorosa (Jerusalem), 38

violence: in cities, 5–7, 23, 26; in George Town, 212, 244–49; in India, 139; in Lhasa, 154, 161, 162, 165, 166, 196, 198; in Malaysia, 237–38; in Tibet, 166, 191, 196, 198. *See also* riots

Vishna Hindu Parishad (VHP) (Indian organization), 136, 138–39, 142

Vishweshwur Temple (Banaras), 108–9, 111, 122, 127, 128–34, 142–48

Visigoths, 69

Vision 2020 (Malaysian organization), 255

Vox Party (Spain), 98

GPSR Authorized Representative: Easy Access System Europe, Mustamäe tee
50, 10621 Tallinn, Estonia, gpsr.requests@easproject.com